# SHOVEL READY

## ARCHAEOLOGY AND ROOSEVELT'S NEW DEAL FOR AMERICA



EDITED BY
**BERNARD K. MEANS**

THE UNIVERSITY OF ALABAMA PRESS
*Tuscaloosa*

Manufactured in the United States of America

Typeface: Bembo

Cover photograph: WPA field crew members wielding shovels at Fort Hill, Somerset County, Pennsylvania, in 1939 or 1940 (Courtesy of The State Museum of Pennsylvania, Pennsylvania Historical and Museum Commission).
Cover design: Gary Gore

∞

The paper on which this book is printed meets the minimum requirements of American National Standard for Information Sciences—Permanence of Paper for Printed Library Materials, ANSI Z39.48-1984.

Library of Congress Cataloging-in-Publication Data

Shovel ready : archaeology and Roosevelt's New Deal for America / edited by Bernard K. Means.
p. cm.
Includes bibliographical references and index.
ISBN 978-0-8173-5718-4 (quality paper : alk. paper) — ISBN 978-0-8173-8625-2 (ebook)
1. Archaeology and state—United States—History—20th century. 2. Archaeology—United States—History—20th century. 3. Historic preservation—United States—History—20th century. 4. New Deal, 1933-1939. 5. United States. Work Projects Administration. 6. United States. Civilian Conservation Corp. I. Means, Bernard K. (Bernard Klaus), 1964-
CC101.U6S56 2013
930.1—dc23
2012025923

# SHOVEL READY

# Contents

# Illustrations

## FIGURES

## TABLES

# Acknowledgments

This volume certainly would not have been possible without Franklin Delano Roosevelt's vision of a New Deal for the American people—putting the unemployed to work rebuilding the nation and exploring America's past. Countless men and women participated in the various archaeology projects we discuss in the following pages. Some individuals became integral to how American archaeology is practiced today, but others labored in anonymity. I would like to thank all of these "Forgotten Men and Women," and the authors in this volume for the incremental steps here toward recalling these relief archaeologists and their legacy.

I would also like to thank Stephen Nash, Denver Museum of Nature and Science, who was chair of the Society for American Archaeology's History of Archaeology Interest Group leading up to the 75th anniversary annual meeting of the SAA. Stephen encouraged my proposed session on New Deal archaeology as part of the Biennial Gordon R. Willey Symposium on the History of Archaeology, which led to this volume. Stephen joined me in that session, as did John Campbell (Hicks and Company), John Cordell (Iowa State Archaeology), David Dye (University of Memphis), John Doershuk (Iowa State Archaeology), Scott Hammerstedt (Oklahoma Archeological Survey), Mark Howe (Sequoia National Forest), Janet Johnson (The State Museum of Pennsylvania), Tim Kelly (Sequoia National Forest), Greg Lattanzi (New Jersey State Museum), Patrick Livingood (University of Oklahoma), Anna Lunn (Weaver and Associates, LLC), Edwin Lyon (retired), Mary McCorvie (U.S. Forest Service), Karen Miller (Sequoia National Forest), Mason Miller (Hicks and Company), Carole Nash (James Madison University), Amanda Regnier (Oklahoma Archeological Survey), and Sissel Schroeder (University of Wisconsin at Madison). Some of these names you will see in this volume.

Judith Knight, recently retired from The University of Alabama Press, was very supportive when I proposed this edited set of papers. Her successor, Joseph Powell, enthusiastically took over the reins of guiding this book to completion and his substantive comments and suggestions are incorporated into this work.

The content and structure of this volume was greatly improved by an anonymous reviewer and a review by Alice B. Kehoe, University of Wisconsin. Beyond her formal review, Alice also freely provided additional suggestions for this volume via a healthy email correspondence. All errors or misinterpretations of the reviewer comments are solely my responsibility.

Finally, I would like to thank Laura Galke, the George Washington Foundation. Laura supported the long hours I put into this volume and offered many helpful suggestions along the way that helped this book eventually see print.

# Introduction

## "Alphabet Soup" and American Archaeology

*Bernard K. Means*

At the time of this writing, the United States remains in the grips of the Great Recession, marked by high unemployment, considerable job insecurity, and thousands of anxious Americans who have lost or may soon lose their homes. Archaeology has been adversely affected as well, with public- and private-sector hiring slowing to a trickle. Government and industry budgets are strained, and, with limited activity in the construction field, there are fewer opportunities for those involved in cultural resource management (CRM)—the largest employer of American archaeologists today—to ply their trade under federally mandated preservation laws. Some have likened the Great Recession of the early twenty-first century to the Great Depression of the 1930s—although today the policies and programs enacted during the Great Depression have ameliorated considerably the impact of the current economic crisis (Krugman 2009:194–195).

Another major distinction between the Great Recession and the Great Depression is that American archaeology's growth during the Great Depression was explosive (Guthe 1952:5). More people were excavating more archaeological sites and in more places across the nation than anyone had ever witnessed before—all made possible by federally funded work relief programs designed to alleviate the crippling and persistent unemployment that characterized the Great Depression. Haag (1985:278) noted that "[t]here has never been a greater revolution in American archaeology than that engendered by the New Deal period." Archaeological investigations across the nation took advantage of virtual armies of relief workers to move tons of soil and uncover thousands of American Indian sites, ranging in size from ephemeral hunter-gatherer camps to large villages and major mound complexes (Dunnell 1986; Fagette 1996; Lyon 1996; Means 1998). Historical archaeology received a tremendous boost during the New Deal as well. J. C. Harrington's pioneering work relief excavations at Jamestown, Virginia, the site of the first permanent English colony in North America, are widely considered to have helped stimulate the development of modern historical archaeology (Little 2009:366; Pykles 2008:32, 2011).

Many people today—including some archaeologists—are unaware of the New Deal's significant contributions to revealing America's hidden past. The New Deal is generally seen as putting the unemployed to work on "brick and mortar" projects like highway construction rather than as a successful combination of scholarship with jobs programs. Partly to address this misperception, I organized a symposium on this topic for the Society for American Archaeology's (SAA) 75th annual meeting, held April 2010 in St. Louis, Missouri. This symposium was sponsored by the SAA's History of Archaeology Interest Group (HAIG) and had the somewhat unwieldy designation as the "Biennial Gordon Willey Symposium on the History of Archaeology: Shovel Ready—Archaeology and Roosevelt's New Deal for America." The focus by the symposium's participants on New Deal archaeology's lasting legacy meshed well with the SAA's 75th anniversary celebration. The SAA was born during the dark days of the Great Depression (Griffin 1985; Meltzer et al. 1986:8) and shares an anniversary with a pivotal development in the history of America and American archaeology—one that transformed and continues to have a significant impact on the practice of archaeology across the United States. I am speaking, of course, of the Works Progress Administration (WPA), later the Work Projects Administration, which also had its 75th anniversary in April 2010. Not coincidentally, the man honored by the HAIG symposium, the late Gordon R. Willey, was himself a New Deal archaeologist. Willey's first professional work after receiving his master's degree involved WPA excavations outside Macon, Georgia (Milanich 2007:16).

Today's twenty-first-century archaeologists, who have a vast array of technologically sophisticated tools at their disposal, might be tempted to view New Deal archaeology as a relic of a bygone era and perhaps best confined to the dust bins of history. The authors collected here do not agree. We do not—and know we should not—ignore the historical role played by New Deal archaeology in the creation of modern archaeology. Instead, we emphasize the continuing relevancy of New Deal archaeology as we draw on the rich information embodied in sometimes musty and brittle field records; we apply new ideas, theories, and techniques to sites excavated more than seven decades ago.

## Dark Days for America

A brief recounting of the economic, political, and social crises that began during the presidency of Herbert Hoover shows why the federal government under his successor, Franklin Delano Roosevelt, created work relief programs that would eventually fund New Deal archaeological investigations across the nation. Americans 75 years ago were faced with an economic calamity that threatened the stability of the country itself (Heilbroner and Singer 1994:283). The Great Depression began in October 1929 and lasted until the onset of World War II (McElvaine 1993; Watkins 1993). Jobless men and women, collectively referred to as "Forgotten Men," wandered the roads and railways during the Great Depression in search of a livelihood (McElvaine 1983). Sometimes, these "forgotten" and forlorn people banded together in cold comfort and lived in squalid and ramshackle "towns" derisively referred to as "Hoovervilles" and located in city dumps or less hospitable places (Biles 1991:11).

One unemployed man noted in 1935 that "[w]e're about down and out and the only good thing about it that I see is that there's not much further down that we can go" (quoted in McElvaine 1983:1). The American work ethic during the 1930s was so deeply ingrained that people were despondent if they lacked gainful employment. The notion of getting on the dole—receiving direct welfare payments—was considered an even more degrading prospect (Watkins 1993:126). Harry Hopkins, one of Roosevelt's top men, noted that "[a] workless man has little status at home and less with his friends," adding that "[g]ive a man a dole and you save his body and destroy his spirit. Give him a job and you save both body and spirit" (both quoted in Bremer 1975:636–637). It was the latter attitude that motivated Roosevelt's administration to emphasize work relief programs as a major strategy for addressing the devastating effect that the Great Depression was having on the American psyche. Roosevelt preferred the idea of work relief over what he saw as demeaning welfare payments (Watkins 1993:126).

## A New Deal for the American People

Economic collapse followed the crash of the stock market on October 24, 1929 (Heilbroner and Singer 1994:277). Unemployment climbed from 1.5 million at the time of the crash (Watkins 1993:51) to 7.5 million 11 months later (Watkins 1993:54–55). Three years after the stock market crash, one in five workers was unemployed—over 12 million people. By Roosevelt's inauguration in 1933, this number had climbed to 18 million (Biles 1991:97; Watkins 1993:51, 54–55). Families were hard hit across the nation, and men and women feared not only for their own livelihoods but also for the future of the country itself (McElvaine 1983:25). The situation changed for many in the 1930s with the arrival of Franklin Delano Roosevelt on the national political scene. Following from successful programs that he pioneered as governor of New York, Roosevelt asserted that the federal government could play a major role in solving the economic and social crises caused by the Great Depression (Biles 1991:13). Accepting the Democratic Party nomination in 1932, FDR pledged a "New Deal" for the American people (Biles 1991:26; Watkins 1993:113).

Roosevelt's New Deal programs were quickly implemented following his inauguration on March 4, 1933, through the creation of work relief programs intended to help build the fabric of the nation, including the construction of roads, bridges, schools, and even zoos (Heilbroner and Singer 1994; McElvaine 1993; Taylor 2008; Watkins 1993). So-called alphabet soup agencies provided the funding for labor projects often administered by local and state organizations (Table I.1). One of Roosevelt's signature initiatives was the creation of the Civilian Conservation Corps (CCC) on March 31, 1933, just weeks after he took office. The first recruit for the CCC was enrolled on April 5, 1933 (Biles 1991:38). Known as Roosevelt's "tree army," the mostly young men of the CCC worked to make nature more accessible by building roads, trails, and camp sites. The CCC lasted for almost a decade, ending on July 2, 1942. Efforts to continue the program beyond that date proved unsuccessful (Paige 1985; Watkins 1993:130–131, 1999:159).

The Federal Emergency Relief Administration (FERA) was formed on May 9, 1933, less than two months after Roosevelt's inauguration. FERA was designed to initiate work relief programs targeted to a broader spectrum of the unemployed than was the case for the CCC (Watkins 1993:51, 124, 1999:170). Lasting just two years, FERA was the shortest lived of the New Deal work relief programs (Watkins 1993:51). This program ended in May 1935 as its final projects were transferred to the newly created WPA (Watkins 1999:259). However, as we shall see below, FERA is notable for funding the first archaeological investigation using work relief labor.

As a program set up under FERA, the Civil Works Administration (CWA) was designed simply to get the unemployed through the winter of 1933 to 1934—expected to be a particularly brutal one—while longer term plans were being made to deal with the deeper structural issues in the nation's economic system revealed by the Great Depression (McElvaine 1993:153; Watkins 1993:128). Gill (1935), as quoted in Watkins (1999:183), noted that "[f]rom a long-term standpoint . . . the chief value of the civil works program may very well prove to be that of effectively demonstrating the possibilities of public work as a means of meeting the needs of millions of destitute unemployed." The CWA ended on March 31, 1934, but, as Gill noted, set the stage for *the* major New Deal work relief program that began just over a year later (Bremer 1975:642; Watkins 1993:126–128, 1999:179–183).

Table I.1. Major New Deal work relief programs in order of their start dates

| Agency | Acronym | Start Date | End Date | Overview |
|---|---|---|---|---|
| Civilian Conservation Corps | CCC | April 5, 1933 | July 2, 1942 | Young men planted thousands of trees, and built campgrounds, trails, and roads to enable people to get closer to nature. |
| Federal Emergency Relief Administration | FERA | May 9, 1933 | May 1935 | Designed to provide work relief programs for a wider spectrum of men and women than allowed under the CCC. |
| Civil Works Administration | CWA | November 9, 1933 | March 31, 1934 | Employed large numbers of workers on a temporary basis during a winter expected to be particularly brutal. |
| Works Progress Administration/ Work Projects Administration | WPA | April 8, 1935 | June 30, 1943 | Intended to build the infrastructure of the nation and also celebrate its heritage, through its writers' and artists' programs. |
| National Youth Administration | NYA | June 26, 1935 | January 1, 1944 | Gave opportunities to a greater variety of youth than seen under the CCC, including programs for women and for African Americans neglected generally in CCC programs. Provided young Americans with work study or vocational training. |

The principal federal work relief program—the WPA—lasted from April 8, 1935, to June 30, 1943 (McElvaine 1993:274; Taylor 2008:549; Watkins 1993:249). During its existence, the WPA employed more than 8 million people on nearly 1.5 million projects in 3,000 counties across the United States (Setzler 1943; Taylor 2008; Watkins 1993:249). Biles (1991:107) detailed the scope of the WPA:

> [O]ne could hardly go to any community in the nation and not find highly visible evidence of the WPA's presence in an improved infrastructure—whether through the repair of existing streets, bridges, and parks, or the provision of new viaducts, culverts, buildings, and sidewalks. A list of notable WPA projects would include New York City's LaGuardia Airport, Boston's Huntington Avenue Subway, Lake Shore Drive in Chicago, and the San Antonio Zoo, among others. In the South the lining of miles of ditches with concrete veritably eliminated malaria as a serious health problem . . . overall the WPA fulfilled Roosevelt's pledge that relief work would serve a useful purpose.

For a celebration and thorough overview of the WPA, Taylor's volume *American-Made: The Enduring Legacy of the WPA: When FDR Put the Nation to Work* (2008) is highly recommended. The WPA did operate with some restrictions and limitations. WPA projects were designed so that they were not competitive with private businesses (McElvaine 1993:267). The WPA paid workers more than they would have received on direct relief, but not as much as they would have been paid by private employers (Biles 1991:105) if there had been work available. WPA funds were distributed to local sponsors and not to states (Biles 1991:105) and this decentralized structure would result in some less-than-adequate archaeological investigations in a few cases. Nonetheless, the impact of the WPA on the American psyche cannot be understated. Close to the one-year anniversary of the WPA, relief workers in Battle Creek, Michigan, pleaded on April 5, 1936: "Please continue this WPA program. It makes us feel like an American citizen to earn our own living" (quoted in McElvaine 1983:127).

Finally, the National Youth Administration (NYA) began in June 1935 and also lasted until 1943. Unlike the CCC, which required young men to leave their homes to work in military-run camps, the NYA gave young men—and young women—the opportunity to work while staying at home. Young people in high school or college were provided with work study opportunities and those unemployed youth who chose not to remain in school worked on local projects designed to have lasting impacts for their immediate communities (Jacobson 1942; Lindley and Lindley 1972; Watkins 1999:267–272; Williams 1939). The NYA also took a stronger stance on ensuring the participation of African Americans in relief programs than was true of the CCC, especially through the efforts of the NYA Division of Negro Affairs, created and headed by Mary McLeod Bethune, the highest ranking African American in the Roosevelt administration (Watkins 1999:271–272).

## Bright Days for American Archaeology

What were dark days for America became bright days for American archaeology when work relief programs were turned toward excavating America's past. All of the "alphabet soup" programs discussed above funded archaeological investigations of one sort or another throughout the United States (Dunnell 1986; Fagette 1996; Little 2009; Lyon 1996; Means 1998; Setzler 1943; Taylor 2008). While the number of archaeological investigations across the United States was fairly minimal in the 1920s, especially after the onset of the Great Depression, scholars were not ignorant of the nation's considerable archaeological potential when work relief monies became available. New Deal archaeology did not begin in a vacuum. The Committee on State Archaeological Surveys (CSAS) was established in 1920 under the National Research Council (NRC) "as a correlating body for archaeological research in North America" (Guthe 1928:501). One major way to meet this goal was to encourage and assist states with surveying their archaeological resources, following the model of surveys already conducted in Ohio, New York, and Wisconsin (O'Brien and Lyman 2001:4). Archaeologists were concerned, in part, about the "absence of any baseline data against which to judge the magnitude of destruction" of sites at the hands of well-meaning amateur societies (O'Brien and Lyman 2001:5).

Carl Guthe assumed the chairmanship of the CSAS in 1929 and played a central role in fostering a national dialogue among archaeologists, including by sponsoring a series of regional conferences (Fagette 1996:7–9). In late 1932, the CSAS under Guthe organized the Conference on Southern Pre-History in Birmingham, Alabama, principally because there was no broad understanding of what archaeological resources were present in the Southeast—and little communication among the region's archaeological community (Haag 1985:273; O'Brien and Lyman 2001:32–35). The CSAS also was involved with pressuring the Tennessee Valley Authority (TVA) to conduct a program of salvage archaeology (Lyon 1996:38; see Dye, Lunn, Schroeder, and Hammerstedt, this volume, on TVA archaeology). Without the activities of the CSAS, New Deal archaeology would certainly not have been "shovel ready" when federal work relief funds became available (see Johnson, this volume, for example). Ironically, the NRC ended the CSAS in 1934 because the federal government was now directly involved in American archaeology through various work relief agencies and the CSAS was viewed as unnecessary (O'Brien and Lyman 2001:63).

New Deal archaeology began in early 1933 with FERA-sponsored excavations at the Marksville mound site in Louisiana (Lyon 1996:1). Success of this project spurred the implementation of New Deal archaeological investigations across the country (Haag 1985:274; Lyon 1996:4; Setzler 1943; Setzler and Strong 1936). We will explore these subsequent investigations throughout the remainder of this volume. Here, I briefly consider in more general terms why archaeology at Marksville mound and, later, thousands of other sites made this then relatively marginal academic field attractive to New Deal administrators—and, conversely, made relief workers attractive to archaeologists.

The initial excavations at Marksville mound demonstrated to federal officials that archaeology readily met the major requirement of work relief programs—large numbers could be quickly employed for lengthy periods (Fagette 1996:53; Setzler 1943:207). Archaeological projects were ideal for work relief because they were, indeed, "shovel ready." The necessary equipment to do archaeology cost relatively little and 85 to 90 percent of funds could be spent on labor-intensive fieldwork (Fowler 1986a:145; Setzler 1943:210; Setzler and Strong 1936). Not only did field workers provide labor, but they also had to supply their own shovels and trowels in many cases. For most workers, archaeological excavations were no more difficult than the farming, mining, or other tasks that they would normally have done if the economic climate were not so bleak (Means 1998, 2000a). Archaeology also did not compete with existing private enterprises in the 1930s and therefore would not harm the "normal" operation of the economy. Archaeological projects produced nothing to compete directly with private industry, but rather were viewed as scientific and educational (Fowler 1986a:145; Setzler 1943:210; Trigger 1986:197–198). Furthermore, it was clear that the richness of the nation's past meant that the work was not likely to run out any time soon.

Who were the New Deal workers? Supervisors of New Deal archaeology projects were not necessarily on relief but sometimes were drawn from existing institutions, such as museums or universities. These supervisors were few in number and faced the challenges of directing large numbers of ordinary citizens who were not formally trained in archaeology (Cotter 1993; Meltzer et al. 1986:8). Gordon Willey, for example, was one such supervisor. Fresh out of the master of arts program at the University of Arizona, Willey became involved in excavating mounds around Macon, Georgia, first working with WPA labor and then with CCC crews when the National Park Service (NPS) took over the project. The Macon project was initially directed by Arthur R. Kelly. Willey recalled in 1984 that "[t]hese operations were considerable. The relief rolls in Macon and surrounding territory were swollen in 1936, the depths of the Depression, and [project director Arthur] Kelly had several hundred men, armed with picks, shovels, and trowels, at his command" (Willey 1984:7). Willey later joined James Ford's WPA project in Louisiana before enrolling in the doctoral program at Columbia (Milanich 2007:18).

The men—and more rarely women—who worked on the work crews were largely drawn from the relief rolls, as Willey recalled, and, because they were not trained archaeologists, were referred to as unskilled or semiskilled. In many images of New Deal archaeologists, workers tend to be elderly or fairly young. This is because, as jobs were being cut, the oldest members of society tended to lose work first and the young had no chance to get one of the rare jobs that were available (Means 1998, 2000a). While men did dominate field crews, there were some notable exceptions. Irene Mound, Georgia, was one of a number of sites excavated near Savannah whose field crew consisted primarily of African American women. Archaeology was no more strenuous for these women than the work they would normally have done as field laborers (Claassen 1999).

What effect did the New Deal have on archaeology? Because large numbers of untrained people were involved, standardized procedures were essential to conducting New Deal archaeology with any hope of maintaining a minimal semblance of order (Dunnell 1986:28). To guide workers unfamiliar with archaeology into recording appropriate information—and to make sure data were collected consistently—preprinted forms became widespread for the first time during the Great Depression. Archaeology grew considerably during the New Deal in response to the need for trained professionals to direct sometimes chaotic archaeological relief projects. Because of the New Deal, archaeology changed from an avocation to a vocation for many of its practitioners (Dunnell 1986:28). We can use forms and reports filed by New Deal archaeologists today to reexamine their past excavations—as is evident by the contributions to this volume.

Only the general prehistory of the country was known before the New Deal sponsored archaeological projects across the United States (Lyon 1996:26). Data produced by Depression-era archaeologists led to the first major cultural syntheses of archaeology east of the Mississippi (Trigger 1986:198). One of these notable works was *Archeology of Eastern United States,* edited by James Griffin (1952) and dedicated to the University of Chicago's Fay-Cooper Cole. Cole trained several of the archaeologists who later went on to direct New Deal–funded excavations (Sullivan and Braly 2011:42). He also employed New Deal relief workers for excavations at the site of Kincaid in Illinois (Cole 1951:vi; Cole et al. 1951). Archaeology at Kincaid and numerous other sites was conducted on a scale unprecedented in America during the Great Depression and rivaled some of the larger excavations in the Old World. Before the New Deal, as is often true today, archaeologists often could only excavate small portions of large sites. With large work relief field crews, substantial areas of sites could be exposed, providing us with a better understanding of how their past inhabitants organized their communities (Lyon 1996:xiii; Means 1998; Trigger 1986:197). Great strides were made in popularizing archaeology and exposing people to the nation's rich past because of the New Deal. New Deal excavations attracted a great deal of public attention while in progress, and relief workers also exposed family members and friends to the archaeological work that they were doing (Fagette 1996:21–22, 30). The incorporation of archaeological sites into tourist guides written by relief workers and intended for travelers across the nation also helped foster the public's appreciation for the past during the Great Depression (Everson 2011).

## End of the New Deal and Work Relief Archaeology

New Deal programs, including those that funded archaeology, would eventually be impacted by American involvement in World War II, although efforts were initially made to prevent this situation from occurring. Reflecting Congress's isolationistic tendencies, the original 1935 legislation authorizing the WPA forbade expenditures of work relief monies on matters related to the military (Taylor 2008:449). As the conflict in Europe and Asia worsened through the latter part of the 1930s, FDR openly challenged the dangers inherent in these isolationistic attitudes and stressed the very real threats to democracy and freedom not only among the country's allies but for the United States as well (Taylor 2008:450–451). Toward the end of the 1930s, WPA funds were increasingly diverted toward military concerns and the NYA began developing vocational programs designed to address the appalling lack of American aviation mechanics (Taylor 2008:453–454). By 1940, New Deal agencies were directing many of their efforts toward preparing America for active participation in World War II. This, of course, meant that less money was available for archaeological investigations. Donald Cadzow, Pennsylvania's state archaeologist, lamented the lack of WPA funds for archaeology in 1940, noting that "archaeological matters have been kicked in the face rather hard by proposed military operations" (Cadzow 1940). An anxious nation was increasingly less concerned with its heritage and more worried about whether there was a future for a free America.

These fears became reality on December 7, 1941, with the devastating Japanese attack on Pearl Harbor. New Deal work relief programs were quickly impacted by this action, including the CCC, which experienced dramatic changes. After war was declared against Japan, for example, the NPS closed all camps not already directly involved in war preparations (Paige 1985). Interestingly, for shuttered CCC camps, the NPS instructed that buildings either be torn down or directed toward another purpose—some camps were converted into Civilian Public Service facilities for conscientious objectors, who performed tasks similar to those of the CCC (Paige 1985), while others eventually became prisoner-of-war camps (Listman et al. 2007:2–7). The global conflict that was World War II generated ripples that directly impacted American archaeology, not only in the loss of relief funds for archaeology but also because many archaeologists were soon sent off to war. Reports on relief work went unfinished—many remain unfinished to this day—as some of those who returned from conflict had lost their interest in the comparatively mundane field of archaeology (Means 2008:3).

Despite the interruption of the war years, American archaeologists did not forget about their experiences with New Deal work relief programs, both positive and negative, after World War II ended (Hawley 2006:487). Their experiences with New Deal archaeology were brought to the forefront with another threat to the nation's past—the planned construction of hundreds of new dams across the United States that would soon immerse thousands of archaeological sites under rapidly rising flood waters (Hawley 2006:487). To address this crisis, archaeologists again sought funds from the federal government, but this time following a model that stressed scientific research instead of work relief (Hawley 2006:487). Those who were employed by what is widely known as the River Basin Surveys (RBS) salvage archaeology program were primarily not ordinary citizens, but rather part of the emerging class of professional archaeologists. The RBS was part of the Interagency Archaeological Salvage Program from its inception in 1945 to its end in 1969 (Thiessen and Roberts 2009:121). The majority of salvage archaeology under the RBS took place in the Missouri River basin (Hawley 2006:488; Thiessen 1999; Thiessen and Roberts 2009:121). Numerous advanced archaeological methods were introduced or developed as part of the RBS to meet the needs of this ambitious salvage program, including aerial photography and the use of powered earth-moving equipment (Thiessen and Roberts 2009:122)—although for an earlier example of powered earth-moving equipment see Schroeder (this volume). The RBS influenced the development of the modern CRM industry (Hawley 2006:488) and can be viewed as a significant link between New Deal archaeologists and those who practice in the field today—an amazing transformation that took place in just half a century. The interested reader is referred to Thiessen (1999), who provides a strong overview of the RBS, particularly for the Missouri River basin.

## Organization, Purpose, and Scope of This Volume

The debt that modern American archaeology owes to New Deal work relief programs was touched on in Edwin Lyon's *A New Deal for Southeastern Archaeology* (1996) and Paul Fagette's *Digging for Dollars: American Archaeology and the New Deal* (1996; see Davis 1997 for an excellent review of both books). These two works provide complimentary overviews of various New Deal programs that funded archaeological projects during the Great Depression but focus their attention on large-scale relief excavations in the southeastern United States. Projects elsewhere are largely neglected, especially those outside the auspices of the Smithsonian Institution or the NPS. Such projects often went unpublished or were limited to narrowly circulated reports in regional and state archaeology journals.

Nevertheless, these unreported or underreported projects significantly influenced our understanding of America's past. The current volume has as its genesis several of the papers presented at the 2010 SAA annual meeting to honor Willey's contributions to the history of archaeology, as well as two additional studies—chapters by Kevin Kiernan and James R. Wettstaed—that were solicited for this volume as complementary to our appreciation of New Deal archaeologists and their legacy. The essays in this volume do not ignore major New Deal projects, but they delve also into the lesser known and forgotten contributions made by work relief field crews. Here, the authors demonstrate how the foundations for archaeological practice in states across America were established during the Great Depression and emphasize the research potential of collections and field records generated as part of New Deal investigations. Systematic procedures followed during relief projects enable old field results to be reinterpreted using new theoretical perspectives or new technologies unavailable to work relief archaeologists. These new analyses of sites excavated during the New Deal also address issues with the collections of records and artifacts generated by these projects. Records produced by New Deal programs not directly involved with archaeology also hold tremendous potential for aiding modern archaeological investigations. Historical archaeologists have long known about and used the slave narratives collected by WPA workers (Fountain 1995), but fewer are likely aware of critical data collected by other agencies, such as the Resettlement Administration (see Wettstaed, this volume).

The themes expressed in individual chapters are overlapping, so the chapters in this volume have been organized geographically (figure I.1). "Part I: Middle Atlantic States" examines the considerable relief investigations conducted at prehistoric and historic sites across this region; this work has often been overshadowed by better known projects in the southeastern United States. Gregory D. Lattanzi, in Chapter 1, considers the New Jersey Indian Site Survey that was directed by staff of the New Jersey State Museum with guidance from members of the Archaeological Society of New Jersey. This WPA-supported survey identified hundreds of important sites across the state and conducted significant excavations at a number of them. Some of these were supervised by Dorothy Cross, who was probably the most prominent and longest serving of the few female archaeologists in charge of New Deal archaeology in the United States.

In Chapter 2, Janet R. Johnson shows how historical archaeology in Pennsylvania grew largely out of the WPA-funded Frontier Forts and Trails Survey. This comprehensive project focused on eighteenth-century fortifications associated with the French and Indian War and drew on archival as well as archaeological data. Johnson also notes that surveys conducted of Pennsylvania's archaeological and historical resources prior to the Great Depression greatly facilitated New Deal investigations across the state.

Next, in Chapter 3, I examine the words and deeds of Edgar E. Augustine, who directed WPA excavations in Somerset County, Pennsylvania, from 1935 to 1940. His painstaking efforts at carefully documenting his findings at a dozen village sites have enabled me to model their community patterns and to obtain radiocarbon assays from their curated collections. The radiocarbon assays have challenged traditional notions of when these villages were occupied—notions that originated from a culture historical framework first developed from New Deal excavated sites.

Next, we turn the reader's attention to "Part II: Midwestern States." New Deal programs in Midwestern states are also comparatively poorly known, such as the support for a museum whose research aims extended well beyond U.S. borders. Stephen E. Nash, in Chapter 4, examines the impact of New Deal programs on Chicago's Field Museum. He documents a shift in museum practices from simple collection of cultural remains to a more scientifically oriented archaeological research program. Few scholars have looked as closely at how the interpretation, presentation, and care of archaeological

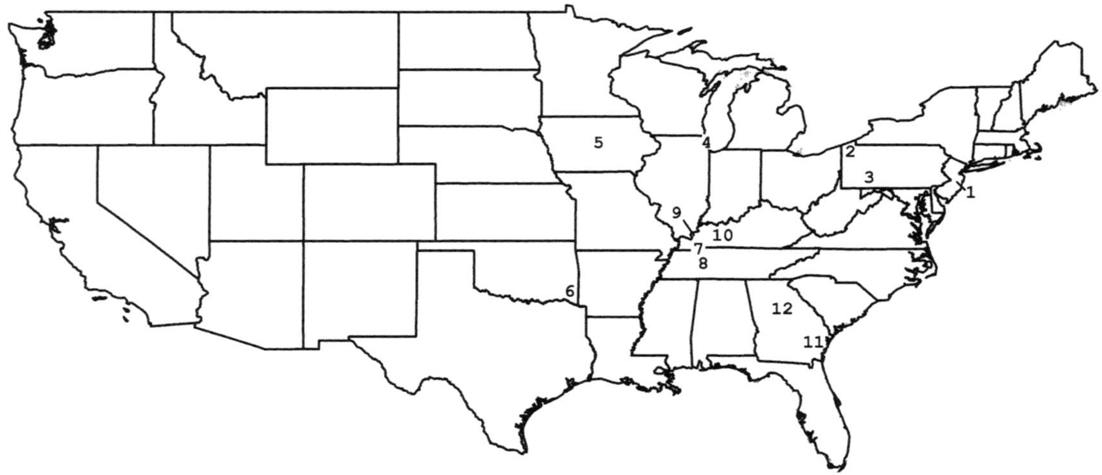


Figure I.1. The locations of major New Deal archaeological investigations discussed within this volume, indicated by chapter number.

collections in museums were affected by the New Deal—including collections generated from investigations outside the United States.

John F. Doershuk and John L. Cordell look at the work relief archaeology conducted in Iowa during the Great Depression in Chapter 5. They emphasize how New Deal archaeological collections continue to provide critical data and influence current research efforts in that state. Archaeologists active since the late nineteenth century in Iowa proved instrumental in guiding FERA and WPA surveys and excavations of an astounding number of sites from 1934 to 1939.

In Chapter 6, Amanda L. Regnier, Patrick C. Livingood, and Scott W. Hammerstedt look at two WPA-excavated mound sites from southeastern Oklahoma. In this area, basic archaeological issues still remain unresolved due to limited excavations that have taken place since the Great Depression. These authors have renewed investigations of these two mound sites, employing sophisticated tools and techniques that complement the coarser New Deal investigations.

The chapters in "Part III: Southeastern States" consider New Deal excavations in the region where the majority of work relief archaeological investigations took place. The University of Kentucky's William S. Webb figures prominently in a number of these discussions, as it was the dynamic force of his personality that drew so much work relief funding to the region. In Chapter 7, David H. Dye considers the underlying personal conflicts between William S. Webb and Thomas M. N. Lewis, University of Tennessee, over the archaeological investigations conducted prior to the construction of the Kentucky Dam along the Tennessee River. These conflicts threatened the overall success of these archaeological investigations for the TVA, which were difficult enough given the constraints of running work relief programs under an accelerated salvage archaeology schedule.

Anna R. Lunn reexamines the Slayden site in Chapter 8, a Mississippian occupation in Humphreys County, Tennessee, that was excavated using a WPA field crew. The site was characterized by a village-ceremonial area, residential mounds, and stone box burials. Lunn's careful delineation of individual house clusters from multiple overlapping occupations is very innovative—especially given the passage of time since the original excavation map was produced.

In Chapter 9, Sissel Schroeder reanalyzes the Jonathan Creek site excavated by a CCC crew prior to the construction of the Kentucky Dam by the TVA. She evaluates the development of innovative field methods and professional practices as archaeologists toward the end of the New Deal shifted their focus from elites and mounds to the exploration of community patterns. Her discussion of the history of New Deal archaeology and its impact across the Southeast expands on the outline I have presented in this opening chapter.

Scott W. Hammerstedt discusses in Chapter 10 the interplay between WPA and modern archaeological techniques at the Annis Mound site, also in Kentucky, excavated first in 1939 to 1940 by the WPA and again in 2002 to 2004 by Penn State University. In a theme echoed by other contributors to the volume, he notes that modern archaeologists are rarely able to conduct archaeology on the same scale as the WPA workers.

Chapter 11, by Kevin Kiernan, highlights the now largely forgotten WPA excavations directed by Preston Holder from 1936 to 1938 along the Georgia coast. In an all too common story, the push by WPA administrators to keep workers continuously employed meant there was little support to publish results while excavations were ongoing. Kiernan reveals that complex machinations curtailed Holder from publishing his findings even after the excavations ceased.

Next, in a departure for this volume, James R. Wettstaed in Chapter 12 does not look at the legacy of New Deal archaeologists, but rather at how a New Deal agency's documentation of its policies can benefit our study of the effects of the Great Depression. Specifically, he examines the importance of records collected by the Resettlement Administration for interpreting historic archaeological sites in Georgia. His analysis of two house sites that left minimal and contradictory material traces was greatly aided by the documentary record created by the Resettlement Administration.

In the conclusion, I consider how we know more about New Deal archaeology today than we did even a few years ago, but I stress that we still have much left to learn. I examine how many archaeologists today are turning their attention to sites discovered directly as a result of New Deal programs. Finally, I explore the question of how New Deal–style work relief programs might work in the current economic crisis—focusing on programs that are effectively using relief funds to employ both professional archaeologists and men and women who have recently returned from combat.

## Why New Deal Archaeology Continues to Inspire Us Today

Many of us who initially turned to the records of New Deal investigations sought to solve a particular issue, to address a specific research question, or to examine the excavation history of a site undergoing renewed scrutiny. As I was finalizing this volume, I was asked by a colleague whether my research or that by the other contributors arose directly out of studies undertaken to comply with the Native American Graves Protection and Repatriation

Act (NAGPRA). This turns out not to be true for any of the case studies presented in the following chapters. However, research conducted into New Deal archaeology has definitely followed from efforts to meet NAGPRA requirements. For example, McConaughy and Johnson (2003) initially examined the records of the Sugar Run Mound site in northwestern Pennsylvania as part of NAGPRA compliance efforts. This site consisted of three overlapping burial mounds and was among several excavated by a CCC crew consisting of members of the Seneca tribe. Ironically, this site is unavailable for study today because it was inundated following construction of a dam that also flooded Seneca homes on land known as the Cornplanter Tract. McConaughy (2005, 2011) has continued his research into the Sugar Run Mound, well after helping complete the NAGPRA inventory of the site. Given the large numbers of graves and burial mounds that were excavated by work relief archaeologists, ongoing NAGPRA inventory efforts will introduce new generations of archaeologists to the world of New Deal archaeology—and its attendant issues (see Doershuk and Cordell, this volume, for a discussion of research in Iowa along these lines).

I began my own studies into the material and scholarly legacy of the New Deal when I planned investigations at the Martz Rock Shelter in 1994—the site was slated to be destroyed through construction of a new highway bypass around Meyersdale, Pennsylvania (Means 2000b, 2000c). The site had first been excavated in 1938 by a WPA crew under the direction of Edgar E. Augustine (see Means, this volume). The records for these investigations were meager, but our modern field crew was guided by several photographs of the 1938 excavations in progress (Figure I.2). Our excavations in 1994 determined that intact strata dating back thousands of years remained at the site despite the early excavations. Further CRM investigations were clearly warranted at this and a companion site also investigated in 1938 but forgotten by modern archaeologists (Means 2000c). We also found two artifacts evocative of the New Deal workers themselves: a broken shovel head and the base of a liquor bottle, the latter found over 3 m below backfill, tucked into a nook in the cliff face (Means 2000b).

At least for myself, I expanded my research into New Deal archaeology only partly because of the questions that could be answered with this considerable and still largely untapped body of data. Truthfully, I was equally drawn toward the story of the people depicted in the stark black-and-white images doing archaeology under very challenging circumstances. I hope the following chapters inspire a new generation of scholars who will appreciate and continue to explore the legacy of these "shovel ready" work relief archaeologists.

Figure I.2. Excavations at the Martz Rock Shelter, Somerset County, Pennsylvania (Courtesy of The State Museum of Pennsylvania, Pennsylvania Historical and Museum Commission).

## Acknowledgments

This chapter benefited considerably from the comments of Alice B. Kehoe, University of Wisconsin, and the anonymous reviewer. Their comments led me to more explicitly contextualize the influence of New Deal archaeology on modern scholars and the impact that events such as World War II had on work relief archaeologists. Marlin Hawley, Wisconsin Historical Society, and Thomas Thiessen, National Park Service (retired), freely provided information that informed my discussion of the River Basin Surveys. Mark A. McConaughy, Bushy Run Battlefield, shared published and unpublished research on mounds investigated by a Seneca CCC crew that contributed to my consideration of New Deal archaeology and NAGPRA, which followed from comments by Alice B. Kehoe. I hope that I did justice to these helpful scholars, but accept all responsibility for any misinterpretations or mistakes that I might have made.

# PART I

# Middle Atlantic States

# 1

# The First Stimulus Package

## The WPA and the New Jersey Indian Site Survey

*Gregory D. Lattanzi*

Between 1936 and 1941, the Indian Site Survey—a federal relief program operated by the Works Progress Administration (WPA)—identified numerous sites and conducted archaeological investigations throughout the state of New Jersey (Table 1.1). These excavations were conducted under the sponsorship of the New Jersey State Museum with the Archaeological Society of New Jersey acting in an advisory capacity and were directed by Dr. Dorothy Cross. This massive project not only identified hundreds of sites but also excavated one of the most significant prehistoric settlements in the Middle Atlantic region—the Abbott Farm National Historic Landmark. Today these older collections, housed at the New Jersey State Museum, are being reexamined by numerous scholars, researchers, and students throughout the region. This chapter looks at the Indian Site Survey program, then and now, and how it provided a more focused and comprehensive picture of New Jersey's prehistoric past.

When one thinks of WPA projects one might immediately envision the Empire State Building in New York or the many arts and writers projects that have left a lasting legacy across the nation. One of the projects that started on the heels of the Empire State Building and other great engineering feats was the New Jersey Indian Site Survey (ISS). Although the project had nothing to do with engineering bridges or roadways, it did contribute significantly to the residents of New Jersey and surrounding states by putting laborers to work. The ISS was considered to be the second archaeologically devoted project in the state—and the largest as well. The first major project was the Alanson Skinner and Max Schrabisch (1913) statewide archaeological survey. This survey was different from the ISS in that it only accomplished the identification and limited excavation of prehistoric sites across the state. The ISS would continue the great work carried out by the 1912 survey and would identify and professionally excavate more than a dozen sites throughout the

Table 1.1. Sites excavated by the WPA in New Jersey

| Site | County | Dates of Excavation |
|---|---|---|
| Abbott Farm | Mercer | March 1, 1936, to February 15, 1941 |
| Bordentown Water Works | Mercer | February 1 to May 13, 1937 |
| Faery Hole Rock Shelter | Warren | November 17 to 19, 1936 |
| Goose Island | Gloucester | April 18 to July 11, 1938 |
| Havens | Ocean | April 8 to May 3, 1940 |
| Indian Head | Camden | March 7 to May 9, 1940 |
| Island Farm | Middlesex | July 21 to August 5, 1937 |
| Koens-Crispin | Burlington | November 29, 1937, to November 7, 1938 |
| Lenhardt-Lahaway | Monmouth | October 14, 1937, to February 25, 1938 |
| Red Valley | Monmouth | June 14, 1936, to October 13, 1937 |
| Riggins | Cumberland | January 18 to March 7, 1940 |
| Rosenkrans Ferry | Sussex | July 12, 1938, to October 26, 1938 |
| Salisbury | Gloucester | March 12, 1937, to March 21, 1938 |
| Stobbe | Mercer | May 12, 1937, to October 17, 1937 |
| Todd Rock Shelter | Sussex | April 1 to May 1, 1940 |
| Tuckerton Shell Mound | Ocean | April 3, 1939 |

*Note:* Adapted from data in Cross 1941 and NJSM site files.

state, although mostly in central and southern New Jersey. From 1936 to 1941, the ISS program was the mainstay of archaeological research and excavation in New Jersey, and the results of this "make work" federal project continue to leave a lasting impression on archaeologists today.

Established on April 8, 1935, the WPA provided each state with great authority over the implementation of its work relief projects. Two New Jersey organizations were stimulated by the archaeological potential of the state and saw the need to direct work relief funds to the state. Those two organizations were the Archaeological Society of New Jersey (ASNJ) and the New Jersey State Museum (NJSM), which together included a handful of very active and influential avocational archaeologists who guided the trajectory of archaeological research in the state.

## Background

The ASNJ and NJSM were the driving forces behind the organization and formulation of the ISS. In order to understand how the ISS played such a pivotal role in the archaeological investigations of the state, an examination of the background of these two organizations and how they joined forces is necessary. The NJSM had its beginnings with the Centennial Exhibition in Chicago in 1876 at which many objects from New Jersey's culture, industry, and agriculture were placed on display. All of those objects from the Centennial were used to help establish the NJSM in 1890. At first, the state museum was a division within the New Jersey Geological Survey. Then the NJSM was formally created as a discrete institution on March 20, 1895, by an act of the New Jersey state legislature. By this act, the state museum was charged with "showing the educational, agricultural and industrial development of the state" (Axel-Lute 2005:2099). The NJSM was the first museum in the country to be founded with an educational mission—one that still continues today.

Next, as noted above, in 1912, an archaeological survey of the entire state was carried out, sponsored by the New Jersey Geological Survey. Alanson Skinner and Max Schrabisch—both of the American Museum of Natural History in New York City—were hired to conduct the survey. At the time, most of the NJSM's collections consisted of geological specimens, collected during the 1825 construction of the Morris Canal. All the earlier Centennial materials as well as the archaeological survey objects were housed on the third floor of the New Jersey State House. In the 1920s, the museum was becoming too big for its original facilities and construction soon started on a new building to house the museum and other state offices. The State House Annex located next to the State House was built to house both legislative and cultural divisions and included numerous murals painted by some of New Jersey's finest artists of the time. In 1929 the museum moved its new headquarters to the State House Annex. These more spacious facilities gave room for expanded exhibits, workrooms, laboratories, classrooms, and lecture halls. During this move, archaeology was added to the museum's program of exhibition and research, relying heavily on the earlier Skinner and Schrabisch statewide survey collections and some donations. Unfortunately, the opening of the newly established state museum coincided with the most devastating period in American history. The opening exhibit, one on colonial New Jersey, was set to open to the public at 10:00 a.m. on Tuesday, October 29, 1929, otherwise known as Black Tuesday. Little did the NJSM or the archaeological community know that this event would benefit them both.

Also at this time, other concerns were surfacing in New Jersey archaeology. Numerous avocational archaeologists, and major artifact collectors—such as Charles A. Philhower, Lanceolet Ely, and Col. Charles Pearsall—were making it a habit to get together and to show off their prehistoric and ethnographic collections. Other individuals also came to participate in these gatherings, including Katherine Greywacz and Dorothy Cross of the NJSM. Because of their desire to promote archaeology in New Jersey and to excavate sites, in 1930 these individuals formed an organization named the Advisory Commission for Indian Research. Based in Trenton, this commission was conveniently located across the street from the state museum. Besides a brief mention of this commission in early publications and newspapers, there is not much else known about it and it appears to have been short lived. The commission's main focus was the promotion and identification of prehistoric and historic American Indian objects from New Jersey. As a result of their devotion, these individuals decided to officially form an archaeological society in order to "bring into close contact persons interested in the natural history of New Jersey, along with holding meetings, conduct excavations and promote the education of New Jersey's Native Americans" (*Elizabeth Journal* 1931). So it was that in April 1931 the Advisory Commission for Indian Research was transformed into the Archaeological Society of New Jersey. In the April 25, 1931, issue of the *Elizabeth Journal* newspaper, the event was recorded in this way: "The committee met in the afternoon in Col. Pearsall's private museum and, after a dinner at the Roosevelt Junior High School in Westfield, formed the Archaeological Society of New Jersey. Members of the committee expressed astonishment at the Pearsall collection of Indian curios, which is one of the finest in the world." This new society would immediately immerse itself in archaeological investigations. In July 1931, just four months after the formation of the ASNJ, its members and staff from the NJSM and the Museum of the University of Pennsylvania together carried out excavations at the Moody and Bevans rockshelters in northwest New Jersey (*Elizabeth Journal* 1931).

During this collaborative effort it was Dr. Dorothy Cross who directed the excavations at the rockshelters, even though Dr. Vladimir Fewkes of the University of Pennsylvania was assigned to supervise the fieldwork. Other individuals who participated in these excavations included known artifact collectors like Mr. Charles A. Philhower, a Mr. Simms, and Mr. and Mrs. J. Havard MacPherson, as well as Katherine Greywacz of the NJSM. Those were the last projects carried out by the State Museum, the ASNJ, or any other organization for the next five years (Lattanzi 2010).

## The Indian Site Survey

The ISS officially started in March 1936 as a New Deal "make work" project. As stated above, the ISS was a statewide federal project, which operated under the Division of Women's and Professional Projects, a subdivision of the Historical Records Survey of Federal One—the main WPA program. The purpose of the Division of Women's and Professional Projects (later renamed the Division of Professional and Service Projects) was to "give employment to women, who usually are the heads of families in need of relief, and to professional and white collar workers" (Findley 2010). White collar and other professionals, both women and men, were employed in fields as diverse as research, the arts, library and museum work, and clerical, medical, dental, and nursing services. The arts projects fell under the control of the Federal One project. The ISS project was sponsored by the NJSM and aided by the New Jersey State Department of Conservation and Development, under which the State Museum operated at the time. The ASNJ acted in an advisory capacity; however, its members played a major role as most were collectors and archaeologists and therefore could direct the ISS to the locations of significant prehistoric sites.

A newspaper article published in 1936 in the *Trenton Sunday Times* stated that the ISS was to have been "headed by Dorothy Cross who has done considerable research work at the State Museum." She was to become the state supervisor of the project and was to start archaeological investigations in Mercer County. The ISS had its headquarters at the State Museum. This project was organized to locate and map Indian trails and sites on which excavation might unearth new data. Another article reported that "the Archaeological Society of New Jersey endorsed the project and has promised that fifteen of the largest collections in the State will be lent to project workers delving into the State's unrecorded past" (*Philadelphia Record* 1936).

During the six years of operation of the ISS, more than 700 new sites were located and surveyed, 58 full-scale excavations were completed, and more than 35,000 objects were added to the museum's collections. At the Abbott Farm National Historic Landmark alone, 663,834 cubic feet of soil was excavated and more than 150,000 artifacts were recovered (Cross 1956; Williams et al. 1981). Many other impressive archaeological sites were excavated all over New Jersey, including a number of rockshelters in the northern part of the state and the Tuckerton shell mound in Ocean County (Cross 1941).

As one can imagine, most states varied in the approach to and implementation of their own archaeological projects and New Jersey was no exception. The excavation procedures employed by the ISS were not typical of other WPA projects in surrounding regions. While contemporary archaeologists in New York and Pennsylvania were excavating in units and in stratigraphic layers, those in New Jersey were digging long trenches, marked out at 10-foot intervals (Figure 1.1). I believe that this style of excavation was a symptom of Dorothy Cross's archaeological background excavating mounds in the Mid-

Figure 1.1. Laborers in a trench engaged in a rather unorthodox method of archaeological excavation (Courtesy of the New Jersey State Museum, Bureau of Archaeology and Ethnology).

west and sites in northern Iraq. Despite this shortcoming, the results achieved through these methods are just as informative now as they were then.

One aspect of the work carried out by the ISS that helps in understanding the excavation techniques and the day-to-day life of excavators during the Great Depression was the documentation they left behind. The copious notes, field maps, photographs, and field diaries paint a picture not only of the laborers but also of the archaeology they conducted on a massive scale. Daily diaries were kept by the "crew chief" on site, who wrote about the weather, visitors on site, any problems with the crew, and the number of artifacts found that day. Some of the many tasks assigned to the staff and crew were the production of overall site excavation maps; making vellum copies of site maps; taking large-format camera photographs not only of excavations but also of artifacts in situ; producing artifact catalog cards; labeling all artifacts; and producing feature forms, burial forms, pit forms, and so on. These records themselves are a treasure trove of information, each a snapshot in time. To organize and achieve these results the ISS worked toward a number of goals attended to by a professional staff as well as a staff of otherwise unemployed laborers from all over the state. The ISS was truly "shovel ready."

## The ISS—Its People and Goals

Accomplishing the goals of the ISS was not easy, so tasks were divided among four divisions: archaeological fieldwork, cataloging, site survey-collection, and research. During the ISS's entire operation a number of interesting individuals were directly involved in either the day-to-day operations or in the final production and completion of all projects. Each division had its own mission, staff, and ways to accomplish the job. The main task of the ISS was to inventory, map, locate, and excavate (Lattanzi 2010) and all the divisions helped to accomplish this task. The ISS had a number of professional individuals to oversee and run the project.

Dorothy Cross was the state supervisor for the WPA from 1936 to 1938, when she resigned to become the museum advisor at the NJSM. This was a surprise as I researched the project, because I had thought that Dr. Cross was in charge of the entire project for its duration, but even more surprising was that she was rarely on site at all. Based on a thorough reading of the diaries written by the field director, Charles A. Scott, Dr. Cross came out to the Abbott Farm site only about once a week.

Dr. Allan H. Smith from Yale University took over as state supervisor for the WPA in February 1939. Dr. Nathaniel Knowles was the next state supervisor in line and took over in September 1939 and stayed to the end of the ISS in 1941. Dr. Eugene Golomstock was site supervisor of the WPA from 1936 to 1939, when he resigned, after which the position was never filled because of budgetary reasons. This list of influential people would not be complete without mentioning Katherine Greywacz, the general director of the NJSM. She was extremely influential in the overall operation of the museum and how it addressed the tasks set before it as part of the WPA requirements for this enormous project. Katherine Greywacz, Dorothy Cross, and the ASNJ were directly involved in the analysis, interpretation, and production of the final aspects of all the WPA investigations, including their eventual publication in two massive volumes (Cross 1941, 1956).

The ISS initially had its main office in the State House Annex but was later moved to North Broad Street in Trenton. Satellite offices for the ISS were established in Camden and Paterson to easily conduct local surveys and excavations out of those offices. At most, 60 to 70 people were employed as part of the ISS team. Wherever an archaeological investigation took place, museum staff hired unemployed workers from within that specific county to help excavate sites. The ISS files at the State Museum show that these laborers were put through vigorous training in the basics of archaeology. Once they mastered a particular skill they were moved up in the ranks and could then train the newest hires. However, since most laborers were not professional archaeologists, problems of "collecting" artifacts certainly existed.

The survey's two main goals were (1) to survey and excavate sites throughout the state, drawing somewhat on the site locations from the earlier Skinner and Schrabisch statewide survey, and (2) to conduct thorough interviews with local collectors, farmers, and anyone who had knowledge of prehistoric artifacts and/or site locations. This "interview process" also included the production of artifact drawings and tables of artifact counts and types. Both of these main goals helped the ISS teams identify significant sites across the state to investigate at a more intensive level, and in addition created a large database of known collectors and their entire inventories.

The fieldwork division focused on the identification and excavation of archaeological sites. These results produced hundreds of files of individual collectors and their collections. Furthermore, it is from these files that ISS team members went out to locate and to produce written and illustrated descriptions of recorded sites. Each collector was interviewed, their collections sometimes photographed, some of the best pieces were taken for further study, and their collections were inventoried in the files of the NJSM. With this information the ISS team identified promising places to excavate. This section of the ISS produced 12 books that included hundreds of archaeological sites indicating the kinds of finds each site contained. While some identifications were loosely based on the Skinner and Schrabisch survey, the bulk of the site inventory came from interviews with known artifact collectors. These 12 books contain rich and amazing information about archaeological sites throughout New Jersey. These books are little gems that hold keys to understanding prehistoric life throughout the state.

Archaeological fieldwork was conducted on those identified sites that seemed the most likely to provide further information on the American Indian cultures of New Jersey. The site that was the most promising and that started and ended the ISS program was Abbott Farm. Initial test trenches up to large full-scale excavation units were dug on most sites, both prehistoric and contact period.

The ISS program would not have been complete without the identification, cataloging, and labeling of all archaeological objects recovered from the excavations. Ms. Dorothy Rickey, an archaeologist, was assigned the task of completing catalog cards for all objects and with the labeling of every specimen. She also worked on pottery reconstruction and human remains identifications. Background research was conducted for the ISS but was not directly associated with fieldwork and excavations. Alice Richards, a social scientist, carried out research on numerous aspects of Delaware Indian history as well as the early colonial settlements of New Jersey. The results of this research went into the many picture drawings of Lenape legends, educational pamphlets, and models and dioramas of American Indian life. Traveling museum exhibits, educational loans, and presentations were all part of the ISS program of educating the public on the prehistoric occupation of New Jersey.

In the end, the fruits of their labors—the artifacts, soil samples, notes, maps, and photographs—were eventually housed at the NJSM. The ISS team made great strides in site survey, collections, art, excavations, drafting, cataloging, research, and photography (Figure 1.2). Objects were loaned to places such as the Field Museum in Chicago, the University of Pennsylvania, the Peabody Museum, and the 1939–1940 World's Fair in New York City.

## The ISS Today

While the ISS excavation practices may not have been up to today's standards, the work carried out by these individuals continues to provide information regarding prehistoric peoples of the Garden State, long after the last shovel hit the ground at Abbott Farm in 1941. Archaeologists today are again taking advantage of the resources at the NJSM, which is the official repository for all the WPA ISS material. Currently, scholars and students are reexamining these old collections, asking new questions, looking for different patterns, and searching for trends that were not apparent to previous investigators. The following are a few examples of current and planned projects that are using the collections of the ISS.

Dr. Michael Stewart from Temple University, Philadelphia, is researching early pottery production in the Delaware Valley. His work analyzing a number of early WPA-excavated sites paints a picture of how ceramics were incorporated into a world where the use of steatite containers was well established. Dr. Stewart is beginning to see that the retention of steatite bowls and integration of steatite as temper into early ceramic vessels was prevalent in much of the Middle Atlantic region (Klein 1997; Stewart and Pevarnik 2008). As part of my own research at Temple University, I am examining copper artifacts from the Abbott Farm National Historic Landmark and other archaeological sites in the Middle Atlantic. Specifically, I am looking at Early to Middle Woodland copper artifacts and examining potential native copper sources and what these may tell us about prehistoric exchange patterns and their influences on social organization (Lattanzi 2008). George Pevarnik (Pevarnik et al. 2008), also at Temple University, is examining prehis-

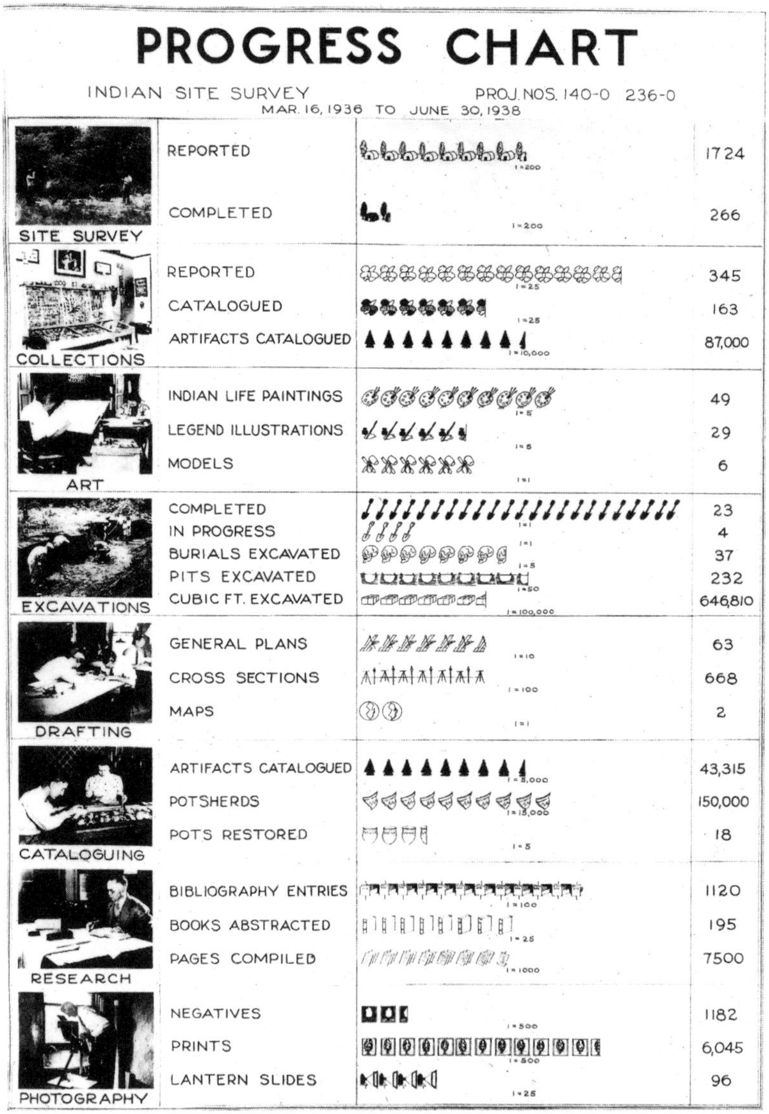


Figure 1.2. Progress chart from 1936 to 1938 showing numbers to date in each of the many categories of the Indian Site Survey (Courtesy of the New Jersey State Museum, Bureau of Archaeology and Ethnology).

toric ceramics from the Abbott Farm National Historic Landmark for geochemical signatures of potential clay sources, the results of which can help to indicate movement or exchange of resources, ideas, or individuals.

Dr. Roger Moeller of Archaeological Services, Inc., has reexamined Upper Delaware Valley Late Woodland pottery and is throwing out traditional ceramic typologies; his reinterpretation of Orient hot rock features is reshaping our notions of Transitional Archaic resource procurement and processing (Moeller 2008). His work has shown that traditional artifact typologies cannot adequately explain the variation seen in the archaeological record and that we need a new model of archaeological explanation. As part of his dissertation research, Dr. Timothy Messner of the University of Wisconsin examined ceramic sherds from the Abbott Farm National Historic Landmark to obtain starch grain and phytolith information (Messner 2008). Along with being the first person to conduct this type of analysis on material from Abbott Farm, Messner also provided the first radiocarbon date from the site. Additionally, under the guidance of Dr. Heather Wholey, undergraduate students from West Chester University in Pennsylvania are conducting trace elemental analysis on steatite bowls from excavated ISS sites and other individual collections from the NJSM to examine possible long-distance trading patterns of this resource throughout the Delaware Valley. Poul Graversen, a graduate student from Monmouth University in New Jersey, is analyzing argillite biface caches located in New Jersey and throughout the Middle Atlantic region. He is trying to determine whether there are any long-term benefits from the burial of these large bifaces to how well they can later be knapped.

As evident from this short list, there are many projects that directly involve the archaeological collections and associated material recovered during the WPA's ISS. That these objects and their associated field records stand the test of time is a credit not only to the professional archaeologists involved with the original WPA project but also to those unemployed laborers affected by the Great Depression who were given "shovel ready" projects in the truest sense.

## Conclusion

WPA archaeology in New Jersey was not a massive work relief program like those in other states. But, as seen from its results, the New Jersey ISS was much more than the jobs it created. It laid the foundation for today's understanding of New Jersey's diverse prehistoric American Indian cultures and their interrelationships with surrounding states. A 1939 quote from archaeologists of the ISS accurately summarizes the purpose of archaeology for scholars and lay people everywhere:

> It must be emphasized that negative conclusions are as equally important as positive ones for the solution of the problem of the nature, development and sequence of the Indian cultures of the State, and the entire eastern seaboard as well. The materials in private collections . . . are being assembled and may well indicate regional differences of culture. In turn the correlation of these with stratified material from the excavations may be of great diagnostic significance. Such analyses are proceeding satisfactorily and although a considerable time will be needed, their value is unquestioned and they offer the only scientific justification for the Archaeological Field work accomplished by the Indian Site Survey [New Jersey State Museum 1939:31].

The economic, scientific, and cultural effects of the massive work relief archaeology program conducted across New Jersey created collections of artifacts and records that are once again shining in the dirt.

Scholars and students, in examining these older collections with new ideas and research problems, are significantly contributing to our understanding of the archaeological past in our own backyard and, more specifically, providing information to those outside the state who can benefit from this new archaeological knowledge. New Jersey's archaeological emergence and its prehistoric prominence in the Middle Atlantic region started during a dark time in our nation's history. Over the years these collections provided and they continue to provide researchers and scholars with the necessary economic and intellectual stimulus to make the whole WPA-funded survey worthy of the effort put into it by the members of the ISS.

## Acknowledgments

I would like to thank Dr. Bernard Means for his invitation to speak at the original Society for American Archaeology session in which the paper resulting in this chapter was presented. Publicizing the great contributions of New Jersey to the field of archaeology, especially for prehistory, is something that has been previously overlooked and understudied. I would like to thank Dr. Lorraine E. Williams, Mr. David Parris, and Shirley Albright who initially published about the potential of the WPA archaeological collections from New Jersey (Williams et al. 1981). All errors and omissions in the current chapter are my responsibility.

# 2

# Historical Archaeology's "New Deal" in Pennsylvania

*Janet R. Johnson*

Massive unemployment as experienced by so many people during the Great Depression was a motivator for the implementation of numerous federal relief projects. Favored were projects deemed as "shovel ready" because they could quickly provide jobs to laborers desperately seeking employment. Federal funds available during the 1930s allowed for research and excavation of numerous archaeological sites throughout the Commonwealth of Pennsylvania and helped launch the melding of historic document research with archaeology. Many of the sites selected for investigation had been identified via previous surveys undertaken by the Pennsylvania Historical Commission (PHC). Guidance and oversight of these excavations was under State Anthropologist Donald Cadzow, who advocated for the solicitation of relief funding by the commission.

## Emphasis on Marking and Recording Pennsylvania's Heritage

From the commission's beginning in 1913 the state legislature charged the PHC with the task of marking historic properties and events, as well as with the preservation of Pennsylvania's history (Nichols 1967:8). With limited funding the appointed commissioners embarked on their first survey in 1914 to identify and mark existing public and private memorials within the state. This early effort linked the PHC with historical societies throughout the state and provided partnership opportunities for future endeavors, including those with the Wyoming Historical and Geological Society, which was based in Luzerne County, Pennsylvania. The Wyoming Historical and Geological Society, under director Frances Dorrance, conducted an organized questionnaire in 1924 of eastern Pennsylvania counties. Miss Dorrance's successful survey aimed at locating and preserving "evidence of Indian culture" and drew support from local museums and state and national professional societies (Dorrance 1931:73). The overwhelming response and productive results from this initial effort resulted in an expanded survey that would eventually encompass the entire state and ultimately include field investigations and bibliographic research. The involvement of the PHC in these surveys and Miss Dorrance's appointment to the commission in 1927 brought a renewed focus on anthropological research (Custer 1996:60). The Dorrance project evolved into the Pennsylvania Indian Survey as a joint venture between the PHC and the Pennsylvania Federation of Historical Societies. Based on these early surveys conducted by the commission, sites associated with the "early Indian period" and the French and Indian War were identified as most in danger of being lost. Concern for these neglected sites and the survey data at hand provided the necessary groundwork for the commission to mark sites and educate the public. These early surveys yielded important site and collection information instrumental in much of the early archaeology subsequently conducted by the commission with WPA funding (Hefner 1980).

The influx of federal relief funding beginning in 1933 provided historical archaeology with its own "New Deal" in Pennsylvania. The onset of federally funded programs combined historical research, the arts, sciences, and engineering in Pennsylvania with a critical common goal—job creation. Funding for archival research and recording of historical documentation was an important catalyst for archaeology in Pennsylvania and would have an impact for more than a decade on archaeology and historic research and on an important byproduct of these two disciplines: publications. Feeling the need to raise the awareness of the local community regarding history and preservation, the PHC noted: "The people living near some of the most historic spots in the State have never had their attention called to them. History, like charity, should begin at home. It should not end there" (Pennsylvania Historical Commission 1915).

## Relief Monies to Fund PHC Initiatives

The pool of relief monies advanced archaeological projects at historic properties across the commonwealth, including Pennsbury Manor under the Civil Works Administration (CWA) (Table 2.1). Prompted in 1931 by the 250th anniversary of the founding of Pennsylvania, the commission had a renewed interest in the Pennsbury Manor site, that of William Penn's manor house, and an awareness of the need to properly mark the property for future generations. A transfer of 10 acres of property to the commonwealth allowed the PHC to move forward with plans to reconstruct the manor house (Allen

Table 2.1. Historic sites excavated as New Deal projects in Pennsylvania

| Site | County | Agency | Dates of Excavation |
|---|---|---|---|
| Pennsbury Manor | Bucks | CWA | 1933 |
| | | WPA | 1936 |
| Fort Muncy | Lycoming | WPA | September to November 1936 |
| Presque Isle | Erie | WPA | August 1937 |
| French Halfway Camp (Fort Mixhaux?) | Erie | WPA | September 1937? |
| Fort LeBoeuf | Erie | WPA | October 1937 to May 1938 |

1991:21). Archaeology was conducted in conjunction with the restoration project using relief funding under the CWA (Allen 1991:20). Although this archaeology occurred on a historic site, there is little to suggest in file documentation that background research of historic records was conducted prior to commencing the excavation. Albert Cook Myers, a well-known authority on Penn, researched historic documents for the reconstruction, but did not begin his research until the archaeology was well under way. Donald Cadzow, who was supervising the investigations, was long recognized for his work along the Susquehanna River at Indian sites and like many other archaeologists of the time was not familiar with employing historic documentation to assist with archaeological excavations (Allen 1991:20). A report of Cadzow's excavations was never produced, which created voids in the documentation and hindered the accuracy of the reconstruction (Weener 1986). Cadzow nonetheless saw the benefit of relief monies and expressed it in a 1934 editorial in the journal for the Society for Pennsylvania Archaeology (Cadzow 1934).

## The Legacy of the Federal Writers Project

In 1935 the WPA was formed along with the Federal Writers Project, and the latter included a division identified as the Historical Records Survey (HRS). The desire to create jobs for thousands of workers launched numerous collaborative opportunities for writers, engineers, artists, clerical staff, archaeologists, librarians, and historians. Newly elected Democratic Governor George Earle III aggressively sought federal relief funds, resulting in the tag "Little New Deal" for Pennsylvania. Earle's success with securing millions in relief funds provided monies for numerous public works programs, including the Pennsylvania Turnpike (Miller and Pencak 2002:298). A growing interest in archaeology in the commonwealth and elsewhere and the need to educate "relic hunters," as well as the development of academic standards, all coalesced during this period and contributed to the formation of the Society for American Archaeology, which held its first annual meeting in 1935 (Griffin 1985:261).

The Federal Writers Project primarily developed and published historical guides for each state, but it also produced a children's science series. The HRS program in Pennsylvania assembled guides to manuscript collections, church archives, and maritime records of the Port of Philadelphia and also conducted historical research into the early forts and trails of Pennsylvania. An important product of this effort was the transcription of the correspondence of Colonel Henry Bouquet from photostats lent by the Library of Congress (Bouquet et al. 1940). These papers and others available from the Public Archives of Canada were essential in providing the documentation necessary for the PHC to later publish numerous titles, such as *Travels in New France, The Wilderness Chronicles of Northwestern Pennsylvania,* and a mimeographed version of *The Papers of Colonel Henry Bouquet.*

Nationally, the HRS received sufficient funding to eventually produce more than 2,000 published inventories before its termination in 1942 (Hefner 1980:1). Today, inventories produced under these state and local sponsorships aid genealogists, historians, and archaeologists alike. Unfortunately, the practice of placing these documents in universities and libraries sometimes proved lethal for their preservation. Some institutions were unable or unwilling to house the volume of materials assembled by the HRS, as was the case in Maine in 1942 where, lacking a facility to house the records, "they were dumped from a wharf in Casco Bay" (Hefner 1980:8).

## Archaeology, Engineering, and Historic Records—A New Recipe

The combined efforts of the HRS and the Federal Writers Project programs facilitated the first organized endeavor to combine research and archaeology in Pennsylvania. Under PHC sponsorship the Frontier Forts and Trails Survey project was begun as a federally funded work relief project in August 1937. The focus of this project was to produce a chronicle of the early history of northwestern Pennsylvania, specifically Erie, Warren, Crawford, and Venango counties. This was a project that the commission had identified at its inception as important; now, with relief funding, the PHC would finally have the resources to research and mark these important sites (Nichols

1967:21). A 1930 survey by Richard and Allyn Wright of Erie County had already produced locational data on American Indian mounds, camp sites, and villages of interest to the commission in this region. This survey combined with the previous research provided "shovel ready" sites in need of labor. Project headquarters were located in the Old Customs House in Erie, Pennsylvania, with departments for editorial, typing, filing, photography, art, and museum staff (Pennsylvania State Archives 2010).

Researchers quickly identified an essential component in the development of the military forts of this region as the Old French Trail or Venango Trail. This trail served French, British, and American troops from the period 1753 to at least 1794 with the establishment of a town at Presque Isle. The earliest use of the Venango Trail was as an American Indian footpath from the Forks of the Ohio to Presque Isle in Lake Erie. This was also referred to as the Frankstown-Venango Path or the Cornplanter-Venango Path. Trader George Croghan wrote to the provincial secretary in 1747 of his trading trip to the borders of Lake Erie and was well aware of American Indian and European use of this trail. He also observed that the American Indians were no longer allies with the French and they would "think a great dail [*sic*] of a little powder and lead at this time" (Stevens and Kent 1940:5). The Venango Trail was an important link for several other trails in the region and would play a key role in the French and Indian War.

Trade routes to the west that were linked to the Venango Trail provided important passage into Ohio and to the Allegheny River. These routes were critical to maintaining control of French territories in Illinois and Louisiana and preventing British forces from aligning with American Indians in these regions. In 1753 the French developed a section of the Venango Trail as the original transport route for carrying canoes and boats between Fort Presque Isle and Fort LeBoeuf, which was located at a fork on French Creek. This route allowed for portage to French Creek, on a route that crossed Mill Creek and Walnut Creek to LeBoeuf (Stevens and Kent 1940:7–9). English traders also utilized this trail to access the Ohio Valley, which the French feared would endanger their domination of the fur trade. The trail to French Creek permitted travel from Lake Erie and eventually to Pittsburgh and the Allegheny River. French control of the route was critical for travel and transport of supplies between the French territories of Louisiana and Canada. The desire of the French to both protect the route and to control the fur trade was the impetus for establishing their fort system. A chain of forts was planned from Lake Erie to the Forks of the Ohio (Stevens and Kent 1940:12). The French recognized Lake Ontario and the lower Niagara River as an important network for trade and communication in North America and established Fort Niagara in 1678 in this area. This fortification facilitated control of the fur trade to the west and would serve as the starting point for the line of defense against the British.

The HRS gathered documents and maps produced by traders and French surveyors and also numerous military accounts from all three occupations of the territory. These documents provided valuable resources in determining the various routes of the trail. A detailed survey completed during the French occupation of the trail provided point-to-point references for use by both the archaeological and engineering divisions of the WPA (Stevens and Kent 1940:15–16).

The Engineering Division of the Frontier Forts and Trails Survey project surveyed the trail from its beginning at Fort Presque Isle (at the foot of Parade Street, in Erie) to the southern boundary of Erie County. The route from Erie to Waterford, the location of Fort LeBoeuf, was almost impassable in 1753 when the French built the first portage, due to "swampy conditions." Recognizing this as a hindrance to their development of a chain of fortifications, the French deemed establishing a passable route a priority. Following the point-to-point measurements as recorded by French engineer De Lery in 1754, the WPA engineers were able to determine the distances and courses of the various routes (Kent 1938). Accounting for conversion of the French units of measurement and the fact that the location of the trail varied, the engineers were incredibly successful in their attempts to record and reconcile points noted in the original 1754 survey. The historic account of this earlier survey enabled recognition in 1937 of key bridge locations, facilitating the identification of landmarks referenced in the 1754 survey (Stevens and Kent 1940:17).

In a 1754 letter, Michel-Jean-Hugues Péan, second in command of the French expeditionary forces, wrote to Governor Duquesne: "I am going to have the entire three leagues of bad road in this portage paved with wood. That will be a lengthy piece of work but it will be durable" (Hunter 1960: 90). The discovery of the remains from a section of the corduroy road in 1937 provided tangible evidence of the immense labor necessary for this endeavor (Kent 1938:5). The Engineering Division also confirmed the shifting of the trail from season to season and year to year as the area was continually plagued by swampy conditions (Kent 1938).

Archaeology was conducted simultaneously with both the research of historic documents and the engineering survey. In addition to surveying the Venango Trail, the Engineering Division also staked the sites for many of the archaeological excavations, providing baselines for mapping (Kent 1938:3). Harry Schoff, who had conducted previous work relief excavations, including that at Fort Muncy in Lycoming County, was hired as assistant project head for archaeology. At one point, a member of the Engineering Division wrote to the PHC complaining of a request from Schoff for them to stop work on the trail in order to assist him in plotting artifacts: "I don't feel that I can interrupt the engineers every time an arrowhead is located to plot it in for Harry." The letter continued with rhetoric regarding "men working haphazardly" and "this might be excusable for a pot-hunter but not an archaeologist" (Mann 1938). Reflected in this letter is the frustration of working with unskilled labor and limited budgets and of attempting to conduct archaeology on sites as dictated by both local and federal sponsorship. The Engineering and Archaeology Divisions were working year round in an area where the average temperature in the month of January is 26 degrees and average snowfall 23 inches—not exactly ideal climatic conditions. Combined with unskilled field crews, this made the survey increasingly difficult.

## The Struggle for Control of a Frontier Wilderness

The French and British forts in western Pennsylvania identified within the scope of research for the WPA-funded project were the fortifications at Presque Isle and Fort LeBoeuf. The French occupied these sites from 1753 to 1759. Both forts were intentionally burned by the French rather than risk use by invading British troops. The British occupation of these sites began in 1760. British Fort LeBoeuf was destroyed, again by burning, during Pontiac's War in 1763 (Harrington 1940).

The area of Presque Isle (later known as the Presque Isle Triangle or Erie Triangle) was occupied by the Seneca throughout the Revolutionary War and was federal property until Congress approved its sale in 1788. Pennsylvania purchased the Triangle's acreage in 1792 from Cornplanter and the other chiefs of the Six Nations who agreed to sell American Indian claims on the land to the Commonwealth of Pennsylvania. Under an agreement with the Seneca the Canandaigua Treaty of 1794 was signed, which provided for a reservation east of Presque Isle known as the Cornplanter Tract. Not all of the Natives living in this area moved to the reservation and the provincial government feared that any attempt to settle the area would be met with hostile attacks by these American Indians. General "Mad" Anthony Wayne overwhelmingly defeated the remaining western tribes of the Six Nations at the Battle of Fallen Timbers in 1794. Wayne and his troops were credited with removing the remaining American Indians and securing Pennsylvania's northwest for colonial settlement (Federal Works Agency 1940).

A detachment of 200 men led by General Wayne's army was sent to the

Presque Isle portage to construct a fort in order to oversee and protect the settlement of the proposed town of Erie. A third Fort Presque Isle was thus constructed by Wayne's troops in 1795. However, unlike the French and British, who built their forts on the west side of Mill Creek, the Americans constructed their fort on the eastern side of the creek (Madlehner 1939).

Historic records transcribed by the HRS describe the position and extent of fortification of the American fort. It was constructed on the high ground to the east of Mill Creek, overlooking the harbor entrance of Presque Isle. A deep ravine to the east of the ground that the fort occupied provided protection from direct attack on all sides except to the south. All timber was cleared for a considerable distance so that an approaching enemy could be easily identified. An extensive stockade was erected with two or three log houses and a two-story blockhouse within its walls. Records indicate this fortification was maintained until the War of 1812 (Federal Works Agency 1940).

Harry Schoff began excavations in August 1937 at the site of the American blockhouse at Presque Isle (Madlehner 1939). In the next 14 months archaeology would be conducted on 22 properties covering 13 sites. The primary focus of the project was on forts of northwestern Pennsylvania, but also included were American Indian sites that had been recorded under previous surveys but never excavated.

Work crews under the supervision of Schoff excavated more than two-thirds of the site of this American fortification at today's Garrison Hill on the grounds of the Soldiers' and Sailors' Home in Erie. An extensive landscaping project was under way and had already exposed features when the archaeology began (Schoff 1938:69). The area was laid out in 5-foot trenches and excavated to an average depth of 2½ feet. Schoff prepared a brief summary of the excavations for *Pennsylvania Archaeologist* in 1938, but a detailed report was never completed. Inventories produced for the 275 artifacts indicate 70 percent of the artifacts were buttons. Since records are incomplete, it is impossible to know whether additional materials were excavated but not retained to explain the disproportionate number of buttons. Unfortunately, poor preservation and the absence of many of the buttons in collections today prevent detailed analysis.

Inventories and photographs were produced at the time of the excavations, after which many of the artifacts were publicly displayed in the Erie Customs House (Madlehner 1939). Catalog records indicate that the collections remained on display in Erie at the Soldiers' Home until the early 1940s before removal to storage. There was overwhelming support of the local community for these investigations not only from interest in the history and artifacts recovered but also because the relief work provided employment for so many in the various projects. Schoolchildren were encouraged to view the exhibits and programs and tours were held for them to observe the artifacts (Madlehner 1939).

The surviving buttons examined for this chapter, of which 90 are present, include cuff buttons and uniform buttons ranging in size from .72 mm to 27.63 mm. Most are white metal or bronze, solid plain flat-faced, and with iron or brass wire eyes. Both spun back and cast back examples are present. Additional buttons are of plain cast white metal with a heavy eye identified by Olsen (1963) as dating from 1750 to 1812. This button was common in households of the period but was also used by the U.S. Army, which would make it appropriate for the site. In 1951 John Witthoft, the state archaeologist for the PHC at the time, requested the return from the Soldiers' and Sailors' Home of buttons on loan from the excavation. Missing from the collections now housed at The State Museum of Pennsylvania, however, are buttons included in the original inventory that were identified only as "eagle" buttons. There were 73 inventoried "eagle" buttons, which is 38 percent of the recovered buttons. Calver and Bolton (1950) report buttons with an eagle motif appear as early as 1780 in the barracks at West Point and this design continued into the War of 1812 and later. Uniform buttons from the War of 1812 are a broad mix of older buttons drawn from supplies and new productions, creating difficulty in linking buttons with troops (Calver and Bolton 1950:147). Of note are buttons identified as "U.S." in the inventory. These artifacts account for 16 percent of the buttons inventoried, but unfortunately they are not present in the collection at the state museum.

Few additional military artifacts beyond buttons were recovered. Of note are nine brass stock clasps. These examples are very similar to those excavated at Fort Stanwix (1758–1781) near Rome, New York. The brass clips were sewn to a cloth neck collar and were part of the uniform of British troops occupying Fort Stanwix (Hanson and Hsu 1975:91). Another artifact of note is a Spanish coin dating to 1784. This artifact is drilled on the edge, possibly for securing in a coat lining, as was a practice during the colonial period. Ceramics recovered include polychrome creamware and annular and mocha pearlware contemporary with the American Presque Isle occupation.

Additional research on the artifacts and historic records may yield further information regarding the manufacture and ownership of several personalized artifacts. Excavators recovered a silver stickpin with engraved initials and an ornate brass fob watch seal. Watch seals were an accessory item to be attached to the watch and dangled from either a chain or cloth outside of the fob pocket (White 2005:132). Watches and accessories were considered status pieces and likely represent an officer at Fort Presque Isle.

In a quarterly progress report of the Frontier Forts and Trails Survey, project head Leo Madlehner summarized the excavations and historic research conducted for the project. Madlehner reported that during the summer months Schoff excavated at multiple sites in the region. Unfortunately, some of these sites had been exposed and partially destroyed prior to Schoff's investigations, requiring salvage archaeology; other sites had been previously identified through the earlier surveys. Included in these investigations were two additional historic sites. Investigations at Misery Bay on Lake Erie sought the location of foundations dating to the War of 1812. The second site was the French Halfway Camp along the portage route identified by researchers of the HRS (Madlehner 1939). In his report Madlehner stated that no artifacts were recovered at these locations, but it is not clear whether positive evidence of site locations was identified.

## Trenching Away at Waterford

From October 1937 through May 1938 Schoff excavated at Waterford, Pennsylvania, in search of the various occupations of Fort LeBoeuf. Excavations at this location would encompass eight properties (Figure 2.1). No documents were located indicating why these were the selected locations for testing, but historic records were undoubtedly referenced given the placement of test units. Schoff (1938) reported that construction from the building of homes and grading of the area had disturbed much of the site prior to excavation. Additionally, repeated episodes of rebuilding Fort LeBoeuf on the remains of previous forts further disturbed the archaeological evidence, making it difficult to interpret (Figure 2.2). This site had three consecutive occupations, French, British, and American fortifications, over a period of approximately 50 years with similar artifacts and little to differentiate them. Further complicating the archaeological record was the burning of all three fortifications.

The American blockhouse at Fort LeBoeuf was the area of the first investigation and was readily identified, as the original cellar foundation was still present adjacent to the Eagle Hotel (Madlehner 1939). This cellar is located on the grounds of the Daughters of American Colonists (DAC), here referred to as the DAC lot. To the rear of the blockhouse cellar foundation, a large refuse deposit as well as another foundation wall was encountered. Additional testing around this second foundation aided investigators in locating the original soil surface at a level of about 2½ feet below the present

Figure 2.1. WPA crew digging an excavation trench in Waterford, Pennsylvania, at the site of Fort LeBoeuf (Courtesy of The State Museum of Pennsylvania, Pennsylvania Historical and Museum Commission).

grade. A concentration of musket balls, gunflints, glass trade beads, and iron tools was recovered here. Work relief crews continued to strip sod on this property and located another thick deposit of wood ash and decayed organic material as well as artifacts similar to those in the first deposit (Madlehner 1939). Adjacent to the DAC lot was an area identified as First Alley. Schoff concluded this was an undisturbed area and an intact ground surface, containing artifacts similar to those in other deposits. Unfortunately, the catalogers of these artifacts grouped the contexts of the DAC lot and First Alley. Depth and trench information is available on the catalog cards prepared by the WPA, but field records of the excavations have not been located to aid in interpreting these deposits.

Madlehner's report continued with a description of excavations in the area of First Alley but across the street and to the northeast. The Johnson property excavations occurred in late December, forcing excavations in small test units, as opposed to the trenches utilized previously. Seventeen pits were reportedly opened, the largest being 15 feet square. At a depth of just over 2 feet, charred timbers were encountered "apparently lying in their original

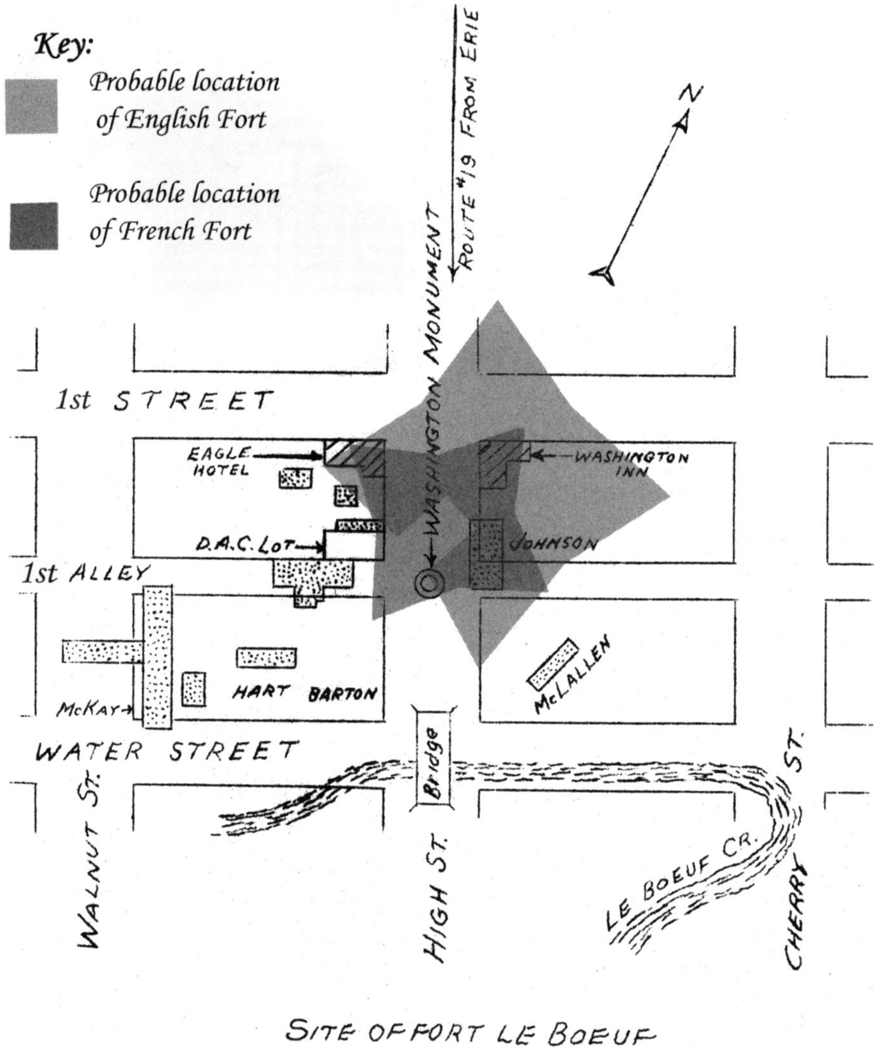


Figure 2.2. The original site map illustrating the units excavated by WPA crews in search of evidence of French and English Fort LeBoeuf. Overlaid images in the center of the map are of proposed locations for both the French and English forts (Courtesy of The State Museum of Pennsylvania, Pennsylvania Historical and Museum Commission).

position." Melted glass, nails, and lead were identified as coming from this area. Associating the artifacts to this excavation area is again difficult due to the cataloging system employed for this site, which did not assign a specific designation to these units.

To the southeast of the DAC lot Schoff excavated the McLallen property. A 1759 map drawn by Lt. Thomas Hutchins of the burned ruins of the French Fort "Le Beauf" (Hunter 1960) identified French Creek to the southeast of the fort. This map further identified a knoll as "Rising Ground that the Fort is Situate on." Schoff's crew opened a trench 12 feet wide and 30 feet long running parallel to a knoll at the rear of this property. Schoff determined that extensive grading had previously occurred in this area based on observations of test unit stratigraphy. Buried refuse from the grading led him to believe that debris from destruction of one of the previous forts had been thrown over the knoll (Madlehner 1939). In some areas the overburden was measured at nearly 8 feet deep and a stratum of fort refuse was identified at just above 3 feet. This layer of refuse was 18 inches thick and contained the greatest quantity of gun parts recovered from the excavations. Schoff's crew observed another possible foundation in the northeast corner of the lot, but conditions in the area prevented further investigations. The report also noted the discovery of a concentration of charred wood containing a piece with a musket ball embedded in it, in addition to a section of a cut silver Spanish coin. The Spanish coin appears to be a Philip V real, which was commonly cut into pieces for use as smaller currency during the eighteenth century (Hume 1969:171). The musket ball, which is still embedded in wood, is on display at the Fort LeBoeuf Museum in Waterford. Artifacts from the McLallen property were cataloged separately from the previous lots and were identified with the letter designation *Z* preceding the catalog number and encompass 208 catalog numbers.

Madlehner's report identified the Hart property as on "the extreme southwestern end of the fort knoll." However, this area had been heavily graded and no intact features were identified. Excavators moved to the McKay property, bounded by First Alley, Walnut Street, and Water Street. A series of trenches dug to a depth of approximately 4 feet, down to gravel subsoil, yielded the highest quantity of Native material, which included points, trade beads, and an Onondaga chert biface (Madlehner 1939). Near the edge of the trench at the edge of the knoll was a deposit similar to that of the McLallen property with musket balls, lead shot, beads, and gun parts. This deposit was not fully excavated due to its location under a large apple tree. Artifacts from this lot also received a separate designation and were cataloged as letter designation *G* and include 136 catalog units.

The last area investigated was the Eagle Hotel property. A trench 3 feet wide and 4 feet deep was dug along the side of the DAC property: a modern cellar was encountered in this trench. Additional testing between the hotel's tennis court and barn consisted of a 15-by-25-foot unit that was also excavated to a depth of 4 feet. This area was deemed as recent fill and did not yield artifacts contemporary with the fort occupations. Additional test pits were excavated between the DAC lot and the Eagle Hotel, encountering what was described as a "comparatively modern foundation" (Madlehner 1939). The repeated method of excavation throughout the properties was trenching; with laborers available to open up these large units, Schoff was able to fully observe soil changes and features throughout the area.

Analysis of the artifacts is admittedly difficult due to the poor cataloging methods employed at the time. However, the artifacts represent a tight concentration of military goods dating over a short time period. They offer an exceptional opportunity to compare fort-period artifacts here with other contemporary artifacts throughout the commonwealth to determine patterns of trade networks and to track the movement of provisions.

Working on residential properties posed issues with "seepage from a septic tank," an apple tree that hindered retrieval of a "large deposit," and a "large spring" that produced conditions too wet for excavations. Despite these obstacles and the winter environment, the excavations yielded important evidence of the frontier forts system. Schoff reported that "the work at Waterford has established beyond all doubt the traditional site of the Le Boeuf forts" (Madlehner 1939).

## Monies May Dry Up, But Heritage Survives

Funding was terminated for the Frontier Forts and Trails Survey of northwestern Pennsylvania in November 1938. The Women's and Professional Projects Division of the WPA expressed concerns with the commonwealth's ability to conduct historic sites excavations. Cadzow wrote to the WPA asking that the program be continued in Pennsylvania. He discounted points raised concerning qualifications of personnel, research problems, and conflict between the HRS and the Frontier Forts and Trails Survey (Cadzow 1938a). Unfortunately, the PHC was unsuccessful in restoring the funding for further historic sites' archaeological excavations in this region, but the study of collections and records generated under this program continued. Publications were not completed until the war years and after. Fortunately, the surviving artifacts continue to have considerable research potential.

There were many issues involved in an undertaking as large as the Frontier Forts and Trails Survey project and this effort was plagued by some of the same political rhetoric that hindered other New Deal programs. However, the records and artifacts excavated under these programs would not have survived if it were not for the caring and dedication of these men and women who were funded by work relief programs. The interest generated in state and local history through these WPA excavations would endure for decades and provides a foundation for historic archaeological research throughout the commonwealth today. I end with a quote from Madlehner's quarterly report filed with the WPA in December 1939: "Historical research, archaeological excavations, engineering surveys and illustrative work have laid the foundations for the writing of the early history of northwestern Pennsylvania."

## Acknowledgments

No acknowledgment for this chapter would be complete without recognizing the efforts of Franklin D. Roosevelt in creating the New Deal. Through his efforts unprecedented funding was provided for historic research and archaeology, facilitating the employment of thousands of unemployed. Many thanks to Bernard Means for his continued interests in curated collections and the research he has shared with the archaeological community. I acknowledge Bernard also for his editorial comments and the coordination of this publication. Special thanks to my colleagues at The State Museum of Pennsylvania and the Pennsylvania Historical and Museum Commission for their assistance with illustrations, editing, and general support of this research.

# 3

# Archaeologist #.00000000000000000

## Edgar E. Augustine and New Deal Excavations in Somerset County, Pennsylvania

*Bernard K. Means*

From the harsh winter of 1934 to the eve of American entry into World War II, ordinary men labored under New Deal work relief programs to excavate American Indian archaeological sites located across the rugged, mountainous landscape of Somerset County, Pennsylvania. The story of these excavations—and their excavators—is told here largely through the words and the deeds of Edgar E. Augustine, who directed most of the Depression-era investigations in Somerset County. Edgar E. Augustine (1898–1973) was born and died in Uniontown, Fayette County, Pennsylvania. He held a number of positions during his life, including serving as a clerk, toiling in the fields as a farmer, and, for a short period, acting as a field director on work relief excavations in southwestern Pennsylvania. As such, Augustine was an archaeologist who played a role in historically significant events but, sadly, is himself not well known today. While more modest in scope than New Deal–funded efforts at Mississippian mounds and villages in the Southeast (Lyon 1996), Augustine's efforts in uncovering Pennsylvania's American Indian past continue to have a profound impact on archaeologists working in the region today—and on the descendants of the relief workers themselves (George 1983; Hart 1993; Johnson 2001; Lepley 2008; Malakoff 2008; Means 1998, 2000a, 2000b, 2000c, 2002, 2005, 2007; Means and Galke 2004). Here, Augustine's contributions are highlighted and the challenges he faced conducting archaeology as government-funded work relief programs are explored.

### The Great Depression and Archaeology in Pennsylvania

Pennsylvania was hard hit by the Great Depression. Central components of Pennsylvania's economy—iron and steel manufacturing, mining, construction, and railroads—saw tremendous losses (Cohen and Filippelli 2003:1). By March 1933, 37 percent of the state's work force was unemployed, and those who still held jobs faced lower wages (Cohen and Filippelli 2003:1, 4). Many lost their homes. In 1934, there were at least 60 Fayette County families who lived in idle coke ovens, and an unknown number lived in caves (Coode and Bauman 1981:161). New Deal work relief programs certainly had an impact on Pennsylvanians from all walks of life. More than 160,000 Pennsylvanians joined the Civilian Conservation Corps (CCC) and served in Roosevelt's "tree army" on projects across the Keystone State (Coode and Bauman 1981:226). A much smaller number would become involved in work relief archaeology.

Even as the Great Depression began to take hold on Pennsylvania, the state agency in charge of archaeological investigations—the Pennsylvania Historical Commission (PHC)—decided in 1932 to launch an ambitious series of excavations in critical areas across the state (*Pennsylvania Archaeologist* 1932a). These excavations sought to capitalize on interest in the state's buried past that had been growing since the early 1920s. In 1924, Frances Dorrance and the Wyoming Historical and Geological Society of Luzerne County, Pennsylvania, had sent out 13,000 questionnaires and received 2,000 answers within a year; 1,900 sites were reported across the eastern part of the state (Dorrance 1931:73–74). The PHC adopted the survey and, still under Dorrance's direction, extended it to the western part of Pennsylvania (Witthoft 1950:303). Pennsylvania's archaeologists enthusiastically supported these survey efforts, partly because they felt that much less was known archaeologically about the state than was true for neighboring New York and Ohio (Mason 1941:27). Sadly, the nascent attempt to draw on the survey results and start an active archaeology program in 1932 was stopped before the year was out as a result of "economies of government made necessary by the [D]epression" (*Pennsylvania Archaeologist* 1932b). Still, as Janet Johnson (this volume) points out, the large number of sites reported by the survey meant that Pennsylvania's archaeology program would be "shovel-ready" when work relief funds became available two years later.

At the founding meeting of the Eastern States Archeological Federation, held February 1934 in Philadelphia, the assembled scholars discussed the implications of Civil Works Administration (CWA) support for archaeological projects in Alabama, Kentucky, and Tennessee associated with the Tennessee Valley Authority (TVA). Donald Cadzow, Pennsylvania's state archaeologist, noted that he had applied for CWA funds for a statewide survey of archaeological sites and urged other states to do the same. A representative from New Jersey indicated that they would follow in Pennsylvania's footsteps (Greywacz 1934:13). As New Deal funding became available, Cadzow was tasked with obtaining work relief funds to restart projects begun earlier in critical parts of the state, as well as finding suitable field directors for those projects (*Pennsylvania Archaeologist* 1935). The selection of Somerset County as a critical area is not surprising. Cadzow was employed by the PHC, one of whose directors was Flora Black. Black was a resident of Somerset County and was quite knowledgeable about the region's archaeological potential. Cadzow may also have been influenced by prominent Somerset banker John Scull, who headed the Somerset County Archaeological and Historical Society.

In October 1934, CWA funds were secured for a "paper" survey designed specifically to document the cultural heritage of Somerset County (Black 1934; Cadzow 1935a:10, 1935b:45). Farmers and others were interviewed to determine the location of archaeological sites encountered during plowing or other activities. Historic cemeteries were also recorded, as were the locations of original historic manuscripts. The survey was performed under the direction of Flora Black (1934) and clearly guided most of the work relief excavations in Somerset County throughout the 1930s and into 1940 (Table 3.1). Flora Black, Donald Cadzow, and Edgar Augustine would all aggressively pursue federal relief funds to explore Somerset County's rich American Indian heritage through the remainder of the 1930s.

The first excavations of an American Indian site in Pennsylvania began in October 1934 with a short-lived project sponsored by the Federal Emergency Relief Administration (FERA) at the Montague site, located in Somerset County. Works Progress Administration (WPA) funding would later allow most of this site to be uncovered. The FERA excavations at this site are not well documented. These excavations do mark, however, the beginning of a major initiative to excavate villages in Somerset County using federal relief funds (Means 1998, 2002). FERA funds, through a local works development grant, were next directed to the Clouse site, another Monongahela village in Somerset County. This site was located through Flora Black's CWA-funded paper survey and she pushed for the site's excavation. According to state archaeologist Donald Cadzow, "ten husky SERB workmen" excavated the Clouse site. Here, SERB stands for State Emergency Relief Bureau, the recipient of the FERA funds. This funding was expended before the site was fully exposed, and excavations were later completed using WPA workers (Adolph 1935:8; Butler 1939; Means 2002).

The majority of Pennsylvania's New Deal relief excavations were conducted under the auspices of the WPA, beginning in November 1935 with excavations at the Hanna site, yet another American Indian village located in Somerset County (Cadzow 1936; Means 1998, 2002). It is with the Hanna site excavations that Edgar Augustine first became a field director on the

Table 3.1. Sites excavated by New Deal work relief crews in Somerset County

| Site | Site Type | Agency | Dates of Excavation |
|---|---|---|---|
| Montague | Village | FERA | October 22 to November 7(?), 1934 |
| | | WPA | March 22 to July 1, 1936 |
| Clouse | Village | FERA | May 5 to July 19, 1935 |
| | | WPA | July 2 to July 7, 1936 |
| Hanna | Village | WPA | November 1, 1935, to March 1, 1936 |
| Peck 1 | Village | WPA | October 13, 1936, to January 29, 1937 |
| Peck 2 | Village | WPA | March 2 to May 18, 1937 |
| Reckner | Village | WPA | May 27 to August 5, 1937 |
| Emerick | Village | WPA | August 27 to October 20, 1937 |
| Troutman | Village | WPA | October 27, 1937, to January 20, 1938 |
| Powell 1 | Village | WPA | January 31 to March 9, 1938 |
| Powell 2 | Village | WPA | March 24 to April 12, 1938 |
| Fort Oak | Camp | WPA | April 27 to May 11, 1938 |
| Martz Rock Shelter | Rockshelter | WPA | June 14 to June 20, 1938 |
| Martz Rock Shelter No. 2 | Rockshelter | WPA | June 14 to June 20, 1938 |
| Fort Hill | Village | WPA | June 26 to October 30, 1939; April 3 to June 18, 1940 |
| Fort Hill Rock Shelters | Rockshelter | WPA | November 6 to November 22, 1939 |
| Gower | Village | WPA | December 20, 1939, to April 2, 1940 |
| Merle Rock Shelter | Rockshelter | WPA | June 6 to June 7, 1940 |

work relief excavations (Butler 1939). He struggled to maintain this role for the next six years in the face of political opposition and intermittent and unreliable federal support (Augustine 1936a, 1936b, 1936c, 1937a; Means 1998, 2000a, 2000c; Scull 1936a). There were even occasional attempts by some of his subordinates to draw on their political connections and usurp Augustine's role as field director (Augustine 1936d).

## Highly Competent in Fieldwork: Edgar Augustine Becomes a WPA Archaeologist

One challenge with conducting archaeology under the WPA—or any New Deal agency—was finding enough qualified supervisors to handle the thousands of unskilled and untrained workers digging at archaeological sites across the United States. Sometimes efforts at locating qualified supervisors failed, and, as a consequence, archaeological sites were destroyed through poorly implemented field procedures and grossly inadequate documentation. Because WPA projects were often decentralized, and depended on local sponsors, the individuals directing the archaeological investigations were not always well suited for the task at hand. For example, a WPA project was begun in August 1936 in Greene County under the direction of Frank B. Jones, director of the Greene County Historical and Archaeological Museum. Jones discovered significant remains from contact-era American Indian sites, but his field methods are best described as crude, and his interpretations are suspect. Jones (1945:746), for example, noted that "the remains of the average Indian will be buried in the earth undissolved several times longer than that of the white race. The same force that will fracture the bones of a white person will have little or no effect on an Indian."

Fortunately, the director of the WPA-funded Somerset County Archaeological Survey—Edgar E. Augustine—was eminently qualified (Means 1998, 2000a). Surviving archival records do not reveal why state archaeologist Donald Cadzow selected Augustine to direct the WPA excavations in Somerset County, or what background Augustine had in archaeology. Much like Athena bursting out of Zeus's skull, Augustine seemingly erupted onto the local archaeological scene with sufficient skills to carry out a well-reasoned program of excavations at American Indian sites—notably at a dozen villages, some of which were multicomponent—and in addition demonstrated the ability to manage men who had little to no prior working knowledge of archaeology (Means 1998, 2000d).

My correspondence with Edgar Augustine's son (now deceased) in January 2000 was only minimally helpful in understanding why Augustine was selected as a WPA field director (Edgar Augustine Jr., personal communication 2000). Augustine's son indicated that his father was employed as a clerk in the Fayette County (Pennsylvania) Commissioner's office until 1932, when he lost his job for political reasons. Augustine was friends with John Scull, and this may have influenced Cadzow to hire Augustine. A letter written by John Scull (1936b) on September 22, 1936, noted that Augustine had been trained by Cadzow and that Augustine was "highly competent in field work, both in regard to the careful excavation and handling of specimens, and in the management of his field force. Mr. Augustine is well regarded locally as a man of integrity and high character." This letter, incidentally, was written to ally political pressure exerted in an effort to force Augustine out of his position as WPA field director. Political interference would dog Augustine's efforts throughout his tenure as a New Deal archaeologist in the selection of sites he would excavate, who he would have to hire, and whether his projects would get their allocated relief funding (Means 1998, 2000a, 2002).

## Full of Sauerkraut and Sausage: Conducting WPA Archaeology in Somerset County

We may never know specifically why Augustine was chosen to direct work relief excavations in Somerset County or the nature of the training he received. Fortunately, Augustine kept careful field records, filed daily reports with his WPA supervisors, and maintained a healthy correspondence with Mary Butler (then Pennsylvania's assistant state archaeologist), Donald Cadzow, John Scull, and others (Means 1998, 2000a, 2002). This archival record reveals that Augustine took quite seriously the goal of keeping a crew of men employed, while simultaneously endeavoring to uncover Somerset County's past (Means 1998). Prior to the New Deal excavations in Somerset County, some scholars had expressed doubt that there had been a substantial American Indian presence in southwestern Pennsylvania (Butler 1936:55). Augustine (1936e) wrote on December 31, 1936: "We try to work the 52½ hour shifts to the best advantage of the excavators, remembering that the first object of work is to provide for these men and their families but we also make every effort to carry out the work to the satisfaction of the [Pennsylvania] Historical Commission and the Works Progress Administration." Augustine made sure that the archaeological work he oversaw was conducted systematically and carefully documented. My detailed examinations of Augustine's field records showed that, while not free of errors, they remain an important resource for modeling village community organization, as well as examining mortuary behavior (Means 1998, 1999, 2000d, 2001, 2006, 2007).

Augustine and his work relief crews focused their attention on excavating American Indian village sites (Means 1998). The bewildering arrangements of postholes—many representing circular floor plan, wigwam-like structures—and other features meant that each village site's excavation involved a lengthy and intensive field effort. In addition to several rockshelters and a camp site, a dozen village sites would be completely or nearly completely excavated by New Deal archaeologists in Somerset County—largely under the direction of Augustine. Very few villages have been completely excavated in the region since the 1930s (Hart 1993; Means 1998).

Augustine likely would have excavated additional villages in Somerset County, except there was a year-long hiatus in his WPA project due largely to political interference. The Somerset County relief project was initially halted in July 1938 over concerns from federal administrators about Augustine's qualifications and also because his project lacked a dedicated repository for the disposition of artifacts recovered during the relief excavations (Woodward 1938). Cadzow (1938b, 1938c) was able to allay federal concerns, but the temporary cessation of the project provided an opening for local political maneuverings. Most WPA archaeology projects were channeled through local sponsors—often county governments or historical societies in Pennsylvania. In Somerset County, the county commissioners—overwhelmingly Republican—delayed the Somerset County Archaeological Survey from summer 1938 to summer 1939, because they felt work relief projects cast the Democratic Party in too-favorable a light in the eyes of voters (Augustine 1938a; Means 1998). When the Somerset project resumed in 1939, the PHC took over direct sponsorship and freed Augustine from many worries related to local political machinations (Cadzow 1939; Nitch 1939).

Augustine endeavored to have two sites picked out ahead of each ongoing excavation to ensure there were no breaks in fieldwork for his crew, noting that "[i]t would be pleasant to have a site or two in advance of the wolves" (Augustine 1936f, 1936g). If he had not been able to keep a sizeable crew busy over an extended period, his work relief funding would have been terminated. Many contemporary photographs show Augustine's men working in the snow, even in raging blizzards, because of the fear that prolonged inactivity would shut the project down (Augustine 1936h) (Figure 3.1, top). Due to days lost to inclement weather, an official time report indicates that Augustine and his men even worked at the Hanna site on Christmas Day 1935. On particularly blustery days, Augustine instructed his men to dress warmly and to take breaks at the camp's fire as often as necessary (Augustine 1935a). The camp fire was typically maintained in two stacked oil drums, tended by the oldest crew member, and sometimes located within a small shelter built on site. Fuel for the fire was obtained by scouring the countryside for firewood during the lunch hour and occasionally by finding coal that had fallen from passing trains (Augustine 1935b, 1936i). At least for some excavations, Augustine purchased canvases that were strung up to shield his men from biting winter winds while they worked and while they ate lunch (Figure 3.1, bottom). Only when freezing rains threatened to soak his men to the skin or when the temperature plummeted to around 0 degrees Fahrenheit did Augustine feel justified in halting work for the day (Augustine 1935c).

Augustine had to fight efforts by federal administrators who wanted to dramatically expand the size of his crews. He correctly argued that the archaeological record would be irreversibly harmed if his crews were not a manageable size (Augustine 1937b, 1937c). To keep trained crew members

Figure 3.1. Top: Winter excavations at the Peck 1 village site. Bottom: WPA workers take a break from excavations at the Hanna site (Courtesy of The State Museum of Pennsylvania, Pennsylvania Historical and Museum Commission).

on his projects, Augustine used his own car—or "flivver"—to drive an experienced core of men from one excavation project to another across Somerset County (Augustine 1939; Means 1998, 2000a). In the hiatus between the excavations at individual village sites, field crews were often reduced to a minimal size, but Augustine used this to his advantage. Writing to Cadzow on August 24, 1936, Augustine (1936j) noted that "[t]aking advantage of the small crew we loaded them in the Flivver and proceeded to just about completely cover the County, making tests and interviewing the native sons" about the locations of potential village sites.

Augustine had to deal carefully with Somerset County's "native sons" as he needed to obtain permission to excavate their land. In a few cases, he had to convince WPA excavators to hire the farmers themselves to excavate village sites on the very farms they had been plowing for years (Augustine 1936k). While Augustine's interactions with the rough and taciturn farmers were not always positive, some farmers responded to Augustine's enthusiasm for archaeology by boarding and feeding him and his core crew when they worked far from their own homes. Augustine (1938b) wrote in March 1938 that "[t]hree of the boys and I live at the Powell homestead during the week and we are full of sauerkraut and sausage."

## Hale and Hearty: Augustine's Field Crew

Augustine and the men who worked for him shared a common characteristic—none of them had formal training in archaeology prior to their involvement with the work relief excavations in Somerset County. Some of them likely were field hands and this may have smoothed relations with the farmers whose land they were disturbing while searching for ephemeral traces of American Indian villages. Others were likely railroad workers or coal miners, the latter a common profession in the region. Augustine's crew ranged in age from 23 to one worker, Marshall Turney, who had "eighty summers on his head" but was nonetheless "hale and hearty" (Augustine 1935d). The relief archaeologists were "drawn entirely from relief rolls" (Augustine 1937b). Although Augustine had say in selecting some workers, others were suggested by prominent Somerset County citizens: "Can't you use some means to get Nyles Romesberg, Confluence, R.D. (lives in Lower Turkeyfoot [township]) placed with the crew engaged in archaeological work near Confluence? This man Romesberg needs the work; has wife and three children, and is a good fellow" (Kooser 1935). No *Nyles Romesberg* is listed as being a member of Augustine's work force, but there is a *Miles Romesburg* who worked for Augustine (Table 3.2); presumably these names refer to the same person.

Table 3.2. List of identified relief workers in Somerset County organized by town

| Town | Workers | |
|---|---|---|
| Confluence | Anderson, William | Mitchell, Robert |
| | Barkley, Glenn H. | Montague, Frank |
| | Chidester, Carl C. | Nagle, Paul Z. |
| | Conway, William W. | Nail, George W. |
| | Dunmeyer, Elwood | Nicholson, Paul E. |
| | Griffith, Merle | Rederick, Ralph R. |
| | Hall, Earl T. | Reid, Edgar F. |
| | Harned, John E. | Reid, Kermit J. |
| | Hyatt, Lloyd | Rowe, Paoli S. |
| | Kemp, Arthur | Rush, Jehu |
| | Kemp, Clyde | Shaffer, Kenneth |
| | Kreger, George A. | Snyder, Albert |
| | Lytle, Carl V. | Ward, Joe |
| | Lytle, Clyde | Williams, George H. |
| | May, Edward | Williams, James I. |
| | Mitchell, Harry L. | |
| Harnedsville | Gillenburger, Melvin | Holt, George |
| Hooversville | Pepley, John | Pugh, Russell S. |
| Listonburg | Burow, Ray J. | Lichtly, Charles |
| | Holt, Joseph | Ward, William |
| | Lenhart, Stanley J. | |
| Meyersdale | Angelo, Samuel | Lief, Robert |
| | Beal, Simon | Martz, James E. |
| | Bowman, John W. | McCleary, William B. |
| | Brenneman, Earl F. | Miller, Edward F. |
| | Brocht, James A. | Murray, James |
| | Brown, Hiram | Porter, William |
| | Gerhart, Clyde | Tipton, Howard |
| | Henry, Brent L. | Yeager, Myron J. |
| | Holzshu, Warren P. | Yommer, Alvin L. |
| | Hutzell, Ernest | |
| Somerfield | Augustine, Edgar E. | Swank, Paul S. |
| | Romesburg, Miles | |
| Somerset | Colvin, Robert B. | |
| Town not listed | Mitchell, Glenn | Turney, Marshall |
| | Sellers, H. Lee | Younkin, Emerson |

In an untitled missive to a WPA official, Augustine (1937d) briefly described the nature of the work expected of his men, referred to as "semi-skilled" laborers: "Excavation accomplished by semi-skilled labor consists of moving top soil and troweling the remaining loam down to hardpan. Semi-skilled labor is required to be able to recognize Indian artifacts, soil stains, post holes, the surface appearance of pits and burial[s] and to have some skill and judgment in the use of fine tools in excavating fragile artifacts and objects." Augustine had to constantly deal with untrained men joining his excavation teams as some members of his crew left for other jobs. Therefore, he made sure he kept a close eye on his workers and he completed many of the field records himself (Augustine 1939:5). Standardized field forms were used here, as they were on work relief projects throughout the United States (Dunnell 1986:28), to guide unskilled laborers and to ensure consistent data recording. In addition to providing their labor for the projects, Augustine's work relief crews had to "supply their own round pointed shovels and four inch pointing trowels" (Augustine 1939:5–6). A more extended discussion of the field methodology employed by Augustine and his crew—and issues with using these field results—can be found elsewhere (Means 1998, 2000d).

Surviving time sheets, daily reports filed by Augustine with his WPA superiors, and names on field records provide a list of 66 different workers who served as Augustine's field crew (Table 3.2). Part of the reason so many different men worked on the Somerset County relief excavations was related to the nature of federal funding. On a number of occasions, workers such as Glenn Mitchell were "Laid off account anticipated lack of funds. Recommended for Transfer," as indicated in a *Notice of Change in Work Status* slip signed July 29, 1936, by Augustine. Other workers left the relief excavations because they found private employment, including Melvin Gillenburger, who took a job with the Western Maryland Railroad in May 1936, and Harry L. Mitchell, who became a concrete finisher on highway projects in May 1938. Some workers left the archaeological investigations because of health issues. Emerson Younkin was transferred to a street project in Confluence because he had arthritis (Lambert 1935).

Augustine's men were largely drawn from the immediate vicinity where individual excavations took place, as the primary goal of WPA administrators was to relieve local unemployment. Men who shared the same last name and lived in the same town were no doubt related in some fashion. With the exception of the small, experienced crew that Augustine drove around in his flivver, this meant that a new crew had to be formed from the ranks of the unemployed each time Augustine shifted to a new location in Somerset County. One of the major reasons Augustine terminated workers was that the "[l]ocation of [the new] project moved making transportation impractical," as he noted on the termination form for Clyde Gerhart on April 26, 1938. Because six of the village sites were located close to the Borough of Confluence, it is not surprising that almost half of Augustine's men came from that small town.

Augustine endeavored to keep his excavations within the same section of Somerset County—and thereby maintain continuity within his work relief crew—but various factors led him to direct his attention to different areas, including difficulties with obtaining excavation permissions from farmers and friendly "suggestions" by politically connected locals. For example, beginning April 27, 1938, Augustine and his men spent 15 days at the behest of the Daughters of the American Revolution looking for a legendary fort that, supposedly, made it "possible for the embattled pioneers to obtain water with safety when attacks from hostile Indians forced them to take refuge in the fort" (Scull 1938). The mythical fort was never located, but at least Augustine could comfort himself with the small American Indian camp that he and his men excavated in that location (Means 2000a). He had less luck when he and his men had to excavate a purported American Indian mound in May of that same year on the land of farmer George Hay. Trenching the mound and excavating to a depth of over 5 feet verified Augustine's initial thought that this was a natural geological formation with absolutely no signs of an American Indian presence (Means 2000a).

Despite his crew's overall dedication, Augustine encountered occasional issues with his workers. The first day of deer hunting season in 1935 saw only 7 of his 18 men reporting for work (Augustine 1935d). The gray-bearded Marshall Turney, who is quite striking in photographs taken of the winter excavations at the Hanna site, apparently found that the bitterly cold winter did not sit well with him; he spent too much time warming himself at the camp's fire and not enough doing the relief work for which he was being paid. Turney was eventually recommended for direct relief. Augustine worked indirectly through his federal superiors to have Turney put on the "dole," because he did not have the heart to carry out this course of action himself (Augustine 1936l). Other workers were terminated because they simply failed to show up for work or because of other workplace issues. Writing to WPA supervisor Sam Kennedy on November 18, 1935, Augustine (1935e) noted that "Joseph Holt, Listonburg, complains of chest pains early in the morning but claims they vanish after an hour or so. This situation, I am told, is largely indisposition (towards work)." Holt was subsequently fired because he "has lost a great deal of time due to illness and is of no value to us when he does report for work" (Augustine 1936m).

## A Lasting Legacy

Meticulous records kept by Augustine formed the basis of a seminal monograph by Mary Butler (1936, 1939; see also Means 2002) that first defined and described the Monongahela culture, an archaeological construct that still guides researchers in the region today (George 1983; Hart 1993; Johnson 2001; Means 2003, 2007). During his time with the WPA, Augustine (1938c, 1938d, 1938e, 1938f, 1940) only published a few short articles on his efforts. This was largely because he was constantly searching for, and then excavating, new village sites to ensure that his crews stayed employed. Furthermore, state officials decided that a Harvard doctoral student, Francis Cresson, was better suited for writing up the final results of the WPA excavations. This report was never completed for reasons outlined elsewhere (Means 2010). However, Augustine's field records exist today, and these are crucial to an understanding of American Indian societies in Pennsylvania (and beyond).

Until recently, few scholars had directed serious attention to the village sites excavated during the Great Depression in Somerset County. Perhaps this was partly because of the negative stigma attached to New Deal archaeology and the assumption that all of these efforts were haphazard and poorly documented at best. Elsewhere I and others have demonstrated the continuing research potential of field records from Edgar Augustine's more than seven-decade-old New Deal work relief efforts. We can employ technological innovations today that might have seemed the province of science fiction in the 1930s. We can also raise questions undreamt of by Augustine and his colleagues, who worked largely within a basic culture historical framework (Means 2003, 2006, 2007).

The preservation of curated organic remains—bone tool fragments, burned beans, and maize kernels and cobs, as well as charred food adhering to pottery fragments—and Augustine's precise field records made it possible to obtain accelerator mass spectrometry (AMS) assays from many of the village sites excavated as New Deal projects in Somerset County (Means 2005). Funded through the National Science Foundation, these AMS assays upended the established chronology for the Monongahela culture, which had placed the New Deal–excavated villages early within the Monongahela temporal sequence, that is, prior to A.D. 1250. This was partly because most ceramic vessels from Somerset County villages were tempered with limestone rather than shell, and it was thought that shell-tempered vessels had replaced limestone-tempered ceramics throughout the area associated with the Monongahela culture by A.D. 1250. The rugged mountainous nature of Somerset County was also considered inhospitable to maize-dependent villagers by this time because of climatic unpredictability resulting from the "Little Ice Age." Surprisingly, given this conventional thinking, the AMS assays revealed that most of the Somerset County villages excavated under Augustine's direction were inhabited at least a century after this region was supposedly abandoned. Further, American Indians produced limestone-tempered ceramics while living in villages well into the early sixteenth century A.D. The choice to regularly live together in villages rather than in dispersed communities apparently represented a deliberate social strategy by the region's American Indians to meet environmental uncertainties associated with the incipient Little Ice Age (Means 2005, 2007).

Even if AMS assays had not been successfully obtained from curated collections, Augustine's determination to completely uncover as many village sites as possible before New Deal funding became unavailable has proved a tremendous boon for modern scholars. Augustine's field methods may not have been as sophisticated as those employed by archaeologists today. However, he labored with his work relief crews to reveal the complete layout of at least 17 village communities—enabling the thorough study of community dynamics in a way that today's partial excavations of village sites cannot. The luxury of having complete or nearly complete plans of so many ring-shaped villages for study proved central to developing methodological approaches and theoretical frameworks that are applicable to circular settlements across the globe and into the far reaches of the past (Means 2001, 2006, 2007).

Studies based on Augustine's field maps, forms, and other records within the context of new theoretical frameworks showed that the inhabitants of villages excavated in Somerset County clearly created their ring-shaped settlement layouts according to cognitive geometric models shared by the entire community. These cognitive geometric models incorporated distinctions between the sacred central plaza and the profane ring of houses—that is, concentric patterning. The profane ring was sometimes divided into clusters of dwellings of varying size—circumferential patterning—and these dwelling clusters may have been analogous to lineages or clans. Overlapping village components show that one impetus for change in the configuration of village social organizations was the sometimes unsuccessful effort to maintain the original cognitive geometric model used to establish a settlement against social pressures to alter a village's layout generated by people living within a dynamic community. The application of graphical analyses based in circular statistics—coupled with the AMS assays—demonstrated that there were considerable differences between settlement layouts within Somerset County over time and space. This variation did not reflect steady progression in social complexity or even settlement size from the earliest to the latest village components in the region. Rather, it would appear that each settlement's initial layout reflected the unique composition of individuals and social groups that established the village community (Means 2001, 2006, 2007).

The Somerset County relief crews excavated not only a maze of the postholes that are a key signature of village layouts but also hearths, storage pits, and graves. Augustine once expressed reluctance in uncovering American Indian interments, and he generally left the remains in situ after their careful and respectful documentation according to the standards of the day (Augustine 1936n, 1936o, 1940:53). While the nearly 200 graves encountered by Augustine's work relief crew were not documented in the greatest detail, the relatively large size of this sample and the information recorded on grave orientations, associated funerary items, and grave locations within village sites provide a welcome insight into the mortuary customs of the American Indians that once inhabited southwestern Pennsylvania (Means 1999). The information collected from American Indian graves by Augustine has also helped my efforts to instruct undergraduate students in the nuances of interpreting mortuary customs using these somewhat incomplete archaeological records. Some students have presented and published their analyses of these mortuary data, thus showing that the New Deal excavations in Somerset County are valuable as an interpretative source and as a teaching tool (Chassé 2007; Gage 2008).

## Conclusion

The archival record reveals that Augustine had a very dry sense of humor, and his daily reports and correspondence on his New Deal excavation efforts are often a pleasure to read. In writing to Cadzow, whom he designated as "Archaeologist #1," Augustine occasionally referred to himself as "Archaeologist #.00000000000000000." Augustine was overly modest and insecure about his own qualifications as an archaeologist. One of two surviving photographs of Augustine depicts him flanked by an elderly gentleman on one side and a young gentleman on the other (Figure 3.2). The back of the image is labeled "the oldest, the youngest, and the poorest" (Means 2000a). The "oldest" refers to Marshall Turney, then either 79 or 80 years of age, the "youngest" is the man standing to Augustine's right, and the "poorest" is the man in the center, Edgar Augustine. Augustine considered himself "poor" in his abilities, but certainly the archaeology of Pennsylvania is richer for his efforts.

Figure 3.2. The oldest, the youngest, and the poorest. Edgar Augustine stands in the center, flanked by two of his field crew (Courtesy of The State Museum of Pennsylvania, Pennsylvania Historical and Museum Commission).

## Acknowledgments

I would like to thank The State Museum of Pennsylvania, particularly Janet Johnson, for the considerable assistance provided in my research on New Deal archaeology in Somerset County, Pennsylvania. The State Museum of Pennsylvania, along with the Pennsylvania State Archives, made available all the original field records and photographs from these work relief excavations that I relied on throughout this chapter. A Pennsylvania Historical and Museum Commission Scholars in Residence grant was a key factor in supporting my review of these original field records. The National Science Foundation funded the AMS dating of Somerset Monongahela villages under Grant No. BCS-0226785, entitled "Modeling Somerset Monongahela Village Organization within a Chronological Framework Developed through AMS Dating of Curated Organic Remains." Edgar Augustine Jr. also graciously provided me with some information about his father that I draw on here.

# PART II

# Midwestern States

# 4

# The Great Depression Begets a Great Expansion

## Field Museum Anthropology, 1929–1941

*Stephen E. Nash*

The Great Depression of 1929–1941 is one of the most important economic, social, political, and now symbolic events in American history (McElvaine 1993). The very term *Great Depression* invokes images of the Dust Bowl and *Grapes of Wrath*–style hardship. The collapse of economic markets and systems beginning on October 29, 1929, ultimately had important ramifications for many North American museums, which at the time were highly reliant on private philanthropy. Yet, perhaps counterintuitively, at least some museums entered a period of enhanced productivity in the 1930s, albeit with radically restructured administrations and finances, research and collections programs, and exhibition and public outreach activities (Colwell-Chanthaphonh 2009:152–154; Haskin et al. 2003; Redman 2011).

This chapter examines archival and published data to contextualize work by the Field Museum's Department of Anthropology between 1929 and 1941 to address the following questions: Did museum-based anthropology, as seen through the Field Museum lens, change appreciably during the 1930s? Were these changes the direct result of the Great Depression and, by extension, the New Deal, or were other forces at play? To address these questions, the data will be considered in three general categories: (1) administration and personnel; (2) research, publications, and collections activity; and (3) exhibitions and public outreach activity.

### The Data

Table 4.1 lists the Field Museum archives consulted for this project. Nash and Feinman (2003:7, 257) made, and reiterated, the point that some of these archives contain data that are difficult to verify from eight decades removed. It

Table 4.1. Field Museum archives consulted for this study

| Archive | Contents |
|---|---|
| Field Museum Director's Office Expedition Files (FMEF) | Correspondence between curators and museum administrators and supervisors. |
| Field Museum Anthropology Correspondence Files (DACF) | Correspondence between the Anthropology Department and external parties. |
| Field Museum Anthropology Expedition Files (DAEF) | Documents including excavation records, artifact tabulations, and some correspondence. |

is not likely that the data contain inaccurate information and are thus wrong, but it is the case that some of the data (e.g., dates of employment for some noncuratorial staff members) are imprecise. Trends in these data are therefore arguably more important than individual cases.

## Administration and Personnel

### *Trustees*

Table 4.2 lists the 37 men who served as Field Museum trustees during at least one of the years between 1929 and 1941. These men constitute a virtual who's who of the Chicago economic elite and include manufacturers, bankers, retailers, railroad magnates, five members of the Marshall Field family, and one Field in-law (Col. Albert A. Sprague II; see Nash and Feinman 2003:268–287). Only three scientists, ethnologist Stephen Chapman Simms and ornithologists Leslie Wheeler and Boardman Conover, served on the board during this important period. Simms was an original staff member of the Field Museum, serving as curator of industrial arts in 1894, assistant curator of ethnology from 1898 to 1912, and curator of the public school extension after 1912 (Almazan and Coleman 2003). His service as a trustee (1928–1937) coincides exactly with his service as director of the Field Museum; he was thus an ex officio trustee and was not appointed by the regular selection process.

In spite of the concentration of trustees in the upper echelons of the socioeconomic continuum and their professional business focus, there was probably some dynamic tension on the board with respect to New Deal economic programs. Marshall Field III was described as a "traitor to his class" because he was an ardent New Deal liberal, but Sewell Lee Avery, the president of the

Table 4.2. Field Museum trustees during 1929–1941, listed by year of first service

| Name | Service Dates | Occupation |
|---|---|---|
| Chalmers, William James | 1894–1938 | Machinery manufacturer |
| McCormick, Cyrus Hall | 1894–1936 | President, International Harvester Co. |
| Ryerson, Martin Antoine | 1894–1932 | Lumberman, banker |
| Field, Stanley | 1906–1964 | First Vice President, Marshall Field & Co. |
| Sprague, Col. Albert Arnold, II | 1910–1946 | Consolidated Grocers Corporation |
| Field, Marshall, III | 1914–1956 | Founder, Field Enterprises |
| Keep, Chauncey | 1915–1929 | Trustee of Marshall Field Estate |
| Wrigley, William, Jr. | 1919–1931 | Wrigley's chewing gum, Chicago Cubs |
| Borden, John | 1920–1938 | Financier and explorer |
| Harris, Albert Wadsworth | 1920–1941 | President, Harris Trust and Savings |
| Simpson, James | 1920–1939 | Chair, Commonwealth Edison of Chicago |
| Smith, Solomon Albert | 1920–1963 | President, Northern Trust Company |
| Crane, Richard Teller, Jr. | 1921–1931 | Plumbing, iron, and brass industrialist |
| Graham, Ernest Robert | 1921–1936 | Architect |
| Markham, Charles Henry | 1924–1930 | President, Illinois Central Railroad |
| Strawn, Silas Hardy | 1924–1946 | Lawyer |
| Rawson, Frederick Holbrook | 1927–1935 | Chair, First National Bank of Chicago |
| Mitchell, William Hamilton | 1928–1987 | Stockbroker |
| Simms, Stephen Chapman | 1928–1937 | Ethnologist |
| Insull, Samuel, Jr. | 1929–1983 | Insurance broker |
| Kelley, William V. | 1929–1932 | Manufacturer |
| Sargent, Fred Wesley | 1929–1939 | President, Chicago & North Western Railroad |
| Richardson, George Adams | 1930–1957 | Trustee of Marshall Field Estate |
| Avery, Sewell Lee | 1932–1960 | President, Montgomery Ward Company |
| Wilson, John P. | 1932–1959 | Corporate lawyer |
| Field, Joseph Nash | 1934–1986 | Son of Stanley Field |
| Wheeler, Leslie | 1934–1937 | Amateur ornithologist |
| Block, Leopold E. | 1936–1952 | Founder of Inland Steel |

*Continued on the next page*

Table 4.2. *Continued*

| Name | Service Dates | Occupation |
|---|---|---|
| Dick, Albert Blake, Jr. | 1936–1954 | Duplicating machinery and office supplies |
| McCulloch, Charles A. | 1936–1945 | President, Frank Parmelee Transfer Co. |
| Gregg, Col. Clifford J. | 1937–1962 | Board, Boy Scouts of Chicago; YMCA |
| Roosevelt, Theodore, Jr. | 1938–1944 | Soldier |
| Armour, Lester | 1939–1970 | Chair, Chicago National Bank |
| Blair, William McCormick | 1939–1984 | Investment banker |
| Cummings, Walter Joseph | 1939–1967 | Chair, Continental Illinois Bank & Trust |
| Wetten, Albert Hayes | 1939–1953 | Realtor |
| Conover, Boardman | 1940–1950 | Soldier, amateur ornithologist |

retail company Montgomery Ward, was arrested when he refused to comply with a government order to recognize the Congress of Industrial Organizations (CIO), a New Deal federation of industrial unions (Nash and Feinman 2003:273–275). As we shall see, the Department of Anthropology benefitted greatly from Works Progress Administration (WPA) funding, so it would be interesting to learn specifically what impact Field's and Avery's divergent perspectives had on other museum programs, but the archives are unclear on this point.

Although some research travel was cut due to economic constraints, the Field Museum's Department of Anthropology was a vibrant and productive place in the 1930s. Such vibrancy likely stands in mute testimony to the financial acumen, wherewithal, and largesse of the museum's affluent trustees.

### *Curators*

Table 4.3 lists the Department of Anthropology curators who served between 1929 and 1941. In 1929, just before the stock market crash, sinologist Berthold Laufer chaired the department and oversaw the work of six curators: Albert Buell Lewis, assistant curator of African and Melanesian ethnology; Henry Field, assistant curator of physical anthropology; J. Eric S. Thompson, curator of Mexican and South American ethnology; T. George Allen, curator of Egyptian archaeology; Wilfrid Dyson Hambly, curator of African ethnology; and the recently hired Paul Sidney Martin, curator of North American archaeology (see Bronson 2003; Codrington 2003; McVicker 2003;

Table 4.3. Field Museum anthropology curators, 1929–1941

| Name | Dates | Title |
| --- | --- | --- |
| Laufer, Berthold | 1915–1934 | Curator |
| Lewis, Albert Buell | 1908–1935 | Assistant Curator, African and Melanesian Ethnology |
| | 1936–1940 | Curator, Melanesian Ethnology |
| Thompson, J. Eric S. | 1926–1935 | Assistant Curator, Mexican and South American Archaeology |
| Hambly, Wilfrid D. | 1926–1935 | Assistant Curator, African Ethnology |
| | 1936–1952 | Curator, African Ethnology |
| Field, Henry | 1926–1935 | Assistant Curator, Physical Anthropology |
| | 1936–1941 | Curator, Physical Anthropology |
| Allen, T. George | 1927–1935 | Assistant Curator, Egyptian Archaeology |
| Martin, Paul S. | 1929–1934 | Assistant Curator, North American Archaeology |
| | 1934–1935 | Acting Curator, Anthropology |
| | 1935–1964 | Chief Curator, Anthropology |
| Martin, Richard A. | 1936–1945 | Curator, Near Eastern Archaeology |
| Wilbur, C. Martin | 1936–1947 | Curator, Chinese Archaeology and Ethnology |
| Spoehr, Alexander | 1940–1941 | Assistant Curator, American Ethnology and Archaeology |
| Collier, Donald | 1941–1942 | Assistant Curator, South American Ethnology and Archaeology |

Nash 2003, 2010; Welsch 2003; Yastrow and Nash 2003). Aside from Field and Martin, all were ethnologists, not archaeologists. Given that Simms, the museum's director, and Laufer were both ethnologists, this is perhaps not surprising. Soon, however, the department would be reconstituted under Martin's tutelage to emphasize archaeology.

The immensely productive but intensely private Laufer committed suicide in 1934 (Bronson 2003). Martin, despite the fact that he was chronologically the junior member of the faculty, was immediately appointed acting curator. One year later, in 1935, he was promoted to curator, the equivalent of today's department chair. The department shrank briefly to four curators under Martin as both Thompson and Allen left the museum in 1935. Martin was almost immediately able to fill both positions, however, and in 1936 he added two archaeologists: Richard A. Martin, curator of Near Eastern archaeology, and C. Martin Wilbur, curator of Chinese archaeology and ethnology. Before the Great Depression ended in 1941, Paul Martin added two more archaeologists to the fold: Alexander Spoehr, hired as assistant curator of American ethnology and archaeology in 1940, and Donald Collier, hired as assistant curator of South American ethnology and archaeology in 1941. In less than a decade, the Department of Anthropology had been markedly reconstituted to emphasize archaeology over ethnology.

This circumstantial evidence suggests that the Department of Anthropology was able to weather the economic storm, at least from the perspective of the curatorial ranks, with only a short-term (i.e., one year) negative impact. Roster changes may more parsimoniously be ascribed to an administrative transition and Paul Martin's desire to reshape the department than to economic difficulties brought on by the Great Depression.

### *Professional and Support Staff*

Reliable and systematic data on professional staff members in museums can be difficult to find, particularly prior to the era of their professionalization in the 1970s. Staff in the 1930s consisted variably of a wide range of positions including collections managers, registrars, conservators, exhibit developers, photographers, and so on, whose tasks ranged from the exciting to the mundane and included cataloging, typing, pest management, handling inquiries from the public, and others. Table 4.4 lists the four (!) professional staff recorded by the department during the 1930s. This table does not list volunteers, nor does it include field staff members on the various field expeditions (see below), records on whom are not well preserved in the archives. Table 4.5 lists the 70 WPA staff members in anthropology from 1933 to 1940 (see Nash and Feinman 2003:265–267). Archived data at the Field Museum are unclear on this murky point. Although the WPA was not founded until 1935, the list of WPA employees found in Field Museum archives includes some with a start date of 1933, which is reproduced here. It is possible that some of these employees were hired before the WPA began and were simply paid from WPA funds after 1935. No matter the case, they were clearly not regular anthropology employees prior to 1933.

Although most of the people appearing on the WPA list toiled behind the scenes and are otherwise not recorded for history, there are exceptions. Elizabeth Willis conducted research on the southwestern United States pot-

Table 4.4. Chronological listing of professional staff members in the Field Museum's Department of Anthropology, 1929–1941

| Name | Dates | Title |
|---|---|---|
| Prasuhn, John G. | 1926–1932 | Sculptor/modeler |
| Ito, Tokumatsu | 1936–1942 | Ceramic restorer |
| Yule, Robert | 1939–1944 | Assistant, archaeology |
| Rinaldo, John B. | 1939–1950 | Assistant to Paul S. Martin |

tery collection and co-authored *Anasazi Painted Pottery in the Field Museum of Natural History* with Martin (Martin and Willis 1940). Although she is listed as the second author, it is likely, given Martin's interests and other obligations, not to mention gender biases in the 1930s, that Willis played the lead role in the volume's production. Four other women, Ann Louise Perkins, Elizabeth Siegrist, Edith Ware, and Mary Warren, and two men, John Plattings and Paul Warner, also held the title of "archaeologist," but the archives are unclear on what they actually did in that capacity, and they did not publish anything during their employment. Louise Bucher, possibly assisted by Miss Christ, typed captions and pasted them on mounted photographs, which were then bound in black binders that still, to this day, prove an invaluable resource for researchers (see Nash and Feinman 2003:310–318).

Aside from the sheer numbers of people involved, the glaringly obvious aspect of WPA work at the Field Museum was the change in staff gender ratios. Of the 233 staff members between 1926 and 2002 on whom records exist, 60 percent (n = 140) were women and 40 percent (n = 93) were men (Haskin et al. 2003:70–71; Nash and Feinman 2003:262–267). If we consider only years before 1933 and after 1940 the gender ratio is even more extreme, with 67 percent (n = 111) women and 33 percent (n = 53) men employed. During the years between 1933 and 1940, however, this ratio is reversed, with a staff that was 57 percent (n = 40) men and 43 percent (n = 30) women (Haskin et al. 2003:71). To be blunt, this reflects the generally pervasive and patriarchal, if erroneous, attitude held by many Americans that working women, especially those paid by government relief efforts, were, by definition, taking money out of the hands of male breadwinners and by extension their families (McElvaine 1993). The Department of Anthropology was indeed a radically different entity during the Depression. From a total of eight recorded employees—seven curators and a sculptor—in 1932, the department grew to five curators and well over two dozen staff members at various times in the late 1930s.

Table 4.5. Alphabetical listing of Depression-era staff in the Field Museum's Department of Anthropology, 1933–1940

| Name | Dates | Title |
|---|---|---|
| Abbinanti, John | 1935–1937 | Object technician |
| Andrea, Henrietta Pier | 1940 | Social scientist |
| Arens, Peter | 1939 | Handicraft worker |
| Austin, Jane | 1933–1936 | Typist/clerk |
| Baron, Sam | 1935–1936 | Object technician |
| Bright, Myrtle | 1937–1940 | Typist/clerk |
| Brin, Ada | 1941 | Librarian |
| Brokaski, Charles | 1935–1937 | Typist/clerk |
| Bucher, Louise | 1934 | Typist/clerk |
| Carlson, Lillian | 1935–1936 | Clerk |
| Christ, Miss | 1934 | Photograph clerk |
| Dahlene, Mrs. | 1934 | Library assistant |
| Daniel, Frazier | 1939 | Handicraft worker |
| Davis, Robert F. | 1940 | Librarian |
| Devaney, John | 1939 | Exhibit cleaner |
| Dickstein, Rudolph | 1938–1939 | Exhibit cleaner |
| Duncan, Ray L. | 1935–1939 | Preparator/clerk/social scientist |
| Eckhart, Carl V. | 1938–1940 | Junior physical scientist |
| Ellerbrook, Dorothy | 1934 | Artist |
| Fortin, Howard | 1938 | Draftsman |
| Gackouski, Mathias | 1938–1939 | Preparator |
| Gerval, Jack | 1939 | Handicraft worker |
| Gino, Frank | 1939 | Senior artist |
| Gray, Joseph | 1939 | Exhibit cleaner |
| Hale, Henry Thomas | 1941 | Artist (dioramas) |
| Hardy, Mary G. | 1938 | Librarian |
| Harrell, Jean | 1941 | Senior typist |
| Harris, Rose | 1939 | Senior typist |
| Hunnicott, Gertrude O. | 1937 | Junior librarian |
| Jacobs, H. Dorothy | 1939–1940 | Librarian |
| Janecek, John J. | 1936–1937 | Artist |
| Kagan, Bella | 1935 | Typist |
| Kahn, Leon | 1939 | Exhibit cleaner |
| Krasovec, William | 1934 | Object technician |
| Lally, Thomas | 1937–1940 | Clerk/handicraft worker |

| Name | Dates | Title |
|---|---|---|
| Lombardo, Vita | 1933–1940 | Typist/clerk |
| Losuredo, Frank | 1939 | Exhibit cleaner |
| Majewski, Michael | 1939 | Exhibit cleaner |
| McCabe, Mary | 1937 | Typist |
| Minghi, Chas. | 1937 | Artist |
| Miotko, Dan | 1939 | Exhibit cleaner |
| Mitros, Harriet | 1937–1939 | Typist/clerk |
| Mueller, Charles | 1935–1937 | Sculptor/modeler |
| Murphy, Anna | 1934 | Photograph clerk |
| Navigato, Mr. | 1934 | Artist |
| Nemec, Charles J. | 1939–1940 | Handicraft worker |
| Occhionero, James | 1939 | Exhibit cleaner |
| Olchawa, Polly A. | 1940 | Senior typist |
| Perkins, Ann Louise | 1936–1937 | Senior archaeologist |
| Pfeiffer, Anna | 1939 | Stenographer |
| Plattings, John | 1935–1939 | Sculptor/modeler |
| Risting, Erling | 1939 | Exhibit cleaner |
| Rosenbaum, Ben | 1940 | Junior physical scientist |
| Royce, Louis | 1939 | Handicraft worker |
| Sands, Thomas | 1938 | Draftsman/physical scientist |
| Scully, Ted | 1938–1939 | Secretary to Henry Field |
| Siegrist, Elizabeth | 1936–1937 | Senior archaeologist |
| Smock, Mary | 1935 | Typist |
| Stewart, Clarence | 1938 | Draftsman |
| Stuth, Harold C. | 1939–1940 | Handicraft worker |
| Tarcov, Oscar | 1938 | Handicraft worker |
| Temple, Jane | 1938–1940 | Librarian/physical scientist |
| Tuch, David | 1938–1940 | Draftsman |
| Turbow, Rose | 1939–1940 | Junior social scientist |
| Ware, Edith W. | 1938–1940 | Archaeologist |
| Warner, Paul | 1937–1939 | Senior archaeologist |
| Warren, Mary | 1934–1939 | Textile conservator/archaeologist |
| Willis, Elizabeth | 1937–1940 | Senior archaeologist |
| Wilson, Grace | 1934–1936 | Typist/clerk |
| Zimmerman, Eunice | 1939–1940 | Copy reader for Henry Field |

## Research and Collections

### *Expeditions*

The number of Field Museum expeditions conducted during the Great Depression dropped dramatically after 1934 (Table 4.6). There were 20 field expeditions conducted between 1929 and 1934 under Laufer's leadership. Under Martin (1935–1941), there were only five, four of which were Martin's own archaeological expeditions to the Southwest (see Nash 2010). It is here that the economic toll of the Great Depression on Field Museum anthropology is most evident. This is not surprising, given that Field Museum expeditions were not funded with operational expenses and were heavily dependent on private philanthropy. It is also here, however, that the economic force of the Century of Progress World's Fair of 1933, held in Chicago, is felt. Fully one-third of the field expeditions conducted under Laufer's leadership between 1930 and 1932 were specifically designed to provision the "Hall of Prehistoric Man" (Henry Field's expeditions in 1930 and 1932) and the "Hall of the Races of Mankind" (Malvina Hoffman's expeditions in 1931 and 1932). Both of these important exhibitions opened coincident with the Century of Progress World's Fair in 1933 (Yastrow and Nash 2003). In the absence of these preparations for the Century of Progress exhibition, the museum's anthropology field expedition activity would have been markedly lower during the Great Depression.

Prior to 1930, private philanthropists supported most of the Field Museum anthropology expeditions (see Nash and Feinman 2003:288–300). In some cases, they took advantage of naming opportunities; in others, they preferred anonymity. Although the evidence is circumstantial, it is thus notable that the last expedition named for its patron occurred in 1930, less than one year after the onset of the Great Depression. It may be that after 1930 patrons sought anonymity in order to not advertise their financial resources while the rest of the nation suffered; the archives are unclear on this matter.

It is notable that expedition activity remained low even after Martin hired archaeologists Richard Martin and C. Martin Wilbur in 1936 and Spoehr in 1940. Only Donald Collier, hired in 1941, conducted a Depression-era expedition under Martin's leadership, and his was a joint expedition with the Institute for Andean Research, plans for which may have already been in place at the time Collier was hired. By conducting four of the five Depression-era field expeditions, Martin thus monopolized the museum's scant anthropology expedition resources largely in support of his own research (Nash 2003, 2010), as well as to attract the talented Collier to the institution (Collier 2003; Staller 2003).

Table 4.6. Field Museum anthropology expeditions, 1929–1941

| Curator/Leader | Expedition |
|---|---|
| 1929 | |
| Various personnel | Excavations at Kish, Iraq |
| Hambly, Wilfrid | Fredrick H. Rawson–Field Museum Ethnological Expedition to West Africa (Angola, Nigeria) |
| Thompson, J. Eric S. | The Second Marshall Field Archaeological Expedition to British Honduras and Guatemala |
| 1930 | |
| Various personnel | Excavations at Kish, Iraq |
| Field, Henry | Marshall Field Archaeological Expedition to Western Europe (England and France) |
| Hambly, Wilfrid | Fredrick H. Rawson–Field Museum Ethnological Expedition to West Africa (Angola, Nigeria) |
| Martin, Paul S. | Archaeological Expedition to the Southwest (Colorado; Ancestral Puebloan sites) |
| Moir, J. Reid | Archaeological Fieldwork at Ipswitch, England, 1930–1931 |
| 1931 | |
| Various personnel | Excavations at Kish, Iraq |
| Hoffman, Malvina | Chauncey Keep Memorial Hall Sculpture Work (France, Germany, Hawaii, Japan, and China) |
| Martin, Paul S. | Field Museum Archaeological Expedition to the Southwest (Colorado; Ancestral Puebloan sites) |
| Thompson, J. Eric S. | The Third Marshall Field Archaeological Expedition to British Honduras and Guatemala |
| 1932 | |
| Various personnel | Excavations at Kish, Iraq |
| Field, Henry | Archaeological Expedition to Europe (France, England, and Germany) |
| Hoffman, Malvina | Chauncey Keep Memorial Hall Sculpture Work (Philippines, Java, Bali, Singapore, Penang, Malaya, and India) |
| 1933 | |
| Burleson, E. L. | Burleson–Field Museum Expedition to Mexico |
| Martin, Paul S. | Field Museum Archaeological Expedition to the Southwest (Colorado; Ancestral Puebloan sites) |

*Continued on the next page*

Table 4.6. *Continued*

| Curator/Leader | Expedition |
|---|---|
| 1934 | |
| Field, Henry | Field Museum Anthropological Expedition to the Near East (Iraq, Mesopotamia, USSR, and Persia) |
| Martin, Paul S. | Field Museum Archaeological Expedition to the Southwest (Colorado; Ancestral Puebloan sites) |
| Thompson, J. Eric S. | Joint Archaeology Expedition of the Carnegie Institute and Field Museum (British Honduras) |
| 1937 | |
| Martin, Paul S. | Field Museum Archaeological Expedition to the Southwest (Colorado; Ancestral Puebloan sites) |
| 1938 | |
| Martin, Paul S. | Field Museum Archaeological Expedition to the Southwest (Colorado; Ancestral Puebloan sites) |
| 1939 | |
| Martin, Paul S. | Field Museum Archaeological Expedition to the Southwest (New Mexico; Mogollon sites) |
| 1941 | |
| Collier, Donald | Joint Expedition of Field Museum and Institute for Andean Research to Ecuador, 1941–1942, Canar Valley |
| Martin, Paul S. | Field Museum Archaeological Expedition to the Southwest (New Mexico; Mogollon sites) |

### *Publications*

There were five publication outlets available to Field Museum employees during the Great Depression. The *Fieldiana* series, intended as the Museum's research journal, published scholarly monographs in anthropology, botany, geology, and zoology. The *Memoirs* series included shorter scholarly monographs but included those, like Martin and Willis's 1940 publication, that required full-sized plates. The *Design* series focused specifically on the study of design elements in material culture; the *Popular* series made complicated topics and museum exhibitions accessible to a wider variety of readers. A *Handbooks and Special Publications* series rounded out the Field Museum offerings.

Table 4.7 lists the 28 *Fieldiana: Anthropology* monographs produced by 11 senior authors between 1929 and 1941. Table 4.8 lists the eight *Memoirs*

Table 4.7. *Fieldiana: Anthropology* publications by Field Museum staff, 1929–1941

| Author | Title | Volume |
|---|---|---|
| 1929 | | |
| Lewis, Albert B. | *Melanesian Shell Money in Field Museum Collections* | 19(1) |
| 1930 | | |
| Hambly, Wilfrid | *Serpent Worship in Africa* | 21(1) |
| Laufer, Berthold | *Geophagy* | 18(2) |
| Thompson, J. Eric S. | *Ethnology of the Mayas of Southern and Central British Honduras* | 17(2) |
| 1931 | | |
| Laufer, Berthold | *The Domestication of the Cormorant in China and Japan* | 18(3) |
| Mason, J. Alden | *Archaeology of Santa Marta, Colombia: The Tairona Culture: Report on Field Work* | 20(1) |
| Thompson, J. Eric S. | *Archaeological Investigations in the Southern Cayo District, British Honduras* | 17(3) |
| 1932 | | |
| Thompson, J. Eric S. | *The Solar Year of the Mayas at Quirigua, Guatemala* | 17(4) |
| 1933 | | |
| Linton, Ralph | *The Tanala: A Hill Tribe of Madagascar* | 22 |
| 1934 | | |
| Hambly, Wilfrid | *The Ovimbundu of Angola* | 21(2) |
| 1935 | | |
| Allen, Thomas G. | *Egyptian Stelae in Field Museum of Natural History* | 24(1) |
| Hambly, Wilfrid | *Culture Areas of Nigeria* | 21(3) |
| 1936 | | |
| Martin, Paul S. | *Lowry Ruin in Southwestern Colorado* | 23(1) |
| Mason, J. Alden | *Archaeology of Santa Marta, Colombia: The Tairona Culture: Objects of Stone, Shell, Bone, and Metal* | 20(1) |

*Continued on the next page*

Table 4.7. *Continued*

| Author | Title | Volume |
|---|---|---|
| 1937 | | |
| Hambly, Wilfrid | *Skeletal Materials from San José Ruin, British Honduras* | 25(1) |
| Hambly, Wilfrid | *Source Book for African Anthropology, Part I* | 26(1) |
| Hambly, Wilfrid | *Source Book for African Anthropology, Part II* | 26(2) |
| 1938 | | |
| Hambly, Wilfrid | *Anthropology of the Ovimbundu, Angola* | 25(2) |
| Laufer, Berthold | *The American Plant Migration, Part I: The Potato* | 28(1) |
| Martin, Paul S. | *Archaeological Work in the Ackmen-Lowry Area, Southwestern Colorado* | 23(2) |
| Thompson, J. Eric S. | *The High Priest's Grave: Chichen Itza, Yucatan, Mexico* | 27 |
| 1939 | | |
| Field, Henry | *Contributions to the Anthropology of Iran* | 29(1) |
| Martin, Paul S. | *Modified Basketmaker Sites: Ackmen-Lowry Area, Southwestern Colorado* | 23(3) |
| Stewart, T. Dale | *Anthropometric Observations on the Eskimos and Indians of Labrador* | 31(1) |
| 1940 | | |
| Field, Henry | *The Anthropology of Iraq, Part I: The Upper Euphrates* | 30(1) |
| Hambly, Wilfrid | *Craniometry of New Guinea* | 25(3) |
| Martin, Paul S. | *The SU Site: Excavations at a Mogollon Site, Western New Mexico, 1939* | 32(1) |
| 1941 | | |
| Spoehr, Alexander | *Camp, Clan, and Kin among the Cow Creek Seminole of Florida* | 33(1) |

published by six senior authors. Only Henry Field and Paul Martin are represented on both lists. Hambly led the way with seven *Fieldiana* publications on a variety of topics, including *Serpent Worship in Africa* (1931), *Craniometry of New Guinea* (1940), and *Skeletal Materials from San José Ruin, British Honduras* (1937). Eric Thompson published four, all of which were on Mesoamerican archaeology and anthropology. Martin published four, and Laufer

Table 4.8. *Memoirs* series publications by Field Museum staff, 1929–1940

| Author | Title | Volume |
|---|---|---|
| 1929 | | |
| Mackay, Ernest | *A Sumerian Palace and the "A" Cemetery at Kish, Mesopotamia* | 1(2) |
| 1930 | | |
| Kroeber, Alfred | *Archaeological Explorations in Peru, Part II: The Northern Coast* | 2(2) |
| 1931 | | |
| Mackay, Ernest | *Report on Excavations at Jemdet Nasr, Iraq* | 1(3) |
| Moodie, Roy L. | *Roentgenologie Studies of Egyptian and Peruvian Mummies* | 3(1) |
| O'Neil, Lila M. | *Archaeological Explorations in Peru, Part III: Textiles of the Early Nazca Period* | 2(3) |
| 1935 | | |
| Field, Henry | *Arabs of Central Iraq: Their History, Ethnology, and Physical Characters* | 4(1) |
| 1937 | | |
| Kroeber, Alfred | *Archaeological Explorations in Peru, Part IV: Cañete Valley* | 2(4) |
| 1940 | | |
| Martin, Paul S., and Elizabeth Willis | *Anasazi Painted Pottery in Field Museum of Natural History* | 5(1) |

published three. All other curators and associates published only one, if any. Taken together, these monographs cover anthropological and archaeological research on all continents except Antarctica and communicate the breadth of research characteristic of a large, classic, and encyclopedic museum like the Field.

Between 1929 and 1934, and under Laufer's leadership, Field Museum anthropologists published 15 monographs—10 *Fieldiana* issues and 5 *Memoirs* issues. Between 1935 and 1941, under Martin, the department published 22 monographs—18 *Fieldiana* issues and 4 *Memoirs* issues. This leads to the inescapable, if still circumstantial, conclusion that diminished field activity after 1934 and large increases from WPA labor pools led directly to an increase in scholarly publication.

The sole contribution to the Field Museum *Design* series published during the Great Depression is Albert Buell Lewis's 1931 study *Carved and Painted Designs from New Guinea*. The *Design* series was short lived and included only five other issues, four by Lewis, one by Laufer, and all during the 1920s. It appears that the *Design* series was a victim of the Great Depression, lack of interest, or both.

Table 4.9 lists the seven publications in the *Popular* series, many of which would go into multiple print runs. Henry Field again led the way with three contributions, on excavations at Kish, Iraq, and on the exhibitions he installed in 1933. Intuitively, it is easy to understand how Richard Martin's *Ancient Seals of the Near East* (1940), Eric Thompson's *Archaeology of South America* (1936), and Hambly's *Primitive Hunters of Australia* (1936) made it into the *Popular* series. Less obvious is the popular appeal of Laufer et al.'s *Tobacco and Its Use in Africa* (1930), although smoking was indeed much more socially acceptable then than it is today.

Hambly and Paul Martin were the only two to publish a handbook or special publication; both did so early in their Field Museum careers. Martin's (1933) contribution was a step-by-step guide to the new Archaeology of North America exhibit that he had helped install, and it provides insights into the Field Museum's exhibition philosophy as well as Martin's understanding of the state of American archaeology at that time (Nash 2010). Hambly's (1930) contribution was a guide to the museum's small Africa exhibit on the ground floor.

All told, Field Museum curators and associates published 48 book-length contributions between 1929 and 1941, an average of four per year. This is an impressive level of scholarly output under any circumstances, but particularly so during the challenging years of the Great Depression. Such prodigious output may, in fact, have been facilitated by the economic challenges of the era, as budget cuts meant that few fieldwork expeditions were conducted, and WPA funding meant more staff to assist with lab work, analysis, and writing. The Field Museum, like the Hearst Museum at the University of California at Berkeley (Redman 2011), appears to have become more productive during the Great Depression.

A thorough analysis of every short, external, popular publication produced by Field Museum curators during this period is beyond the scope of this chapter, but those of Paul Martin demonstrate the Field Museum's scholarly output during the trying years of the Great Depression. During the 1930s, Martin published more than two dozen popular contributions, book reviews, and articles not considered in the above tabulation (see citations in Nash 2010). Given that both Field and Hambly were as prolific as Martin in

Table 4.9. Field Museum *Popular* series publications, 1929–1940

| Author | Title | Volume |
|---|---|---|
| 1929 | | |
| Field, Henry | *The Field Museum–Oxford University Expedition to Kish, Mesopotamia, 1923–1929* | 28 |
| 1930 | | |
| Laufer, Berthold, Wilfrid Hambly, and Ralph Linton | *Tobacco and Its Use in Africa* | 29 |
| 1933 | | |
| Field, Henry | *The Races of Mankind* | 30 |
| Field, Henry | *Prehistoric Man—Hall of the Stone Age of the Old World* | 31 |
| 1936 | | |
| Hambly, Wilfrid | *Primitive Hunters of Australia* | 32 |
| Thompson, J. Eric S. | *Archaeology of South America* | 33 |
| 1940 | | |
| Martin, Richard A. | *Ancient Seals of the Near East* | 34 |

monograph output, it is possible that the museum's public relations department pushed their work out to an interested media and the general public as they had done with Martin's, particularly given Field's installation of the "Hall of the Races of Mankind" and the "Hall of Prehistoric Man" (Codrington 2003; Nash 2003; Yastrow and Nash 2003).

*Collections*

Although none of the collecting expeditions listed in Table 4.6 returned to the museum empty-handed, two expeditions—the Kish Expedition and the Archaeological Expedition to the Southwest—merit special attention because of their sheer size and the fact that the collections they amassed were not properly and completely processed for more than seven decades.

The Field Museum's annual expeditions to Kish, Iraq, began in 1923, long before the start of the Great Depression, and ended in 1933, before the start of the New Deal. Conducted jointly with the Ashmolean Museum at Oxford University and the Iraq Museum in Baghdad, the actual excavations were probably affected by Great Depression economics only in 1933, when the Field Museum elected not to participate. At the end of a season's excavation, representatives of each institution would gather to divide the spoils. The Iraq Museum took the unique and exceptional pieces; the Field Museum got the archaeological remains (pottery, stone tools, human remains, animal remains) and a sample of the cuneiform tablets; and the Ashmolean Museum conversely took the vast majority of the cuneiform tablets and a sample of the archaeological remains. Unnamed department staff cataloged a small fraction of the Kish materials on their arrival in Chicago, and WPA-funded employees John Abbinanti and Sam Baron were charged with cleaning the famous arched gateway from Kish, which remained on display into the 1960s.

Paul Martin was hired by the Field Museum in 1929 to resuscitate, after a two-decade hiatus, the Archaeological Expedition to the Southwest (Nash 2010). In 8 of the next 12 years, Martin mounted expeditions to southwestern Colorado (1930–1938) and west-central New Mexico (1939, 1941). From the museum's perspective, and to a lesser degree Martin's, an expedition's purpose was to recover exhibition-quality material for display purposes. Illustrating the dynamic tension that sometimes confronts curators, Martin also expressed interest in conducting scientific research to answer specific research questions (Martin et al. 1936). From a collections-based perspective, these expeditions were indeed successful, as exhibition-quality material was recovered and returned to the museum. Martin and his crew were less than successful in cataloging and properly caring for the archaeological remains they returned to the museum, however, in spite of the added WPA labor. For example, Martin et al. (1936) published data on 1,377 objects from floor contexts at Lowry Pueblo but cataloged only 598, or 43 percent, of those objects. Since then, the collection has suffered significant losses through attrition, possible petty theft, and probable curatorial culling. Of the 598 artifacts mentioned above, only 520 (87 percent) were found during inventory in 1998.

Through concerted and focused efforts funded by the National Science Foundation, the National Endowment for the Humanities, and the Department of Defense, the artifact assemblages from both the Kish Expedition and the Archaeological Expedition to the Southwest were completely cataloged in the late 1990s and early to mid-2000s and are now available for scholarly research (Pestle et al. 2006; see Nash 2010). The archives are unclear about what, exactly, the WPA laborers did at the Field Museum between 1933 and 1940, but they certainly did not focus their attention on the complete cataloging of the collections made by the field expeditions.

# Exhibitions and Outreach

## *Permanent Exhibitions*

The Field Museum moved to its current location in Grant Park in 1921, after spending 28 years in Jackson Park, on Chicago's south side. Most exhibition cases were moved intact. Very little new exhibition development occurred in the decade prior to the move; after the move, staff focused on securing the collections in the new facility. By the late 1920s and early 1930s, however, the institution entered a new phase in exhibition development, particularly as citywide efforts intensified in preparation for the Century of Progress Exhibition of 1933 (Collier 2003; Yastrow and Nash 2003).

Two major, and ultimately world-famous, exhibitions were designed and installed to open concurrently with the Century of Progress exhibition, held on Northerly Island, a small spit of landfill located a short distance east and south of the Field Museum. The "Hall of the Races of Mankind" included bronze sculptures by Malvina Hoffman, a sculptor and artist commissioned in 1930 to travel the world, find the archetypical representative of hundreds of "races," sculpt them, and cast them in bronze. Hoffman's commission cost $125,000 in 1930, the equivalent of $1.6 million in 2009 dollars. Clearly, the Great Depression had not yet affected all the Field Museum's coffers. The "Hall of the Races of Mankind" exhibit enjoyed a prominent place on the museum's exhibition floor until it was deinstalled in 1968, when the typological concept of race had become anathema to anthropologists and other scientists, if not the general public.

The "Hall of Prehistoric Man" was largely the result of Henry Field's efforts. Planning began, like that for the "Hall of the Races of Mankind," in 1927, when Laufer encouraged Henry Field to begin thinking about ideas for new exhibitions. They lobbied museum President Stanley Field for support; it did not hurt matters that Henry was Stanley's nephew. The "Hall of Prehistoric Man" included eight dioramas depicting the then-current understanding of human evolution, beginning with *Homo erectus,* continuing to the famous Neanderthal diorama, and concluding with the Swiss Lake Dweller diorama. This installation also remained on display for more than four decades.

Henry Field was not the only museum curator working on permanent exhibitions in the early 1930s. One of the considerations Laufer made when hiring Martin in 1929 was the installation of a new archaeology hall, organized according to the culture area and culture history paradigms then prevalent in Americanist anthropology. Martin did indeed lead the effort to reinstall the North American archaeology exhibit in 1933, but complete reinstallation did not occur until the 1940s, after Martin had matured in his role as department chair.

### *Temporary Exhibitions and Outreach*

A complete analysis of the many small, temporary exhibitions offered by Field Museum anthropologists between 1929 and 1941 is beyond the scope of this chapter, and in any case good records on temporary exhibitions did not exist until 1940 (Haskin et al. 2003). It appears that the Field Museum exhibition floors were indeed dynamic places during the 1930s. To name just a few, in 1931 Martin installed a display of the Peregrine figure, a rare, fluorite, anthropomorphic figurine found in extreme southern Illinois (Martin 1931). In 1932, he introduced a new display of Navajo blankets (Martin 1932). In 1934, it was Eskimo toys (Martin 1934), and in 1936, Martin recognized the psychic unity of humankind and alluded to the economic challenges of the Great Depression by placing on display an ancient promissory note, in the form of a cuneiform tablet from Kish, that indicated a usurious charge of 100-percent interest on a loan (Martin 1936).

In 1933, in conjunction with the opening of the "Hall of Prehistoric Man," Henry Field put on display the Cap Blanc skeleton, affectionately known as Magdalenian Girl. This Upper Paleolithic skeleton was discovered in the Dordogne region of southwestern France but had never been on public display. The public presentation of Magdalenian Girl harkens back to the worst eras of sensationalism, if not outright misrepresentation, in museum exhibitions. Field reported that an ivory harpoon point was found near her ventral cavity and that this object might have been the cause of her death. The titillating hint of violence was too much to resist; she was presented to the visiting public, in newspapers and advertisements, as having possibly been killed by a jealous lover. The first Saturday she went on display 22,000 people lined up to see her; extra security was required to hold back the throngs. Unfortunately, archived correspondence indicates that Monsieur Grimaud, the man who discovered the skeleton, did not remember any such harpoon being found in direct association with the skeleton. Her public presentation was therefore more hype than fact and casts an unseemly shadow on Field's work at the museum.

The dozens of short articles published and temporary exhibitions installed by Martin and other Field Museum curators helped keep museum visitors engaged in, and hopefully excited by, new developments in anthropological and archaeological research both inside and outside the institution. To use today's parlance, it is likely that many Chicagoans were practicing "stay-cations," and these installations helped the Field Museum remain a prime tourist destination.

## Conclusion

To return to the questions proffered at the start of this chapter: Did museum-based anthropology, as seen through the Field Museum lens, change appreciably during the 1930s?

The number of curators on staff fluctuated after Laufer's suicide, but this is more easily accounted for by changes in departmental leadership than economic difficulties. The orders-of-magnitude change in the number of professional staff working in the Department of Anthropology is, however, due directly to WPA funding. The mark of these staff was felt on a wide variety of tasks, from custodial to clerical to analytical, and the coincident increase in the production of scholarly monographs is very likely due, at least in part, to their assistance.

The Department of Anthropology was remarkably prolific, producing 48 monographs in a 13-year span. Some of this productivity was likely due to travel restrictions brought on by economic hardship, and it was bolstered by the presence of a large WPA-funded staff. It is virtually certain that Field, Martin, and Hambly, among others, would not have been nearly as prolific if it were not for the extra staff. Unfortunately, the WPA staff's productivity did not transfer over to the arena of collections processing, as many objects received in the 1930s would not be properly processed until seven decades later. Field expeditions were most negatively affected by the Great Depression, as no anthropology field expeditions were conducted in 1935, 1936, and 1940, and only five such expeditions occurred in toto after 1934. On the exhibitions front, visitors to the museum were treated to a series of new, permanent, exhibitions tied to the Century of Progress exposition of 1933 and to dozens of smaller installations throughout the decade.

With the Century of Progress exposition, Laufer's suicide, and the transition to Paul Martin's leadership, the Field Museum was indeed a radically different place after 1933, but the effect of New Deal legislation on the Department of Anthropology was felt almost exclusively behind the scenes and on scholarly production, not on the public side of the institution. Nevertheless, the immense productivity and great expansion of the Department of Anthropology in the 1930s established an entirely new course for Field Museum anthropology in the 1940s and beyond, one in which Americanist archaeology would come to dominate its activities.

## Acknowledgments

Many Field Museum colleagues, particularly collections management assistant Sarah Coleman and archivist Armand Esai, helped me compile and analyze the data for this chapter. Bernard K. Means deserves thanks for organizing the Shovel Ready symposium at the Society for American Archaeology meetings in St. Louis in 2010 and for all his work in preparing this volume for publication. Finally, I thank, in retrospect, those prescient employees of the Field Museum in the 1930s who were thoughtful enough to document their activities.

# 5

# Project 1047

## New Deal Archaeology in Iowa

*John F. Doershuk and John L. Cordell*

New Deal funding for Iowa archaeological projects permanently transformed the essential character of archaeology in the state, pushing research in a new direction and to a new level of intensity from its 1920s surface-only orientation. First Federal Emergency Relief Administration (FERA) and later Works Progress Administration (WPA) funds were put to work through Project 1047 for the excavation of sites (Figure 5.1) that were expected to be representative of Iowa's "rich and complex archeology" (Iowa State Planning Board 1934:154). The methods utilized in these 1930s digs lacked many of the excavation controls and documentary procedures that evolved in later decades and that are now viewed as standard archaeological practice. Nonetheless, these federally funded excavations of ancient village sites and burial mounds generated remarkable data of lasting significance. Indeed, the intensity of the archaeological field effort supported from 1934 to 1939 by New Deal funding in Iowa went unmatched for several decades. Tellingly, when substantial excavation efforts were eventually once again initiated in Iowa during the mid-1950s and thereafter by professional archaeologists, the targeted sites were either locations New Deal archaeology had previously explored—such as the Kimball site in northwestern Iowa or the Hartley Terrace site complex in northeastern Iowa—or related sites such as Wittrock or Phipps (Anderson 1975, 1985; Bryson and Baerreis 1968; Henning et al. 1968; McKusick 1973, 1979; Ruppé 1955). This tendency appears to reflect recognition by these researchers of the importance of the earlier work as well as the need to address research questions prompted by the existing body of data.

Modern large-scale cultural resource management (CRM) efforts in Iowa during the past several decades have—not surprisingly—led to the accumulation of far more archaeological material recorded in far greater detail than resulted from any New Deal–funded project. However, despite the hiatus in

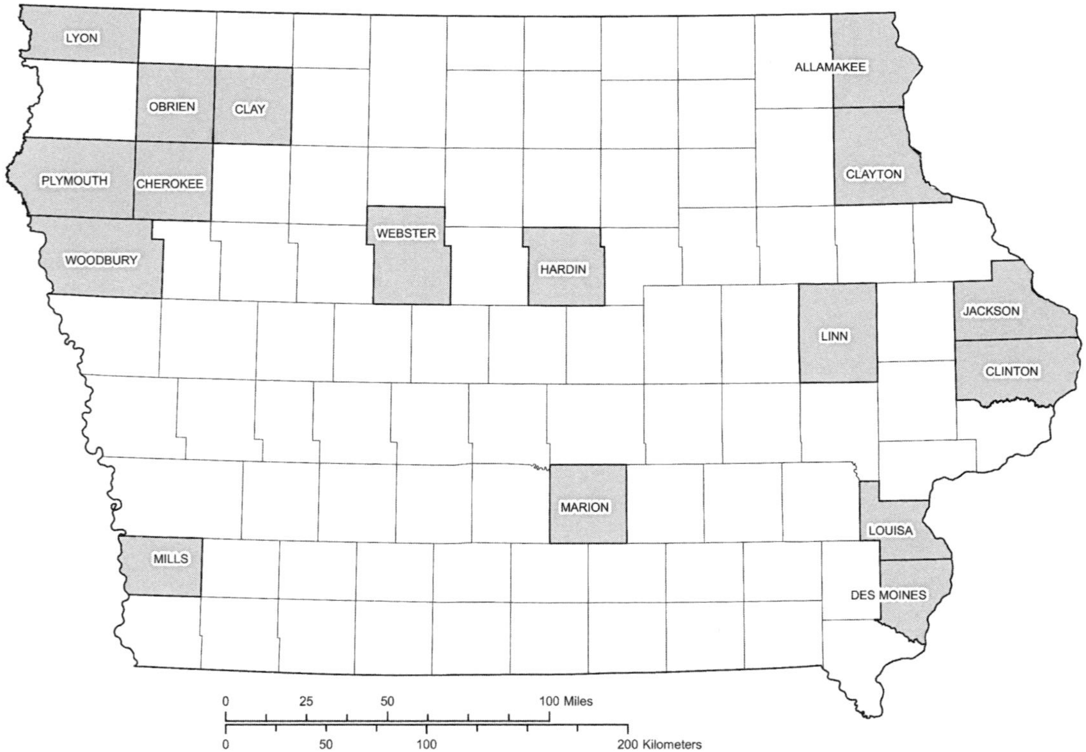


Figure 5.1. Locations of all archaeological sites investigated in Iowa through FERA and WPA funding, 1934–1939.

Figure 5.2. Inset portrait: Charles R. Keyes (1949), supervisor of Iowa FERA- and WPA-funded archaeological projects, 1934–1939. Excavation image: Ellison Orr (1938), assistant supervisor and primary field archaeologist of Iowa FERA- and WPA-funded archaeological projects, 1934–1939 (Courtesy of the State Historical Society of Iowa, Iowa City).

field activities following the end of 1930s federal support and despite the fact that New Deal funding in Iowa did not lead *directly* to the establishment of well-organized, financially sound, institutionally based archaeological research programs, there is little doubt that the legacy of New Deal archaeology continues to be of fundamental importance in Iowa.

New Deal funding for Project 1047 in Iowa could not have become available at a more propitious time. Although the summer of 1934 proved the hottest on record for Iowa, so archaeological excavation conditions were more than challenging, especially for relative newcomers to such endeavors, the time was absolutely right from an archaeological research perspective because the achievements of the Iowa Archaeological Survey, and its director Dr. Charles R. Keyes (Figure 5.2), effectively peaked in the early 1930s. To put 1934 to 1939 New Deal Iowa archaeology into proper context requires a brief digression into the history of the discipline in the state.

## Historical Overview of Early Iowa Archaeology

Publications documenting early archaeological inquiries in Iowa first began to appear with some regularity beginning shortly after the Civil War. Former State Archaeologist of Iowa Duane Anderson (1975) has labeled this the "Pioneer Investigations" period of Iowa archaeology, commencing in his schema around 1870 and lasting to 1920. While dominated as elsewhere in the country by "treasure hunters, romantics, and curiosity seekers" (Anderson 1975:71), important exceptions including Frederick Starr, T. H. Lewis, and Duren Ward were evidence that archaeology as a nascent scientific discipline was beginning to find a foothold in Iowa (Alex 2000:17; Lewis 1899; Starr 1897; Ward 1903, 1905). Another former State Archaeologist of Iowa, Marshall McKusick, has framed the early beginnings of Iowa archaeology slightly differently, choosing to distinguish the period from 1841 to 1881 as the era of the "Iowa Mound Explorers," followed by the period "Scientific Origins," which he brackets from 1881 to 1897. McKusick's next identified stage of development for Iowa archaeology is the "New Fieldwork Methodology 1903–1914," during which a handful of individuals, including the aforementioned Ward, emphasized the importance of sophisticated field techniques and interdisciplinary research (Harlan 1910, 1914), certainly visionary ideals for archaeology anywhere at the time (McKusick 1979:4). Regrettably, inopportune personnel shifts coupled with the waning of what little institutional support existed at the time for Iowa archaeology led to an almost complete interruption of research in the state until around 1920.

Anderson (1975:73) identifies the period from 1921 to 1951 as the "Keyes-Orr Period" in Iowa archaeology, recognizing the seminal importance of efforts by Charles Keyes and his associate Ellison Orr in the growth of archaeological knowledge. McKusick (1979:5) also gives preeminence to Keyes, especially his early work on prehistoric ceramic sequences, labeling 1920–1928 as the "Definition of Ceramic Cultures" intellectual stage. The astounding feature of the Keyes-Orr collaboration is that neither was trained as a professional archaeologist. Iowa's fourth state archaeologist, William Green (1992:80), has described Keyes thus: "His principal claim to recognition as an eminent scholar derives from work he did largely in his spare time in an entirely different discipline. From [1922] to 1950 Keyes directed the Iowa Archaeological Survey, a systematic statewide program of investigations which put Iowa on the nation's archaeological map." For much of this period, Keyes held a full-time academic year appointment at Cornell College as a professor of German language and literature, the discipline in which he was formally trained. His activities as the director of the Iowa Archaeological Survey were restricted to the summer months and what time he could spare for correspondence and weekend visits with the vast network of avocational collectors he developed over the years. Green (1992:80–81) has documented Keyes's many contributions to the transformation of American archaeology into a recognizable scientific discipline (see also Tandarich and Horton 1976 for an extensive list of relevant source material). Suffice it to say that Keyes participated as Iowa's primary (and often only) representative in many of the developments that advanced the discipline to professional status. This progress included organizing Iowa survey efforts on behalf of the National Research Council's Committee on State Archaeological Surveys as well as becoming a member of the newly established Society for American Archaeology and a regular contributor of field reports to *American Antiquity* (Keyes 1935, 1937a, 1940).

Keyes began a catalog of Iowa archaeological materials as early as 1897 (Perry 2008), an important methodological precursor to the statewide Iowa Archaeological Survey cataloging efforts that matured in the 1920s. Happily for modern researchers, Keyes retained copies of a great deal of his outgoing correspondence, greatly enriching—and informing—the responses he received from those with whom he corresponded. Keyes was a regular participant in regional and national conferences, attending the first and second Plains Conferences in 1931 and 1932. He organized the third of these conferences, held in 1936 at his home institution, Cornell College, Mount Vernon, Iowa. He participated in the influential 1935 Indianapolis Archaeological Conference (Keyes 1937b) and was organizer of the 1937 joint session of the Central Section of the American Anthropological Association with the Society for American Archaeology held at the Old Capitol, Iowa City. This remains the only occasion when either of these two important organizations has met in Iowa. In reviewing Keyes's record of archaeological activity, it is a wonder he ever found time to keep up his German language skills.

As with Keyes, archaeology for Ellison Orr (Figure 5.2) began as an avocational pastime. Archaeology for Orr was one of many interests "expertly pursued and often published" (Alex 2008). Orr retired in 1930 at age 73 after a long career as a Bell Telephone Company manager based in Waukon, Iowa (McKusick 1979). After retirement, archaeology became Orr's full-time passion and ultimately a second occupation. Beginning in the 1870s, Orr had become a progressively more avid amateur naturalist and archaeologist whose keen observations on northeastern Iowa's driftless area brought him increasingly into the scientific circles of the day. Likewise, and particularly after 1920, Keyes's archaeological interests were bringing him into the same circles. A passing reference by Keyes (1934:324) suggests he and Orr were acquainted by no later than 1918. The relationship between these men solidified through the 1920s, building on their mutual archaeological interests, and culminated in 1934 with Keyes hiring Orr, then "76 years young" (Perry 2007:103), as assistant supervisor of Project 1047.

Being financially remunerated to conduct archaeological research is certainly one valid hallmark of being a professional and by this measure Charles Keyes became at least a part-time professional archaeologist when appointed director in 1922 of the Iowa Archaeological Survey (Anderson 1975; Green

1992; McKusick 1979; Schroder 1981). Keyes conceived and compiled a plan for the survey that was "highly ambitious yet achievable within the expected limits of resources" (Green 1992:81). The plan was endorsed by Benjamin Shambaugh, superintendent of the State Historical Society of Iowa—now part of the Iowa Department of Cultural Affairs—which today also houses the Iowa State Historic Preservation Office. Resources were scarce, with Keyes as the director and only employee—and then only part time—drawing a modest summer salary from the Historical Society to complement his college academic year salary. Shambaugh arranged a research associate appointment for the summer employment of Keyes through the State University of Iowa (now the University of Iowa), which at the time also housed the State Historical Society in Schaeffer Hall on the Pentacrest in Iowa City. Until federal relief money became available in the early 1930s, Keyes spent his time corresponding and visiting with collectors all across the state, recording sites and familiarizing himself with Iowa's diverse and rich surface archaeology, effectively preadapting him for the prospects offered by Roosevelt's New Deal.

## Iowa's New Deal Excavations

Keyes tapped Orr to join him as a paid professional to tackle the job of leading FERA and then WPA excavations at numerous major prehistoric village and mound sites across Iowa from 1934 to 1939 (Alex 2000:21). McKusick later wrote that Orr's efforts in the 1930s represent "the first well-controlled and representative excavations made in Iowa" (McKusick 1971:532-533). Keyes (1934:324) described his thinking at the time: "When the opportunity came this last spring to conduct archaeological explorations in Iowa on a scale not heretofore possible, the previous work of Mr. Orr pointed clearly to the valley of the Upper Iowa as the place where the digging tools should be put in motion. With the organization of the Iowa State Planning Board, and with FERA support as an important item of its equipment, men became available for the heavy work of excavation. The first years of the Iowa archaeological survey had necessarily been limited to a State-wide search for archaeological sites. Now there was the opportunity *to look beneath the surface of things* and do an intensive bit of work" [emphasis added].

There can be no doubt that Keyes and Orr shared a palpable excitement at the prospect of finally having the opportunity to engage in serious field excavation. Keyes (1934:331) wrote, "Cultural stratification—the goal of every archaeologist! Up to 1934 not a single case had ever come to light in Iowa. Always the old sites of the five prehistoric cultures known to have occupied Iowa lay in the same general plane, side by side frequently, but never superimposed. If one could only be found directly beneath the other, their time sequence would be established beyond any possibility of doubt." Keyes leaned heavily on Orr's decades of experience in northeastern Iowa, utilizing him as guide, advisor, and assistant regarding the local archaeology (Perry 2008). Orr's extensive surveying skills proved especially important to the success of Project 1047. Happily for subsequent generations of Iowa archaeologists, Orr mapped in careful detail the locations of archaeological sites and features, routinely tying the excavations he supervised to the section and quarter-section markers with which he was familiar from his telephone company days.

## Project 1047

Administratively, Project 1047 was the conduit through which New Deal funding initially flowed into Iowa archaeological research. This project was one of many in Iowa described by the Iowa State Planning Board in its *A Preliminary Report of Progress* published in late 1934 and provided to the National Resources Board. The range of resources covered by the report is impressive; archaeological resources were grouped in Project 1047 with scenic and recreational resources. In retrospect, it is clear that if chance had led to assignment of a supervisor with more concern for landscape vistas or fly-fishing opportunities rather than Keyes's archaeological interests, the funding might have been put to very different uses than excavating "ancient village sites and Indian mounds now threatened with destruction" (Iowa State Planning Board 1934:153). No doubt in the absence of New Deal funding, Keyes and Orr would have continued their 1920s-style surface-oriented archaeological data collecting. They might even have figured out an alternative source of support if their vision for Project 1047 had been sidetracked by the funding being used for other endeavors. It is doubtful, however, that anywhere near the quantity or quality of archaeological fieldwork could possibly have been accomplished in Iowa during the 1930s if the New Deal funding for Project 1047 and its subsequent iterations had not been available.

Iowa's New Deal archaeology started in 1934 with a dig planned for the New Galena mound group, known to Keyes as site Ae-5 and in modern nomenclature as 13AM108. This group had been frequented by Orr on various previous mapping and surface collection missions and was known to originally consist of 32 conical mounds. As of June 11, 1934, the first day of fieldwork, Keyes reported that "after many years of cultivation, only fifteen mounds can be identified and the largest of these so flattened out that they scarcely reach an elevation of two feet" (Keyes 1934:340). Unlike in subsequent years, Keyes participated daily in the fieldwork as supervisor and with Orr "planned the various points and methods of attack [and used] small hand trowels or brushes" to uncover features or particularly noteworthy artifact clusters (Keyes 1934:340). Excavation squares, generally 5 by 5 feet, served as the basic provenience unit and it was not uncommon for depths of 6 to 8 feet to be reached. Sieves with half-inch mesh screens were selectively used as an aid in artifact recovery; Keyes estimated 100 cubic yards were screened out of that summer's hand-excavated total volume of 4,000 cubic yards (Keyes 1934:338).

Although Keyes noted that Project 1047 was planned to involve the "supervision of certain unskilled work" (Keyes 1934:332)—by necessity to meet FERA program requirements that unemployed individuals be put to work in order to receive economic relief—there was a substantive archaeological research design, too. Orr documented that he and Keyes were well aware from their extensive surface surveys in northeast Iowa that many late prehistoric large Oneota culture village locations were known in the Upper Iowa River valley on high terraces and that "practically one hundred percent" of the pottery sherds recovered were shell tempered; only "once in a while among the field finds of sherds would a small piece covered with 'string' impressions and tempered with crushed granite or sand" be discovered (Orr 1936a:A-2). The question driving the research by Keyes and Orr was, "were the builders of these mounds [e.g., such as at the New Galena mound group] the ones who made and lost or threw away the bits of grit-tempered ware? Only by thorough scientific excavation could we find out" (Orr 1936a:A-2). Incidentally, McKusick (1979), Anderson (1975), and Green (1992) correctly cite Orr's series of reports documenting New Deal archaeology endeavors as "Orr 1963," as until recently these volumes were only available as original manuscripts on file at Effigy Mounds National Monument or as a microcard series (Orr 1963). The University of Iowa Office of the State Archaeologist now electronically archives high-resolution scans of the original manuscripts, which are thus cited here by the dates Orr assigned to them (Orr 1936a, 1936b, 1936c, 1942a, 1942b, 1942c, for volumes 1–3, 5, 10, and 11, respectively).

In addition to Keyes and Orr, the 1934 crew included as regulars the latter's 51-year-old son, Fred Orr, and Harrison Toney, also of Waukon, who were given the positions of field workers. Toney, who owned a car, also furnished transportation. Keyes (1934:338) noted, "numerically our organization was never a large one . . . ordinarily we picked up three to four men . . . occasionally as many as six or seven . . . a few times only, through error or some unexpected happening, we got down to one . . . we thus had a working force that was never under five and never over eleven." The Allamakee County "relief engineer" was responsible for identifying and assigning the one to seven workers provided for the New Galena dig beyond the four regulars; the fieldwork was conducted six days per week but the assigned workers were rotated so that no one man got more than three days of work in a single week. Compensation was 30¢ per hour. Keyes (1934:335–336) noted that "all were willing to learn and nearly all were strictly honest . . . during the entire summer only four men were assigned to us who were confirmed shirkers . . . word sent in to the Relief Engineer resulted in the disappearance of the four names from the work sheets." Orr (1936a) confirmed the opinion Keyes expressed, noting that although "during July and August the weather was extremely hot . . . the men stayed by it . . . [with few] exceptions the workmen furnished by the FERA were trustworthy and careful and did a day's work that was satisfactory to us." The value of New Deal funding for Iowa archaeology is perhaps best expressed by Keyes (1934:354), who chose to close his account of the 1934 effort with the following: "what an enormous amount of honest working power might society have left beside the road during the summer of 1934! How fortunate for the workers and for us, at least, that tools were placed in idle hands!"

Additional federal funding provided to Project 1047 allowed Keyes to dispatch Ellison and Fred Orr, along with driver Harrison Toney, to northwestern Iowa. This work began in mid-September 1934 with the aim of investigating sites of the Mill Creek culture. Keyes desired to conduct "a test of their possibilities" or what archaeologist Michael Perry (personal communication 2010) has described as the "first Phase II testing in Iowa." From September 24 to November 26, 1934, while also excavating several sites, Orr and his team mapped the details of 11 mound groups located in nine counties distributed across the length and breadth of Iowa. This is an accomplishment few modern CRM archaeology crews could match even with the availability of modern equipment and the current transportation system.

Project 1047 continued through the winter of 1934–1935 with Orr and his colleagues visiting numerous sites to evaluate their potential for preservation by the state. Several that they describe (Orr 1936b), including Blood Run, Toolesboro, and Malchow Mounds, were eventually purchased as state-owned historic sites or made part of the State Preserves system. By spring of 1935, Project 1047 entered its last phase with the focus through that summer on mound sites along the Mississippi River bluffs northwards from Clinton, Iowa. Keyes and Orr were both early and persistent proponents for a National Park Service unit in Iowa (Iowa State Planning Board 1935). Notably, a portion of the mound-rich landscape near McGregor investigated by Project 1047 eventually became, in 1949, Effigy Mounds National Monument. Establishment of this National Park Service unit was critical in bringing an additional professional archaeologist to Iowa and Wilfred Logan served as the Effigy Mounds archaeologist for many years. Logan drew heavily on the New Deal–funded excavation assemblages generated by Keyes and Orr for his dissertation on Woodland complexes (Logan 1976). Logan's seminal work defining ceramic assemblages in eastern Iowa continues to be routinely cited today.

Keyes wrote a letter to the Iowa State Planning Board summarizing the 1935 field season. He noted that a "Mr. James B. Griffin of the University of Michigan, a specialist in the study of the ancient pottery of the eastern United States, began a study of the pots and potsherds collected by us . . . Griffin pronounced the materials as first class and of great interest." Keyes used Griffin's observations to advantage, moving on in the same letter directly to a funding request: "it is highly desirable . . . that our Project continue its work, if possible, on a somewhat enlarged scale and with even better equipment and organization" (Orr 1936c:15).

## Project 962

Keyes's request was met, albeit under a new project number, 962, assigned by the Iowa State Planning Board and supported by WPA funds. Project 962 returned Orr and his crew to northeastern Iowa, where several sites were investigated, including the "enclosed area or 'Old Fort' . . . on the Lane Farm Terrace" (Orr 1942a:v). Orr documented that up to 10 WPA "common laborers" were assigned to Project 962 in addition to the two Orr regulars and driver Toney. Work started September 1 and was completed December 4, 1935, with "a total of 3800 cu. yds of earth handled during the working hours allotted to us during that time, at a cost of a fraction over 30 cents per cu. yd." The most important result of Project 962 was one that immediately influenced the archaeological research of the time—and one that remains of central importance today—that is, establishing cultural affiliation. Orr (1942a:v) wrote that the results of Project 962 "establish that the people who occupied the Area up to an early contact with the white traders, probably about the beginning of the 17th century, were of the Oneota aspect of the Upper Mississippi river phase of the Siouan culture as defined and designated by Keyes, and that the builders of the mounds were an Algonkin [*sic*] people preceding them." Mildred Mott (1938), studying at the University of Chicago, extended this line of research, linking archaeological cultures to historic Indian tribes that occupied Iowa, particularly the Ioway (Wedel 1959). More recently, NAGPRA-driven compliance (Schermer et al. 1998) and related cultural-affiliation studies (Benn and Stadler 2004; Green et al. 2001) continue to build on the New Deal–generated results.

## Project 3600

New Deal funding continued through the later 1930s for Iowa archaeology with Keyes and Orr ultimately conducting federally funded archaeological investigations at 155 sites in 16 Iowa counties and at one Illinois site (11WT1), with excavation work at 53 of these sites (Table 5.1). Major excavations took place in Allamakee, Clayton, Mills, and Plymouth counties. Efforts culminated with WPA Project 3600 in 1938 and 1939, which funded multiple site excavations in the Glenwood area of southwestern Iowa in 1938 (Orr 1942b) and major trenching investigations at sites in northwestern Iowa in 1939 (Orr 1942c). The Glenwood sites investigated included National Register of Historic Places (NRHP) eligible earthlodges of the Nebraska phase of the Central Plains Tradition; Orr (1942b:4) noted that A. T. Hill and Paul Cooper were excavating related Central Plains Tradition sites in Nebraska, work also based on New Deal funding. Orr supervised 10 WPA-funded workmen between April 8 and December 5, 1938, for a total of 12,800 work hours; wages by this time had risen to 40¢ per hour (Orr 1942b). Orr as supervisor of fieldwork was compensated $1,042.50 for the same period but wrote his report free of charge! The "Glenwood culture" sites that Orr documented have received continuing professional attention in recent decades. This includes a 1970s-era 18-lodge data recovery excavation sponsored by the Iowa Department of Transportation during U.S. 34 highway construction in Mills County that represents one of the earliest large-scale Section 106–driven archaeological mitigation projects in Iowa (Hotopp 1973, 1977). John Hotopp, the project director, based his dissertation on the data collected in this undertaking, noting that in addition to the excavation of 12 lodges as part of the 1938 New Deal–funded archaeology in the Glenwood area, Orr "located 71 lodge sites . . . [and] more than 10,000 archaeological specimens were shipped to Iowa City for analysis. This material . . . is an essential component for the study of Central Plains archaeology in Iowa" (Hotopp 1978:22–23).

The 1939 portion of Project 3600 focused on two Mill Creek culture sites, the aptly named Broken Kettle (13PM1) and Kimball (13PM4), both near Sioux City in northwestern Iowa. By this time, the New Deal funding was flowing from the federal government to the Graduate College of the State University of Iowa, reflecting subtle changes in Keyes's relationship

Table 5.1. Archaeological sites investigated via FERA and WPA funding in Iowa, 1934–1939

| Site | Site No. | Investigation | Reference |
|---|---|---|---|
| Big Spring Mound Group | 13AM94 | Survey & excavation | Orr 1936a |
| Elephant Terrace | 13AM59 | Survey & excavation | Orr 1936a |
| Harper's Ferry Mounds: Big Mound (Mound Group 4) | 13AM151 | Survey & excavation | Orr 1936a |
| Harper's Ferry Mounds: William Cota Mound Group (Mound Group 13) | 13AM160 | Survey & excavation | Orr 1936a |
| Harper's Ferry Mounds: Martell Mounds | 13AM158 | Survey & excavation | Orr 1936a |
| Harper's Ferry Mounds: Brazell's Island Mounds (Mound Group 1) | 13AM81 | Survey & excavation | Orr 1936a |
| Hammel Mounds | 13AM95 | Survey & excavation | Orr 1936a |
| Lane Farm Mound Group | 13AM104 | Survey & excavation | Orr 1936a |
| Lane Enclosure | 13AM200 | Survey & excavation | Orr 1936a |
| New Galena Mound Group | 13AM108 | Survey & excavation | Orr 1936a |
| O'Regan Bench | 13AM21 | Survey & excavation | Orr 1936a |
| Sixteen Rock Shelter | 13AM122 | Survey & excavation | Orr 1936a |
| Waterville Rock Shelter | 13AM124 | Survey & excavation | Orr 1936a |
| Weymiller Mound Group | 13AM88 | Survey & excavation | Orr 1936a |
| Wines Bluff Mounds | 13AM149 | Survey | Orr 1936a |
| Slinde Mound Group | 13AM120 | Survey & excavation | Orr 1936a |
| Ward Mound Group | 13AM129 | Undetermined | Orr 1936a |
| Blood Run Mound Group | 13LO2, 13LO5 | Survey | Orr 1936b |
| Broken Kettle Mound | 13PM1 | Excavation | Orr 1936b |
| Burge Mound Group | 13LN244 | Survey | Orr 1936b |
| Brushy Creek Mound Group | 13WB130 | Survey | Orr 1936b |
| Buck Creek (Bluff) Mound Group | 13CT34, 13CT36 | Survey | Orr 1936b |
| Bellevue State Park Mound Group | 13JK9 | Survey | Orr 1936b |

| | | | |
|---|---|---|---|
| Clancy Lake (Peterson) Mound Group | 13CN7 | Survey | Orr 1936b |
| Caldwell Mound Group | 13HA1 | Survey | Orr 1936b |
| Cross Mound Group | 13WD3 | Survey | Orr 1936b |
| Eslick Mound Group | 13WB131 | Survey | Orr 1936b |
| French Town (Eckards) Mound Group | 13CT166/A-C, 13CT99 | Excavation | Orr 1936b |
| Hook Mound Group | 13LA40 | Survey | Orr 1936b |
| Hawbaker (Wickwire) Mound Group | 13WB132 | Survey | Orr 1936b |
| Hill Mound Group | 13OB22 | Survey | Orr 1936b |
| Leheigh (Lehigh) Mound Group | 13WB80 | Survey | Orr 1936b |
| Lewis Martin Mound Group | 13OB24 | Survey | Orr 1936b |
| Maquoketa River Mound Group | 13JK15 | Survey | Orr 1936b |
| Martin Johnson Mound Group | 13LO2 | Survey | Orr 1936b |
| Malchow Mound Group | 13DM4 | Survey | Orr 1936b |
| Patterson-Cornell Mound Group | 13DM5 | Survey | Orr 1936b |
| Patterson Mound Group I | 13OB20 | Survey | Orr 1936b |
| Patterson Mound Group II | 13OB71 | | |
| Paulina Mound Group | 13OB25 | Survey | Orr 1936b |
| Pleasant Creek Mound Group, Section Corner Mound Group | 13JK17 | Survey & excavation | Orr 1936b |
| Quinby Mound Group | 13CK73? | Survey | Orr 1936b |
| Red Rock Mound Group | 13MA7 | Survey | Orr 1936b |
| Sny Magill Bluff Mound Group | 13CT18 | Survey | Orr 1936b |
| Toolesboro Mound Group | 13LA29 | Survey | Orr 1936b |
| Wittrock (Enclosed Camp) | 13OB4 | Survey | Orr 1936b |

*Continued on the next page*

| Site | Site No. | Investigation | Reference |
|---|---|---|---|
| Webb Mound Group | 13OB28 | Survey | Orr 1936b |
| Albany Mounds | 11WT1 | Survey | Orr 1936c |
| Bellevue Mound Group | 13JK10 | Survey | Orr 1936c |
| Deppe Mound Group | 13JK11 | Survey & excavation | Orr 1936c |
| French Town Mounds | 13CT166 | Survey & excavation | Orr 1936c |
| Finger, Henry Mounds (Finger Mound Group or H. Finger Mound Group) | 13CN5 | Survey | Orr 1936c |
| Finger, L. Mounds (Finger Mound Group or Louis Finger Mound Group) | 13CN6 | Survey | Orr 1936c |
| Gudovissy Mound Group (1) | 13CT11 | Survey & excavation | Orr 1936c |
| Gudovissy Mound Group (2) | 13CT44 | Survey & excavation | Orr 1936c |
| Green Island Mound Group | 13JK12 | Survey | Orr 1936c |
| Harvey's (Harveys) Island Mound Group No. 1 | 13CT45 | Survey | Orr 1936c |
| Harvey's (Harveys) Island Mound Group No. 2 | 13CT66 | Survey & excavation | Orr 1936c |
| Harvey's (Harveys) Island Mound Group No. 3 | 13CT67 | Survey | Orr 1936c |
| Jennings-Liebhardt Mound Group (Pleasant Ridge Mound Group) | 13CT26 | Survey | Orr 1936c |
| Lemenselzar Mounds | 13JK13 | Survey | Orr 1936c |
| Marshall Mound Group | 13JK14 | Survey | Orr 1936c |
| Mound Group Sec. 5 T83 R7E | 13CN8 | Survey | Orr 1936c |
| Mound Group Sec. 32 T84 R7E | 13JK19 | Survey | Orr 1936c |
| McMahan Mound Group | 13JK16 | Survey | Orr 1936c |
| Pleasant Creek Mound Group | 13JK17 | Survey & excavation | Orr 1936c |
| Peterson Mound Group | 13CN7 | Survey & excavation | Orr 1936c |
| Pleasant Valley Bluff Mounds (Pleasant Creek Bluff Group) | 13JK2 | Survey | Orr 1936c |
| Sabula Mound Group | 13JK18 | Survey | Orr 1936c |
| Turkey River Mound Groups—Pete Adams Group 1 | 13CT5 | Survey & excavation | Orr 1936c |
| Turkey River Mound Groups—Pete Adams Group 2 | 13CT10 | Survey | Orr 1936c |

| | | | |
|---|---|---|---|
| Turkey River Mound Groups—Pete Adams Group 3 | 13CT2 | Survey | Orr 1936c |
| Turkey River Mound Groups—Pete Adams Group 4 | 13CT3 | Survey | Orr 1936c |
| Turkey River Mound Groups—Matt Adams Mound Group | 13CT12 | Survey | Orr 1936c |
| Bear Effigy, Brazell's Island, Harper's Ferry (Brazell's Island Mound Group) | 13AM81 | Excavation | Orr 1942a |
| Bolles' Terrace Cache, 3 mi. north of Harper's Ferry (Bolles' Terrace) | 13AM259 | Excavation | Orr 1942a |
| Burke's Mound Burial Place, New Galena (Burke's Mound Cemetery) | 13AM67 | Excavation | Orr 1942a |
| Hill Mounds, 3 mi. north of Harper's Ferry (Hill Mound Group) | 13AM105 | Excavation | Orr 1942a |
| Hog Back Mounds, New Galena (Hog Back Mound Group) | 13AM86 | Excavation | Orr 1942a |
| Lane Farm Terrace Enclosed Area, "Old Fort" (Lane Farm Enclosure) | 13AM200 | Excavation | Orr 1942a |
| Lane Farm Terrace Mounds (Lane Farm Mound Group) | 13AM104 | Excavation | Orr 1942a |
| Luth (Hennessy) Mounds, 2 mi. north of Harper's Ferry (Luth [Hennessy] Mound Group) | 13AM150 | Excavation | Orr 1942a |
| Mud Hen Joe (Wines' Camp) Mound Group, 2 mi. north of Waukon Junction (Mud Hen Joe Mounds) | 13AM116 | Excavation | Orr 1942a |
| New Galena Mound Group | 13AM108 | Excavation | Orr 1942a |
| Woolstrom's Burial Place, New Galena (Woolstrom Cemetery) | 13AM61 | Excavation | Orr 1942a |
| Ryan and Houlihan Mounds, Harper's Ferry | 13AM117 | Excavation | Orr 1942a |
| H.S.A. | 13ML64 | Excavation | Orr 1942b |
| H.S.G. | 13ML79 | Excavation | Orr 1942b |
| H.S.N. | 13ML232 | Excavation | Orr 1942b |
| H.S.X-16 Pitzer | 13ML239 | Excavation | Orr 1942b |
| H.S.F. | 13ML67 | Excavation | Orr 1942b |
| H.S.Q. | 13ML234 | Excavation | Orr 1942b |
| H.S.J. | 13ML229 | Excavation | Orr 1942b |

*Continued on the next page*

| Site | Site No. | Investigation | Reference |
|---|---|---|---|
| H.S.O. | 13ML233 | Excavation | Orr 1942b |
| H.S.X. McGanigal | 13ML235 | Excavation | Orr 1942b |
| H.S.X-10 Marshall | 13ML236 | Excavation | Orr 1942b |
| H.S.X-11 | 13ML237 | Excavation | Orr 1942b |
| H.S.X-15 Henry Lohse | 13ML238 | Excavation | Orr 1942b |
| Mound Group 4, Terry Mound Group | 13ML49 | Excavation | Orr 1942b |
| Mound Group 10, Boyce Mound Group | 13ML246 | Excavation | Orr 1942b |
| Mound Group 2, Hunt Mound Group | 13ML245 | Excavation | Orr 1942b |
| Mound Group 7, Wells Mound Group | 13ML117 | Excavation | Orr 1942b |
| Mound Group No. 1, Tipton Village Mound | 13ML193 | Survey | Orr 1942b |
| Mound Group No. 3 | 13ML194 | Survey | Orr 1942b |
| Mound Group No. 5, Case Mound Group | 13ML282 | Survey | Orr 1942b |
| Mound Group No. 6, Picnic Mound Group | 13ML283 | Survey | Orr 1942b |
| Mound Group No. 7, Wells Mound Group | 13ML117 | Excavation | Orr 1942b |
| Mound Group No. 9 | 13ML195 | Survey | Orr 1942b |
| Mound Group No. 11, Sayles Group | Unassigned | Survey | Orr 1942b |
| Mound Group No. 12, Sayles Group No. 2 | 13ML197 | Survey | Orr 1942b |
| Mound Group No. 13, Barbour Group | 13ML247 | Excavation | Orr 1942b |
| Mound Group No. 14, Wilson Group | 13ML198 | Survey | Orr 1942b |
| Earth Lodge B | 13ML294 | Survey | Orr 1942b |
| Earth Lodge C | 13ML558 | Survey | Orr 1942b |
| Earth Lodge E? | 13ML560 | Survey | Orr 1942b |
| Earth Lodge H, Marcia Williams (Starbuck) | 13ML228 | Survey | Orr 1942b |
| Earth Lodge I | 13ML189 | Survey | Orr 1942b |
| Earth Lodge L | 13ML295 | Survey | Orr 1942b |

| | | | |
|---|---|---|---|
| Earth Lodge M | 13ML231 | Survey | Orr 1942b |
| Earth Lodge X-36 | 13ML254 | Survey | Orr 1942b |
| Earth Lodge R, Terry House | 13ML409 | Survey | Orr 1942b |
| Earth Lodge S | 13ML296 | Survey | Orr 1942b |
| Earth Lodge T, Wickersheim | 13ML80 | Survey | Orr 1942b |
| Earth Lodge U | 13ML81 | Survey | Orr 1942b |
| Earth Lodge V | 13ML406 | Survey | Orr 1942b |
| Earth Lodge W | 13ML199 | Survey | Orr 1942b |
| Earth Lodge X-1, West Henderson House | 13ML191 | Survey | Orr 1942b |
| Earth Lodge X-2, East Henderson House | 13ML191 | Survey | Orr 1942b |
| Earth Lodge X-3 | 13ML298 | Survey | Orr 1942b |
| Earth Lodge X-5 | 13ML299 | Survey | Orr 1942b |
| Earth Lodge X-7 | 13ML410 | Survey | Orr 1942b |
| Earth Lodge X-8 | 13ML300 | Survey | Orr 1942b |
| Earth Lodge X-9, Stille Site No. 1 | 13ML301 | Survey | Orr 1942b |
| Earth Lodge X-12, Stille Site No. 2 | 13ML102 | Survey | Orr 1942b |
| Earth Lodge X-13, Stille Site No. 3 | 13ML116 | Survey | Orr 1942b |
| Earth Lodge X-14 | 13ML302 | Survey | Orr 1942b |
| Earth Lodge X-17, Pitzer House No. 2 | 13ML303 | Survey | Orr 1942b |
| Earth Lodge X-18, W. C. Lohse House | 13ML5 | Survey | Orr 1942b |
| Earth Lodge X-19 & 20, Knickman House | 13ML219 | Survey | Orr 1942b |
| Earth Lodge X-21 | 13ML192 | Survey | Orr 1942b |
| Earth Lodge X-22, Case House | 13ML284 | Survey | Orr 1942b |
| Earth Lodge X-24 | 13ML285 | Survey | Orr 1942b |
| Earth Lodge X-25 | 13ML290 | Survey | Orr 1942b |

*Continued on the next page*

| Site | Site No. | Investigation | Reference |
|---|---|---|---|
| Earth Lodge X-26, Plumer House Site No. 1 | 13ML289 | Survey | Orr 1942b |
| Earth Lodge X-29 | 13ML293 | Survey | Orr 1942b |
| Earth Lodge X-30, Nell Bogart House Site No. 1 | 13ML240 | Survey | Orr 1942b |
| Earth Lodge P | 13ML297 | Survey | Orr 1942b |
| Earth Lodge X-33, Sayles House Site No. 2 | 13ML286 | Survey | Orr 1942b |
| Earth Lodge X-34, Sayles House Site No. 3 | 13ML179 | Survey | Orr 1942b |
| Earth Lodge X-35 | 13ML306 | Survey | Orr 1942b |
| Earth Lodge X-37, Ed Hoover House | 13ML241 | Survey | Orr 1942b |
| Earth Lodge X-40 | 13ML307 | Survey | Orr 1942b |
| Earth Lodge X-38 | 13ML155 | Survey | Orr 1942b |
| Earth Lodge X-39 | 13ML288 | Survey | Orr 1942b |
| H.S.X-45 | 13ML275 | Survey | Orr 1942b |
| H.S.X-46 | 13ML190 | Survey | Orr 1942b |
| H.S.X-47 | 13ML308 | Survey | Orr 1942b |
| H.S.X-50 | 13ML309 | Survey | Orr 1942b |
| Earth Lodge X-42 | 13ML255 | Survey | Orr 1942b |
| Earth Lodge X-48 | 13ML87 | Survey | Orr 1942b |
| Earth Lodge X-43 | 13ML287 | Survey | Orr 1942b |
| Earth Lodge X-44 | Unassigned | Survey | Orr 1942b |
| Earth Lodge X-49 | 13ML310 | Survey | Orr 1942b |
| Earth Lodge X-51 | Unassigned | No location survey | Orr 1942b |
| Camp Site A | 13ML564 | Excavation | Orr 1942b |
| Camp Site B | 13ML83 | Excavation | Orr 1942b |
| Broken Kettle | 13PM1 | Survey & excavation | Orr 1942c |
| Kimball | 13PM4 | Survey & excavation | Orr 1942c |

with the State Historical Society of Iowa and in turn that of this institution with the university. In his preface to the volume he wrote on these excavations, Orr included his thanks to other WPA-funded colleagues in adjacent states "where like archaeological work was being carried on in Minnesota, S. Dakota, and Nebraska" (Orr 1942c). As before, "ten WPA men were made available as shovel men for the work of excavation during the summer of 1939" (Orr 1942c:2). To gain landowner permission to excavate at the Broken Kettle site, Keyes agreed Orr and his crew would refill old pit silos on the farmyard that straddled the archaeological deposit with fill from a new silo (i.e., archaeological excavation) that was to be 10 feet wide, 8 feet deep, and 45 feet long with a ramp of 20 feet at the northeastern end. This is an early example of a typical fact of life impacting many federally funded or permitted CRM archaeology projects today: that of non-archaeological constraints dictating the parameters of how much excavation a project may undertake and where.

Following completion at Broken Kettle of the agreed-upon earth moving and the collection of copious archaeological specimens, the crew relocated to the Kimball site, which, while frequently surface collected by locals, had not previously been excavated (Orr 1942c:68). Orr discovered intact house floors, lines of postholes, and spectacular artifacts. Archaeologist Michael Perry (2007:108) has observed, "following up on Orr's ground-breaking work, archaeologists of the 1950s, 1960s, and 1970s would reveal the layout of Mill Creek houses, study the development of Mill Creek settlement mounds, define the variety of Mississippian trade goods, examine changes in how they farmed and hunted, investigate the possible effects of climate change on people of the Great Plains, and debate Mill Creek origins and possible reasons for abandoning northwestern Iowa."

The data generated by Project 3600 continue in their importance in archaeological research conducted today. For example, a large grant-funded project focused on elevating the Iowa Loess Hills National Scenic Byway to "All-American Road" status is under way, and archaeological resources were tapped as one of the "intrinsic qualities" of especially notable importance. In particular, Glenwood earthlodges and the Kimball site became the focal points of new research to provide the clinching details for recently submitted National Register nomination documents (Merry 2009). Multiple Property Documents such as the "Central Plains Tradition in the Loess Hills Region of Iowa" and the "Initial Variant of the Middle Missouri Tradition in Iowa" establishing the significance of these archaeological foci are currently under review at the national level; acceptance will result in NRHP listing for the Kimball site.

## The Legacy of the Keyes-Orr New Deal Investigations

While space constraints do not allow review of all the significant archaeological details with which Keyes and Orr were involved, it bears noting that many of the professional archaeologists subsequently involved with Iowa research have sought out the opportunity to comment on and affirm the importance and continuing influence of the 1930s Keyes-Orr New Deal–funded archaeological work. These luminaries include, from the 1950s, National Park Service archaeologist Wilfred Logan (1951), Smithsonian archaeologist Waldo Wedel (1952), and the first State Archaeologist of Iowa Rey Ruppé (1953); the aforementioned Marshall McKusick in the 1960s (McKusick 1979); Duane Anderson in the 1970s (Anderson 1975); Joseph Tiffany in the 1980s (Tiffany 1981, 1986; Tiffany et al. 1990); William Green in the 1990s (Green 1992); and, more recently, Lynn Alex (2000), David Benn (2001), and Michael Perry (2007). These archaeologists are in general agreement—McKusick perhaps being more critical than others—that while the New Deal investigations were hardly perfect by any modern standard, Iowa archaeology would be considerably poorer if not for the efforts of Keyes and Orr. In particular, early Orr maps and site descriptions and notes on artifacts and collections by Keyes have provided modern archaeologists with critical data on locations that have become obscured by development, erosion, and vegetation changes (Perry 2007). As Benn (2001:33) observes, "He [Keyes] and Orr did magnificent work amassing a public record of antiquities and archaeological sites, saving what was fast disappearing to the looters."

William Green (personal communication 2010) has noted that the prolific fieldwork of Keyes and Orr appears to have created two sorts of legacies in Iowa. On the one hand, New Deal archaeology laid the foundation for the emergence of professional, systematic, scientific investigations. This can be easily seen in work supported by institutions like the Sanford Museum in northwestern Iowa and Effigy Mounds National Monument and Luther College in northeastern Iowa at relatively early dates and leading eventually to formal programs at the University of Iowa, Iowa State University, and elsewhere. At the same time, elsewhere in Iowa, the prominent visibility of Orr's extended field projects encouraged nonprofessional digging where perhaps preservation would have been preferred. Certainly, post-1939 work in Mills County on earthlodge sites by Frances McDowell and even Paul Rowe was inspired by Orr, but these individuals lacked mentorship and they continued with field methods that could be characterized in modern terms as substandard far longer than was practiced elsewhere (Benn 2001). On the plus side, however, Green (personal communication 2010) observes, "Depression-era funding generated a huge database that many people, notably and initially Mildred [Mott Wedel], mined for theses, dissertations, articles, books, exhibits, etc. The fieldwork and Keyes's summary articles developed much of Iowa's culture historical framework. I think Orr was frustrated that more of the work wasn't published during his and Keyes's lifetime . . . but later scholars made good use of the data."

Under a curatorial agreement with the State Historical Society of Iowa, the University of Iowa Office of the State Archaeologist took physical possession of the Keyes Collection in 1998 following the move into the current facility at 700 Clinton Street in Iowa City. The resulting enhanced accessibility of the Keyes Collection has led to an increase in the use of the materials, especially for comparative purposes. Planned curatorial rehabilitation of the collection involving repackaging, additional cataloging, and extensive digital photography—including 3-D scanning of particularly important artifacts—promises to make the Iowa materials collected through New Deal funding even more accessible and useful in the future.

## Acknowledgments

Marshall McKusick and Duane Anderson, both long-time State Archaeologists of Iowa, laid the foundation in their respective looks at the history of archaeological practice in Iowa for our appreciation and understanding of the impact of WPA funding. Bill Green, another distinguished former State Archaeologist of Iowa, provided much valued commentary on our efforts to fairly position the work of Keyes and Orr vis-à-vis modern methods. Dale Henning and David Gradwohl, both "senior scholars" of the Iowa archaeology scene, also provided helpful perspectives as did Steve Lensink and Jerome Thompson. Mike Perry deserves special recognition as probably the best-informed archaeologist on the work of Keyes and Orr; he pointed us to several important references. Lastly, we would like to thank Bernard Means for the opportunity to participate in both the SAA symposium and this edited volume; errors, gaffs, and omissions remain our responsibility.

# 6

# The Last of WPA Archaeology in Oklahoma

## The Clement and McDonald Sites

*Amanda L. Regnier, Patrick C. Livingood, and Scott W. Hammerstedt*

By 1941, federally sponsored archaeology in Oklahoma had been ongoing for nearly eight years. As part of economic relief intended to mitigate the economic collapse of the early 1930s under the weight of the Dust Bowl droughts and the Great Depression, sites had been identified and tested in 12 counties. Beginning in 1933, the bulk of the archaeology had taken place at sites in the Arkansas River drainage system, culminating most notably in the cleanup of the regrettable looting and destruction of the Craig Mound at Spiro. As federal funds continued to be poured into work relief programs, field crews moved to nearby Mississippian mounds and villages and a series of Late Archaic and Woodland midden mounds along Fourche Maline Creek. In May 1941, University of Oklahoma archaeologist David Baerreis started operations in McCurtain County in the southeast corner of Oklahoma. For the next nine months, Baerreis directed excavations at two prehistoric Caddo sites along the Glover River, the mound center at Clement (34Mc8–10) and what was presumed until recently to be the much smaller McDonald site (34Mc11/12). The excavations came to a halt in early 1942 when the United States entered World War II and the Great Depression ended. Federal funds were shifted to the war effort, and workers, including Baerreis himself, were sent overseas (Rogers 1978).

Although they lasted only nine months and involved just two sites, the McCurtain County excavations were the first to address a crucial gap in Oklahoma prehistory (Table 6.1). The house patterns and artifacts recovered solved the puzzle of who lived in the region between the Mississippian mound center at Spiro and the similar sites of northeast Texas, southwest Arkansas, and northwest Louisiana. Based on these excavations, for the

Table 6.1. Archaeological sites investigated using WPA funding in McCurtain County, Oklahoma, 1941–1942

| Site | Site No. | Dates of Excavation |
|---|---|---|
| Clement I | 34Mc8 | June 2 to December 9, 1941 |
| Clement II | 34Mc9 | July 25, 1941 |
| Clement III | 34Mc10 | November 17 to 29, 1941 |
| McDonald I | 34Mc11 | December 10, 1941, to March 4, 1942 |
| McDonald II | 34Mc12 | December 10, 1941, to March 4, 1942 |

*Note:* Dates for excavations obtained from WPA notebooks on file at SNOMNH.

first time Baerreis was able to document the presence of prehistoric Caddos living in this portion of southeast Oklahoma between approximately A.D. 1000 and A.D. 1600. Prior to this foray into southeast Oklahoma, the many Caddo mound and village sites in the Red River drainage system were known only to local residents. Both sites studied by the Works Progress Administration (WPA) are located along the Glover River near its confluence with the easterly flowing portion of the Little River. Physiographically, both sites are in the narrow Piedmont region that lies between the southern Ouachita Mountains and the western Gulf Coastal Plain. Many published summaries of WPA work have looked at broad histories; we believe a focus on the nine months of work in this one county near the end of the WPA era is illustrative of the methods and goals WPA researchers like Baerreis had developed through many years of experience with the program. In this case it also shows increasingly less attention to documentation by archaeologists rushing to complete work before the WPA program ended. These rushed notes proved challenging when the Oklahoma Archeological Survey reexamined the Clement and McDonald sites in 2008 and 2010, respectively.

## Field Methods of the Oklahoma WPA

Before describing excavation at the sites and details of what was recovered by the WPA and our own recent investigations, we will take a moment to consider the standard methods developed by Oklahoma WPA archaeologists, which we have determined from examining unpublished field notes. After a potential site was located, a small crew dug a number of test units to further evaluate the site. At Clement and McDonald, testing efforts generated numerous artifacts. After the testing, the site was gridded arbitrarily into either

5- or 10-foot squares, so artifacts from testing, which are typically labeled with descriptions such as "under the large peach tree," essentially are unprovenienced. In some cases, this includes hundreds of sherds and pieces of lithic debitage. At McDonald two areas were identified and excavated separately. A 5-foot grid was used to excavate the midden and cemetery in the western portion of the site, while the midden and house 250 feet to the east were excavated using a 10-foot grid. As will become a theme, during the waning months of the WPA work the quality of documentation declined; in this case the excavators failed to note the size of the grids on excavation sheets or the structure map. Initially, the switch in grid size caused a great deal of confusion in our recent work when we looked at the map of a structure from the eastern midden and, presuming a continuation of the 5-foot grid, puzzled over what appeared to be the smallest Caddo round house on record at only 8 feet across. Non-mound contexts were excavated in 12-inch levels. Mound contexts were excavated by slicing the mound gradually back row by row along the 5-foot grid (Figure 6.1).

Grids were reported to be oriented to magnetic north and labeled with row (generally north–south) and alley (generally east–west) numbers. However, as we have discovered in our subsequent work at the Clement site, orientation of the grid varied. At Clement, our 2008 geophysical survey using magnetic gradiometry encountered rectangular patterns presumed to be WPA trenches (Hammerstedt et al. 2010). We were puzzled, however, by the orientation of these units, clearly off magnetic north. Again, reviewing a field notebook, we discovered the original documentation of magnetic north grid orientation, which was written in David Baerreis's handwriting, had been crossed out at some point and a slightly different orientation was written above in different handwriting, presumably that of crew chief Jess M. Jones. Furthering our confusion, row and alley numbers were not always assigned consistently. In the middle of the grid at the McDonald site, row and alley designations reversed, and the artifact distribution maps made no sense until we eventually discovered half of the grid was rotated 90 degrees.

Much of the information we have about the Oklahoma WPA excavations comes from the Quarterly Reports of Activities on file in the Sam Noble Oklahoma Museum of Natural History (SNOMNH) and in the Western History Collections of the University of Oklahoma Libraries. In the first quarterly report of the WPA excavations, written in 1938, five years after relief efforts started, Oklahoma University anthropologist Dr. Forrest Clements provided examples of the standard recording forms. Two different forms were used. One was for features such as burials, caches, and piece-plotted artifacts, and the other was for elevation readings from a transit. At most of the

Figure 6.1. Workers slicing into the mound at the Clement site. Each of the stakes marks the corner of a 5-×-5-foot grid square (Courtesy of the Sam Noble Oklahoma Museum of Natural History).

sites the excavators drew mound profiles at least once during excavation and plan maps of post patterns associated with structures (Clements 1938). In general, the quality of the quarterly reports seems to have declined through time. Early versions included photographs, profile maps, extensive feature and burials descriptions, and artifact drawings. The reports from McCurtain County had no attached images and are the least detailed of the reports. Presumably, the recording quality declined with a growing sense of urgency to complete the excavations as the relief effort wound down.

A handful of photographs from the McCurtain County sites and the excavation forms are on file at the SNOMNH. In addition, three field journals from David Baerreis and crew chief Jess M. Jones are also kept on file there. One appears to be dedicated solely to Clement and seems to have remained at the site throughout the course of the excavations. A similar field journal for the McDonald site is also on file. The main notebooks from Clement and McDonald largely consist of daily entries of what was found in each open unit, accompanied by scattered sketches of interesting features encountered during the day. The Clement notebook also includes a detailed roster of every posthole encountered; descriptions of associations, burials, and caches; and rosters of and lists of the hours worked by the 22 crew members between May 29 and November 6, 1941. The McDonald notebook has the same daily entries of what was found in each unit, along with detailed descriptions of the burials excavated at the site. It lists the hours worked by the crew between December 5, 1941, and March 4, 1942, which appears to be the last day for which they were paid. No units are logged in the notebook after February 24, 1942. Another notebook appears to be David Baerreis's personal field notebook, and this includes a few notes from Clement and McDonald, along with some notes from sites in Bryan County. Another notebook details Jess M. Jones's work in July and August 1941 with a crew of three field workers testing the excavation potential of several nearby sites. Some vital information definitely has been lost. Probably the biggest issue is the lack of site maps. The files include transit elevation readings for the base of a number of units, but in most cases the surface elevations are not present or the forms instruct the reader to refer to a now missing map, making the elevations frustratingly useless.

From the McCurtain County field journals and a few sources chronicling earlier WPA efforts, we have been able to reconstruct some of the financial details of the WPA efforts. One clue about archaeology budgets is taken from an address given by Alfred Reed Jr., the first president of the Oklahoma State Archaeological Society, at the society's annual banquet in 1937, later published in the *Oklahoma Prehistorian* (Reed 1938). From the summer of 1936 to February 1937, the federal share of the archaeological work conducted in Oklahoma by 70 men was $18,000. From February 1937 through June 1938, $75,000 in federal funds were to have been supplemented with $11,000 from the Universities of Oklahoma and Tulsa and a $6,000 donation from the Phillips Oil Company, leading to a total of $92,000 to conduct excavations and employ approximately 100 men for 18 months. To break this down further, this means a budget of approximately $5,111.11 per month for the entire state.

Because of dwindling funds and the looming American entry into World War II, the McCurtain County archaeological crews were substantially smaller than they had been during much of the 1930s. Between May 29 and November 6, 1941, the field crew consisted of 22 men, who received three different levels of pay. Two crew chiefs, including Jess M. Jones, made 43¢ per hour, or $17.20 per 40-hour work week. Below the crew chiefs was a group of five more-experienced excavators, who made 33¢ per hour, or $13.20 per 40-hour work week. The remaining 15 workers made 27¢ per hour, or $10.80 per 40-hour work week. In December 1941, the workers received a raise, but the crew size was dropped to 16 men. It is unclear whether this was due to purposeful layoffs or general employee attrition. The hourly rate for both crew chiefs went up to 46¢ per hour. The three remaining experienced excavators made 37¢ per hour at McDonald, and the remaining 11 field workers made 31¢ per hour. For comparison, the mean annual income for hourly wage earners in the United States in 1940 was $1,276 (Dugan 1942:347). Assuming a full year of 40-hour work weeks, this works out to approximately 61¢ per hour, which is nearly 50 percent more than the highest pay for WPA archaeological laborers. In McCurtain County, where the local timber industry had collapsed a decade earlier after forest resources were depleted, this seemingly meager pay was certainly better than nothing (Benson et al. 2004). The record of hours worked by the crew in the field journal shows that in the five and a half months, 14,204 man-hours were spent excavating at Clement. This works out to an outlay of $4,288.37 for labor over that period.

Baerreis's journals also give us an idea of some of the day-to-day working conditions, including how much (or little in this case) equipment the crew had to work with, the number of levels the crew could dig in a day, and some of the challenges accessing a site. At the outset of the McCurtain County project, in late May, Baerreis and Jones noted numerous days lost from both rain and flooding. The work stoppage dragged on for several days when the crew was unable to cross the flooded low-water bridge on the Glover River to access the Clement site. On the morning of June 2, frustrated with not being able to pay the crew for work, Jones sent two members of his crew out to find a boat and by noon was able to ferry nine workers across the river to start working on one of the mounds. The next day the entire crew was able to make it out to the site, thanks to the boat. The Clement journal also includes an inventory of the tools used by the field crew of 22. On October 26, Jones listed 12 trowels, 10 needles, 3 brushes, 1 100-foot tape, 1(!) 6-foot tape, 16 long-handled round-point shovels, and 9 little picks.

## The Clement Mound Site (34Mc8–10)

The first McCurtain County site Baerreis tackled was Clement, named after the mortgage company based in Norman that owned the property. In addition to the field journals, remaining records from the site include numerous feature forms describing associations, burials, and caches; roughly 30 elevation sheets; about a dozen photographs; maps of three structures; and a very rough mound profile sketch. During the testing stage, the site was divided into three sections, McCl-I, II, and III, later assigned the trinomial designations 34Mc8, 9, and 10. The bulk of the Clement excavations took place at 34Mc8, which included a "large domiciliary mound" and a midden area north of the mound with two superimposed structures. The excavations at the McCl-I portion of Clement are discussed in greater detail below.

At McCl-II (34Mc9), Jones placed a few test units and noted the presence of structures and burials before abandoning the site. In his September 1941 quarterly report, Baerreis described 34Mc9 as located on "a high 'island' on the North bank of Glover Creek. The 'island' is separated from the mainland by a dry channel containing numerous springs and becomes one in actuality in times of high water. Test pits revealed here abundant cultural remains, wattle and traces of a baked clay floor." Jones also noted it was in the woods on an "isle" in his brief paragraph documenting testing at the site on July 25, 1941. In the December 1941 report, Baerreis reported that excavation of the house at McCl-II was never completed because it straddled a property line and the landowner of the adjoining property denied permission to excavate. Because only one test pit was excavated, no grid was established at McCl-II. There are no notes from this portion of Clement in the files at the museum, and we are still unclear where this portion of the site is actually located. In the September report, it is listed south and east of 34Mc8, but Jones's July 25, 1941, journal entry places it southwest off the main grid at Clement, furthering our confusion about its location relative to the mounds at Clement.

Three houses and several burials were excavated in the McCl-III (34Mc10) portion of the site between November 17 and 29, 1941. Again, there is confusion as to where the site is located. Baerreis's notebook places the site at the eastern edge of the Clement property, while the September 1941 quarterly report and Jones's journal entry place it on the western edge. In this case, we have reason to believe Jones and the quarterly report are correct. During our 2008 field project, we tested the fields to the east and found no evidence of any occupation. We are still unclear where this site boundary was in 1941. Our contour map from the 2008 excavations shows these fields are about 13 feet lower in elevation than the 34Mc8 portion of Clement, which runs counter to Jones's August 7, 1941, description of the site, in which he stated: "Testing on CL3 in west side of [Clement] farm on ridge in the timber. Put four large test pits in small mound got fine pottery sherds but [the mound] seems to be natural. But found house on north east end off ridge at the road." If McCl-III was on a ridge, it certainly was not east of McCl-I.

As with McCl-II, it appears that no grid was ever created in this portion of the site. The Clement notebook includes a page and a half of descriptions of 7 of the 10 burial pits excavated, with descriptions of bone preservation and associated grave goods. The remainder of the McCl-III records consist of a map of House 1, a rectangular structure with a central hearth and two intrusive burials, along with data sheets from 10 burials, including two from House 1 and eight from House 2. In the corner of the House 1 map there is a small, single-line drawn map with the locations, orientation, and distance between the three houses, but it provides no information where they are in relation to McCl-I and McCl-III (Figure 6.2). The data sheets reference a map of House 2 that presumably has been lost. Baerreis's personal journal includes a profile sketch of the hearth from House 2 and notes that it measured 7.5 feet east–west by 7.2 feet north–south. No depth is listed. Presumably, the eight burials in the structure area postdate House 2, although this is not made clear in the notes. No information from House 3 is found in the files; however, in the September 1941 quarterly report, Baerreis described finding portions of a clay floor with this structure.

The bulk of the Clement excavations were conducted at McCl-I (34Mc8). The quarterly reports mentioned one large domiciliary mound in this portion of the site, where it is described as measuring 100 feet in diameter and 7 feet 10 inches in height with a roughly conical shape. Baerreis (1941a:2) also reported that "at the beginning of the excavations the symmetry was marred in the East central portion of the mound by a shallow pit approximately 30 feet in diameter marking the area excavated in the mound by Mr. George T. Wright, an amateur archaeologist from Paris, Texas." Baerreis ascertained that Wright found evidence of a house pattern in this area, prob-

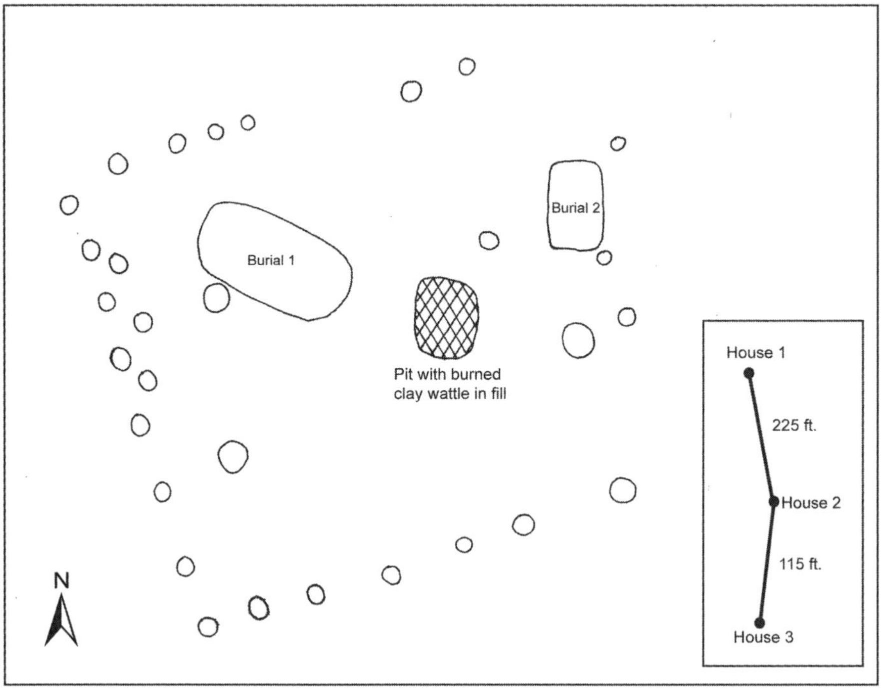


Figure 6.2. Plan view of House 1 at McCl-III (34Mc10) with sketch map depicting the location of all three houses in the lower right corner. Adapted from a sketch on file at the Sam Noble Oklahoma Museum of Natural History.

ably at a depth of 3 to 4 feet, before he stopped his excavations. It is not clear whether he actually spoke with Mr. Wright or simply observed the exposed features in the mound profile. In the field journal, Baerreis noted that the Clement I area was rented by a local farmer, Jasper Parker, who cooperated with the crew by leaving a strip of land between this mound and the road unplanted to accommodate the archaeology. In the December quarterly report, Baerreis (1941b:1) reported a second domiciliary mound located several hundred feet to the west, which was cut through by a road along its eastern margin.

Baerreis's mound descriptions in the quarterly reports left us somewhat perplexed when we initially visited the site in March 2008. In the main field, two slight rises separated by approximately 60 m and oriented along an axis of roughly 45 degrees are visible from the road. Initially, we presumed the larger of these was the excavated mound and the smaller mound, located to the southwest, was the second domiciliary mound. Upon rereading the quarterly report, we realized that this did not in any way match Baerreis's description, since the smaller mound lacked a road through the eastern margin and was entirely too close to the bigger mound. Everything became clearer when we spoke to the current landowner, who informed us that before he leveled it out, the southern mound was the larger of the two. It was once so large that, as another local told us, a mule and a cart could hide behind the mound and not be seen from the road. During our field season at the Clement site in June 2008, another local resident came by to visit us and directed us to a mound on an adjacent property with a road through the eastern edge. This clarified one issue but left the lingering question of why Baerreis never mentioned the second mound in the main McCl-I field in his quarterly reports. The second mound is mentioned in the 1951 article "A Survey of Oklahoma Archaeology" that summarized the materials from both McCurtain County sites into a McCurtain focus (Bell and Baerreis 1951:53).

The bulk of the Clement field journal consists of a list of units worked each day at McCl-I and accounts of what was recovered. Since Baerreis was not always present in the field, most of the daily logs and archaeological data sheets were actually recorded by crew chief Jess M. Jones, which we realized when we compared the handwriting in his survey and testing journal with that in the official Clement journal. The field journal allows us to get an idea of how much soil was moved by the crew in an average day and a better idea of what they found than the archaeological data sheets, the bulk of which are devoted to burials. On June 24, 1941, according to the hour logs, the entire crew of 22 was present, and the crew excavated 27 12-inch levels in 16 different units on the mound. Notable discoveries in these units, aside from "pottery sherds"—which seems to be the default entry when nothing else of interest was recovered—included fragments of a deer jaw and turtle shell, a burned dirt dauber's nest, "crystal quartz," "a crude ground celt," "brown rotten slate," points, and a "paint stone." While on the surface this information may seem to be of little use, because we have the artifacts labeled by provenience, the field notebooks are crucial for understanding the mound construction sequence, since no detailed profiles were ever completed.

For example, on June 24, 1941, an interesting soil zone was encountered across units 21:9 through 21:12, described variously as consisting of "fragment of charred corn cob[s] in black mixture," "crystal quartz from black mixture—ap[p]rox[imate] d[epth] 30 [inches]," "fragment of mussel shell from dark mixture," and "animal bone fragments from heavy charcoal mixture." Only a small portion of this area, the concentration of burned corn cobs, was assigned a feature number (A14-2). If we had only the archaeological data sheets, we would understand this as an isolated smudge pit. When combined with the information in the notebook, this feature becomes less of an isolated phenomenon. A few days later, on July 2, the crew was excavating in units 22:8 through 22:13, where artifacts at depths of between 39 and 50 inches were noted in a zone of charred material mixed with ash. This zone of charred material and dark soil continues into units 23:8 through 23:13, where the crew encountered this mix in and above postholes, but it is not noted in row 20, which was excavated June 13–14. After July 9, the crew moved approximately 100 feet (20 rows) away and worked in the area where the overlapping structures were exposed.

The next mention of this zone in the mound occurs on August 21 and is recorded in Baerreis's handwriting, suggesting that Baerreis heard about this discovery from Jones and, wanting to work on it himself, instructed Jones to move elsewhere on the site until Baerreis could return. Unit 25:12, recorded in Baerreis's handwriting, included an ash mixture, and more burned corn cobs were located in unit 25:9. In an entry for unit 25:23 Baerreis intriguingly wrote "Broken points" and "foyer" at a depth of 30 inches. From all of this information, we can infer a charred zone in the mound between 30 and 50 inches below surface measuring approximately 30 feet by 20 feet and underlain by post molds. The use of the term *foyer,* which Baerreis placed in quotation marks in the notes, most likely implies an entrance trench. In the second quarterly report, Baerreis (1941a:3) reported the bulk of the mound likely was capping a structure he was unable to define, although they had located posts and portions of a clay floor. Until we reviewed the journals and found the above information, it was unclear where in the mound and at what depth the structure was located, since it is not mentioned on any of the archaeological data sheets.

The technique of cutting vertical slices into the mound allowed Baerreis (1941a:2) to surmise it was built in three stages. The lowest level consisted of dark midden soils approximately 5 to 7 inches thick. The midden deposit extended well beyond the edges of what would eventually become the mound, implying the mound was built over an earlier occupation zone. The earliest mound construction stage consisted of a thin layer of dark ashy soil over a patchy baked clay floor. The partial structure that Baerreis was unable to define was located atop this thin layer. Baerreis (1941a:3) reported they did locate the hearth from this structure. It measured 30 inches across with ash and charcoal fill to a depth of 20 inches, although it is not described or sketched in the field notebooks. The final mantle of the mound was constructed over and around the burned structure. It consisted of a homogeneous clay cap showing no signs of loading, leading Baerreis (1941a) to conclude it was constructed in a single, brief episode.

Sometime after the mound was complete, a shaft tomb was dug from the summit of the mound, at least 7 feet 10 inches above the original ground surface, through all strata to sterile subsoil. The shaft tomb measured 130 inches north–south by 69 inches east–west and contained 10 burials, 20 whole vessels, an engraved shell gorget and several shell discs, 3 pipes, a celt, small projectile points, stone earspools, pearl and seed beads, and green pigment (Baerreis 1941a). The shaft tomb also had a cedar post located in each corner. Another later intrusive burial was recorded near the southern edge of the mound, one of only five burials with any preservation of bone excavated at the site. Two of the well-preserved burials were post-removal Choctaw individuals. Seventeen additional clusters of whole vessels were excavated in the non-mound midden. Baerreis correctly believed these were burials with no bone preservation. Other features recorded in the McCl-I midden included several shallow, basin-shaped pits. One of these was a large feature associated with the historic Choctaw occupation and filled with charred animal bone and nineteenth-century European ceramics.

In the midden area north of the mound, the excavation crew encountered two overlapping rectangular structures. The larger of these, and likely the earlier, was a roughly square single set-post structure with four central support posts and a southwest-facing entrance trench. The house measured 25.5 feet on a side with a 6-foot entrance trench. A prepared clay step was constructed at the entrance trench to the house, which is common in structures in the Arkansas Valley (Kay and Sabo 2006), but this is the only known example in southeast Oklahoma. The charred northwestern central support post, measuring .9 feet in diameter, was preserved in the four-post structure. Baerreis (1941b) noted the presence of a prepared clay floor in this house but no evidence of any hearth. The later, overlapping house was rectangular, measuring 18.7 × 17.1 feet, with two central support posts and a 15-foot-long southwest-facing entrance trench. After excavating the two houses, Baerreis elected to leave the site, both because it became difficult to secure permission for further work and because, he argued, "it is felt that we have more than a good sample of the artifact types at this site and since sites are very abundant in this region, it would be more profitable to sample the artifact types and features of other sites in the region" (Baerreis 1941b:1).

## The McDonald Site (34Mc11/12)

On December 10, 1941, the crew moved approximately 11 miles upstream to the McDonald site. Survey of one area of the site, which was on land owned by George McDonald, was done by Jones on July 21, and another area was tested on September 26. During the July testing, Jones described the area as "sandy land, looks fine," "maybe prehistoric dwelling place," and "lots of spoils, this is a high sandy field." Jones provided a sketch map showing the river on the west side of the site, a lake to the north, and a ford of the Glover River. The lake is likely a cutoff channel remnant that appears on the U.S. Geological Survey quad map north of the site location as it is currently plotted. Jones reported finding "worked stone, pottery, and points" during the July testing. Presumably these were on the surface, since he noted that McDonald had corn and cotton crops growing at that time. In September, Jones took a crew of three and excavated three test pits at a different location on the McDonald property, which he described as "in woods," but he did not reference the location with respect to the first McDonald site in his notes. He described the test pits as follows: "1. Seems to be house floor. 2. Is 36" deep with mixture in bottom. 3. Is 32" deep with crushed pots in it." Beyond giving a single location of "near the peach tree," he did not specify where these pits were located on the site. He concluded his assessment of the site by noting, "black sand and found sherds in nearly all the pits we have dug." This information was enough for Baerreis to select the McDonald site for further investigation over 12 other McCurtain County sites tested by Jones between July and September. The field notebook from McDonald shows us the crew spent a total of 6,443 man-hours excavating at McDonald, which works out to a total labor outlay of $2,190.69.

Until the spring of 2010, the only pieces of documentation known to exist for the site were Baerreis's and Jones's notebooks, the burial association sheets, maps showing the placement of the McMd-I units and the McMd-II structure, and the brief description of the site in the Bell and Baerreis (1951) synthesis. Based on this information, the site was interpreted as a small hamlet, probably outlying the Clement mound center. The nagging question, however, was where the 32 people buried in the McDonald midden areas actually lived. Surely they could not have occupied just one small structure, given the relatively short use life of structures in the humid environment of southeast Oklahoma. There was some speculation they may have lived downstream at the Clement mounds (Dowd 2008) or, alternatively, that McDonald served as a central cemetery for the residents of other nearby hamlets. This issue was resolved when we recently found an original copy of the final WPA report from southeast Oklahoma, dated March 31, 1942, in a box of carbons from Baerreis's files. This report was not on file at the SNOMNH nor was it included in the WPA archives in the Western History Collections. In the report, Baerreis clearly regrets having to abandon future work at the site, noting that "a sparse mantle of refuse appears to cover the edge of the same terrace upon which unit I was located for at least a mile up the river." Baerreis noted that the crew found portions of additional square houses while excavating test pits in the McMd-II portion of the site. Based on the new evidence, McDonald clearly was much more than a small midden, cemetery, and single household.

Faced with an enormous scatter of artifacts at McDonald, Baerreis considered the results of Jones's testing and decided to focus excavations on two portions of the site. The first, McMd-I (later 34Mc11), consisted of a midden and an intrusive cemetery. In the report Baerreis (1942:1) described this area as never having been cultivated and covered in a heavy growth of brush and timber, suggesting that it may be the area Jones tested in September 1941. However, in addition to the 32 Caddo burials with 80 whole vessels, as well as a single historic burial, Baerreis reported the McMd-I midden area yielded "no trace of house floors, but a sparse quantity of sherds, stone artifacts, and bone refuse with a few areas of ash . . . scattered through a deposit two to three feet in thickness." It is possible that Jones misidentified the possible house floor in his test pit 1, or McMd-I may be an altogether different portion of the McDonald property.

The McMd-II (later 34Mc12) portion of the site was located 250 feet from McMd-I on the same terrace. At one point in his report, Baerreis (1942:4) referred to this area as being in a field, suggesting that it may be the area Jones first visited in July 1941. Here the crew excavated a round house, a cache pit, two confirmed burials, and two possible burials from a sparse midden. In the report, Baerreis (1942:5) noted that the two confirmed burials were quite deep, extending 45 to 48 inches below the surface, while the two possible burials were very shallow, 9 to 12 inches below the surface. The round structure measured 18 feet in diameter with a north-facing entrance trench (Figure 6.3). The entrance trench measured 11 feet in length and was described as slightly V-shaped in cross section (Baerreis 1942:6). In the report, Baerreis (1942:7) noted this was the first round house ever excavated in McCurtain County and suggested it might be similar to structures of the Belcher focus identified by Clarence Webb for northwestern Louisiana. The center of the structure had a large concentration of ash, along with two metates. A round fired clay object with corn cob impressions was recovered from the center of the hearth. Fragments of four vessels and four bifaces were found on the house floor. Baerreis's personal notebook includes a sketch of the hearth area, depicting the hearth and the locations of some of the surrounding artifacts. The sketch also shows a large flat rock slab adjacent to the hearth, which we have observed in other Caddo structures in southeast Oklahoma (Dowd 2011). The presence of these artifacts on the house floor suggests the house burned

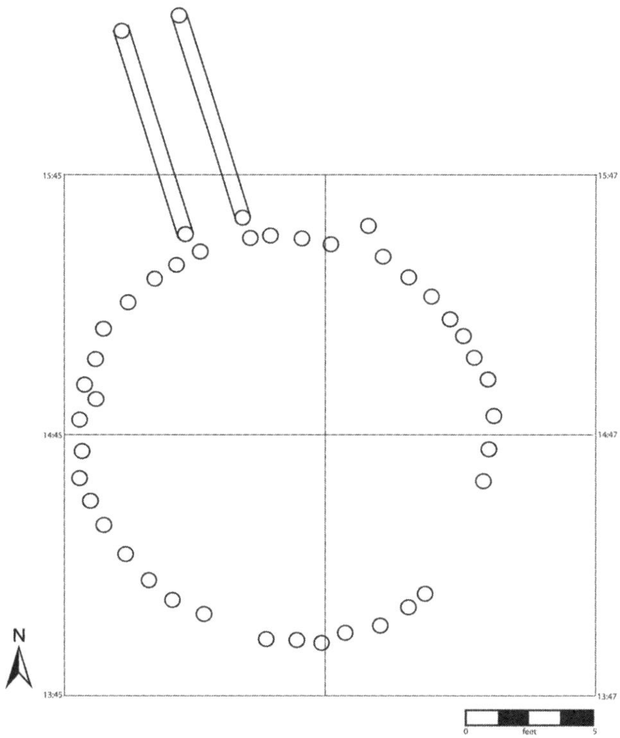


Figure 6.3. Plan view of the round structure excavated at McMd-II (34Mc12). Adapted from a sketch on file at the Sam Noble Oklahoma Museum of Natural History.

accidentally. In contrast, the intentionally burned structure we excavated in 2008 at Clement was so thoroughly cleaned that even the hearth and interior features were scooped out prior to burning (Hammerstedt et al. 2010).

Baerreis's personal notebook also includes a description of the McMd-II cache pit, which measured 85 inches at the top and tapered to a flat bottom measuring 49 inches across located 6 feet below the ground surface. At the base of this pit, a whole vessel and three large quartz chunks were recovered, along with a leaf-shaped biface in the pit fill. A profile of this pit and a plan view of the base are sketched in Baerreis's personal journal, where he simply noted it as a possible burial and did not provide any dimensions. Without the dimensions from the report, we assumed he was depicting another burial; however, the size and shape of the cache pit are different from those of a typical Caddo burial.

## Lasting Contributions of the Oklahoma WPA

In 1941, the excavation of these two sites in a remote corner of southeast Oklahoma filled an immense gap in knowledge of the prehistory of Oklahoma. Just a few years earlier, WPA archaeologists took over the ravaged mounds at Spiro and recognized the spectacular archaeological remains were more similar to prehistoric Caddo sites in northeast Texas, southwest Arkansas, and northwest Louisiana than to anything to the west and north, but separated from these sites by the Ouachita Mountains. At Clement and McDonald, Baerreis found a "culture [that] will provide another link between the Spiro Aspect and sites in northeast Texas and western Arkansas" (Baerreis 1941a:5). The McCurtain excavations were the first professionally excavated Caddo sites along the rivers that flow south out of the Ouachita Mountains, and Clement is one of the largest and most politically significant mound sites in this portion of the Little River drainage system. With the analysis of this material and the subsequent collaboration with Dr. Bell to create the McCurtain focus, the WPA excavations in southeast Oklahoma laid the groundwork for decades of subsequent archaeological research.

The excavations at the Clement and McDonald sites were conducted in the waning days of federally funded WPA archaeology. By 1941, the quality of recording had declined substantially, meaning that mound profiles, site maps, and sketches of archaeological features from later excavations are rare. This corresponded with a growing sense of urgency to get as much excavation finished as possible before the flow of federal funds for large labor crews dried up. The research also illustrates the pinnacle of a test-first strategy developed over the years of experience with large WPA crews. One consequence of this strategy is that the Clement and McDonald localities were exposed with several discontinuous blocks of excavation. This is a fairly modern approach to site testing and excavation that stands in contrast to large blocks of excavation found at many other WPA sites. Unfortunately, a lack of attention to the production of a master map has created a problem out of this otherwise laudable approach.

Although the notes from both sites are incomplete and the quality of recording is not up to modern archaeological standards, the collections and notes from the Clement and McDonald sites still hold enormous research potential. For better or for worse, excavations exposing as much area of sites as at those conducted by the Oklahoma WPA archaeologists are rarely undertaken by modern archaeologists, so the field notes and artifacts from larger exposures opened during the WPA excavations remain essential to our understanding of broad patterns of site structure and mound construction. Unlike many of the WPA sites in eastern Oklahoma and the rest of the Southeast, Clement and McDonald were not in areas scheduled to be flooded by impoundments for dams. The Glover River remains Oklahoma's largest undammed river, making it possible to address some of the lingering questions about both sites. While Baerreis was able to complete some preliminary analysis of the pottery from both sites (see Bell and Baerreis 1951), the bulk of the material remains unanalyzed. New research projects drawing on the WPA excavations and artifact collections, including fieldwork and reanalysis of the collections from Clement (Hammerstedt et al. 2010) and analysis of the collections from the McDonald site (Dowd 2008, 2009; Regnier and Dowd 2010), have been undertaken in just the past few years. Over 70 years after the WPA excavations ended, they are still guiding and informing the study of Oklahoma's past.

## Acknowledgments

None of the renewed research at Clement and McDonald would have been possible without an agreement with the Caddo Nation of Oklahoma, via Bobby Gonzalez and Robert Cast. In addition, we would like to thank Elizabeth Leith and Don Wyckoff of the Sam Noble Oklahoma Museum of Natural History for allowing us access to the artifact collections and WPA notes.

# PART III

# Southeastern States

# 7

# Trouble in the Glen

## The Battle over Kentucky Lake Archaeology

*David H. Dye*

New Deal archaeological investigations have long been recognized for their valuable contribution to scientific archaeology (Davis 1997; Dye 1991; Fagette 1996; Guthe 1952; Haag 1985; Lyon 1996; Sullivan 1999). Lesser known or appreciated are the battles waged and compromises hammered out among archaeologists, field supervisors, landowners, and politicians, as well as federal, state, and local administrators. New Deal archaeology was conducted in an atmosphere of rapidly emerging laws and procedures that generated varying degrees of cooperation and conflict among the individuals and agencies involved. Laws were passed, proposals were written, and fieldwork was approved, often within a matter of weeks, leaving little time for research proposal preparation. Strained nerves and intense competition often characterized these difficult times as everyone involved scrambled to make the evolving, imperfect system work.

Inevitably, personalities clashed among the various New Deal stakeholders and participants. While it is not always pleasant to relive personal conflicts of key personalities in archaeology, the study of prehistory in particular, and science in general, is sometimes plagued by such battles and they are often overlooked as an important and intangible process of scientific investigation. This chapter is presented not as criticism of individuals or an exposé of personal weakness, but rather to provide a glimpse into the human component, if not foibles, that helped form and shape the foundation of present-day archaeology. It also gives insight into the frustrations that dedicated and hardworking archaeologists faced during the New Deal era. Such intellectual and personal battles were not unique to either the individuals portrayed here or the times in which they labored, but understanding the nature of these conditions, both personal and administrative, helps us better appreciate the accomplishments that they made in the face of sometimes unimaginable obstacles.

Two prominent North American archaeologists, Thomas M. N. Lewis and William S. Webb, found themselves as primary protagonists in an unfolding drama over Tennessee Valley archaeology in the late 1930s. The feud had its beginnings as early as April 1937 concerning publication rights of recently excavated, unpublished data. Their story is one of profound frustrations, misunderstandings, personality conflicts, and often petty rivalries that grew out of the tumultuous times. Lewis's and Webb's personal conflicts entangled professional archaeologists and government officials. The role of personality was significant in these early days of professional archaeology, and this incident in the Tennessee Valley underscores the importance of individual agents and participants in scientific research.

The two archaeologists differed from one another in background, education, personality, and temperament. In two respects they were well matched: both possessed convictions in their sense of proprietary jurisdiction, if not outright ownership of the archaeological resources in their respective states, and they envisioned their research plan as the most appropriate and professional way to conduct the archaeological investigations. Lewis had acquired both field experience and laboratory skills working under the guidance of his mentor, W. C. McKern of the Milwaukee Public Museum, and he had taken anthropology and archaeology graduate courses at the University of Wisconsin. Webb, on the other hand, had no undergraduate or graduate experience in either anthropology or archaeology, but he had accrued considerable fieldwork and a solid publication record. With prior military backgrounds in World War I, Lewis, as a naval officer, and Webb, as an army officer, over time formed implacable lines of engagement and charged headlong into the fray.

Congressional plans for construction of Kentucky Dam in May 1938 and the archaeological work that would ensue from the anticipated research opportunities considerably aggravated the disagreement. The "dark and bloody ground" of Kentucky and Tennessee became an arena for the struggle over who would oversee the mammoth archaeology project to be undertaken in the Kentucky Basin. Such battles were not unique to either Lewis or Webb, or to Tennessee Valley archaeology, but the potential benefits of the Kentucky Basin research were significant: unprecedented research opportunities in an almost unknown archaeological area of eastern North America. In addition, both Lewis and Webb believed he alone was capable of conducting a modern, scientific approach to the archaeological investigations in question. While Lewis envisioned the application of current anthropological theory as the driving force behind detailed report preparation on specific archaeological sites, Webb was primarily interested in summary reports (Lyon 1996:146). As Sullivan (1999:72) notes, the argument between Lewis and

Webb "was mainly over whether the reports should be comprehensive and analytical as Tom and Madeline [Kneberg] wished, or abbreviated and descriptive as Webb requested."

The quarrels between Lewis and Webb were played out between April 1937 and September 1939 and involved federal, state, and Tennessee Valley Authority (TVA) officials and the most influential, powerful, and respected archaeologists of the time, including Fay-Cooper Cole of the University of Chicago, Carl E. Guthe of the National Research Council (NRC), and W. C. McKern of the Milwaukee Public Museum. The results of the struggle would determine the quality of the TVA excavations and the subsequent publications. The conflict would have a major impact on future research in the region, access to data for generations of researchers, and interpretations of eastern North American archaeology.

The Kentucky Basin's location was at the root of the problem between Lewis and Webb. The impounded Tennessee River would create a massive reservoir that extended from Kentucky upstream into west-central Tennessee, the two states in which the two men reigned in archaeological matters. Although the dam was to be built in western Kentucky, the main reservoir would cut through Tennessee, inundating the Tennessee River floodplain almost to Pickwick Dam at the Alabama, Mississippi, and Tennessee borders. Lewis, as head of the anthropology program at the University of Tennessee, envisioned the major Tennessee portion of the Kentucky Lake operation as being within his jurisdiction. Webb, as consultant to the TVA and having been recently in charge of the investigations in the Norris (Webb 1938a), Wheeler (Webb 1939), and Chickamauga (Lewis et al. 1995) basins, viewed the entire Tennessee Valley as his turf: sharing the valley, over which he was the sole consultant, was out of the question. Webb and Lewis marshaled their forces for an all-out frontal assault (Lyon 1996:145). Their struggle was a conflict that drew colleagues, friends, and government officials into the fray. Fay-Cooper Cole went so far as to visit Lewis in the spring of 1939 in an unsuccessful attempt to defuse the acrimony brewing between Lewis and Webb (Cole 1939; Lyon 1996:159).

## The Construction of Kentucky Dam

The Lewis and Webb feud over archaeological state's rights had its origins in Washington's concerns about economic development, flood control, and river navigation. Congress had expressed interest in various initiatives throughout the nineteenth century that might improve economic transportation on the Tennessee River, especially the lower river portion between Muscle Shoals in northwestern Alabama and the Ohio–Tennessee confluence in western Kentucky. Increased electricity generation and improved navigation would help alleviate the dire economic circumstances rampant throughout Appalachia (TVA 2010).

In the early 1900s the U.S. Army Corps of Engineers took steps to survey the Lower Tennessee River in anticipation of the proposed Gilbertsville Dam at Aurora Landing in Kentucky, but in the end the project was shelved. With the Mississippi River flood of 1927, however, Congress passed the Flood Control Act of 1928 (Barry 1997). Attention turned not only to the Mississippi River but also to its major tributaries, such as the Arkansas, Missouri, Ohio, and Tennessee rivers, for possible flood control and navigation. Thus, the Tennessee River became a primary focus of federal and state attention. Unfortunately, interest once again waned with the deepening economic depression of the 1930s and subsequent government cutbacks in federal programs (TVA 1951).

The Ohio River flood of 1937 and its aftermath impelled Congress to reconsider impounding the Lower Tennessee River. Recent research demonstrated that some 4 percent of the water in the Lower Mississippi River originated in the Tennessee Valley watershed. Thus, flood control and navigation of the Tennessee River rose once more as a congressional issue, but this time it assumed national priority, not only because of flooding but also in light of the fast-approaching, massive needs for increased energy and transportation. The United States was headed for inevitable involvement in the war brewing in Europe, and power and efficient movement of goods would be the key to the country's wartime footing (TVA 1951).

After selecting and approving the dam site location in 1937, Congress authorized funding for the Kentucky Dam project on May 23, 1938. The dam would be the seventh main-river impoundment and the largest of the 23 multipurpose Tennessee River reservoir projects operated by the TVA for economic development, flood control, hydroelectric power generation, improved navigation, and numerous forms of recreation. At more than 200 feet in height and almost 8,500 feet long, Kentucky Dam would reduce flood damage on some six million acres of the Lower Ohio and Mississippi rivers and limit the frequency of flooding on another four million acres. Kentucky Dam would have a flood storage capacity of over four million acre-feet, more than two and a half times the capacity of the next largest TVA reservoir, Guntersville Basin in northeastern Alabama (TVA 1951, 1964, 1983, 2010).

Acquisition of some 320,000 acres of land and easement rights began soon after Congress authorized the project. Not only was the earthen dam construction massive in scope, but the ancillary projects also required a Herculean effort and massive funding. Altogether the TVA "cleared more than 48,000 acres, moved 1,609 families, built more than 60 new bridges, and moved 3,390 graves and 578 monuments in 397 cemeteries" (Lyon 1996:158). The budget for the archaeology component was minuscule in comparison to that of the overall construction program. Nevertheless, the funding earmarked for archaeology constituted a major research effort in eastern North America and one that would prove to be of enduring significance for decades to come.

Originally named Gilbertsville Dam after the nearby town, the dam's name was later changed to Kentucky Dam. This hydroelectric dam was the most expensive TVA dam project to date, amounting to nearly $118 million, and was the longest and largest of the TVA reservoirs, covering some 160,300 acres of water surface and impounding the Lower Tennessee River for some 184 river miles (TVA 1964, 2010). Construction on the Kentucky lock and dam began July 1, 1938. The project was scheduled for completion in the summer of 1945, but, due to impending war and the anticipated navigation and power needs for national defense, the opening was shortened by a year, with completion taking place on August 30, 1944 (TVA 1964:34). The change in plans would ratchet up the already elevated state of tension between Lewis and Webb, who were struggling to write proposals, complete overdue reports, and manage field crews.

## New Deal Archaeology and the Kentucky Basin

The archaeological resources within the proposed Kentucky Basin were largely unknown in the late 1930s. In the upper end of the proposed reservoir, J. Parish Stelle (1871a, 1871b) had mapped and excavated a series of mounds in 1870 for the Smithsonian Institution (Welch 1998). Clarence B. Moore conducted two seasons of excavations throughout the Tennessee Valley between January 1914 and April 1915 (Moore 1915). With funding through the Civil Works Administration (CWA), Frank H. H. Roberts and Moreau B. Chambers investigated the Shiloh National Military Park mounds, also in the upper portion of the basin, from late December 1933 to the end of March 1934 (Table 7.1). This early New Deal archaeology project was under the aegis of the Smithsonian Institution (Roberts 1935; Welch 2006).

From November 1935 to May 1936, Lewis, along with Charles H. Nash and Georg K. Neumann, carried out major excavations in the Buffalo and Duck river confluence area with Works Progress Administration (WPA) funding (Table 7.1), first at the Slayden site (Inman 2007; Lunn, this volume) and

Table 7.1. Archaeological sites investigated for the TVA using New Deal funding

| Site | Location | Dates of Excavation |
|---|---|---|
| Eva | Benton County, Tennessee | September to November 1940 |
| Gray Farm | Stewart County, Tennessee | April to September 1939 |
| Hiwassee Island | Meigs County, Tennessee | April 1937 to March 1939 |
| Hixon | Hamilton County, Tennessee | June to October 1936 |
| Jonathan Creek | Marshall County, Kentucky | March to April 1939 |
| Link Farm | Humphreys County, Tennessee | March to May 1936 |
| Mound Bottom–Pack | Cheatham County, Tennessee | July 1936 to February 1937 |
| Peachtree Mound | Cherokee County, North Carolina | December 1933 to April 1934 |
| Shiloh Mounds | Hardin County, Tennessee | December 1933 to March 1934 |
| Slayden | Humphreys County, Tennessee | November 1935 to February 1936 |
| Williams | Henry County, Tennessee | April to July 1939 |

then at the Link Farm site (Dye 2002, 2003). The seven months of fieldwork on the Lower Buffalo and Duck rivers provided Lewis with an early sense of proprietary rights to Tennessee archaeology within the Kentucky Basin.

With the exceptions of Moore's work, which was the most comprehensive survey and excavation program in the Kentucky Basin to date, and of Roberts and Chambers's investigations, which were the most intensive excavation of a single site, Lewis and Webb had little information on which to base their research strategies in the Kentucky Basin. Moore's excavations, though well reported, did not meet the improved archaeological standards of the late

1930s. Roberts and Chambers's work was incompletely reported, even for the time. Thus, it would have been virtually impossible to anticipate the nature of the sites to be found in the basin, especially the large number of Woodland and Archaic sites. While both Lewis and Webb had considerable experience in the region, the specifics of the archaeological record would elude them in the planning and proposal preparation stages. Jennings (1994:89) notes, "so little was known about Tennessee's prehistoric resources that probably no one, let alone Lewis, could have architected a research plan at the time."

## Biographical Sketches of the Key Combatants

Thomas McDowell Nelson Lewis was born in Chambersburg, Pennsylvania, on March 27, 1896, but grew up in Watertown, Wisconsin, where his grandfather had earlier established the G. B. Lewis Company. Lewis is described as "a trim, handsome man with polish gained from education at Princeton and service in the Navy" (Sullivan 1999:66). Lewis attended Northwestern College, now Martin Luther College, in Watertown for five years and then enrolled in the Lawrenceville School, a prestigious prep school near Princeton University, for one year. Attendance at the Lawrenceville School paved his way for admission to Princeton. After two years at Princeton he took an 18-month leave of absence to serve in the Great World War, participating in the Naval Reserve Force from the end of May 1917 to mid-December 1918 (National Archives and Records Administration 1918).

During the war he served as a boatswain's mate first class and was for six months in charge of a gunnery crew aboard the 110-foot, wooden-hull submarine chaser, the SC-52. He was one of two officers on board the subchaser as it patrolled the North American Atlantic Coast in search of German submarines. Lewis was awarded the Victory Medal for his military service (National Archives and Records Administration 1918). Writing in January 1934 to Walter B. Jones, director of the Alabama Museum of Natural History, about the anticipated demands of running field crews in the Norris Basin, Lewis (1934) noted: "I had charge of a deck force for a year and a half during the World War and as a result of handling that tough bunch of hoodlums I don't believe that I would encounter many difficulties with a bunch of college boys and unemployed."

After returning to Princeton and completing his bachelor's degree in 1919, he took anthropology graduate courses at the University of Wisconsin in 1920 but was forced to drop out and work in the family business because of his father's declining health (Herskovits 1950:110; Sullivan 1999). Lewis soon worked his way up to sales manager and his coast-to-coast travels allowed him the opportunity to visit a variety of archaeological sites. He also had a close working relationship with W. C. McKern, head of the Anthropology Department at the Milwaukee Public Museum. In correspondence with McKern, Lewis (1933) confided his hopes of someday becoming a professional archaeologist: "If I am able to transform this avocation into a vocation it will be providential more than anything else."

There are few descriptions of Lewis's personality, but Jesse D. Jennings (1994:89) offers us his opinion that Lewis "had no professional credentials, either academic or in experience, that qualified him to be employed by the state of Tennessee in such an operation." Fagette (1996:107) also portrays Lewis in a negative light: "Lewis proved himself basically incapable of organizing and managing a large-scale archaeological project. Problems quickly emerged that revolved around failures to process material and Lewis's sometimes vitriolic personality." Sullivan (1999:70), however, notes that "Tom set up a lab in Knoxville to catalog materials brought from the field. He was hoping to spend a large sum of TVA funds on this lab, but Webb (still serving as the TVA consultant) did not approve the expenditure." Despite these problems Lewis's hard work and determination, along with that of his colleague, Madeline D. Kneberg, helped create a program at the University of Tennessee that profoundly affected the course of Tennessee archaeology during his tenure from 1934 to 1961. Kneberg had completed all but her dissertation prior to moving to Knoxville in June 1938 (Sullivan 1999). Trained as a physical anthropologist under the guidance of Fay-Cooper Cole at the University of Chicago, she never intended to become an archaeologist. However, her interpretive approach drew a great deal of praise. Lewis and Kneberg's work, despite the problems of the times, "was the innovative edge of archaeological research at its time" (Sullivan 1999:87).

William Snyder Webb was born on January 19, 1882, in Greendale, Kentucky, only a few miles outside of Lexington. Webb expressed his pride in being a Kentuckian in his characteristic homespun style: "My grandfather was a Presbyterian minister; he was a Democrat and he owned a still right here in the county" (Thierman 1955). Graduating with a bachelor's degree in physics from Kentucky State College, now the University of Kentucky, in 1901, he received a master's degree, also in physics, the following year. He pursued post-master's work in physics at Cornell University and later at the University of Chicago, but never completed the doctoral degree (Haag 1965).

From 1904 to 1907 he was legal secretary to the commanding officer for the Indian Territory Land Office. Charged with overall responsibility for law enforcement in the Seminole Nation, he eventually rose to the position of deputy United States marshal, riding with the Seminole light horse troops, issuing warrants, and camping with them. During these outings he regularly heard stories around the campfire told by the 85-year-old Seminole troop captain about life in the Everglades. Webb soon developed a passion for American Indian studies that stayed with him for the rest of his life (Schwartz 1967). In 1907 he returned to Lexington and began teaching in the Physics Department. He was appointed department head in 1915.

Webb took a leave of absence from the university to join the army, becoming a first lieutenant in the 1st Field Artillery of the 84th Infantry Division at Fort Benjamin Harrison, Indiana. He was trained as an artillery officer because of his background in mathematics and physics. Later promoted to captain, he served with the 325th Field Artillery at Camp Zachary Taylor, Kentucky. By the end of the war he held the rank of major, an epithet he carried throughout his life. He was also assistant director of the School for Fire of the Field Artillery at Fort Sill, Oklahoma (Schwartz 1967:43).

In 1936 Webb related a story about his service years to Jennings when the two had a chance meeting during the Hixon site excavations in the Chickamauga Basin. According to Jennings, the governor of Kentucky had offered full and unconditional pardons to prisoners who would volunteer for active military service. Webb was to train some 400 convicts for overseas war duty. Once his regular army sergeants got the "tough-looking and unruly lot" under control, Webb then took over and began to build an artillery troop that served with bravery and distinction in France (Jennings 1994:85–86). After the war Webb returned to his former position as head of the Physics Department and in 1926 he also became head of the Archaeology and Anthropology Department. In late 1933, after more than 10 years of archaeological field research in Kentucky, Webb was tapped by the NRC and the Smithsonian Institution to serve as consultant for the TVA archaeological program.

Schwartz (1967:44–47) perhaps best summarizes Webb's complex personality: "[he] was a many-faceted man whose nature and personality are difficult to describe. He was humble but stubborn (hence the nickname 'Bullneck'), kindly but aggressive, affectionate but aloof, a dilettante yet a scholar, droll but serious, a disciplinarian but with warmth, a gregarious and delightful raconteur who could also enjoy his own company long enough to write many highly detailed descriptive reports, an extremely effective and productive administrator knowing at the same time how to enjoy leisure, even though his hobbies were pursued with as much vigor as his job. Perhaps only those who knew him personally could appreciate these coexisting contrasts." Haag (1965:471) adds that Webb was a man of boundless energy and varied interests. He was a "vivid and vigorous man . . . not without certain faults. As is always the case with a strong personality, enemies were made, and the Major certainly had his share."

Lewis and Webb had equivalent status in the profession. They were both talented avocational archaeologists who had undertaken research through personal means, rather than public funding, prior to their work with the TVA (Fagette 1996:107). While Lewis lacked the dynamism and field capabilities of Webb (Fagette 1996:107), Webb did not have Lewis's interest in the new avenues emerging for a more scientific archaeology. Nor did he have an associate of Madeline Kneberg's caliber, whose creative and innovative aspirations provided new perspectives for reconstructing the past. This latter issue was perhaps primary in Lewis's success. Kneberg was a self-reliant researcher who was a full partner with and major influence on Lewis's theoretical approach to archaeology (Sullivan 1999). Kneberg provided a creative edge, professional balance, and an informed sounding board for Lewis. Together Lewis and Kneberg worked to investigate past lifestyles based on continual input from W. C. McKern. Webb lacked someone who could alter or critique his descriptive methodology.

## New Deal Archaeology and the Tennessee Valley Authority

With the creation of the Tennessee Valley Authority on May 18, 1933, archaeological resources in the Tennessee Valley were immediately threatened with destruction and inundation, creating both opportunities and problems for archaeologists. A number of professional and avocational archaeologists pressured the TVA as early as August 1933 to begin an archaeological program that would salvage as much information as possible from the planned reservoirs. The NRC in the fall of 1933 created a subcommittee on Tennessee Valley archaeology within its Committee on State Archaeological Surveys, acting on advice from Arthur E. Morgan, chair of the TVA, and in cooperation with the National Research Council's Science Advisory Board and the Smithsonian Institution. The subcommittee was composed of Matthew W. Stirling of the Smithsonian Institution's Bureau of American Ethnology, who served as chair, and members Neil M. Judd, curator of archaeology at the Smithsonian's U.S. National Museum, and Burnham S. Colburn, president of the First National Bank and Trust Company of Asheville, North Carolina (Lyon 1996:39). The Committee on State Archaeological Surveys was chaired by Carl E. Guthe, University of Michigan.

In December 1933 representatives of The University of Alabama, TVA, and University of Tennessee met in Knoxville to discuss plans for future archaeological work and to select a full-time consultant to the TVA (Lyon 1996:39). Judd recommended McKern, but he refused because of his current workload (McKern 1933). Webb was next offered the job and he accepted. Webb acted as the TVA consulting archaeologist for the two reservoirs being planned for immediate construction: Norris Basin in the Clinch River Valley of eastern Tennessee and Wheeler Basin in the Tennessee River Valley of northern Alabama. Webb in turn picked Lewis, on the basis of McKern's strong recommendation, to oversee the Norris Basin work and David L. DeJarnette, presumably stemming from Walter B. Jones's endorsement, to serve as overall field supervisor for the Wheeler Basin. McKern at the time was head of the Anthropology Department at the Milwaukee Public Museum and Jones was director of the Alabama Museum of Natural History.

Concerns with Webb's appointment began to surface almost from the beginning. DeJarnette, writing in 1941, pointed out some of Webb's shortcomings: "He knew very little archaeology when he took over the TVA program in 1934 and had a very different attitude towards archaeology than he does today. We managed to do good field work then in spite of his influences to the contrary" (DeJarnette 1941). Webb envisioned salvage archaeology as a battle, with the site being the unwary enemy (Schwartz 1967:43).

In early January 1934, fieldwork had begun in the Norris Basin with a staff of 19 field supervisors and more than 1,000 laborers under the CWA (Guthe 1952:5). When the CWA was terminated on March 31, 1934, Webb arranged for Federal Emergency Relief Administration (FERA) funds until the Norris fieldwork program was closed on July 1, 1934 (Lyon 1996:66; Sullivan 1999:67–68; Webb 1939:2). Guthe and Judd aided Webb in selecting supervisors and in seeking advice in locating competent supervisors and formulating plans for the initiation of an archaeological survey (Webb 1939:5).

By the end of the Norris Basin project in the summer of 1934, Webb saw the need for an archaeology program in Tennessee that would allow him to continue future TVA work, especially in the anticipated Guntersville, Kentucky, and Watts Bar basins. He recommended to University of Tennessee President James D. Hoskins that the university establish an archaeological research program for the state of Tennessee under the direction of Lewis, who had been out of a job since the completion of the Norris Basin project. Webb undoubtedly envisioned an amicable working relationship with Lewis, operating within a chain of command similar to that he enjoyed with David L. DeJarnette and Walter B. Jones at the Alabama Museum of Natural History (Lyon 1996).

On September 1, 1934, following Webb's advice and Hoskins's recommendation, the University of Tennessee established the Division of Anthropology within the History Department and Lewis was named director (Sullivan 1999:68–69). In November 1935 Lewis hired Charles H. Nash and Georg K. Neumann to work with him on a WPA project that included a site survey of the Lower Duck and Buffalo rivers in Humphreys County, along with the excavation of the Link Farm and Slayden sites. In July 1936 they moved the operation to the Mound Bottom and Pack site complex on the Harpeth River in Cheatham County, working there for an additional seven months (Lyon 1996:140–141). Thus, from November 1935 to January 1937 Lewis had been proceeding on his own by sending field crews to sites in Cheatham, Davidson, Humphreys, and Perry counties in central Tennessee, in addition to his 1934 work in the Norris Basin and subsequent eastern Tennessee surveys in 1934 and 1935. In addition, in early 1936 he had been planning for the Chickamauga Basin excavations, hiring a number of students from the upper Midwest.

Webb was still in overall charge of operations as the TVA consulting archaeologist, but he may have begun to feel threatened by Lewis's growing independence. In April 1937 Lewis wrote to McKern that he greatly admired Webb, but he had gained the impression that Webb was becoming sensitive to any criticism (Lewis 1937a). Webb had earlier complained to Lewis that he believed Lewis was trying to undermine him and his connection with the TVA (Webb 1937). Lewis was perplexed by these allegations, lamenting to McKern that he did not understand why Webb was so miffed. Lewis confided that he realized Webb's likes and dislikes for people could be extreme and that he had been careful to avoid antagonizing him, but by late spring of 1937 he had become aware of a "diminishing friendliness" during Webb's visits to monitor the Chickamauga Basin fieldwork (Lewis 1937b).

The open rupture between Lewis and Webb took place over one of the most vexing problems in scholarship: joint authorship of scientific publications. Even though Lewis supervised all the fieldwork and report preparation in the Norris Basin (Webb 1938a), as DeJarnette had done in the Wheeler Basin (Webb 1939), Webb assumed sole authorship for both volumes, rather than editorship, which would have been more appropriate. There was a widespread and entrenched pattern of senior supervisors having sole or top billing on publication bylines. Jennings (1994:78), for example, in 1936, excavated the Peachtree site and wrote the resulting report, but his supervisor at the Smithsonian Institution, Frank M. Setzler, argued for and received senior authorship (Setzler and Jennings 1941).

In November 1937 Lewis had published a short, popular monograph, *Annotations Pertaining to Prehistoric Research in Tennessee,* in which he summarized his previous four years of archaeological investigations in central and eastern

Tennessee, outlining TVA's sponsorship of the extensive archaeological program in Tennessee in the Chickamauga and Norris basins. He had assembled a mass of information and proposed that a portion of it would be published by the TVA and the remainder issued by the University of Tennessee when funds became available (Lewis 1937c:28).

Webb resented Lewis's writing the pamphlet, which included photographs from the ongoing Chickamauga excavations. Webb believed, as consulting archaeologist to the TVA, that only he had the right to publish research stemming from the Chickamauga Basin project, as he had done earlier with the Norris and Wheeler basin work. He complained to Lewis that it was a blow to his prestige as the TVA consultant. Lewis's statements concerning the University of Tennessee's sponsorship of archaeological investigations, claims of ownership of collections, rights to publication, and the anticipated display and interpretation of the artifacts in a future University of Tennessee archaeological museum, vexed Webb.

By late December 1937, Webb's angst and frustration were escalating. Guthe wrote Lewis urging him to try to work with Webb: "For the sake of American archaeology and of your many mutual friends, sit down with Professor Webb and talk the matter out reasonably and eliminate the present confusion" (Guthe 1937). Lewis explained to Webb that the original agreement he and the TVA had made with the University of Tennessee mandated that he prepare and write the overall field report and that he planned to submit it to Webb for discussion and publication. He further informed Webb of his intentions to conduct a detailed study of the archaeological materials as soon as he was able to acquire a laboratory assistant. Upon completion of the field reports, laboratory analyses, classificatory groupings, and photographic work, Lewis would send the material to Webb as co-author for his input and to make arrangements with the TVA for publication. Lewis added, "When I made this agreement with you I was fully aware of the amount of time which each one of us would devote to the investigation of and the preparation of the report on the Chickamauga Basin would compare as 99 to 1, but I could see no objection to that, since I felt that such collaboration might result in a better report" (Lewis 1938).

To further compound the rivalry, late in 1938 the TVA, following Webb's request, asked for a proposal to conduct archaeological work in the Kentucky Basin. Webb hoped to control all work in the basin, so when he learned of Lewis's intent to send field parties there the following spring, he advanced his schedule for fear Lewis would disrupt his plans. In reaction to Webb, in March 1939 Lewis sent Nash to the Kentucky Basin to prepare for their proposed long-term investigation. Nash had George A. Lidberg begin work at the Williams site in April, while he initiated excavations at the Gray Farm site in May. To thwart Lewis's activity, Webb in turn sent James R. Foster to the basin to carry out an archaeological survey from March 22 to April 29, 1939, in the hope that he could forestall Lewis from obtaining a permanent toehold in the area (Lyon 1996).

In May 1939, Webb, feeling increasingly frustrated over Lewis's work in the basin, wrote Lawrence L. Durisch of the TVA Department of Regional Planning Studies stating that there should be no "cooperation between the University of Kentucky and the University of Tennessee" (Lyon 1996:158). In the meantime, Lewis met with Setzler and Stirling at the Smithsonian Institution in mid-June to plead his case. He explained the laboratory procedures in detail to Setzler and went over the problems he was experiencing with Webb (Lewis 1939a).

On June 27, 1939, Lewis was summoned before three TVA officials who tipped him off that Webb was attempting to establish a TVA-CCC camp with the mission to investigate the entire Kentucky Basin and that all work would be under his direction. Lewis, on the other hand, would be requested to select only two or three sites for investigation, in addition to the current work at the Gray Farm and Williams sites. Lewis was also told he would need to complete the work on the Kentucky Basin sites within a year's time and redirect his efforts to the Watts Bar Basin. Lewis (1939b) confided to McKern that the state WPA director was also a member of the University of Tennessee Board of Trustees and that he would support the University of Tennessee's interests. He was also concerned that problems would arise if two reports were compiled by staffs working independently of each other. Overall, he thought the outcome would be detrimental to American archaeology if Webb's plans were to prevail.

Lewis (1939b) also mentioned that University of Tennessee President Hoskins was a strong believer in state's rights when it came to archaeology and that Hoskins was considerably aroused over the frequent interferences by Webb. Hoskins agreed to take the matter before Harcourt A. Morgan, TVA board member and former president of the university. Lewis vented his frustrations to McKern, noting that with Webb's projects "in progress throughout Kentucky and a hand in the Alabama pot, we hardly think there is any need for the TVA consultant to disturb the Tennessee set-up in order to occupy his spare time" (Lewis 1939b). Frustrated by Webb's lack of capitulation or compromise, Lewis was becoming less conciliatory and requested an appointment as state archaeologist in order to direct Tennessee's share of Kentucky Basin archaeology and to be freed from Webb's "annoying interferences" (Lyon 1996:159).

In July 1939, Lewis and Madeline Kneberg learned from Arthur R. Kelly, archaeologist with the National Park Service (NPS), that Webb was discussing plans with Arno B. Cammerer, director of the NPS, for crafting a cooperative archaeological project among the University of Kentucky, the NPS, and the TVA (Lewis 1939c). In a later note to McKern, Lewis (1939c) outlined his argument. If Webb intended to block his work and the archaeological materials were turned over to the University of Tennessee without the accompanying records, as the TVA officials suggested, then Lewis would have "nothing but a lot of 'relics' to stow away in the hold, and there will be another incomplete report published." He had already mentioned to Kelly that Webb's preliminary reports on the Norris and Wheeler basins would preclude funding the publication of a final report. Lewis reasoned that a detailed and thorough analysis of the excavated materials would necessitate a complete revision of any preliminary report. He knew that the TVA would not fund an additional $8,000 or $10,000 for publication of a final report whose preface would have to recommend that the owners of the preliminary report "toss it into the waste basket and substitute the new one!" Lewis thought the NPS should cooperate with both the University of Tennessee for work conducted in Tennessee and with the University of Kentucky for work carried out in Kentucky. He reasoned that with 14 months' experience in the Kentucky Basin, he, rather than Webb, would be better able to produce a report closer to the one that Guthe and McKern expected (Lewis 1939c).

With renewed anxiety, Lewis (1939d) again pleaded his case to President Hoskins. Earl S. Draper, director of TVA Land Planning and Housing, had earlier stated that the TVA would authorize its cooperation only in the Watts Bar Basin, as land acquisition had not yet begun in the Tennessee portion of the Kentucky Basin. The TVA could not give Lewis any help until these land purchases had commenced. Lewis understood that if he could not secure TVA's cooperation at once in the Kentucky Basin, he would be forced to discontinue his work there, because he did not have the funds to pay property owners for crop damages. In addition, cessation of work would necessitate discharging his laboratory personnel as their employment hinged upon the number of certified WPA workers employed in the field. Through the TVA's withdrawal of funding, he would lose approximately 120 people currently working under Nash's supervision in the Kentucky Basin. Lewis's program in the Kentucky Basin would collapse if the TVA followed through with its proposal.

On August 7, 1939, Lewis, Hoskins, and University of Tennessee business manager James P. Hess appeared before the TVA Board of Directors at the request of TVA chair Harcourt A. Morgan (Lewis 1939e). After hearing a statement prepared by Lewis, but read by President Hoskins, the board agreed that Lewis should continue his work in the Kentucky Basin. The TVA would provide Lewis with the necessary engineering services, field laboratory rental, supplies, and surveying instruments (Lewis 1939d). In an effort to rectify the soured relationship with Webb and to ameliorate any hard feelings, Lewis (1939d) wrote President Hoskins suggesting that Webb might be invited to a meeting during which an effort would be made to dispel the ill feeling that had existed over the past several years.

Webb did travel to Knoxville, but only conferred with the TVA authorities and University of Tennessee Business Manager Hess on August 9. Hess reported the meeting to Kneberg, who in turn passed the information on to Guthe, as Lewis was in the Kentucky Basin consulting with Nash about ongoing field operations. Kneberg (1939) was incensed about the turn of events: "The root of the objection to our doing the work in the Dam Basins appears to be that we are considered as incapable of turning out reports acceptable to the professional group of archaeologists."

In hopes of regaining control of the situation, Lewis (1939f) dispatched a letter to Guthe the following week, noting that two TVA officials had visited the lab, informing him of comments made by Webb during a recent visit. Although the TVA officials were willing to assist the university, Webb's accusations seemed valid and would have to be addressed in order to justify the TVA's continued financial assistance. They proposed that Lewis compose a letter that they could direct to Guthe, requesting someone to render an opinion on the quality of work now in progress and the likelihood that Lewis could produce an acceptable report.

Webb was summoned to a meeting in Knoxville on August 21 by the TVA and informed that Guthe would be requested to recommend a professional archaeologist who could make an appraisal of Lewis's operation. Webb pointed out that in his estimation Lewis's laboratory procedures and field techniques were satisfactory but that Lewis's operation was "utterly incapable of compiling an acceptable report" (Lewis 1939g). On September 17 and 18, 1939, Guthe inspected the University of Tennessee archaeological laboratory. Guthe was impressed with the laboratory arrangements and procedures and "astounded at the amount of subterfuge which has been going on here" (Lewis 1939g). On the eighteenth, Guthe conferred with President Hoskins and the TVA officials, and the next day conferred with TVA chair Harcourt A. Morgan. During Lewis's meeting with TVA officials on the twenty-second, he was offered full cooperation and support. Guthe agreed to send his report to President Hoskins with copies to Kelly, Setzler, and Webb.

## Postscript

Webb continued to serve as consultant to the TVA until 1942 and produced co-authored reports on the Pickwick Basin (Webb and DeJarnette 1942) and Guntersville Basin (Webb and Wilder 1951) investigations. Although a site report was prepared for the Jonathan Creek site in the Kentucky portion of the basin (Webb 1952), Webb did not issue a comprehensive report for the overall University of Kentucky investigations, the only TVA basin in which he worked that lacked a report. Webb died in Lexington, Kentucky, on February 15, 1964.

Lewis and Kneberg also did not publish comprehensive reports for the Chickamauga, Kentucky, or Watts Bar basins. The Chickamauga Basin report was completed in draft form, and although a mimeograph summary (Lewis and Kneberg 1941) was circulated, the manuscript was not published due to funding limitations until 1995 through the efforts of Lynne P. Sullivan (Lewis et al. 1995). Lewis and Kneberg's outstanding publication was the report on the Hiwassee Island site in the Chickamauga Basin (Lewis and Kneberg 1946), partially based on Charles Nash's field notes. *Hiwassee Island* became a much lauded report and gained Lewis and Kneberg professional admiration and respect. Walter Taylor, one of Americanist archaeology's major postwar critics, praised the book as "quite possibly the best archaeological report I have had the occasion to read" (Taylor 1948:9).

Although Lewis and Kneberg did not publish a report of the Kentucky Basin investigations, they collaborated on several summaries of the Archaic components in the basin (Lewis and Kneberg 1947, 1959), including a major report of Douglas Osborne's excavations at the Eva site (Lewis and Lewis 1961). Lewis and Kneberg retired from the University of Tennessee in 1961 and married shortly thereafter. Thomas M. N. Lewis died in Winter Haven, Florida, on August 18, 1974, and Madeline Kneberg Lewis passed away on July 4, 1996.

The feud between Lewis and Webb was certainly painful for the profession and for the parties involved. Sullivan notes: "More than fifty years later, Madeline was visibly uncomfortable discussing these problems" (Sullivan 1999:72). But as Lyon (1996:144) points out, the conflict between Webb and Lewis was more than a personal battle between two archaeological luminaries. Their battle was a many faceted and multidimensional conflict over the control of archaeological resources, including collections and documentation. The conflict was part of a national debate over differing conceptions of how archaeology should be carried out and reported. It centered on arguments that are as viable today as they were during the New Deal era. How do we interpret archaeological data and what are the standards of archaeological reporting? While their battles may be reduced to personal feuding, their stances reflect a major paradigm shift in archaeology and indicate how two capable, diligent, and thought-provoking New Deal archaeologists transformed the conduct of modern archaeology.

## Acknowledgments

I would like to thank Jefferson Chapman and Lynne Sullivan for their help in obtaining copies of the Charles H. Nash letters, curated at the WPA Archives, McClung Museum, University of Tennessee, and Claudia Jacobsen for her help in obtaining permission to cite the W. C. McKern letters housed in the Anthropology Department, Milwaukee Public Museum. Also, my appreciation to Marlin Hawley for making available copies of the W. C. McKern letters. My sincere thanks to Marlin Hawley, Charles McNutt, Patty Jo Watson, and the two anonymous reviewers for their constructive editorial comments on an earlier draft of this chapter. In addition, Charles and Marlin also provided suggestions concerning Kneberg's role in the conflict between Lewis and Webb. Thanks also to Bernard Means for his invitation to participate in the symposium and in this resulting volume, and for his helpful suggestions on various chapter drafts.

# 8

# WPA Archaeology at the Slayden Site, Humphreys County, Tennessee

*Anna R. Lunn*

Modern perceptions of archaeology frequently view excavation and data recovery as the field's heart and soul—the driving force that keeps archaeology alive. Large-scale excavation is certainly the most direct and exciting way of discovering what lies beneath the ground's surface, and archaeologists draw hypotheses and conclusions in extensive reports based on their current fieldwork. What many people may not realize is that large amounts of equally useful data are gathering dust in museums while archaeologists continue to unearth more artifacts than can be properly stored, much less sorted, analyzed, and reported.

During the New Deal era alone, dozens of archaeological sites were excavated in the Tennessee River Valley prior to the creation of reservoirs designed to improve navigation. Archaeologists and field crews labored to recover thousands of prehistoric and historic artifacts, writing an endless stream of field notes documenting every stage of the work. Although the excavations greatly increased researchers' knowledge and understanding of American prehistory, few reports were generated from the many hours in the field, due to budget constraints and America's involvement in World War II. Working with old collections from these New Deal excavations can be somewhat daunting, since one is faced with the prospect of locating the artifacts and records, deciphering another person's field notes and reports, and quantifying the data in a manner that is both useful and significant to modern archaeological objectives. However, the end result is well worth the effort as valuable information is added to the archaeological record.

One of the earliest sites excavated in Tennessee during the New Deal era was Slayden (40HS1) in Humphreys County, a Mississippian period settlement characterized by stone box burials, a village-ceremonial area, and five residential mounds later redefined as house circles (Nash 1968). Feature forms, burial forms, photographs, field notes, and a number of personal letters are available from these excavations, which took place during the winter months of 1935 and 1936. These records—written primarily by archaeologist Charles H. Nash and physical anthropologist Georg K. Neumann—are archived at the Frank H. McClung Museum, University of Tennessee, Knoxville. By transcribing the notes and recreating the field maps, I was able to reconstruct a timeline of the excavations and the archaeological field methods that were employed. Additionally, a modern analysis of the artifacts recovered during the 1935–1936 fieldwork yielded significant information about prehistoric peoples living in Humphreys County and provided indications of the site's age.

## Site Location and Description

Slayden is located near the center of Humphreys County on the Duck River, which is the Tennessee River's largest tributary. This particular area is within the Western Highland Rim physiographic region and is characterized by steep hills underlain by limestone and outcrops of shale and chert, including Fort Payne chert. Many of the lithic artifacts recovered from Slayden were crafted from local materials, although exotic materials such as greenstone and rhyolite were also used. Natural rises, which were modified by people living at the site, exist on the periphery of an open area that Nash referred to as the village-ceremonial center. Residential mounds are situated a short distance away, as are the burials. The site's components are spread across several acres at the top of the bluff, overlooking the Duck River floodplain to the east. At the present, the village area lies in a field that was once used for agriculture but that is now fallow. The remainder of the site, including the residential mounds and the burials, extends into a section of woods south and east of the field.

Excavations at Slayden began in November 1935 when Thomas M. N. Lewis, Charles Nash, and Georg Neumann arrived in Humphreys County. Using Works Progress Administration (WPA) funds, they organized a group of local workers with the intention of digging at the Link Farm site, located a mile north of Slayden on the Duck River (Table 8.1). However, the landowner would not give them permission to dig right away, and Lewis opted to work at Slayden in the meantime. Work officially commenced on November 20, 1935, and excavations conducted across the site revealed a number of structures, as well as pits, post molds, and hearths. The site was divided

Table 8.1. Archaeological sites investigated using New Deal funding in Tennessee

| Site | County | Dates of Excavation | Reference |
|---|---|---|---|
| Slayden | Humphreys | 1935 to 1936 | Nash 1935 |
| Link Farm | Humphreys | 1936 | Dye 2002, 2003 |
| Shiloh | Hardin | 1933 to 1934, 1998, 1999 | Welch 2006 |
| Obion | Henry | 1913, 1940 | Garland 1992 |

into three main sections—village, cemetery, and residential (Figure 8.1). Four units (1, 3, 4, and 5) were excavated in the village area, while the stone box burials were excavated as one unit (2). Four units (6, 7, 8, and 9) were placed in the residential area on small mounds. A tenth unit was planned for the residential area but was never excavated (Nash 1935).

The investigations at Slayden were wrapped up quickly after March 1, 1936, when permission was finally granted for the WPA archaeologists to work on three mounds at Link Farm. As a result, Units 4, 6, 7, 8, and 9 were excavated with a sense of urgency that is reflected in the feature data forms and notes. Many features were not fully exposed, and others may have been overlooked. Unit 10 was never excavated, although it was assumed to be a continuation of the Slayden site (Nash 1935). However, the WPA crew conducted thorough excavations within the main village and the cemetery south of the village (Unit 2). These two sections of the project yielded a significant amount of data relevant to Mississippian sites in the Lower Duck River valley.

## Field Methods

Data collected from the units were recorded on standard burial, feature, and field specimen data forms issued by the University of Tennessee and included the same details typical of modern excavations such as elevation, grid coordinates, and associated features and artifacts. A 10-foot grid system was established across the site, and measurements were taken in tenths of a foot. Features were recorded onto large plats at regular intervals, and photographs were taken of each unit once features were exposed. Past experience led the archaeologists to adopt horizontal stripping as the best technique for revealing features and determining their extent (Lewis and Lewis 1995:610), and

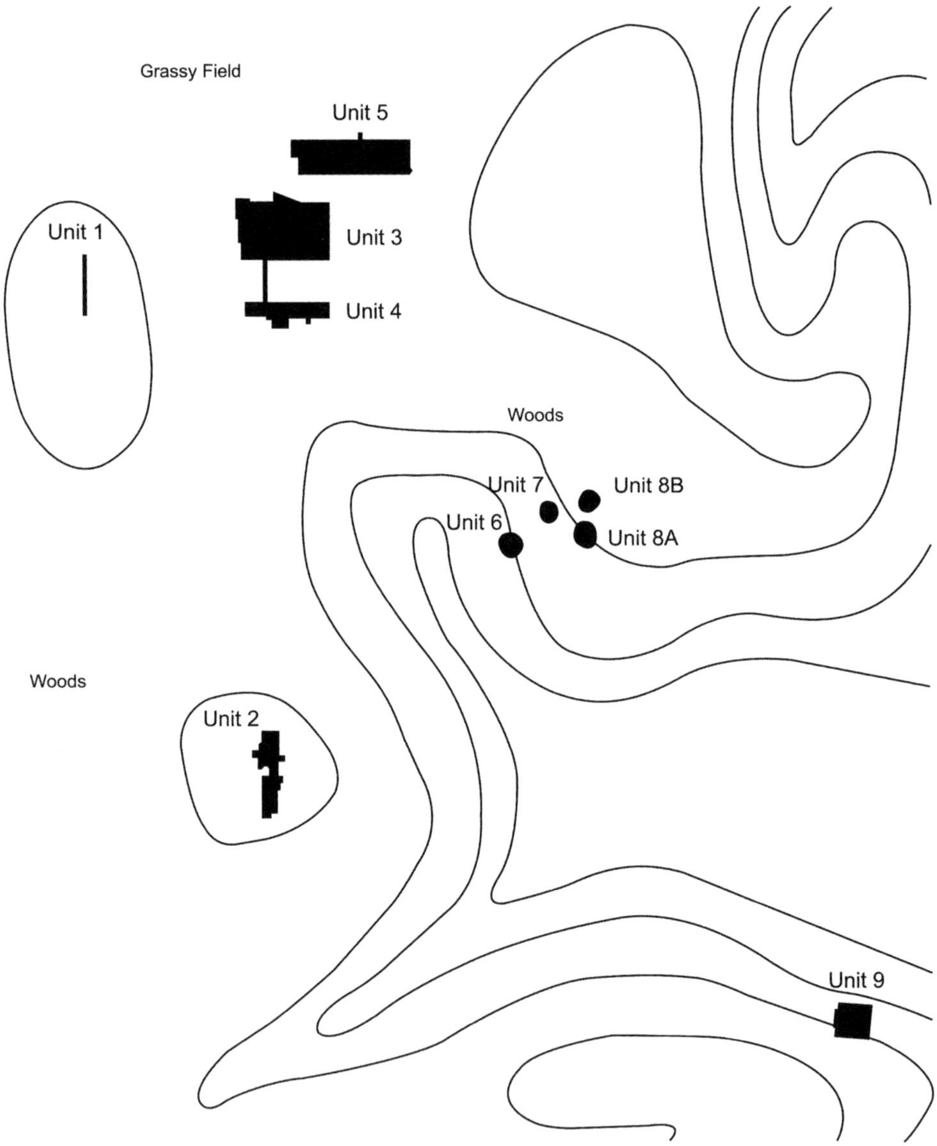


Figure 8.1. Unit locations at the Slayden site.

Nash excavated units in 1-foot levels. Each feature was assigned a number and described on feature data forms with special attention devoted to structures.

## Summary of Unit Excavations from a Review of the Field Records

### *Village*

Investigations at Slayden began in the village area, and excavations performed across the area revealed a number of structures, both rectangular and circular and of varying sizes, as well as cache pits, refuse pits, and hearths. Despite soil erosion due to agricultural and timbering practices during the historic period, the excavations revealed a surprising amount of information. Artifacts recovered from the main village area included pottery and chipped stone tools that Nash and Neumann estimated to be Mississippian.

Unit 1 was a trench 5 feet wide and 75 feet long placed on the western edge of the village to determine its extent (Figure 8.1). Level 1 consisted of topsoil, and few artifacts were uncovered before workers encountered sterile subsoil 20 inches below the modern ground surface. The only feature unearthed in Unit 1 was a refuse pit containing a few pottery sherds and charcoal fragments. The sparse artifact distribution and lack of significant features seem to indicate that Unit 1 was on the western periphery of the site.

Unit 3 began as a 5-foot trench placed in the main village area east of Unit 1 (Figure 8.1). Numerous post molds, house floors, and other features were revealed in the first 10-foot section, prompting Nash to extend the unit boundaries. Evidence of human occupation can be seen to a depth of 22 inches below the surface on four different levels. A total of six structures were identified in Unit 3, and all of these had associated features such as hearths, pits, post molds, and/or wall trenches (Figure 8.2).

The oldest structures were recorded in Level 4 as Features 11 and 40. Nash interpreted Feature 11 as a rectangular structure measuring 63 feet by 24 feet—by far the largest structure at the site. Feature 40 is also rectangular and was situated just west of Feature 11 at the same elevation. The walls of both structures are somewhat irregular, especially those associated with Feature 11, which may actually be two smaller structures located adjacent to one another. Two structures were identified in Level 3 as Features 14 and 21. Feature 14 measured 43 feet by 28 feet, and Feature 21 measured 42 feet by 31 feet. Pits were identified in both structures, but Feature 14 also had two associated hearths. Only one structure was identified in Level 2—Feature 19. This structure is rectangular with rounded corners, and a portion of the northwest floor was burned. Finally, the most recent structure in time was

Figure 8.2. Unit 3 structures at the Slayden site.

identified in Level 1 as Feature 23. This structure has the distinction of being the only round structure in the village area at Slayden. Three hearths were associated with Feature 23. Artifacts recovered from Unit 3 included pottery, projectile points, blades, chisels, hoes, and charred corn cobs. Many of these were associated with specific features or structures.

Unit 4 began as a 5-foot trench south of Unit 3 in the center of the village area (Figure 8.1). Unlike Unit 3, which had rich evidence of human occupation at several levels, excavations at Unit 4 revealed only two distinct levels—one just beneath the modern ground surface and one approximately 2 feet below that on the original ground surface. Between these two levels, Nash recorded a layer of artificial loading that was used to level the slope after the earlier structures were abandoned. While both levels displayed evidence of structures in the form of post molds and wall molds, no intact structures were recorded at Unit 4. Three sides of a rectangular structure were identified in Level 1 (Feature 14), and a hearth was identified in the northwest corner of the structure. Two structures were revealed in Level 2 (Features 35 and 37), between which were a large number of cache pits. Feature 35 was only partially excavated but was defined as a rectangular post mold structure with square corners. Feature 37 was a square structure delineated by post molds set inside a wall trench. Fifty additional post molds were scattered throughout the unit, but no definitive patterns emerged to indicate specific structures. Other features at Unit 4 included five charcoal pits, 11 cache pits, and several hearths and refuse pits. Associated with many of these features were numerous artifacts, including projectile points, chisels, hoes, hammerstones, a stone pipe, split cane, and a drilled mussel shell.

Unit 5, measuring 140 feet by 90 feet, was located in the main village area north of Units 3 and 4 (Figure 8.1). Because time was limited, Nash changed his methods slightly for Unit 5, staking the entire unit off in 10-foot squares and excavating within a grid system. Features and artifacts from Unit 5 were referenced with the stake numbers in the documentation. Artifacts were scarce in Level 1, but 2 inches below the plow zone workers uncovered several features and four stone box graves. Portions of three structures were identified in Unit 5 by the presence of wall molds (Features 1, 19, and 21), but no intact structures were revealed. As with Unit 4, post molds were scattered throughout Unit 5 but without any clear patterns. The burials, all adults, were located near the modern ground surface and may have been interred after the area was abandoned by the population. Specific artifact types recovered in Unit 5 included hoes, stone beads, a stone pipe, projectile points, celts, stone discs, a drilled stone, and a knife. Artifacts specifically associated with burials were uncommon in Unit 5. Pottery fragments were present in Burials 1, 2, and 3, but these may have been the products of plowing or other disturbances. Burial 4 contained a celt along with the bones of an adult unidentified as to gender.

### *Cemetery*

Unit 2 was located across a raised area in the woods south of the village and encompassed a number of burials (Figure 8.3). Excavations revealed 64 stone box features, which were "constructed by setting narrow shale slabs on the ground and keeping soil over the whole after the body was placed into it" (Neumann 1936). Two features did not contain any human remains and may have been postholes rather than burials, though evidence of looting was noted across the unit. Of the 62 confirmed burials, only 12 were completely undisturbed. At least 12 had been looted at some point in time, and the remainder had suffered damage from rodents, vegetation, and other taphonomic processes.

The majority of the bodies were situated in an extended position oriented east to west, with the head toward the west. Most of the ornamentation and pottery recovered from Unit 2 was found in graves of women and children (Neumann 1936). Few males were interred at Slayden; only five males were identified at Unit 2 and only one of these burials contained funerary items. Another unusual aspect was the high ratio of infants and children to adults; of more than 60 burials, 33 were infants, 5 were children, and 1 was a juvenile. Though Neumann was able to identify the age for most of the skeletal remains and sex for the majority of adults, to date no one has studied specific causes of death among the population at Slayden. Nor have any studies been conducted to locate additional human remains in other parts of the site or to determine whether some individuals may have been buried at other nearby sites, such as Link Farm.

Associated funerary items were discovered in 11 burials from Unit 2. Among these burials, five were infants, one was a child, three were adult females, and one was an adult male. Artifact types recovered represent a variety of materials and included a two-hole shell gorget on the chest of an infant, 18 spherical fluorite beads around the left wrist of a mature female, and various ceramic vessels and projectile points.

In addition to burials, one feature was recorded at Unit 2, located slightly underneath the stones associated with Burial 50 and probably dating earlier in time. The feature was classified as an "area of fire-cracked stones" and measured approximately 30 inches long and 26 inches wide. The feature was bowl shaped with the deepest portion (16 inches) at the center and was filled with fire-cracked sandstone and other rocks (none more than 1 inch

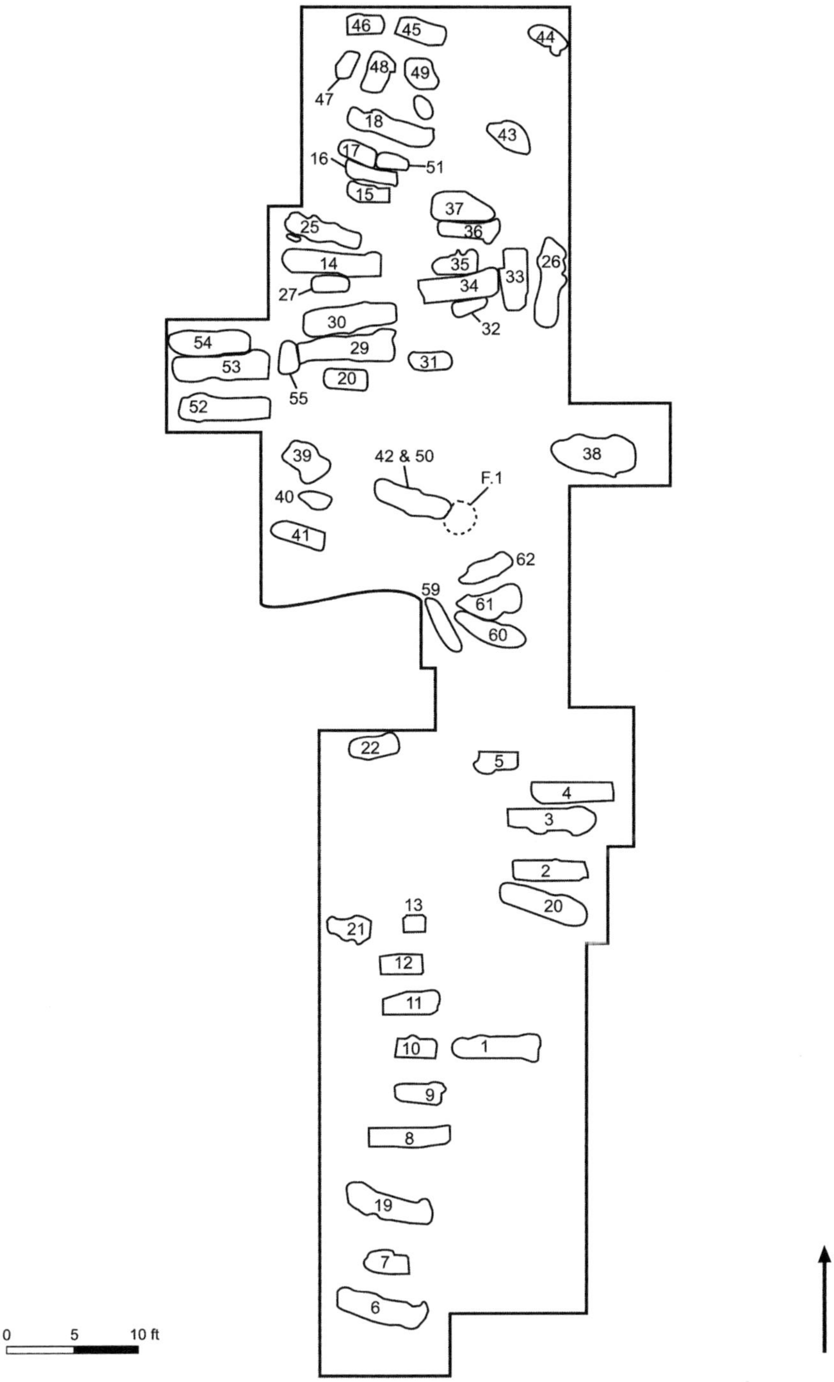


Figure 8.3. Plan of Unit 2 burial locations at the Slayden site.

in diameter) and black clay soil that may have been discolored by charcoal, although no fragments were actually found.

*Residential Area*

Units 6, 7, and 8 were grouped together on the same natural elevation south and slightly east of the village (Figure 8.1). These units were located on top of small mounds (the largest was 30 feet in diameter and 3 feet in height) characterized by a depression in the center of the mound. Nash (1935, 1968) refers to these as house circles and theorized that they were built up naturally over time as a structure was burned or torn down and the area swept clean for a new structure to be erected.

Nash began by excavating a 5-foot trench on the west side of Unit 6, though he later changed to a horizontal method of excavation. Just beneath the modern ground surface, burned clay, charred logs, and charcoal comprised of split cane and grass indicated the presence of a structure that had burned (Feature 3), though the remains were too delicate to attempt a reconstruction of the building. Once the burned materials had been cleared, post molds were revealed depicting a square structure (20 feet on all sides) with rounded corners. Below this was a smaller rectangular structure measuring 10 feet by 15 feet (Feature 4). Excavations illustrated that building materials associated with Feature 4 were swept outward once the structure was abandoned and that artificial fill was spread over the area to create a floor for the next structure (Feature 3). Unit 6 did not yield many artifacts, though several were associated with the structures.

Unit 7 was similar to Unit 6, though no artificial fill was evident. Only one small square structure (Feature 2) measuring 18 feet on each side was identified in Level 1, and features associated with the structure included post molds set inside a wall trench. Two of the walls were unique: the west wall, which was made up of a double row of post molds set in one wall mold, and the south wall, which was reinforced by a row of post molds outside the wall mold. The only other features associated with Unit 7 were three refuse pits (Features 1, 4, and 5)—two inside the structure and one outside—and a burned area (Feature 3) in the center of the structure's floor. Few artifacts were uncovered at Unit 7, though shell-tempered pottery was associated with the structure.

Unit 8 cut across two small residential mounds located adjacent to each other and labeled Units 8A and 8B. Workers identified a burned square post mold structure measuring 17 feet on each side (Feature 2) in the first level of Unit 8A. Unlike the case with the other burned structures recorded at Slayden, numerous artifacts were recovered both inside and outside Feature

2, providing circumstantial evidence that the burning was unintentional and that the building was abandoned in a hurry. Charred logs, burned red clay, and fragments of cane matting were identified inside the structure. Beneath this house, workers uncovered a second, earlier structure (Feature 5), which measured 14 feet by 15 feet. The building was delineated by a wall mold on the west side and post molds on the other three sides. Unlike the other residential structures excavated at Slayden, Feature 5 contained a number of miscellaneous post molds inside the building. No other features were definitively associated with the structure, though a refuse pit (Feature 6) filled with charcoal and ashes was identified just west of it. One additional square structure (Feature 4) measuring 23 feet on each side was identified just below the ground surface south of the mound, though no features or artifacts were associated with this structure.

Excavations at Unit 8B revealed a small square structure (Feature 1) measuring 15 feet on each side just beneath the modern ground surface. The structure was delineated by post molds and a wall trench, and a central hearth (Feature 2) was noted. Two large burned logs were recovered inside the structure and apparently served as a support for the posts. As with Unit 8A, a smaller structure (Feature 4) was uncovered beneath the top structure, though no features were associated with this earlier structure. Feature 4 measured 14 feet square and was defined by wall trenches and post molds. Artifacts recovered from Unit 8 included pottery, projectile points, celts, and a chisel.

Unit 9 was located directly south of Units 6, 7, and 8 and was the largest of the residential mounds, measuring about 30 feet in diameter (Figure 8.1). The eastern portion of the mound was situated on the natural rise of the bluff, while the western side was artificially raised to the same elevation. Excavations revealed a circular structure 20 feet in diameter on the original ground surface before the mound was leveled (Feature 5). When the western half of the structure was destroyed, that edge was built up with clay loam fill, and a new structure (Feature 6) was erected using the existing eastern wall of the earlier structure. Other features at Unit 9 included two hearths (Features 2 and 4), one 6 inches below the other, in the center of the structures.

## Ceramics

No discussion of Mississippian sites would be complete without an examination of ceramics that were curated from the site, which often have temper and stylistic changes that can provide tentative dates for sites. Based on my analysis, the ceramic assemblage from Slayden contains both decorated and undecorated sherds whose pastes include grog, shell, and mixed grog and shell as tempering agents. The assemblage was first separated according to style: plain, decorated, and indeterminate. The indeterminate style category consists of sherds whose exterior surface was worn away, as well as sherds that are decorated but that have become smoothed to the point that differences between cord-marked and fabric-impressed pottery could no longer be determined. The decorated sherds were further subdivided by surface treatment: cord marked, fabric impressed, incised, or some combination of these. Decorated sherds make up the majority of the collection (64 percent) with cord-marked and fabric-impressed styles making up 94 percent of the decorated category. Plain sherds account for 26 percent of the assemblage, with the remaining 10 percent being indeterminate.

Once stylistic categories were established, each was then subdivided by temper type (Table 8.2). Grog, shell, and mixed grog and shell tempers are the most common temper types (98 percent). Only six sherds are tempered differently: four with a combination of shell and fiber and two with an indeterminate temper. If the assemblage is representative of the ceramics used by inhabitants of Slayden, then grog was the preferred choice (66 percent) for temper (Table 8.3). Only 14 percent of sherds are tempered with shell alone, while 18 percent of sherds contain a combination of grog and shell temper.

The most common vessel shape, regardless of temper type or stylistic variation, appears to be the globular jar. Most were no more than 25 centimeters in diameter, though two jars were more than 40 centimeters in diameter at the widest part of the body. Several effigy water bottles were also noted on feature and burial forms, though these were not available for my analysis. Variation can be seen in rim styles more than in vessel shape. The two most common rim types are straight and flared. The straight rims typically sat on open-mouthed, neckless globular jars. Where the rim ends, the body of the vessel curves outward and is rounded. Some of the vessels have rims that gently flare outward, giving the vessel a smooth, curved appearance. Others have sharply flared rims, where the neck would have been constricted. Some of the rims are notched along the edge and some are plain; punctations are seen on several sherds. A number of the rims are folded—a characteristic of grog-tempered pottery noted by Berle Clay (1963) in the Tennessee-Cumberland region and by Paul Welch (2006) at Shiloh. Eight rims have loop handles, one of which is flattened.

A full discussion of ceramic types is not possible here, but every effort was made to sort the artifacts into a type-variety system. A review of the literature for ceramic typologies of the region covered areas around Slayden, but there was nothing specific to the Lower Duck River valley. The ceram-

Table 8.2. Ceramic types by temper from the Slayden site

| Type | Temper | Count |
|---|---|---|
| Plain | Grog | 37 |
| | Shell | 13 |
| | Grog/shell | 49 |
| *Total plain sherds* | | 99 (25.3%) |
| Decorated | | |
| Cord marked | Grog | 113 |
| | Grog/shell | 6 |
| Fabric marked | Grog | 74 |
| | Shell | 34 |
| | Grog/shell | 10 |
| Incised | Grog | 10 |
| | Shell | 1 |
| Other | Grog | 3 |
| *Total decorated sherds* | | 251 (64.2%) |
| Indeterminate | Grog | 22 |
| | Shell | 8 |
| | Grog/shell | 5 |
| | Fiber/shell | 4 |
| | Unknown | 2 |
| *Total indeterminate sherds* | | 41 (10.5%) |
| *Total sherds* | | 391 (100%) |

ics at Slayden display varying degrees of similarity to those of the Lower Mississippi Valley (Phillips 1970), the Tennessee-Cumberland region (Clay 1963), West Tennessee (Garland 1992), and the Middle Tennessee River valley (Haag 1942; Heimlich 1952; Welch 2006). Grog-tempered ceramics include varieties of Baytown Plain, Mulberry Creek Cord Marked, and Matthews Incised. Additionally, a number of grog-tempered ceramics are fabric impressed, which seems to be unusual. Of the other sites examined, only the Obion site yielded similar sherds (Garland 1992). Shell-tempered ceramics include varieties of Mississippi Plain and Kimmswick Fabric Impressed, while mixed temper types include Mississippi Plain, Kimmswick Fabric Im-

Table 8.3. Comparison of temper types from the Slayden site

| Temper | Count | Percentage |
|---|---|---|
| Grog | 257 | 66 |
| Shell | 55 | 14 |
| Grog/shell | 71 | 18 |
| Fiber/shell | 4 | 1 |
| Unknown | 2 | <1 |
| *Total sherds examined* | 389 | 100 |

pressed, Mulberry Creek Cord Marked, Matthews Incised, and Coles Creek Incised. Other ceramic artifacts recovered from Slayden include pottery trowels, ceramic discs, a bead, pipes, and rim appliqués.

## Stone Artifacts

My analysis of the lithic assemblage for Slayden shows that it includes both chipped and ground stone artifacts, with bifaces, hammerstones, celts, and hoes being a few of the more common tool types. The majority of the pieces were formed from local chert types, though a few key pieces were crafted of more exotic materials. Regardless of the raw material used, the Slayden lithic artifacts cover a wide time range (Table 8.4). Points dating anywhere from the Early Archaic period to the Mississippian period were recovered, providing evidence that Slayden is a multicomponent site. The Early Archaic is represented by Big Sandy and Lost Lake points, while Benton and Pickwick points fall into the late Middle to Late Archaic periods. Two Turkey-tail cluster points provide a transition between the Late Archaic and Early Woodland periods, followed by Adena (Early Woodland) and Copena (Middle Woodland) point types. Finally, several small, triangular Madison points suggest a Late Woodland to Mississippian period occupation.

While the projectile points offer a fascinating glimpse into Slayden's chronology, some of the site's more interesting artifacts are not diagnostic of a specific time period. Seven large blades, one of which was made of mottled pink rhyolite, were identified in the lithic assemblage and illustrate an impressive attention to detail in their manufacture. These tools may be what Brown (1976:148) has termed "socio-technic" weapons. Additionally, several ground stone celts or celt fragments were recovered from the site. The

Table 8.4. Chipped stone artifacts from the Slayden site

| Description | Count |
|---|---|
| Big Sandy Side Notched | 2 |
| Lost Lake | 2 |
| Benton | 3 |
| Pickwick | 2 |
| Turkeytail-Harrison | 2 |
| Adena | 6 |
| Adena blade | 1 |
| Copena | 3 |
| Madison | 4 |
| Fort Ancient | 1 |
| Miscellaneous blades | 7 |
| Bifaces | 14 |
| Utilized flakes | 7 |
| Preforms | 17 |
| Cores | 3 |
| Drills | 4 |
| Hoes | 19 |
| *Total chipped stone artifacts* | 97 |

most interesting of these, recovered from Burial 4 in Unit 5, has the classic spatulate shape and was made of nonlocal green slate. Other chipped stone tools include bifaces, utilized flakes, preforms, cores, drills, and hoes. Ground stone tools include hammerstones, celts, abraders, and chunkey stones (Table 8.5).

## Chronology

A number of artifacts in the Slayden assemblage are diagnostic of specific time periods. Though the types and dates suggested may be modified in years to come, a general outline of chronology can be created based on current knowledge. Radiocarbon dates, which should be the next research goal, will allow the chronology to be refined further and will provide a means of comparing the vertical distributions of ceramic types. For example, the transition from grog temper to mixed temper to shell temper is not well un-

Table 8.5. Ground stone artifacts from the Slayden site

| Description | Count |
|---|---|
| Hammerstones | 13 |
| Celts | 10 |
| Club heads | 2 |
| Burnishing stones | 1 |
| Grinding stones | 1 |
| Abraders | 3 |
| Weights | 2 |
| River rocks | 8 |
| Pebble mortars | 6 |
| Fire-drill hearths | 5 |
| Chunkey stones | 4 |
| Discs | 3 |
| Stone rings | 3 |
| Stone beads | 2 |
| Effigies | 4 |
| Miscellaneous ground stone | 13 |
| Stone chunks | 2 |
| *Total ground stone artifacts* | 82 |

derstood, and the period of overlap, if any, is unknown. Calibrated radiocarbon dates may assist in the development of a ceramic morphology based on temper type.

Overall, the Slayden ceramics indicate a primarily Early Mississippian period occupation, which probably dates somewhere between A.D. 1000 and A.D. 1200. The majority of the sherds were tempered with grog, which is mostly typical of Woodland period cultures. However, overlap into the Mississippian period has been documented at Obion, an Early Mississippian site near Slayden characterized by Mississippian structures and grog-tempered pottery (Garland 1992). The Obion site dates to A.D. 1000 or later based on radiocarbon analysis. Because of the strong similarities in both structures and artifacts between Slayden and Obion, the two sites may be contemporaneous. In addition to grog-tempered pottery, the presence of loop handles on ceramics is characteristic of the terminal Late Woodland or Early Mississippian period (Garland 1992; Welch 2006), and flared rims and folded rims also point to an early occupation (Clay 1963; Welch 2006).

The lithic assemblage also reflects a multicomponent use of the site. A total of 26 projectile points were examined—10 Archaic, 11 Woodland, and 5 Mississippian. This suggests that the site was regularly used through time, which makes sense given the abundance of water, food, and lithic resources in the area. Many of the structures at Slayden are Mississippian in nature, composed of post molds set into wall trenches, a late innovation arising with the development of large stone hoes that made digging easier (Milner 2004). Furthermore, stone box graves are characteristic of the Mississippian period in the region.

## Site Summary

One of the most fascinating aspects of Slayden is the distribution of artifact types, and a brief examination of these may shed light on how the site was used through time. For example, nearly all the grog-tempered pottery was recovered from the main village area, possibly indicating that the earliest inhabitants settled in the area of today's large field before spreading out to the south. Mixed grog-and-shell-tempered sherds were recovered from both the village and the residential areas, while shell-tempered sherds were recovered from all three areas. The distribution of lithic artifacts shows a similar pattern. Woodland points were concentrated in the village area, while Mississippian points were recovered from both the village and residential areas. Archaic points were also recovered from the village area and from Unit 9. Based on the evidence, it appears that Slayden has two Archaic components, one Woodland component, and one Mississippian component.

The Mississippian occupation was apparently not long, based on current evidence. Most of the excavated units yielded only one or two levels of habitation and no more than four levels. The lifespan of structures built of wood and cane was not extensive, and a long-term occupation would be characterized by more residential levels (Nash 1968). Additionally, the low number of burials reflects a limited occupation, as does the lack of rich middens characteristic of larger sites. However, it should be noted that no archaeological investigations have occurred in the floodplains surrounding Slayden, and no excavations have been conducted since the original WPA work to test the extent of the site in all directions.

In many ways, Slayden is a typical Early Mississippian site, exhibiting some aspects of the more impressive Middle Mississippian chiefdoms yet retaining many Woodland period traits. In fact, the development of chiefdoms is not well understood in the Lower Duck River valley, and it may be that the Mississippian period needs to be redefined in this region. Indeed, archaeological sites in Humphreys County have enormous research potential because so few projects have been undertaken since the New Deal era. For the region immediately surrounding Slayden, future research should begin with a systematic survey of the Duck River valley to identify unrecorded sites and to check known sites for integrity. A comparison of artifact types, common architectural elements, and radiocarbon dates at these sites would provide a substantial addition to our knowledge of prehistory in this region—a knowledge rooted partly in the New Deal excavations at Slayden.

## Acknowledgments

I would like to gratefully acknowledge Lynne Sullivan and Bobby Braly at the Frank H. McClung Museum, University of Tennessee, for their invaluable help during my research.

# 9

# Culture, Time, and Practice

## The Shifting Interpretive Potential of New Deal–Era Collections

*Sissel Schroeder*

The field investigations conducted with New Deal funds in the eastern United States significantly expanded the quantity of excavated sites, many of which serve as type sites or yielded type specimens for archaeological taxa still in use today, provided a rudimentary understanding of chronology, and were pivotal to the initial construction of a synthetic culture history for eastern North America. The key components of the New Deal–era archaeological research programs in the Southeast were a shared systematic field and laboratory methodology that produced comparable results of scientific integrity; the conservation of heritage resources; development of a research agenda that coalesced around the question of chronology, thereby challenging the perceived timelessness of the Native American past; and an expanded view of archaeological cultures that led to the investigation of habitation as well as mound sites (Dunnell 1986:30; Fowler 1986a; Haag 1986; Jennings 1986:56; Setzler and Strong 1936). The public investment in research also provided substantial and lasting benefits for the nation and its people through efforts to preserve ancient monumental construction, villages, and other sites. At national parks, national monuments, and state parks—like Ocmulgee National Monument and Moundville—mounds and earthworks that were excavated were subsequently reconstructed to aid public interpretation and ensure that the research and preservation legacies of the past endured for future generations.

Nearly 80 years after the first New Deal–sponsored archaeological projects, the quality, integrity, and comparability of collections (at least those excavated following similar field methods) are important factors contributing to the continuing value and research potential of these materials. Across the southeastern United States, there are many current and recent reinvestigations of these old collections that serve to highlight aspects of the New Deal projects that placed them at the forefront of archaeological investigations in the 1930s, stress the important legacy of these collections, and demonstrate their potential for studies that pose fresh questions, revisit the conventional interpretations derived from the New Deal work, apply new analytical methods, use new inferential frameworks, and support the reworking of interpretative narratives presented to the public. Over the past 20 years or so, the collections from sites identified as Mississippian have been an especially rich source of innovative research ranging from the instability of chiefdoms to questions about gender and status to subjects of daily practice and ritual life, reflecting the diverse interests of contemporary archaeologists (e.g., Coe 1995; Hally 1994; Hammerstedt 2005a, 2005b, this volume; Lunn, this volume; Peebles 1981; Regnier et al., this volume; Schroeder 2005, 2006, 2009, 2011; Sullivan 1987, 1995, 2007, 2009; Welch 2006; Wilson 2008).

Throughout this chapter, I weave examples derived from William S. Webb's research at the Jonathan Creek site, situated in the Tennessee Valley in western Kentucky, in with results from my own ongoing analyses of the collections to trace the research potential and significance of New Deal–era collections. In particular, I contrast Webb's use of architectural evidence from the site to investigate chronology and culture, two key research questions of the 1930s and 1940s, with my ongoing reanalyses of the same data to demonstrate the promise that these legacy collections hold for inquiries that look at chronology from a more nuanced perspective, eschew simplistic trait-list approaches to the definition of culture, draw on more recent developments in anthropological theory that allow for both external and internal sources of change, and rely on practice theory to build inferences about the origins of architectural variability. The remnants of perishable architecture at the site were the foundation for the original interpretation of site chronology, which has not withstood the test of time. In addition, new analyses of the architectural data provide unanticipated insights into everyday life, including the engineering of roofed space and diversity of the above-ground appearance of buildings.

## The Beginnings of Professionalism in American Archaeology

The community of American archaeologists in the 1920s and early 1930s was small and, at least in terms of the amount of dirt moved each year, dominated by amateurs. Formal training in archaeology was available at about a half-dozen institutions, mostly private universities located in the Northeast. This mixed composition of the field at the beginning of the New Deal is evident in the backgrounds of the 31 individuals who signed the constitution that created the Society for American Archaeology (SAA) in 1934.

About one-third of the signatories had been formally trained in ethnology and physical anthropology, about one-third had some formal training in archaeology, and about one-third were students and avocational archaeologists (Griffin 1985:266–267; Guthe 1935). By the time the first annual meeting of the organization was held in 1935, the organization had attracted 328 dues-paying members, 75 of whom were able to attend the conference (Griffin 1985; Guthe 1936; Meltzer et al. 1986). Only a dozen or so of the individual members were nationally recognized and well-respected archaeologists engaged with fieldwork in the eastern United States prior to the New Deal (Griffin 1985). In contrast, the SAA today has more than 10 times the members it had in 1935, most have some professional training in the discipline, and they come from all over the world.

With the sudden and dramatic increase in the amount of federal funds available for archaeology through various New Deal agencies, most of the prominent archaeologists in the East assumed leadership roles for the disbursement of money and implementation of fieldwork. Principal among these was Major William S. Webb, a physics professor at the University of Kentucky, who was largely self-trained as an archaeologist. Webb forged a strong relationship with the Tennessee Valley Authority (TVA), one of the few New Deal programs unaffiliated with financial reform that still exists today, to establish a program of archaeological documentation, research, and stewardship in the parts of the Tennessee drainage basin that would be impacted by the agency's mandate to construct hydroelectric dams. Under the direction of Webb, as well as T. M. N. Lewis at the University of Tennessee, sites ranging from Archaic tradition shell mounds to Copena sites associated with Hopewellian ceremonial practices to large Mississippian town-and-mound centers were excavated (see Dye, this volume; Lewis et al. 1995; Webb 1938a, 1939, 1952; Webb and DeJarnette 1942; Webb and Wilder 1951). The evidence recovered from these projects, which employed comparable excavation methods, mapping procedures, and field forms, was critically important for achieving two of the primary research goals for American archaeologists of the 1930s: chronology building and the formation of a synthetic culture history.

## A Brief History of Interpretive Frameworks

### *A Timeless View of the Past*

Before the Great Crash of 1929, antiquarians and nascent archaeologists in the eastern United States were entrenched in a descriptive approach that was largely limited to the investigation of mound and earthwork sites and to debunking the "Myth of the Moundbuilders" (Thomas 1894; Willey and Sabloff 1995). Many of the survey, mapping, and excavation projects at these strikingly visible places were designed to develop a system of classification for the mounds, address the question of who built them and when, and acquire representative samples of artifacts from both mortuary and habitation sites (e.g., Jefferson 1782 [1784]; Jefferson et al. 1799; Schoolcraft 1854:135–136; Thomas 1894). These early institution- and government-sponsored archaeology projects were directed by individuals with strong backgrounds in the natural sciences, but little to no formal training in archaeology, who relied on observational methods associated with the disciplines in which they had received their education and who often developed approaches to fieldwork and collections management that suited their particular needs (Hinsley 1976; Hodge 1931:98; Meltzer 1985).

By about 1890, a number of self-taught archaeologists were providing formal education in archaeology and anthropology departments at Harvard University (beginning in 1890, with F. W. Putnam providing the archaeology training), the University of Pennsylvania (starting in 1886, with courses taught by D. G. Brinton), Clark University in Worcester, Massachusetts (through course work taught by A. F. Chamberlain, a student of Boas, beginning in 1892), and the University of Chicago (shortly after 1891 with the first archaeology course taught by Frederick Starr) (Dorsey 1894; Hinsley 1992). In 1901, Putnam helped Alfred Kroeber establish the anthropology program at the University of California, Berkeley, with archaeology as a key constituent part, especially in its affiliated museum.

The young archaeologists trained in these early programs were willing and eager to develop and apply to their research standardized and meticulous field and laboratory techniques (Dunnell 1986), many of which became systematized during the New Deal and remain basic tools that we use today, yet the products were fundamentally descriptive and typological, with some occasional interest in functional explanations of certain artifact forms (Cushing 1886; Hough 1916; Willey and Sabloff 1995). One of the major interpretive contributions from this late nineteenth- and early twentieth-century disciplinary condition was the establishment of rudimentary archaeological culture areas using the geographic distribution of different mound types and stylistically distinctive ceramics recovered during survey and excavation (Holmes 1903, 1914; Kroeber 1939; Mason 1895, 1905; Stirling 1932; Thomas 1894). Much like Clark Wissler's culture area concept for ethnographically documented societies, the archaeological culture areas provided a *non-evolutionary approach* to the comparison of archaeological materials and supported a *timeless* view of pre-Columbian Native Americans (Wissler 1914; see also Holmes 1914 for culture areas defined on the basis of the ceramics). In 1913, when Roland Dixon tried to make sense of the shards of prehistory from eastern North America, he admitted to being defeated by the "baffling complexity" of the archaeological record known at the time, prompting him to explain similarities and differences in terms of migration and displacement (Dixon 1913:550, 555, 559).

### *Progress in Time and Space*

In a response to Dixon's comments about the state of archaeology in eastern North America, Berthold Laufer astutely observed, "*chronology* is at the root of the matter, being the nerve electrifying the dead body of history. It should be incumbent upon the American archeologist to establish a chronological basis of the pre-Columbian cultures" (Laufer in Dixon 1913:577; emphasis added). When Laufer spoke these words at the annual meeting of the American Anthropological Association in 1913, two important methods used by Old World archaeologists to sort out chronological relationships were just beginning to be employed by American archaeologists: stratigraphic excavation and ceramic seriation (Jones 1873; Kidder 1931; Kroeber 1916; Meltzer 1985; Meltzer et al. 1986; Petrie 1899; Phillips et al. 1951; Spier 1917; Trigger 2006:121–129, 135, 278–281; Walker 1883; Willey and Sabloff 1995; Wyman 1868, 1973 [1875]). After Manuel Gamio and Nels Nelson successfully applied these methods in the Basin of Mexico and in the Galisteo Basin in New Mexico (Gamio 1913; Nelson 1914, 1916), archaeologists across the Americas began to focus on the issue of chronology using strictly archaeological methods (Dunnell 1986:29; Willey and Sabloff 1995).

### *Archaeology in the Southeast before the Great Crash of 1929*

For the southeastern United States, archaeological endeavors prior to the 1930s had been limited by a weak economy that persisted from the Civil War until the New Deal and by the absence of any established formal academic programs in archaeology before World War I (Patterson 1991). This situation, in combination with the "baffling complexity" (Dixon 1913:555) of the archaeological record of eastern North America, contributed to the reputation of the Southeast as an intellectual backwater, known for its mounds and a few stunning finds from the excavations of C. B. Moore, Frank Hamilton Cushing, and other self-trained archaeologists but not recognized as a place of methodological or theoretical innovation in archaeology. Ironically, some of the first stratigraphic excavations in North America that identified sequences of change in material culture had been conducted in the Southeast, but they did not have a direct or persistent impact on the practice of archaeology in the region, nor did they stimulate an interest in the development of regional culture history or chronology (Jones 1873; Walker 1879, 1883, 1885; Willey and Sabloff 1995; Wyman 1868, 1973[1875]). Even Cushing's report of his 1895 and 1896 excavations at Key Marco, which led to the recovery of an astonishing collection of well-preserved wooden artifacts that captured international attention, did not clearly influence the research interests of other archaeologists in the Southeast (Cushing 1896; Table 9.1).

In the 1920s, the Smithsonian Institution and the Bureau of American Ethnology began to channel more of their limited resources to archaeological work in the Southeast (e.g., Fewkes 1924, 1925, 1928; Myer 1921, 1924, 1928). Around 1920, the National Research Council also began supporting archaeological surveys in the Midwest, which accelerated efforts to systematically inventory and document archaeological sites in a number of other states (Griffin 1985; Lyon 1996:17), notably Kentucky (see Funkhouser and Webb 1928; Webb and Funkhouser 1932). Most of the publications related to these field projects are largely descriptive and fairly entrenched in a timeless view of the past, a consequence of the absence of a strong synthetic interpretive framework in the region and the lack of a centralized effort to develop regional culture histories and chronologies. Archaeologists working in the Southeast were hamstrung by the poor provenience of many ceramic assemblages in museum collections and shortage of known stratified sites, two conditions that significantly constrained the development of a ceramic/cultural chronology of the sorts being developed by Kroeber, Spier, and others in the Southwest; by Parker and William Ritchie in New York state; and by Strong in Nebraska (Kroeber 1916; Parker 1920; Spier 1917; Strong 1935; for the Southwest, see also Gladwin and Gladwin 1930, 1931, 1934; Kidder 1924).

Elsewhere in the United States, a few archaeologists were beginning to employ what became known as the direct historical approach as a mechanism to gain some control over time by linking historic-era Native American groups with more ancient monuments and sites in the same region (e.g., Cushing 1896; Kroeber 1916; Parker 1916). The approach did not gain widespread use until the 1930s (and even then, it was relatively short-lived), when archaeologists began explicitly seeking ways to link historic Native American tribes and material culture with prehistoric archaeological cultures and artifacts as a way of investigating chronology and identifying change through time (e.g., Strong 1933, 1935; Wedel 1938).

Table 9.1. Southeastern archaeological sites mentioned in the text

| Site | Location | Dates of Excavations | References |
|---|---|---|---|
| Key Marco | Collier County, Florida | 1895–1896 | Cushing 1896 |
| Jonathan Creek | Marshall County, Kentucky | 1940–1942 | Webb 1952 |
| Marksville | Avoyelles Parish, Louisiana | 1933 | Setzler 1934 |
| Moundville | Hale County, Alabama | 1930–1941 | McKenzie 1964; Peebles 1979; Wilson 2005 |
| Ocmulgee/ Macon Plateau | Bibb County, Georgia | 1933–1941 | Fairbanks 1946, 1981 |
| Shiloh | Hardin County, Tennessee | 1933–1934 | Roberts 1935; Stirling 1935; Welch 2006 |

### *The Development of Archaeology in the Southeast after Black Thursday*

Following the Wall Street crash in October 1929, economic circumstances across the country grew increasingly dire. When President Roosevelt was inaugurated on March 4, 1933, one-quarter of the American workforce was unemployed, and roughly two million people were homeless (Lebergott 1964: 512; Mitchell 1947). Roosevelt quickly set in motion a number of economic programs focused on reforming the financial system, providing work relief for the unemployed and poor, and stimulating the recovery of the economy (Leuchtenburg 1963). The Smithsonian Institution, with its long history of engagement with the antiquities of the United States, was given the job of providing scientific guidance to archaeology projects sponsored by relief agencies, which began almost immediately with work at the Marksville site in Louisiana sponsored by the Federal Emergency Relief Administration (FERA) (Setzler 1934; Setzler and Strong 1936). In the first season of archaeological fieldwork in the Southeast, more than 90 percent of the work relief funds were allocated to labor, fully in keeping with the philosophy of the New Deal back-to-work programs (Setzler and Strong 1936:306). It has been estimated that in each six-month span of time during the New Deal, more archaeological data were generated by federally funded programs in the Southeast than had accumulated during the several decades leading up to the Great Depression (Williams 1960:3).

Archaeology on the massive scale conducted with New Deal funding had never before been attempted in the United States. The excavation projects sponsored by the Works Progress Administration (WPA), Civilian Conservation Corps (CCC), and other federal relief agencies of the 1930s and early 1940s were the conduits through which consistent archaeological field procedures were established, repeated, and refined. Because each field project required supervisors with formal training in archaeology, there was a great demand for university-educated archaeologists. The University of Chicago was one of the few institutions, and the only one in the midcontinent, with a formal structured program that provided students with hands-on experience doing archaeological fieldwork of a nature that was comparable to what would be encountered in the Southeast (Haag 1986:65). At the University of Chicago, Fay-Cooper Cole had been for several years training students in methods that formed the foundation of the standardized field and lab procedures used on New Deal archaeology projects. Within any given project, forms were used so that observations and measurements were consistently recorded, facilitating analyses and comparisons with other excavation projects at similar sites. The general approach was later published by Robert Heizer in 1949 as *A Manual of Archaeological Field Methods; Prepared for Use by the California Archaeological Survey of the University of California and the Department of Anthropology at Berkeley* (Dunnell 1986:28)—a volume revised and reissued a number of times, and its influence is still evident in the practice of archaeology today.

Importantly, "the existence of a coherent, widely-shared methodology produced comparable products that could be integrated with one another, not only over time and space, but conceptually" (Dunnell 1986:30). At a local or regional level in the Southeast, chronological understandings of sites and ceramic assemblages were linked with ethnohistoric information to identify and explore change over time (e.g., Collins 1927; Ford 1936; Stirling 1940). In 1941, as a direct consequence of the massive archaeological investigations supported by New Deal agencies, including the application of stratigraphic excavation methods and the seriation of regional ceramic assemblages, James Ford and Gordon Willey were able to construct the first synthetic interpretation of the prehistory of the eastern United States (Ford and Willey 1941). This chronological framework, which relied on diffusion and migration as external causal mechanisms for the geographic spread of archaeological cultures, was quickly followed in 1946 by the publication of

James B. Griffin's chronological and cultural synthesis for the Eastern Woodlands, which did not rely as strongly on diffusion and migration and has had a more enduring impact on archaeologists working in this region (Griffin 1946, 1952, 1967).

## Archaeology at the University of Kentucky

### *Before the Great Crash of 1929*

The early history of archaeological research at the University of Kentucky, which played a pivotal role in New Deal archaeology in the Southeast, shares much in common with the history of the discipline, albeit lagging in time behind developments elsewhere in the United States. The leading advocates for archaeology in Kentucky were two professors at the University of Kentucky who epitomized the nineteenth-century antiquarian—trained in the physical and natural sciences and with an interest in archaeology that they pursued with determination and passion—William S. Webb and William D. Funkhouser. Much like Cyrus Thomas and Frederic Putnam had done decades earlier, Webb and Funkhouser conducted some of their own fieldwork but also relied heavily on individuals scattered across the Commonwealth to send them information on sites and artifacts, what Curtis Hinsley (1999:144) called the "correspondence school" approach to data acquisition (see also Browman 2002; Gruber 1986; Meltzer 1985). Webb's approach to publication of the results of their fieldwork focused on a limited inventory of the materials that were recovered, stressed functional interpretations, and avoided accepted typologies (Schwartz 1967)—a trait-list approach to archaeological classification that came under heavy criticism after World War II (Lyon 1996:42; Milner and Smith 1986:15–16; Spaulding 1985).

After several years of somewhat haphazard investigations, Webb and Funkhouser persuaded the university to establish the Department of Archaeology and Anthropology in 1926, with Webb as the chair, so they could qualify for a truck from the National Research Council (Dye, this volume; Haag 1965:470; Hammerstedt, this volume; Schwartz 1967). Additional funding from the Smithsonian Institution enabled Webb to expand the emergent program, conduct excavations at a larger scale, and increase his involvement in archaeology at a national level. Although Webb and Funkhouser had an understanding of time depth that was limited to several hundred years before European contact, they were perceptive enough to recognize that changes in material culture and mound form had occurred over that time (Funkhouser and Webb 1928:73; Lyon 1996:22), intellectually placing them among their contemporaries in the region who, on the eve of the Great Depression, were still on the cusp of major advances in archaeological chronology building that occurred in the wake of New Deal–sponsored archaeology in the Southeast.

### *The Tennessee Valley Authority, Salvage Archaeology, and William S. Webb*

Archaeological excavations at key mound sites in the Southeast were among the first New Deal–supported projects implemented to bring employment to rural America. Most of the early projects, which were sponsored by FERA, the WPA, and the Civil Works Administration (CWA), were targeted at known sites already deemed significant by the Smithsonian, archaeologists, and local communities—places like Marksville in Louisiana, Ocmulgee/the Macon Plateau in Georgia, and Shiloh in Tennessee (Fagette 1996; Fairbanks 1946, 1981; Lyon 1996; Setzler 1934; Setzler and Strong 1936; Welch 2006). Preservation and interpretation plans were already in the works for these sites when federal funds became available to support archaeological field investigations, which were undertaken to augment and expand scientific knowledge of these places and the ancient Southeast. Indeed, letters were periodically sent to archaeologists involved in FERA-, CWA-, and WPA-sponsored fieldwork to remind them that "[t]he WPA is anxious that archaeological projects make real contributions to scientific research in this country" (Davis 1937).

In addition to seizing the opportunity to expand archaeological research projects at sites of recognized significance, archaeologists, who were well aware that many of the largest sites in the Southeast were situated in river valleys, also were deeply concerned about the potential destruction of archaeological resources that would occur in the wake of dam construction. In May 1933, Roosevelt created the TVA. The agency was charged with the job of planning for and constructing dams across the Tennessee River that would provide flood control, facilitate navigation, and produce hydroelectric power (TVA 1983). In August 1933, Webb and David DeJarnette, of the Alabama Museum of Natural History, traveled to Knoxville to meet with the chairman of the newly created TVA, A. E. Morgan, to express their concerns about archaeology and to present a clear and concise proposal to mitigate a sample of prehistoric sites through survey and excavation (Olinger and Howard 2009:18). Shortly after this meeting, Webb was hired by the TVA to provide supervision over the archaeological investigations conducted in the river basins that would be impacted by dam construction, including Guntersville, Norris, Pickwick, Wheeler, and Kentucky Lake (see Dye, this volume; Webb 1938a, 1939, 1952; Webb and DeJarnette 1942; Webb and Wilder 1951). "[A]cting in response to pressure from the Smithsonian (SI) and later [the SAA]," Webb became "the prime visible force in creating government awareness of its responsibility for preservation of cultural resources as he directed the TVA program" (Jennings 1986:56).

Before the creation of the TVA archaeology program, little archaeological research had been done in the Tennessee drainage and most had been concentrated on mounds and mortuary contexts (e.g., Moore 1915; Myer 1924, 1928; Roberts 1935; Stelle 1871a). In selecting sites to be excavated, Webb balanced a number of competing needs that included potential archaeological significance, accessibility of roads for trucks, the positive attitude of the owner, and the availability of a large labor supply within a reasonable distance of the site (Webb 1937).

While the criterion of archaeological significance placed a lot of emphasis on mounds, Webb also was involved in the disciplinary debates that were coalesced around the questions of chronology and culture from an archaeological perspective. In December 1938, Webb received a letter from James Foster, a graduate student at the University of Chicago: "Dr. Cole has assigned for his course in North American Archaeology, instead of a final examination a problem that has me tearing my hair and I am supposed to be a 'specialist' in the Southeast, in these parts, anyway. He wants a paper organizing the archaeology of the Southeast into the McKern Classification similar to the way Roberts has done in the Southwest, and Ritchie in the Northeast. Have you any suggestions?" (Foster 1938). In his response, Webb wrote: "My frank opinion is that we know so little of the southeastern United States that we are not prepared as yet to make a classification [in reference to the McKern system]. When that is done the 'non-pottery' people of Alabama shell mounds will undoubtedly be the oldest. You know what I think of the order of occurrence of pottery in the Southeast. This is a clue to chronology. This is all I have and I do not know of anyone who has any more" (Webb 1938b).

After five years of intensive excavation work in the Tennessee Valley and tributary drainages, certain other gaps in the kinds of information available to archaeologists were becoming clearer. One of these gaps was ancient community life in a Mississippian town-and-mound site. A few months after his correspondence with Foster, Webb was able to identify a site in western Kentucky called Jonathan Creek that held the potential to fill the gap in knowledge regarding community design and that possibly also would be useful in chronology building.

## The Jonathan Creek Site: The End of the New Deal

### *The Field Project*

In March 1939, the TVA approached Webb about conducting an archaeological survey of the Kentucky portion of the Tennessee River Valley prior to the construction of Kentucky Dam at Gilbertsville, Kentucky (see Dye, this volume; Lyon 1996:158; Milner and Smith 1986:19). Webb gave the job to James Foster, who interrupted his studies at the University of Chicago to undertake the survey. In one month of survey in 1939, Foster identified 47 sites in the Kentucky portion of the Tennessee River basin (Webb 1952). The largest and one of the most significant sites was Jonathan Creek, a Mississippian-era town-and-mound center that had been initially documented in the late nineteenth century during a geological survey of western Kentucky (Loughridge 1888). Jonathan Creek became the first Mississippian town-and-mound center investigated with the explicit goal of revealing the complete community plan.

Webb's excavations at the site began in October 1940 using CCC labor. For Webb and the four site supervisors, James R. Foster, Glenn E. Martin, Harold Dahms, and Joseph Spears, the traces of domestic architecture they unearthed rapidly overshadowed the mounds in significance. The scale of the project soon became overwhelming, especially in light of the growing conflicts in Europe and Asia. By 1941, much of the U.S. labor force was diverted to defense preparedness and the CCC camp enrollment became significantly reduced. On July 26, 1941, the site foreman wrote to Webb:

> As we are getting almost nothing in the way of pottery out of the plow zone I hit upon the idea of using slip scrapers to remove the plow zone. I made this suggestion to Wilder and he agreed that we should speed up our work in the village area. I rigged up three scrapers behind a dump truck and started removing the plow zone. The process worked so efficiently that I surprised myself as well as Wilder . . . If we are able to get larger scrapers from the Park Service, I will put the tractor into operation. This will speed up excavations even more. Wilder seem[s] to think we will be criticized for using this method of excavating, but I believe this is the best method to open a large village area such as this one [Spears 1941].

Wilder's concerns were not unfounded. "The use of heavy machinery . . . was contrary to the WPA philosophy of putting men to work," wrote Haag (1986:70). However, the anticipated outcome, broad exposure of a significant portion of the site to reveal the spatial relationships among numerous archaeological phenomenon, such as structures and palisades, and to focus excavation efforts on these features, must have been a sufficient incentive for the supervisors to continue using heavy equipment to remove the disturbed plow zone, a field strategy commonly used today (Figure 9.1).

Excavations at Jonathan Creek were terminated in March 1942, when the remaining CCC crew was mobilized for World War II. Although the project

Figure 9.1. Slip scraper used to strip the plow zone during excavations at the Jonathan Creek site in August 1941 (Courtesy of the William S. Webb Museum of Anthropology, University of Kentucky, Neg. No. 7170).

did not result in the excavation of the entire site, as originally planned, the efforts of the excavators had exposed 89 structures with a variety of foundation styles and eight stockade lines with bastions that also varied in form (Figure 9.2). At the time of the excavation, the finds at Jonathan Creek were unprecedented. There had been no investigation of sites so intensively protected by massive, sequentially built defensive constructions and Webb's detailed descriptions of the stockades, in particular, remain a major contribution to regional culture history. He, and the archaeologists working with him, also recognized that the architectural diversity of structures at the site was significant—the diversity of structure types was unlike anything recognized elsewhere in the Southeast up to that time. Webb harbored hope that superimposed features would assist him in sorting out the history of occupation at the site.

*Webb's Architectural Interpretations*

Following World War II, Webb, who had overseen the excavation project from Lexington, Kentucky, briefly visiting the site only a few times, produced a short report on the excavations (Webb 1952). While Webb is com-

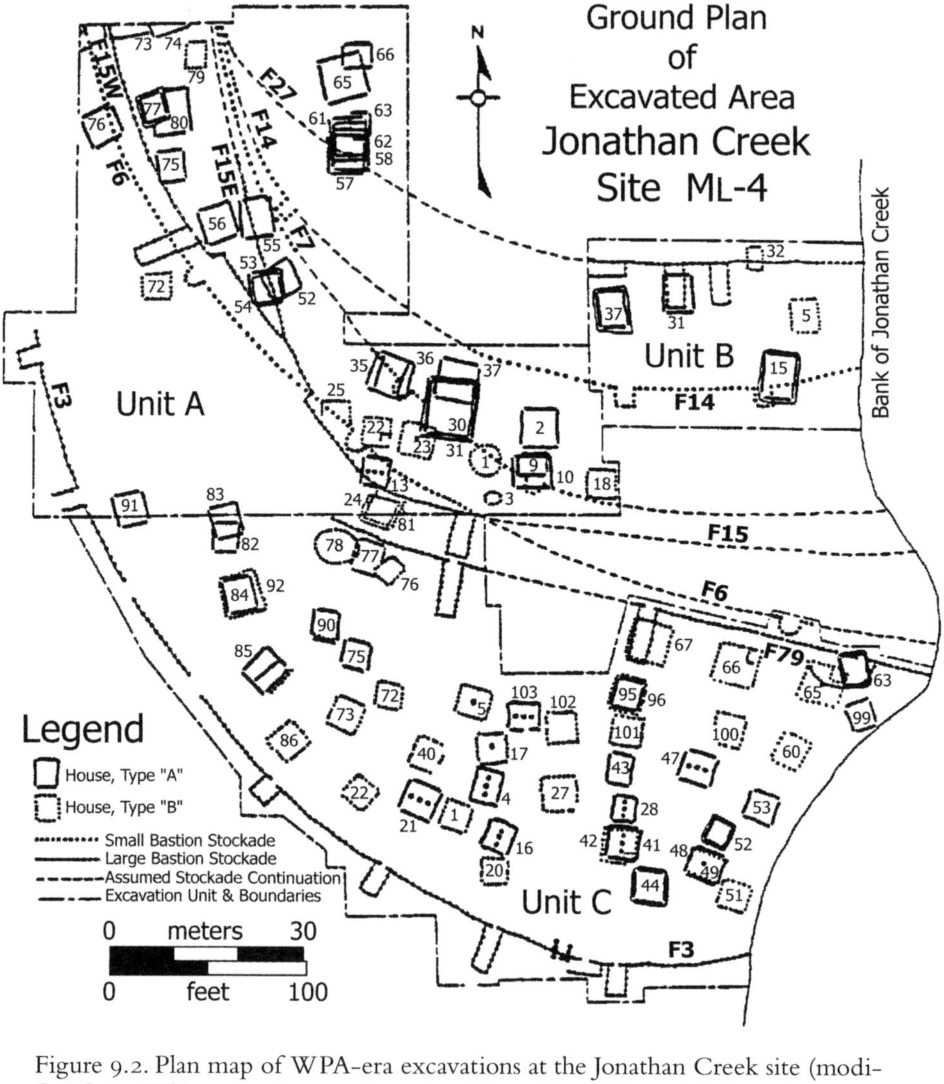


Figure 9.2. Plan map of WPA-era excavations at the Jonathan Creek site (modified from Webb 1952:16–17 and reprinted from *Leadership and Polity in Mississippian Society,* edited by Brian M. Butler and Paul D. Welch. Copyright © 2006 by the Board of Trustees, Southern Illinois University. Used with permission of the Center for Archaeological Investigations).

monly acknowledged for his strong commitment to producing reports soon after a project was completed, he often is castigated for achieving his goal with fairly superficial products that were largely descriptive and relied on trait lists (see Dye, this volume). In his defense for the Jonathan Creek project, he could not have done more given the circumstances. The New Deal labor had departed long before the artifacts were processed and cataloged, and no federal funds were available after World War II to complete the lab work. Without a comprehensive artifact inventory and because the site lacked stratigraphy, Webb focused his energies on architectural features of different forms as the key to unlocking the occupation history of the site.

Webb's interpretive efforts for Jonathan Creek were strongly influenced by the paradigms that guided and emerged from the New Deal era in Southeastern archaeology: chronology building and migration and diffusion as sources of change. Webb applied the direct historical approach to associate certain archaeological phenomena with historically documented Native American tribes, reflecting an interpretive framework entrenched within the foreshortened sense of time depth that had characterized American archaeology prior to World War II and before the first applications of the radiocarbon dating method. Webb argued that the Jonathan Creek site had two major periods of occupation, and he drew on the chronicles of the sixteenth-century de Soto entrada and ethnohistoric accounts of the Chickasaw and Natchez as analogues for each occupation (Bourne 1904; Jennings 1941; Le Page du Pratz 1976 [1774]; Swanton 1911, 1946; Vega 1951; Webb 1952:134–138; see also Schroeder 2005). The first occupation, which was represented by wall trench structures, pit houses, and palisades with long rectangular bastions, Webb speculatively attributed to the Chickasaw. The second occupation of the site, which was represented by square single-post structures, started out small and grew over time during which the residents experimented with several bastion designs: small square bastions, reinforced circular bastions, and small square bastions with rounded corners. Webb assigned this second occupation of the site to the Natchez.

## The Jonathan Creek Site and Its Interpretive Potential Today

Some of Webb's reluctance to expand the Jonathan Creek report to include reconstruction of ancient lifeways, or to fit the site into the emerging culture historical nomenclature for eastern North America (e.g., Griffin 1946, 1952, 1967), may have been an outgrowth of his lack of formal training in anthropology and archaeology and the fact that he had never earned a doctorate (e.g., Milner and Smith 1986; Schwartz 1967). Webb was certainly a scholar of his times, and his scientific conservatism, stubbornness, and, perhaps, intellectual insecurities likely constrained his interpretive efforts (see Dye, this volume).

In my own work with the evidence of perishable architecture at Jonathan Creek, I have identified examples of structure superpositioning that are the reverse of Webb's posited sequence. I have noted at least two wall trench foundations that postdate single-post buildings—for a systematic critique of Webb's inferences about the occupational history of Jonathan Creek, see Schroeder (2005). Accelerator mass spectrometry (AMS) radiocarbon dates obtained on several samples of corn and wood (fortuitously saved by the excavators and never treated with preservatives) are tightly clustered, statistically indistinguishable from one another, and fall, at the 2σ level, within the thirteenth century A.D. (Table 9.2; Schroeder 2006, 2009). My currently limited reanalysis of ceramics supports this chronological placement for at least a significant part of the site (Schroeder 2007). These analyses, which really were not an option for Webb when he was preparing the site report, weaken the direct historic analogies that he made with the eighteenth-century Chickasaw and Natchez. Furthermore, the contradictory architectural evidence that I have identified undermines his argument in support of two separate and distinct occupations of the site.

Because the evidence for significant temporal differences in structure architectural style at the site is ambiguous, explanations for architectural variability need to be sought elsewhere. For example, the different building styles may reflect functional distinctions such as houses designed for occupation during different seasons, menstrual huts, public buildings, and small storage structures or sweatlodges as described in a variety of ethnohistoric sources (e.g., Baird 1974; Bartram 1791; Galloway 1997; Grinnell 1919; Hall 1976 [1801]; Mehta 2007). Alternatively, some of the distinctive architecture may symbolize membership in a particular social group or status differentiation, or it may represent ethnic or other differences among contemporaneous occupants of the site (Schroeder 2011). For reasons detailed elsewhere (Schroeder 2005), the functional explanations of seasonality, storage, sweatlodge, and menstrual hut are not well supported by the available data from Jonathan Creek.

Among the 89 structures uncovered and mapped at Jonathan Creek, 86 have a square or rectangular floor plan (Figure 9.2). Of these, 31 were erected with single-post foundations, and the remaining are variations on wall trench construction, including five unusual buildings that had three massive postholes evenly spaced down the centerline of the structure. In addition, the ex-

Table 9.2. AMS radiocarbon dates from Jonathan Creek

| Sample No. | Context | Conventional Radiocarbon Age | Intercept | 1σ Calibrated Result | 2σ Calibrated Result |
|---|---|---|---|---|---|
| Beta-180074 | Pit in House Fea. 13 | 790 ± 40 B.P. | Cal A.D. 1260 | Cal A.D. 1220–1270 | Cal A.D. 1180–1290 |
| Beta-180075 | Floor of House Fea. 31 | 780 ± 40 B.P. | Cal A.D. 1260 | Cal A.D. 1230–1280 | Cal A.D. 1190–1290 |
| Beta-180076 | Midden Fea. 38 | 820 ± 40 B.P. | Cal A.D. 1230 | Cal A.D. 1190–1260 | Cal A.D. 1160–1280 |
| Beta-180077 | House Fea. 44 | 800 ± 40 B.P. | Cal A.D. 1250 | Cal A.D. 1210–1270 | Cal A.D. 1180–1280 |

*Note:* Calibration according to Stuiver et al. 1998.

cavators identified three distinctive post circles that I consider to have been ritual, nondomestic features. In an effort to identify the origins of some of the variation in perishable architecture at the site, I undertook an analysis of floor plan, floor area, post mold and posthole diameter, post mold and post-hole depth, post spacing, number of posts per structure wall, wall trench width and depth, post slant, and location within the community (the details are presented in Schroeder 2011). The interpretations derive from an acceptance that most Mississippian societies had a form of political organization called "chiefdom"; the recognition that the social, political, and economic conditions of these societies were dynamic and highly variable, which also implies that the physical and social boundaries of these societies varied in permeability; and an interest in approaching the investigation of everyday life through architecture and landscape.

To briefly summarize, a restricted range of floor plans and technological approaches to engineering rigid walls structured both the domestic architecture in the village and the larger buildings on the summits of two low platform mounds. Evidence from the diverse wall trench foundations in the village, including the slant of posts in the ground, supports an inference that both hipped and gable roof forms were used, and it is possible that some of the rigid walls supported a separate curved roof. The variation in the above-ground appearance of domestic buildings in the village might be associated with social or ethnic identity, but basic engineering knowledge of construction technology, such as how to excavate a wall trench and the size of saplings appropriate for the walls, was shared among their builders. Single-post structures with square/rectangular floor plans were erected using techniques that were derived from a different system of shared knowledge. For both wall trench and single-post buildings, however, there is enough variation in the execution to suggest that individual households created structures for their own use within the constraints posed by the values and traditions of their social identity and the tools available to them, and that the community may have been filled with houses of diverse external appearance.

The location and size of mound summit buildings, which may have been more elaborately decorated than non-mound structures, signaled the political, social, and ritual distinctiveness of these buildings, and yet they were erected using the same practices, tools, and materials that were applied to constructions in the village. Because mound summit architecture in the Southeast is typically associated with elite members of society, the individuals of high rank at Jonathan Creek enjoyed some of the privileges of their rank as recognized at the local level, but they shared in many of the vernacular traditions of the community, making them simply the first among many (e.g., Gougeon 2006).

## How Far We Have Come

The interpretive frameworks that today guide and structure archaeological research in the eastern United States have evolved considerably from the eighteenth- and nineteenth-century antiquarian concerns with museum-quality artifacts and colonialist speculations about the origins of the moundbuilders. In the two decades leading up to the New Deal, a relatively small number of archaeologists working in the eastern United States struggled to make sense of the scattered and baffling pieces of prehistory that lined the shelves of museums, departments of anthropology, and state and local historical societies, and began to confront thorny problems about archaeological cultures and time, moving beyond the interpretive limitations created by a timeless view of the past. The excavations conducted with money from New Deal relief agencies produced such massive amounts of comparable and systematically collected data that regional patterns became discernible, while stratigraphic excavations and ceramic seriations helped archaeologists gain some control over chronology, making it feasible, at last, for the development of synthetic overviews of the culture history of eastern North America (Ford and Willey 1941; Griffin 1946, 1952, 1967).

Although I have not done justice to the impact of cultural ecology, neo-evolutionary thought, and the New Archaeology on archaeological research after World War II (see Willey and Sabloff 1995), I recognize that these perspectives still inform much of the work being done today in the Southeast, as do the synthetic culture histories sketched out by Ford and Willey and by Griffin. In recent years, many archaeologists in the region have turned their attention to trying to understand the origins of variation and diversity in archaeological phenomena—the kind of "white noise" that was disregarded during the years that archaeologists were seeking to establish a cultural historical structure for the region and to identify cross-cultural commonalities in the human experience—and in so doing, they have drawn on practice theory and concepts of agency to guide interpretations about the lived experiences of people in the past. Since the New Deal era, the disciplinary landscape of archaeology has grown increasingly complex and multidimensional, and more numerous in terms of practitioners, and yet our practices, whether research driven, mandated by federal compliance, or focused on heritage preservation and outreach, continue to engage stakeholders and the public through discourses on identity, history, land rights, education, heritage preservation, and scientific research.

## Acknowledgments

I would like to express my thanks to Bernard Means for the invitation to join the session he organized for the Biennial Gordon R. Willey Symposium on the History of Archaeology at the 2010 SAA meetings and for his interest in having me prepare a contribution to this volume. Comments and suggestions from Bernard Means, Larry Nesper, Alice Kehoe, and one anonymous reviewer helped me to polish my prose and refine the focus of the chapter. The architectural research all too briefly summarized in this chapter benefited from the assistance of Tanya Treptow and Bryan Haley; the encouragement of George Milner, Nancy O'Malley, and George Crothers; and financial support from the Vilas Associates Program, the Wisconsin Alumni Research Foundation, the Graduate School, and the Vilas Life Cycle Professorship Program, all at the University of Wisconsin. I am especially grateful to Matthew Harris and his staff in the Special Collections Library at the University of Kentucky for facilitating my access to William S. Webb's correspondence and files.

# 10

# New Deal Archaeology in West-Central Kentucky

## Excavations at Annis Village

*Scott W. Hammerstedt*

The New Deal archaeological program in Kentucky, directed by William S. Webb, conducted fieldwork at more than 70 sites between 1937 and 1941. While only about a quarter of these excavations were published, New Deal archaeology made tremendous contributions not only to contemporary knowledge of Kentucky's prehistory but also to the professionalization of archaeology. New Deal excavations were unique because of the scale of the work, including the amount of earth moved, the money available, and the size of the work crews. While the techniques used do not always measure up to modern standards, the resulting collections are often all that remains from these sites and, when used in tandem with current methods, can be extremely valuable.

Here I review work conducted by the Works Progress Administration (WPA) from 1939 to 1940 and by the Pennsylvania State University from 2002 to 2004 at Annis, a single-mound Mississippian site along the Big Bend of the Green River in Butler County, Kentucky. The combined excavations exposed well over 5,000 m$^2$ of the site (including the complete excavation of the platform mound), plotted several hundred features, and recovered thousands of artifacts. The high quality of WPA field notes allowed me to relocate previous grids and trenches to tie together excavations conducted more than 60 years apart. The combined strengths of WPA and modern archaeological techniques complement one another in this case, permit an "archaeology of archaeology," and result in a meaningful reconstruction of the site's occupation.

### A Brief History of Pre–New Deal Kentucky Archaeology

It is not possible to fully understand New Deal archaeology in Kentucky without first summarizing earlier work in the state. Early accounts were speculative in nature and favored the view that the earthworks found in Kentucky were beyond the capability of American Indians and may have been constructed by an unknown race of Mound Builders (Schwartz 1967). This was a common belief in the United States at the time and one that would not be refuted until the publication of a major report at the end of the nineteenth century (Thomas 1894). A partial exception to this was provided by Rafinesque (1824), who generated a list of known sites from across the state but still speculated wildly on the origin of American Indians. By the late nineteenth and early twentieth century, systematic attempts were made to record archaeological sites in Kentucky and adjacent states, with Squier and Davis's (1998 [1848]) landmark description of earthworks serving as an early example. Most published archaeological reports at this time were site-specific and descriptive (Lewis 1996; Schwartz 1967), although Young (1910) discussed a range of categories of archaeological remains from multiple sites, and Smith (1910) produced what Schwartz (1967:20–21) calls the "first organized archeological report on a Kentucky site." In these reports, the authors attempted to move beyond simple description of a single site to provide broader information on categories of artifacts, their potential uses, and comparisons with nearby areas.

Also at this time, Clarence B. Moore, a wealthy philanthropist from Philadelphia, was engaged in his long-term study of American Indian mound sites in the southeastern United States. Moore, sponsored by the Academy of Natural Sciences of Philadelphia, traveled the Southeast every fall through spring from 1891 to 1918 aboard his steamboat, the *Gopher of Philadelphia,* to excavate sites identified by his workers the previous summer (Knight 1996; Polhemus 2002). Each summer, he returned to Philadelphia and prepared at his personal expense detailed and well-illustrated reports, albeit still largely without interpretation. In 1916, Moore visited the Green River region of Kentucky, including Annis, publishing his results later that year (Moore 1916).

Despite the efforts of Moore and a handful of others, early twentieth-century archaeology in Kentucky was still largely nonprofessional. Published information was still largely speculative and often tied solely to description. New developments, however, were about to provide the impetus for rapid leaps in the quality of Kentucky's archaeological work.

## The New Deal Archaeological Program in Kentucky

The professionalization of archaeology in Kentucky was largely due to the influence of William S. Webb, a professor of physics at the University of

Kentucky and a co-founder of the university's Department of Anthropology. Along with William D. Funkhouser, Webb founded the Department of Anthropology in 1927, in part so they could obtain funding from the National Research Council and buy a field truck (Haag 1965; Lewis 1996; Schwartz 1967). Webb's contributions to Kentucky archaeology have been discussed in preceding chapters (Dye, this volume; Schroeder, this volume); therefore I will provide only a brief outline here.

New Deal excavations in Kentucky were run primarily under the auspices of the WPA, although Civilian Conservation Corps (CCC) laborers were used at the Jonathan Creek site in the Kentucky Basin (Schroeder 2005, this volume; Webb 1952). Projects were done statewide but were focused on Adena sites in the Bluegrass, rockshelters in the Knobs and eastern Kentucky mountains, and Archaic shell mounds and Mississippian villages along the Tennessee, Cumberland, and Green rivers. Archaeologists focused on obtaining stratigraphic information to decipher cultural sequences, expose village and house plans, and recover skeletal remains (Lyon 1996; Milner and Smith 1986). Following the goals of the federal WPA program, projects were primarily conducted in rural counties with high unemployment (Milner and Smith 1986). A total of 72 sites in 17 counties were excavated under the auspices of the New Deal. Twenty-two of these excavations were subsequently published (Milner and Smith 1986).

The program was coordinated from Lexington and relied on supervisors who directed the day-to-day aspects of field projects (Milner and Smith 1986). These men had attended college and were trained in archaeology, history, or a related field and were expected to have experience in museum work and mapping. Many had worked on WPA or Tennessee Valley Authority (TVA) projects in other states, and several had attended the University of Chicago's field school at Kincaid. Supervisors were to know local prehistory and be able to follow orders. They were responsible not only for the fieldwork but also for photography, field records, supply and tool inventories, and excavation summaries (Milner and Smith 1986). Additionally, supervisors occasionally met as a group with Webb to hash out important issues: "August 3–7. Lexington. A series of round-the-table discussions where a number of perplexing questions concerning fieldwork were battled to a finish. As a result some of the forms (burial, feature, and field specimens) will be changed" (Brown 1939–1940:15).

Crew sizes varied from 10 to 50 men, accompanied by several supervisors, a timekeeper, and a tool checker. Laborers served as "shovel men" or "trowel men," depending on their level of expertise, and were paid accordingly. Shovel men removed overburden and pushed wheelbarrows while trowel men excavated features and burials. In this manner, large groups of men were trained and put to work despite high turnover. The total statewide workforce sometimes approached 300 (Milner and Smith 1986:62).

With the beginning of World War II, funding for archaeological projects vanished and most of the laborers found themselves in military service or in other war-related industries. By March 1942, all New Deal archaeology in Kentucky had come to a halt. As a result, many of the sites excavated during this period were not studied (let alone published) and, in many cases, the artifacts remained unwashed and uncataloged.

## The WPA Archaeological Program at Annis, 1939–1940

The WPA excavations at Annis took place from February 11, 1939, to April 10, 1940, and were supervised by Ralph D. Brown. Brown received his bachelor's degree from the University of Minnesota in 1929 and had previous experience in Algeria, France, Minnesota, and New Mexico. He was hired by Webb in 1938 and eventually became the state WPA supervisor (Lyon 1996:96; Milner and Smith 1986:22). Brown was an above-average excavator who took high-quality field notes; unfortunately, the notebook of his daily observations from February 11 to May 29, 1939, is missing. However, feature forms and maps from that time are available to fill in some of the gaps.

Features were mapped, described, and photographed before excavation. Maps were carefully plotted, often at night when excavation was done for the day. Doris Annis Tichenor, whose family Brown boarded with during the excavations, recalls him working late at night on notes and piecing together potsherds by the light of kerosene lamps; most Kentucky supervisors routinely worked 12- to 13-hour days (Milner and Smith 1986:23–24). In addition, on at least one occasion, Brown gave a tour of the site to local schoolchildren. A report on this visit entitled "The Indian Village Site," written by a child in late November 1939, was found in the personal papers of Lena Grey Annis and is now in the possession of Doris Tichenor. Shortly thereafter, on December 5, Brown "regaled the students of Morgantown with an illustrated talk on Kentucky archaeological excavations. They were rapt. I heard not a whisper" (Brown 1939–1940:46). Events such as these clearly would have added to Brown's workload.

Brown remained in touch with the Annis family for many years until his death; a 1947 letter to the family sent from Tokyo (where he was stationed as part of the U.S. occupation force) inquired whether there was "a way for you to get and send to me one of those fine old Kentucky country hams. Such things are unprocurable and almost unthinkable over here" (Brown 1947). There is no record to indicate whether this request was met.

Figure 10.1. Obtaining water to wet down extremely dry soil (UKMA negative #3279; Courtesy of the William S. Webb Museum of Anthropology, University of Kentucky).

It is clear from Brown's notes that he faced numerous obstacles during the Annis project. Chief among these were weather, personnel, and equipment. Fieldwork was carried out during all seasons, including the cold winter. He managed to retain some good humor: the description accompanying one photograph showing the site covered in snow reads simply, "Winter work is sometimes carried on under drawbacks." This good humor would have come in handy during the cold winter of 1940, when the temperature was sometimes as low as 2 degrees. Brown's comment on that day: "Cold enough." Photographs taken during the excavation of the platform mound show that the Green River had frozen over and the crew had lit fires in drums to keep warm and thaw the ground, which had sometimes frozen nearly a foot beneath the surface. Brown's notes indicate that on at least one occasion (January 31, 1940) he sent a worker to the site at 3:00 a.m. to start the fires in order to thaw the ground enough to be able to start excavating at 6:00 a.m. (Brown 1939–1940:61). On several other days men were tasked simply with removing snow (Brown 1939–1940:51, 55).

The crew faced a different set of adverse conditions during the summer and fall of 1939, when extremely dry conditions made excavations difficult. Figure 10.1 shows an ingenious method of obtaining water from the Green River to wet down baked soil. According to the description found on the back of the photo, the bucket was weighted and lowered itself to the water's edge. The winch was equipped with a hand brake and a Ford crank, 42 turns of which would return the full bucket. The project supplied the bucket, rope, and nails, the boards were scavenged from the river, and the men supplied the remaining materials.

Personnel issues were also a common problem, notably in terms of the number of workers and the duration of their employment. WPA regulations stated that workers could only be employed for 18 months, could only be reappointed after a further 30 days (Lyon 1996:73–74), and were only allowed to work a certain number of hours per week. Therefore, retaining experienced workers was a constant problem. Brown was keenly aware of this issue, as these excerpts from his field notes attest:

> July 24. [John] Cotter came in morning—went to Morgantown with him to check upon assignables. There seemed to be sufficient to permit this unit to operate in spite of any devastation the 18-month regulation may perpetrate [Brown 1939–1940:12].
>
> Aug. 8. This is the last day for 13 men who are being dropped on account of the 18-month regulation. And I notified them. My crew will now number only 24 or 23 depending on the length of stay allowed to the timekeepers [Brown 1939–1940:15].
>
> Oct. 31. Had a crew which worked its time out in two hours, after that only 4 men remained to finish the day [Brown 1939–1940:38].

He apparently had at least one worker who was not up to par: "Nov. 3. To Morgantown with payroll for sacking the timekeeper" (Brown 1939–1940: 39). In several other cases, however, he mentions that new workers were performing well. Because of issues such as these, the crew ranged from just a handful of men to over 30 depending on the day.

Finally, equipment was in relatively short supply and in some cases was inferior: "is very slow, since I can get no mattocks and have only two . . . To town with payroll and to change 5 bad shovels for better ones, which I finally got" (Brown 1939–1940:20). However, Brown was able to devise a system to get around some of these issues when working in a confined space in the mound: "One mattock man loosens the dirt for 4 shovelers, the 4 shovelers tend 4 wheelbarrows, which, going into one side and out the other to minimize traffic problems, form a fairly even and continuous line—two coming and two going" (Brown 1939–1940:37).

One of the strengths of nearly all WPA archaeological projects in Kentucky is the scale of the excavations, and Annis is no exception. The Annis site complex consists of three components (Figure 10.2): a platform mound (which was eroding into the river), a palisaded village, and a low sand mound, each of which was given its own site number and excavated separately. Brown's crew excavated the platform and sand mounds in their entirety along with much of the village, exposing more than 5,000 m$^2$ of area, producing more than 25,000 artifacts, and recording several hundred features. These excavations are described in more detail elsewhere (Hammerstedt 2005a).

Excavation procedures followed Webb's general statewide plan. An arbitrary 0-foot stake was placed south of the sand mound and a north–south baseline extended from it to the river, with half of the site falling on each side of the line. Grid north roughly corresponded with magnetic south. The site was then staked out at 5-foot intervals, labeled with a northing coordinate and then L1, L2, etc. and R1, R2, etc. depending on whether the square was to the left or right of the baseline; e.g., 150L3 was 150 feet north and 15 feet west of the 0-foot stake. In general, workers excavated in 5-×-5-foot blocks in 6-inch levels, although there were some exceptions (Hammerstedt 2005a).

Brown did not always easily recognize features in the soil at Annis, which ranged from "a veritable quicksand" (as described on some feature forms) to very dry: "Excavation is becoming quite difficult on account of extreme dryness of soil, hindering both digging and noting of contrast of fill with surrounding soil. It slows the work noticeably" (Brown 1939–1940:9). We had the same issues in 2002–2004.

*Annis Sand Mound (15BT21).* Excavation began on the Sand Mound in the winter of 1939. This low mound, built largely of sand, was directly grid south of the outermost palisade (Figure 10.2). Unfortunately, Brown's field notebook for this time period has been lost, although individual feature forms are still available. The mound was 1 m high and approximately 35 by 30 m in diameter. The WPA excavators dug in 9-inch levels and a combination of 5- and 10-foot squares. Soil was not screened. Five burials, several features, and numerous artifacts, primarily flaked stone, were found. Only 10 sherds were recovered; nine of these were in the top 1 to 1.5 feet. Based on the lack of ceramics and the projectile points found, I believe that the sand mound is likely Archaic and predates the rest of the site by several thousand years.

*Annis Village (15BT20).* Once the sand mound excavations were completed, work moved north to the village. The excavations were done in 5-foot squares and 6-inch levels. The units extended to a fence line to the west. It is unclear why Brown and his crew did not excavate farther to the east

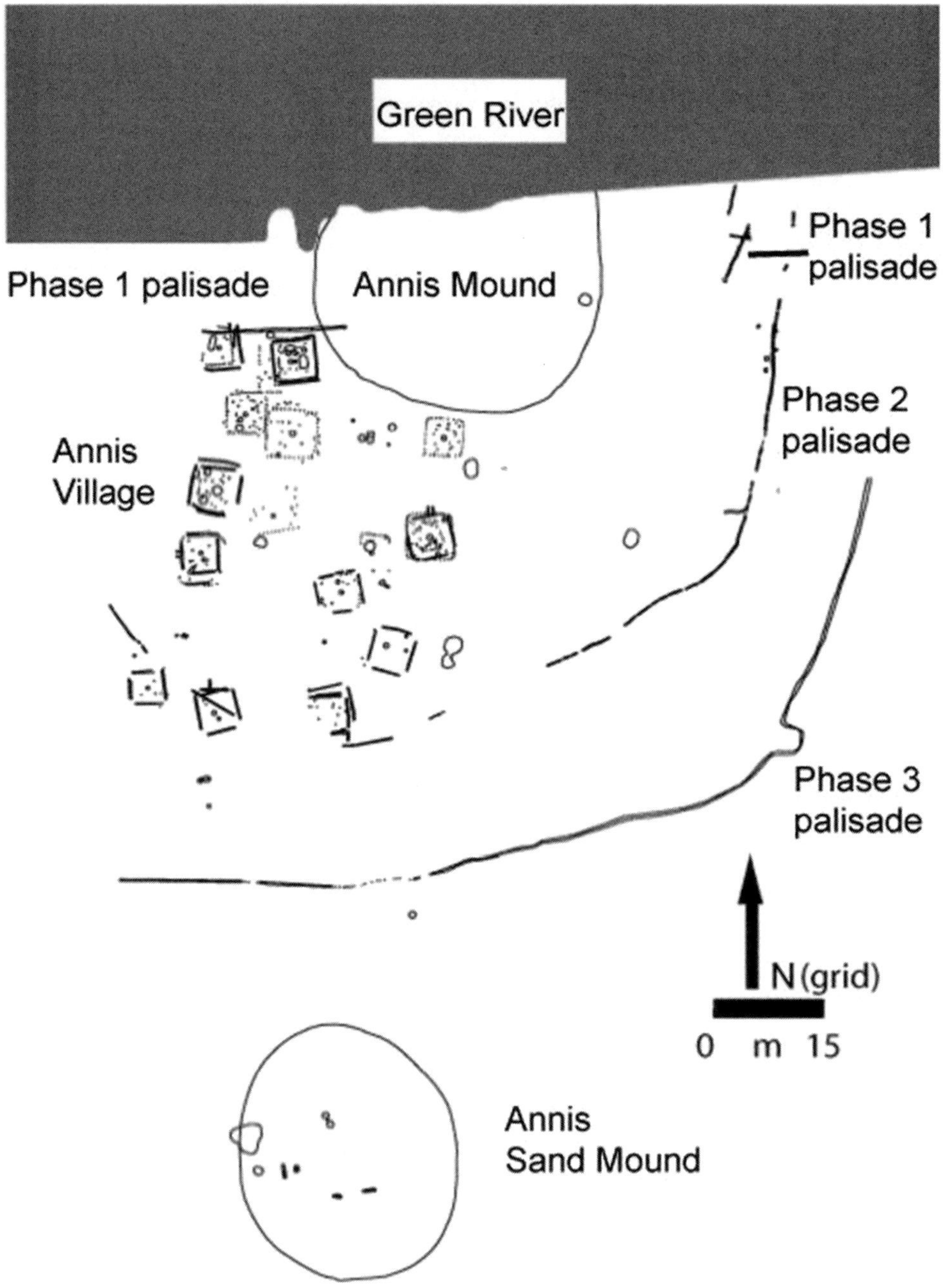


Figure 10.2. Annis site plan.

(perhaps time constraints were an issue) but they did follow out several palisade lines in that direction.

The work in the village area revealed 16 structure areas (Figure 10.2); many of these were rebuilt at least once. Both single set-post and wall trench structures were present and nearly all possessed a central hearth and one or more interior pits or post molds. Some of these had been burned. Walls and features were usually pedestaled, an issue I will return to below. Although no earth was screened during the excavations, interesting or unusual objects such as vessel fragments, refuse deposits, and caches were often piece plotted, photographed, and described in situ.

Parts of three concentric palisades that surrounded the site were found. These have been named Phase 1, 2, and 3 to correlate with mound construction stages. Some sections of these were excavated but others were simply exposed, mapped, and backfilled. One bastion was identified on the outermost (Phase 3) palisade (Figure 10.2). Curiously, this was the only bastion recorded, raising the possibility that its function may not have been solely defensive and it may have served as a watchtower.

*Annis Mound (15BT2).* The platform mound was the final part of the site to be excavated. It was 3.7 m tall and measured roughly 33 m on a side before erosion took its toll (Figure 10.3, top). As with so many other mounds in the southeastern United States, Clarence B. Moore had previously tested the mound in 1916. He proclaimed it to be "the largest mound seen of or heard of by us on Green river" (Moore 1916:480). Moore excavated a "trial hole" 17.5 $m^2$ in area and nearly 4 m deep in the center of the mound. He reported one hearth in this unit but did not find anything of interest to him and moved on. Brown's crew recorded Moore's pit and it appears in several maps and photographs.

Mound excavation began on August 23, 1939. The early excavation trenches followed the classic "slicing" method in which vertical slices were removed sequentially. However, one of these slices revealed several post molds in profile and Brown abandoned this method in favor of a horizontal clearing operation (Brown 1939–1940:30). This was a fortunate development as this change in strategy identified multiple summit structures. Brown clearly believed that soil for the mound was obtained locally as the fill was a "sandy clay, such as would be produced by a mixture of soils in the neighborhood, chiefly to the west and northwest, from whence the soil from the mound was probably got" (Brown 1939–1940:21).

Based upon Brown's notes, maps, and photographs, it is clear that there were four occupation levels present within the mound (Figure 10.3, bottom). The earliest of these consisted of two clusters of post molds located beneath

Figure 10.3. Top: The platform mound at Annis before excavation, 1939, facing grid northeast. The Green River lies behind the mound in this photo (UKMA negative #3250; Courtesy of the William S. Webb Museum of Anthropology, University of Kentucky). Bottom: Annis Mound stage schematic (Courtesy of *Southeastern Archaeology*).

the mound, in Brown's premound "Old Humus," but they form no discernible pattern. An additional post was found to the west but was determined to be part of a later construction episode (Hammerstedt 2005a:107, 133).

The first phase of mound building was named the Sub-Primary mound by Brown. I have renamed it Phase 1 to correlate with the palisade that was likely constructed at the same time. This mound was 24 × 15 m in area and was raised to a height of 70 cm. A large structure, with a floor area of at least

88 $m^2$, was uncovered on the mound summit. The exact size of the structure is unclear because of erosion. It was rebuilt at least once and numerous hearths and trash-filled pits were found within the walls. Two large middens were on the western flank of the mound. These primarily consisted of processed animal bone, but sherds and stone artifacts were also present. The recording of these middens as separate features is testament to Brown's skill as an excavator. Flank middens were rarely noted by WPA-era investigators—even though they must have seen many of them.

The second stage of the mound, called the Primary mound or Phase 2, measured 30 × 18 m at its base and nearly 1 m of soil was added to make the entire mound 1.6 m tall (Figure 10.3). Another structure was built on the surface; this one encompassed at least 250 $m^2$, although erosion once again took its toll. The sheer size of this building suggests that the outer line of posts was a fence or enclosure that screened an interior building. Hearths and other fire-related features were the only features found on the summit and only a handful of artifacts were present.

The final stage of the mound was called the Secondary mound or Phase 3. This stage brought the mound to its final size of 33.5 m on a side and 3.7 m tall (Figure 10.3). A wall trench structure was constructed on the summit. Erosion is once again a problem, but the structure was at least 105 $m^2$ in area. A narrow entryway was present on the eastern wall. A large patch of burned earth, charcoal, and charred cane and roof pole fragments suggests that the building was burned. Only a handful of artifacts were recovered from features; most are from mound fill. It is possible that the features were cleaned out before the structure was burned.

Once the excavation of the mound was completed in April 1940, the mound was rebuilt to its original dimensions at the request of the Annis family. The rebuilt mound was placed roughly 60 feet grid south of its original location to protect it from further erosion, and a mulberry tree was planted on the summit to replace one that was removed when the project began. The mound still stands in that spot today, although Mr. Annis remarked until his death that he much preferred the original location (Doris Tichenor, personal communication 2002).

## The Penn State Archaeological Program at Annis, 2002–2004

Apart from a few University of Kentucky graduate student projects, including one master's thesis (Fryman 1967; Stokes 1995; Young 1962), the Annis collection lay mostly undisturbed for the next 60 years. I became interested in the site in 2001 and it was the subject of my doctoral dissertation (Hammerstedt 2005a, 2005b, 2007). While there are problems with the collection, the scale of the excavation—although typical for many WPA projects—is simply not feasible today due to the cost of fieldwork. The strengths of the WPA work lie in the exposure of much of the village and the complete excavation and mapping of the mound. Weaknesses lie in the lack of modern techniques, such as screening, flotation, and radiocarbon dating. Since Annis, unlike so many other New Deal sites in the Southeast, was not inundated by a reservoir after excavation, a return to the site seemed profitable. Focused excavations to locate WPA trenches and to collect biological material complement the strengths of the WPA effort and make up for some of its deficiencies.

From 2002–2004, Penn State field schools and volunteer crews directed by George Milner and myself conducted excavations at Annis that exposed a total of 251 $m^2$. The 2004 excavations did not encounter any WPA excavations and are not discussed here. In the more than 60 years between the WPA work and our arrival at the site, the 0-foot stake used by Brown was lost. However, as mentioned above, the western edge of the WPA excavations stopped at a fence line that is included on all their maps. I noticed that the fence bisected one particular pit, Feature 67, within a structure just west of the mound. Brown had photographed this feature and both the fence and the pit are clearly visible. On my first visit to the site in the summer of 2001, remnants of this fence were still in place, although they had been absorbed by nearby trees. In 2002, George Milner and I took a crew of Penn State student volunteers to Annis. Using the locations of the platform mound and the sand mound as a guide, we decided to excavate along the fence in an effort to find the remnants of Feature 67. We opened up a number of test units in this area; nearly all proved to be in WPA backfill.

After some initial failures, we managed to relocate an unexcavated portion of Feature 67. Excavation was difficult in this area due to a combination of wet soils and roots, yet the feature was clearly visible. This gave us one known point to match the WPA grid. However, we still needed more. I mentioned above that Brown's crew pedestaled structures while excavating and that the wall trenches were not always completely removed. We decided to branch out to see whether any remnants of the structure and palisade located near Feature 67 could be found. Excavation was once again a bit of a challenge, but the pedestaled trenches were identified as intersecting bands of light soil surrounded by WPA backfill. Further testing also identified the previously excavated remnants of a hearth, part of the Phase 1 palisade, and a corner of Structure 15 (Figure 10.4). The combination of these

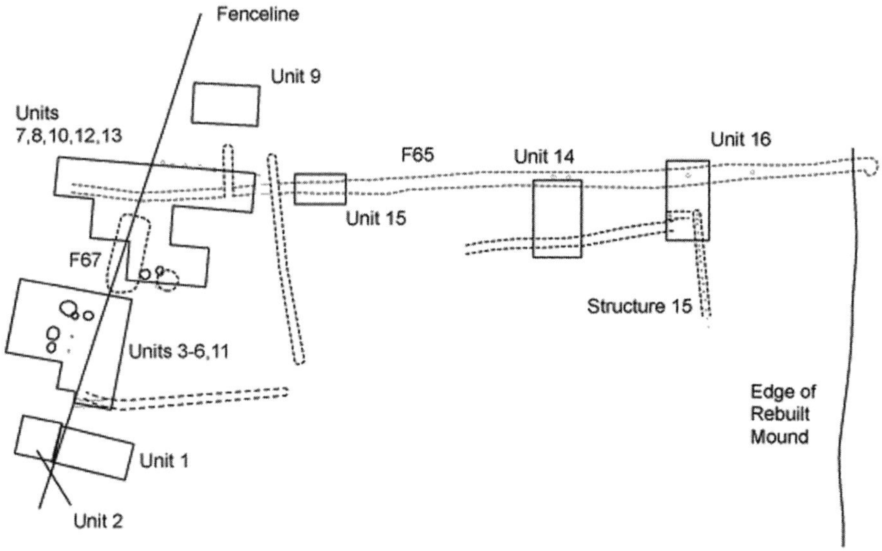


Figure 10.4. The 2002 Penn State excavation units at Annis in the vicinity of Feature 67. Relocated features originally exposed by the WPA are shown as dotted lines.

points gave us a reasonably good idea of how the WPA grid was laid out and we regarded the 2002 season as a success (Hammerstedt 2005a:81–86).

In 2003, a Penn State field school returned to Annis, focusing efforts on an area east of the mound. We hoped to identify portions of the palisade and structures to further reconcile the grid systems. We successfully relocated one palisade (the Phase 2 construction) precisely where we thought it might be. Additionally, in and around one of our test units at the southern edge of the exposed palisade, we found a clear trace of the WPA excavation. In this area, we documented a large patch of grayish-brown fill above the palisade. Part of an eyeglass lens, metal objects (including an overalls clasp), and large pieces of sandstone were found in this fill. This disturbed area was nearly 2 m long and followed the same path as the underlying, but unexcavated, palisade. According to Brown's notes, the WPA excavation of this area took place in February 1940 during several days of rain (Brown 1939–1940:66). The palisade was not excavated at that time but was exposed, mapped, and reburied. The appearance of the soil was consistent with dirt churned up and packed by many pairs of boots. That is, it looked just like compacted backdirt. Matching up the end of the WPA-excavated palisade with the segments we located in 2003 gave us another fixed point to reconcile the two grids (Hammerstedt 2005a:87–93). One other piece of evidence gave us the final piece of the puzzle. One of our test units near the mound bore clear evidence of historic disturbance—a deep trench in the profile of the northern half of the unit. Examination of Brown's maps showed that this was the edge of an area dug in 1940 (Hammerstedt 2005a:93–94).

The combination of WPA points identified in our 2002 and 2003 seasons confirmed that the WPA grid and our arbitrary grid were off by only slightly more than 3 degrees. By rotating features around known points in AutoCAD, we were able to fully reconcile the grids and securely plot the locations of WPA and Penn State–excavated features with respect to one another. As I discuss elsewhere (Hammerstedt 2005a), this proved crucial to understanding the site and its occupational history and was only possible because of the quality of Ralph Brown's notes. As Brown moved on to other projects and the WPA archaeological program in Kentucky came to a close shortly after the Annis fieldwork, a final report was never produced. The following interpretations come directly from my examination of Brown's field notes and insights and the combination of WPA and later work by Penn State crews.

## The Occupational History of Annis

Space does not permit me to discuss my interpretation of the site's occupational history and social organization in detail, but this has been presented elsewhere (Hammerstedt 2005a). I will simply provide a brief summary here. The earliest use of the site was likely during the Archaic period when the sand mound was constructed. However, the primary occupation was during the Mississippian period. I have divided the Mississippian occupation into four subperiods: Premound and Phases 1–3. It is important to note here that these phases are strictly internal; that is, they do not represent true archaeological phases. The entire Mississippian component at Annis falls within what has been termed the Tinsley Hill phase in southern Indiana and western Kentucky and the Thruston phase in central Tennessee (Butler 1991; Smith 1992).

*Premound.* The Old Humus premound deposit is the earliest of the Mississippian deposits. Based on the presence of a Ramey Incised sherd at this level, the Old Humus tentatively dates to the twelfth to thirteenth century (Fowler and Hall 1972; Milner et al. 1984). It consists solely of two scatters of post molds that do not form any pattern.

*Phase 1.* Phase 1 consists of the Sub-Primary mound and the innermost palisade. As mentioned above, the Sub-Primary mound was just under a meter tall and a large structure was built on its summit. Based on the presence of hearths, trash-filled pits, and two flank middens, I interpret this as a residential building, probably for a locally important person or family.

The inner palisade was also likely built at this time. This palisade enclosed .3 ha of the site and consisted of large posts set into a nearly 1-m-deep trench. Two radiocarbon assays were obtained from the 2003 excavation of the eastern portion of this palisade: Beta-181396 (660 ± 30 B.P.; cal 2σ A.D. 1278–1392); and Beta-181398 (630 ± 30 B.P.; cal 2σ A.D. 1287–1398). These assays were statistically identical and created a pooled radiocarbon date of 645 ± 21 B.P. (cal A.D. 1285–1391). Although I do not have corresponding dates from the Sub-Primary mound, diagnostic sherds (Ramey Incised, Powell Plain, and Matthews Incised, *var. Manly*) from feature fill support this date.

*Phase 2.* During Phase 2, the mound's footprint was increased and its height was raised to 1.6 m. The enlarged mound (the Primary mound) covered parts of the Phase 1 palisade. The sheer size of the summit structure means that the outer wall was likely an enclosure surrounding an interior building. I have interpreted this structure as nonresidential based on the low numbers of artifacts present and the lack of pits (all features were hearths or patches of burned earth that may have been surface fires).

At or about this time, the middle palisade was constructed. It enclosed approximately .8 ha, more than doubling the size of the previous enclosure. It was also built by setting posts into a deep trench. A radiocarbon date (Beta-181397) of 710 ± 30 B.P. (cal 2σ A.D. 1256–1385) was acquired.

*Phase 3.* At this time, the mound was enlarged to its final height of 3.7 m. Another summit structure was erected; this one once again seems to have been residential based on the reappearance of trash-filled pits and domestic debris. The structure was likely burned and, since only a handful of artifacts were found in features, it may have been intentionally and thoroughly cleaned before the fire was set.

The outermost palisade was likely contemporaneous with the final phase of mound construction. It enlarged the enclosed village to 1.3 to 1.8 ha (depending on the unknown extent of riverbank erosion). We were unable to relocate this palisade in 2004, but WPA photographs suggest that it was built in the same way as the previous two. This palisade is unique in that it has one bastion. This bastion, however, would not have been particularly effective alone. I suggest that it may have served as a watchtower or fortified gate.

*Summary.* An initial settlement of the riverbank was present before mound construction began. Each identified construction phase saw an enlargement of the mound and the area circumscribed by the palisade, although I have only been able to assign a handful of village houses to particular phases (Hammerstedt 2005a:207–216). I believe that the use of the mound shifted over time from residential to ritual/communal and back again based on the nature of summit buildings and artifacts. However, the mound likely remained the focus of the community through time no matter which specific activities may have been occurring on it.

## Conclusion

New Deal archaeology has had a lasting positive impact on research in Kentucky. Its initial contribution was to create a set of standards and to professionalize the discipline, an impact that cannot be overstated. Webb's emphasis on publication resulted in more than 20 monographs that, while representing fewer than half of the total number of sites excavated, in many cases still provide the only published information available from these sites. These and other WPA monographs served as a model for later professional contributions to the literature, including the FAI-270 project volumes (George Milner, personal communication 2010).

While many WPA collections in Kentucky and elsewhere were left unanalyzed at the onset of World War II, this has proven to be a mixed blessing. Modern researchers are now taking advantage of these collections and are studying them using modern methods and techniques. While WPA excavators did not collect flotation samples or screen their soil, and they did not have access to radiocarbon dating, the large-scale exposure of village plans has proven to be of immense value since few projects have the necessary time, money, and labor available today.

We were able to take full advantage of the strengths of the WPA documentation provided by Ralph Brown and his crew. The large area exposed (more than 5,000 m$^2$) and the careful recording of features and structures made the targeted smaller-scale excavations by Penn State crews possible. Brown's willingness to alter excavation strategies in the face of the data allowed much more information to be gleaned from the mound than would otherwise have been the case. Without his skill, the reconstruction and interpretation that I have outlined above would not have been possible. This project illustrates the continued value of these older collections to current archaeologists and I am heartened to see that many researchers continue to use them.

## Acknowledgments

I would like to thank Carroll and Doris Tichenor for serving as gracious hosts during three summers of fieldwork, for protecting the Annis site for many years, and for sharing their firsthand knowledge of Ralph Brown. Thanks also to George Crothers and Nancy O'Malley for granting permission to use photographs and facilitating access to the collections at the William S. Webb Museum of Anthropology. A final thank you to Bernard Means for his invitation to contribute to this volume.

# 11

# Preston Holder's WPA Excavations in Glynn and Chatham Counties, Georgia, 1936–1938

*Kevin Kiernan*

The history of New Deal archaeology on the Georgia coast has remained obscure, because the foremost archaeologist of the coast, Preston Holder, was not permitted to publish the major results of his excavations. His superiors at the Smithsonian Institution in Washington, D.C., at the Ocmulgee National Monument in Macon, Georgia, and at the Works Progress Administration (WPA) offices in Savannah, Georgia, did not allow him to publish his highly detailed progress reports and strongly discouraged and effectively prevented him from developing a Columbia University dissertation on the entire Georgia coast. Because he always expected to publish a final report and to use his findings in his doctoral work, however, Holder has left researchers meticulous and extensive documentary and material evidence. These resources include official and unofficial reports and correspondence; step-by-step methodologies for archaeologists working under WPA constraints; detailed field notes, burial lists, faunal lists, graphs, and contour and profile maps; statistical sherd analyses; artifact displays requisitioned for local interests and tourists; a wide range of photographs, including ceramic keys; and at least 33 large bins containing many thousands of mostly decorated ceramics. These now far-flung resources all manifest Holder's successful, pioneering campaigns, not only in Glynn County but also in Chatham County, Georgia, from May 1936 through January 1938 (Table 11.1). By the time he was done, Holder had discovered at one site and confirmed at another the first unambiguous ceramic chronology in Georgia, had helped to found the Southeastern Archaeological Conference, and had widely distributed unpublished reports on all his excavations from Brunswick to Savannah among his sponsors, su-

Table 11.1. Holder's WPA Excavations in Georgia

| Site Name | Site No. | Location | Dates of Excavation | WPA Project No. |
|---|---|---|---|---|
| Airport | I | St. Simons Island, Glynn County | May 1936 to February 1937 | 165-34-3338 and 165-34-8031 |
| Sea Island Mound | II | Sea Island | May to June 1936 and February to May 1937 | 165-34-3338 and 165-34-8031 |
| Charlie King Mound | III | St. Simons Island, Glynn County | December 1936 and February to March 1937 | 165-34-3338 and 165-34-8031 |
| Gascoigne Bluff | IV | St. Simons Island, Glynn County | April to May 1937 | 165-34-8031 |
| Cannon's Point | V, A–E | St. Simons Island, Glynn County | April to July 1937 | 165-34-8031 |
| Evelyn Mounds | VI, A–E | Brunswick, Glynn County | July to August 1937 | 165-34-8031 |
| Irene Mound | [VII] | Savannah, Chatham County | September 1937 to January 1938 | 165-34-8037 |

periors, and fellow archaeologists in Washington, D.C., as well as in Macon, Brunswick, and Savannah, Georgia.

## Holder Becomes a New Deal Archaeologist

Preston Holder earned a bachelor's degree in anthropology with minors in zoology and paleontology in 1935 from the University of California, Berkeley. Knowing his extensive training and experience in the field with the archaeologist Duncan Strong, Matthew Stirling, chief of the Bureau of American Ethnology at the Smithsonian Institution, hired Holder to supervise excavations of two prehistoric Indian mounds near Tampa, Florida, in 1935–1936. Based on his excellent, relevant work, Holder won the confidence of Stirling and the Smithsonian Institution. When Stirling's colleague Frank M. Setzler, then acting head curator of the Department of Anthropology at the National Museum in Washington, D.C., was looking for an experienced archaeologist to supervise excavations on St. Simons Island, Georgia, and Stirling's brother was unavailable, Holder was the obvious choice (Compton 1936a; Setzler 1936a; Stirling 1936a; Wetmore 1936).

In early March 1936, the Smithsonian had dispatched Setzler on a reconnaissance mission after bulldozers leveling a runway for a New Deal–funded airport on St. Simons Island uncovered ancient human and canine remains beneath a shell wall (Compton 1936b). After a three-day exploratory excavation, Setzler was impressed by the scope of the site, as well as by the many potential sites his hosts showed him on St. Simons and the sea islands to the north and south. After Setzler's return to Washington, Stirling advised Holder to make the 400-mile drive to Macon, Georgia, and confer with Arthur Kelly; Kelly was supervising the excavation of what was soon to become the Ocmulgee National Monument (Stirling 1936b). The Society for Georgia Archaeology (SGA) paid the expenses for the two archaeologists to drive down to St. Simons Island to meet with potential sponsors from the Sea Island Company, the Brunswick Board of Trade, and the SGA (Mallory 1936a), a coalition enticed by the promise of a surge in tourism, jobs, and knowledge of the past. Holder accepted the assignment to supervise excavations on St. Simons and in Glynn County with the understanding that the Sea Island Company would supplement his meager WPA salary for six months (Stirling 1936c; cf. Harrold 1936). After that, Holder expected to be in graduate school.

Setzler was determined to get the St. Simons excavations under way at once. The paperwork moved swiftly through Washington, D.C., and Brunswick, but then languished for many weeks in the Savannah WPA district office. D. G. Nichols, the district director, threw up continual obstacles to the project on St. Simons Island (e.g., Holder 1936a, 1936b, 1936c; Kelly 1936a, 1936b; Nichols 1936a, 1936b). The shrewd and persistent James M. Mallory, a founding member of the SGA, was particularly effective in galvanizing the Sea Island and Brunswick authorities, if not Nichols (Mallory 1936b, 1936c, 1936d). By the end of April, Mallory informed Setzler that "the Sea Island Company, with the cooperation of the Board of Trade and the County Commissioners, agreed to finance the salary of Mr. Holder until the project can be approved, which it was thought would take two or three weeks" (Mallory 1936a). Holder had already left his job as the supervising archaeologist in Tampa, on the assurance that the Sea Island Company and the SGA would pay his salary on the St. Simons excavations until the WPA paperwork cleared Savannah (Setzler 1936b; Stirling 1936c).

## Following the Paper Trail on Holder's WPA Excavations

Despite continuing delays in Savannah, Holder began work at the Airport site on May 4, 1936, without WPA funding, and sent Setzler a three-page preliminary report by the weekend (Holder 1936d; Mallory 1936e). Naturally assuming that he would be making his reports to Setzler, who had recruited him, Holder described the work he had accomplished in the first five days at the site, including his early analysis of the pottery, which he pointed out did not yet support Kelly's hope "for an eastward extension of his Macon groups into this area" (Holder 1936d). Setzler informed Holder within the week that he would be reporting directly to Kelly. Setzler requested, however, that Holder send him or Matthew Stirling carbon copies of all reports. Setzler wrote to Kelly, reassuring him that he had instructed Holder "that he is working under your immediate direction, because in the final analysis you will be the one who will make the conclusions for the Institution" (Setzler 1936c). Less than a month later Setzler reminded Kelly that "any published announcements must emanate from you" and specified that this position "holds good for the work on St. Simons Island" (Setzler 1936d).

Following Setzler's orders, Holder submitted, still without WPA funding, his first official report on June 2 for work accomplished to his titular supervisor, Arthur Kelly, at the Ocmulgee site in Macon. He also sent carbon copies to J. D. Compton at Sea Island, Richard Job at the Brunswick Board of Trade, and Setzler at the Smithsonian (Holder 1936e). It is fortunate that Holder always made carbon copies of his reports, because Kelly apparently kept none of them. In a 1973 interview with Marilyn Pennington, Kelly said, "I don't think Holder's material has ever been analyzed or written up, you know, and I am not sure I even know where it is" (Williams 1997:6). Negating previous agreements among Glynn County commissioners, the SGA, and the Smithsonian Institution (McKinnon 1937; Townsend 1936a, 1936b), Lucy B. McIntire, the WPA supervisor of archaeological projects under Nichols, imperiously appropriated the Glynn County materials, which incongruously ended up in the keeping of the Savannah Chamber of Commerce. Where they went from there is not well documented. The Brunswick Chamber of Commerce (formerly Board of Trade) tried to locate some of the artifacts in 1968 and wrote to Holder, who was then chairing the Department of Anthropology at the University of Nebraska (Newham 1968). Holder informed them that "the records of the excavations, along with photographs and final reports were forwarded via WPA channels through the Savannah Office (Mrs. Lucy McIntire was in charge). I am sure copies were forwarded to the Smithsonian Institution in Washington where they are probably lost in the files. More importantly, I am sure copies and specimens were forwarded to Macon, where Dr. A. R. Kelly was in charge" (Holder 1969). Finally, the Glynn County materials went from Macon to Tallahassee, Florida, when the National Park Service (NPS) center moved there in 1972. The ceramics and other artifacts are now on loan from the NPS and are cataloged as "Glynn County Acc. 562" in the Archaeology Laboratory at the University of Georgia.

As for his records in the National Anthropological Archives (NAA) in Suitland, Maryland, Holder may have deposited the five boxes that make up Manuscript 3301 with the Smithsonian Institution, as he is named as creator. Holder wrote to Setzler on December 14, 1938, about depositing his papers at the Smithsonian for safekeeping. The obscure method of cataloging Holder's papers, in any event, may well account for their neglect by researchers. As of January 2011, an online search for "Preston Holder" or "Preston Holder papers" in the collections of the Smithsonian Institution (http://collections.si.edu/search/) gives the surprising result of "Antonio Waring Papers." If one happens to know that Holder's papers are "MS 3301," a search for the manuscript number will yield the rather opaque result "Records of archeological excavations in Glynn County, Georgia for Work Projects Administration 1936–37." It is noteworthy that these records do not include his five-month archaeological excavations at the Irene Mound in Chatham County from 1937 to 1938.

The two major studies of WPA archaeology, Paul Fagette's *Digging for Dollars: American Archaeology and the New Deal* (1996) and Edwin A. Lyon's *A New Deal for Southeastern Archaeology* (1996), do not use in their studies, and may be forgiven for not knowing about, the anonymous Preston Holder papers of MS 3301 at the NAA. Moreover, neither author consulted the Preston Holder archive at the University of Nebraska at Lincoln. The latter collection was not at all well known, was not yet fully organized, and was in remote storage when I first contacted the University Archives and Special Collections in November 2007. As is evident from citations throughout this chapter, the Holder archive at Nebraska provides critical information, particularly through his correspondence, for understanding his contributions to the archaeology of coastal Georgia.

Judging by his notes on Holder's work on the coast, Fagette relied on superficial, second-hand summaries of Holder's reports that were compiled in the mid-1940s for the NAA "WPA Index" of MS 4844, Box 1 (Fagette 1996:189). The index was created to provide a finding list for WPA projects throughout the United States. Holder's full reports, from which the summaries purportedly derive, are missing from MS 4844, Box 5, where all of the Georgia reports are supposed to reside. The summaries themselves are no substitute. For example, the summary of the important excavations at Evelyn, where Holder finally established the first chronological sequence of ceramics in Georgia, makes only the banal observation that "the pottery obtained included cord-marked ware and a complicated stamp ware different from that encountered at the Airport site" (McCoy 1946).

Even without consulting the Holder papers in MS 3301 and the Holder archive at the University of Nebraska–Lincoln, Lyon (1996) is far better informed than Fagette about Holder's work. Unlike Fagette, Lyon did not rely on sparse, second-hand summaries, but rather on the fecund sources of information both in the Frank M. Setzler Papers, where he found copies of Holder's original reports to Arthur Kelly, and in the Antonio J. Waring Papers. Lyon's overall account, while generally accurate, has some mistakes and misconceptions. For instance, Holder isolated 3,000 post molds at the Airport site, not "thirty thousand" (Lyon 1996:109). Also, probably unfamiliar with the island, Lyon distinguishes the Hampton River Mound on Sea Island and the Sea Island Mound (Lyon 1996:108, 109), which are both Site II. As with Site I, the Airport site, Holder excavated Site II in two stages, once before and once after the WPA project was funded in July 1936. After briefly describing Holder's excavations in Glynn County, Lyon mentions that a comprehensive report was not published at the time (Lyon 1996:109). However, he correctly suggests that Kelly was to blame for never writing the synthesis that Setzler expected only Kelly, not Holder, to write (Lyon 1996:108–110).

At some point after the formation of the NAA in 1968, the Smithsonian provided the NPS with a copy of Holder's archive, MS 3301. The NPS moved fairly quickly to disseminate the archive by hiring Marsha Chance (1974), a master's student in archaeology at Florida State University, with Hale G. Smith as principal investigator, to organize and publish them in the early 1970s. There is not sufficient space to discuss this 1974 thesis, but because many archaeologists now rely on it for information about Holder's work on the Georgia coast, it is necessary to mention in passing some of its inaccurate representations. The thesis includes appendixes that purport to summarize or replicate Holder's records. However, Chance's summaries are sometimes inaccurate and misleading. Scholars should consult Holder's own vast records in order to see the breadth and depth of his work and understand his contribution to the cultural prehistory of the Georgia coast. Holder's field notes and typed records of burials always included coordinates, making it easy to orient precisely all skeletal remains and to assign exact proveniences for all funeral furniture. For example, Holder's record for Burial 32 from the

Airport site is reflected in Table 11.2. As the table indicates, Holder used comprehensive burial forms in the field, so that each burial and any associated artifacts are precisely located on his grid by trench, station, and depth. He compiled exhaustive records like this one for all burials at all sites he excavated. All of the records combined provide an extremely rich and detailed overview of burial practices at these sites on the Georgia coast.

## Holder's Pre-WPA Excavations on the Georgia Coast

Even before his WPA salary began, Holder distinguished himself as a resourceful, conscientious, and methodical scientist on St. Simons Island. He shared his research with his fellow archaeologists and trained his assistant, Antonio Waring, in how to undertake professional archaeology. These qualities are what make his surviving correspondence, reports, and records important to researchers today. As Setzler said in replying to his first report, "I was very much interested in reading your detailed report, and feel confident that all of my recommendations concerning you for the position have not been exaggerated. Let me congratulate you on the manner in which you have handled the project" (Setzler 1936e). Whereas Kelly worked with hundreds of laborers, Holder began excavating at the airport in May 1936 with a "force" of "two very intelligent Negro shovelmen," named George Life and Charles King (Holder 1936d, 1936f), and one "technical" assistant, C. O. Svendsen, the son of the St. Simons Island lighthouse keeper (Holder 1936e). Though an integrated crew was extraordinary in the South in the 1930s, Holder never even commented on it and was himself "no stranger to a shovel" (Holder 1937a).

Although he called it a "brief summary," Holder (1936e) in fact provided in his first formal report on June 2, 1936, many details of 22 burials, including types of burials; orientations of bodies; proportions of men, women, and children; and a complete itemization of burial offerings. In three weeks at the airport (May 4–25, 1936) his small crew managed to dig 12 10-foot-square exploratory pits and four exploratory trenches, one of which he described as 4 feet wide, 4 feet deep, and 200 feet long. Observing that these old plantation grounds had been thoroughly plowed over generations, Holder explained why there would be no stratigraphy for pottery types at this site. He nonetheless was able to furnish a surprisingly detailed analysis for such a short time in the field:

> The percentage of plain ware is about seventy-five percent. The plain ware is, in general, quite crude, showing a high percentage of sand or

Table 11.2. Burial 32 at St. Simons Island Airport, Georgia

| Burial #32 | |
|---|---|
| Location | Square: T18S10<br>Skull top: T19 plus 1', S10 plus 8'<br>Lower ends of tibia-fibula: T18 plus 5', S10 plus 8½' |
| Depth | Below surface: 18"<br>Below contact: 10" |
| Matrix | Sand. |
| Type | Primary. Full-extended. |
| Orientation | Trunk: prone<br>Skull: on right side, facing S.<br>Arms: extended alongside<br>Legs: extended<br>Axis: anterior W, posterior E. |
| Postmortem movement | Feet missing; perhaps disturbed by excavations for secondary burials in adjacent square. |
| Condition | Poor. Bone badly disintegrated. |
| Age and sex | Adult female. |
| Associated objects | 4 small seed pearls (I F17); three found in oral cavity, and one in right eye socket. Undrilled. Small flint fragment (11 166). |
| Bones recovered | Fragmentary cranium and maxilla mandible<br>2 humerus (frag.)<br>2 femur "<br>2 tibia "<br>2 radius "<br>2 fibula " |
| Comments | First occurrence of pearls at this site. |

*Source:* Holder 1936–1937.

> grit, and vegetal tempering . . . The decorated ware consists of at least five types of stamped ware—check-stamp is quite rare; your "delta" and a "herringbone" stamp seem to predominate—three types of cord-marked ware, three types of "thong" marked ware, and ware incised and punctate sherds (not done, certainly, with the usual Timucuan finesse). Rims are usually of the simple turned type, although occasional incised, punctate, and rounded rims occur, and at least one example has been found of the reed-punch beaded type . . . The bottoms (that is, the "hole in the doughnut") of at least three "killed" pots have been found [Holder 1936e].

After listing all of the artifacts other than pottery, Holder concluded the section of his preliminary report on the Airport site by discussing the structural details that appeared from the long trench across the eastern part of the shell area. Noting that he would require additional labor before excavating the deep shell middens and pits, he ended by observing that the discrete layers of shell intentionally placed over the burials were often covered by deep layers of sand, which pointed to "a time-lapse between a period when the area was used for burying-grounds and a time when it was intensively occupied" (Holder 1936e).

Holder and his small, but effective, crew accomplished all of this work at the airport in 15 working days, before moving to the Sea Island site. No doubt beginning to fear that the WPA funding would never come, the Sea Island Company on May 25 directed Holder and his few workers from the dig at the Airport site to the small mound at the northern tip of Sea Island. Within the next week Holder had analyzed the mound as three layers of burial mounds, which had been badly pitted by amateurs before he arrived. On his preliminary expedition from May 25 to May 31 to the Sea Island mound, Holder excavated eight burials, described their types and individual orientation, and noted that one burial included an apron of shell beads, a type of artifact that came to distinguish this site from all the others.

When the Sea Island Company ended its payments on May 31, 1936, the SGA picked up Holder's salary for the next couple of weeks, until its funds also ran out (Holder 1936g). After six weeks of waiting in a penniless limbo for his WPA salary to commence, the WPA district office in Savannah treated him with callous indifference when he inquired about his status (Nichols 1936a). Nichols maintained that he had to wait for Ray Morris, the WPA foreman at the airport, to confirm that there would be sufficient labor available for the excavation, while Morris kept forgetting to send confirmation to Nichols. Holder, who had helped Kelly write the WPA application, knew that the delaying tactics in Savannah were unjustified, and he perceptively suggested to Setzler, and later to Kelly, that the delays might be sabotage by Nichols (Holder 1936a). On July 13, 1936, exactly a month after the pre-WPA funding stopped, Holder brought Kelly up to date: "There will be no monthly report this time," he began, "for the good and simple reason that there has been no work done since the first of last month at which time available funds for my salary ran out." Perhaps wondering why Kelly had not written, Holder remarked that "the past month's silence on my part is due to the fact that I did not wish to worry you with the myriad and irritating details of WPA procrastination" (Holder 1936h).

Though forced to live on his meager savings, Holder was not idle but worked for free in his lab after funds to pay his salary dried up in mid-June (Holder 1936a). It was presumably at this time that he drew up his "Pottery Lab Book—Site I—Airport, St. Simon's [*sic*] Island," an extraordinarily detailed, 16-page guide to help his lab assistants document pottery types (Holder 1936i). In the guide all potsherds are classified according to rim type, plain or decorated surface, and temper. Holder classified 11 distinct rim types, with pictures illustrating cross section, outside surface, and inside surface for each type. He divided the thousands of sherds he had already collected into the broad categories of plain ware and decorated ware, and subdivided the decorated ware into (a) imprinted ware and (b) incised and punctate ware. He then subdivided the imprinted ware into "designs involving a repeated and definite motif or decoration—probably carved on a wooden paddle" and "designs involving undifferentiated pattern—probably made by wrapping various materials around a paddle." Holder carefully classified the tempering medium as grit, ground sherd, sand, or vegetal (or fiber), as well as noting the presence of air holes and seemingly untempered clay. He noted that there was some overlapping, when tempers combined, for example, both grit and sand. He even provided in the lab book a statistical table showing for the plain ware the percentages of the 11 rim types that showed grit, sherd, sand, and vegetal tempering.

The excellent work Holder accomplished before the WPA funding came in is representative of the conscientious, scientific approach he took from beginning to end. Holder applied the same method of pottery analysis to every site he excavated, and included statistical overviews in his reports to Kelly. One can get a clear overview of the meticulousness of his work from the series of six reports on all the St. Simons sites that he diligently sent to Kelly, before and after funding was authorized on July 22, 1936, as WPA Project No. 65-34-3338. There is neither space nor need to discuss in detail these reports on the St. Simons and Sea Island sites. Daniel Elliott has recently compiled copies derived from the NAA in "The WPA Glynn County Excavation Project: Phase I—Preston Holder's Paper Trail" (Elliott 2010). Elliott (2010:1) provides digital images of exactly what Holder did indeed write in 1936–1937, commenting that "it is a story that should have been written by Preston Holder before he died in 1980." Readers will see that Holder's reports stand very well on their own. As welcome as their dissemination now may be, however, researchers who wish to understand Holder's signal contributions to Georgia archaeology must go behind his reports and investigate the surviving materials on which they are based.

## Holder's WPA Excavations

When the WPA project was at last funded, Holder resumed his excavation of the Airport site "with a force of ten laborers." Setzler had reassured him a month earlier that he could accomplish more with 20 laborers than he could with the 50 or 75 he was originally promised, so Holder's 10-man crew was small by anyone's reckoning. Notwithstanding, Holder eventually excavated and methodically documented 85 graves containing 200 burials at the site. Using standard burial templates, he carefully recorded the trench and station locations on his grid for all burials and the provenience of all the artifacts found with the burials. Holder also made a determined effort to identify a distinct house pattern. In his reports covering the Airport site, he cumulatively recorded 300 post molds on August 31, 1936, a total of 935 on October 5, 1936, and about 2,500 in the December 12, 1936 report (Holder 1936e); he presumably located another 500 by the end of January, when progress on the airport forced him to abandon the Site I excavation (Holder 1937b), because the total eventually reached about 3,000 (Holder 1938a). Despite the large number of post molds and convincing signs of part of a stockade wall, Holder was unable to identify a distinct house pattern. The chaos of post molds that he recorded might indicate seasonal occupation, intermittent destruction of a village site in the sandy soils by the ferocious storms and hurricanes that have always hit the island, or other disasters.

It is hard to know how much more work Holder was able to do at the Airport site after the December report. He might not have had money or time for any more work in December. Nichols and McIntire in Savannah sent him a dismal note on November 17 informing him that he had $218 left for his payroll at the end of the month, $30 less than he needed. Their advice was to knock off early to leave enough money for himself and his white men (Nichols 1936b), but Holder was not likely to shortchange his black laborers. Renewed WPA funding with a new project number, 65-34-8031, came through on January 13, 1937 (Holder 1937b). At the end of the month he drew up a signed contract with Charlie King, one of the original two black workers, to allow excavation of a mound on King's property, a short distance from the Airport site (Holder 1937c). Holder excavated the mound as Site III in February and early March 1937. The characteristic pottery he encountered was cord marked, whereas the predominant pottery at the Airport site showed that American Indians used paddles with complicated carvings to imprint the clay. The difference revealed both a time lapse and a change of cultures in the area before the arrival of Europeans.

An indication of the enduring value of Holder's minutely detailed profile records may be seen in a handsome, professionally drawn, location, contour, and profile map I unearthed at NAA in 2007. The inventory to the Waring Papers listed its final item as "Map of St. Simons Island, Georgia—Chirby King Mound," an obvious misspelling of the Charlie King Mound. The map was too fragile to unroll and I had it professionally restored before I examined it. After restoration, the map indeed proved to be a grid with contours and profiles of the excavated area of the Charlie King Mound, with the unexpected bonus of a profile and grid of the Sea Island mound and village (Kiernan 2008). Using Holder's trench and station locations on the burial forms, as well as the proveniences recorded on the artifacts from these sites, one can locate on the maps precisely where the burials and artifacts were excavated (Kiernan 2009, 2010). In the bottom right corner of the map, the draftsman, M. O. Bellingrodt, left his initials and the date October 22, 1937, which was when Holder was at Irene. Holder told Waring in a letter in early November that "Bellingrodt is doing some beautiful drafting work, making tracings of profiles from St. Simons and will prove very useful in keeping a detailed drafting record of the work here [at Irene]" (Holder 1937d). What happened to the other profile maps of the sites from St. Simons Island and the ones he planned for the Irene site remains, for now, a mystery, but with today's technology it is possible to use Holder's data to create even more valuable location, contour, and profile maps.

By mid-March 1937 Kelly had received five reports, mainly covering Sites I–III: Airport, Sea Island Mound, and Charlie King Mound. As Kelly at this stage had shown scant interest in what was happening on St. Simons Island and vicinity, Holder waited until late July to report on the remaining sites. Holder next moved his crew back to the Sea Island Mound, to complete the interrupted excavation there. As he relayed to several people, including Setzler in early April, he was continually astonished by the excellent state of preservation of the skeletal material, which included the tiny bones of a stillborn child (Holder 1937e). Nearly a third of the burials were of adolescents

Figure 11.1. Sea Island Mound (Courtesy of the National Anthropological Archives, Smithsonian Institution, MS 3301).

and children, including two babies interred on the backs of adults. The outstanding funeral furniture was made up of nearly 1,500 shells, including pendants, bangles, aprons, and shrouds for babies. The original mound was a natural sand dune, not basket-laid, while the adjoining village was short-lived, to judge by its thin middens (Figure 11.1). More than 2,000 sherds, about 25 percent of them decorated, were found in the excavated section of the village. Of the decorated sherds, three-quarters were "wrapped paddle ware," boldly marked by a fabric with knots "as in a fish-net," and all of these were uniquely sherd tempered. Holder later tentatively placed this ware at the top of his ceramic stratigraphy, coeval with Lamar, in his Evelyn Daybook (Holder 1937f).

At the bottom of the same ceramic stratigraphy diagram Holder tentatively placed the "Early Swift Creek" Sites I and IV, Airport and the Gascoigne Bluff site. Today one thinks of Gascoigne Bluff, Site IV, as a relatively small area on the north side of the causeway from the marina. In his late July report Holder found evidence of occupation for two miles or more along the bluff on the Frederica River. It seems strange, then, that Holder stopped excavating after only four 10-foot pits for the putative reason that no burials were found. After all, the shell midden, as he reported, was "amazingly rich in pottery fragments," and it seems more, not less, interesting that the 1395 sherds were "virtually identical in every respect" to the ceramics from the Airport site. Perhaps he was ordered to move on, considering the "recent building excavations" he alluded to in the report, conceivably a reference to the new Coast Guard boathouse, another WPA project. In any case, he proceeded to Cannon's Point, Site V, which, he said, "may well have been the most extensive site" on the island, a surprising assessment after leaving one that seemingly sprawled for at least two miles, from the Airport site to upper Gascoigne Bluff. Holder excavated five locations, designated VA–VE, at Cannon's Point. He concluded that Site V, as was true of St. Simons Island as a whole, seemed to represent in its pottery at least two different cultures, one characterized by complicated stamped ware (VA and VE, as at the Airport site and Gascoigne Bluff) and the other by cord-marked ware (VC and VD, as at the Charlie King and Sea Island mounds).

## Holder's Brief WPA Publication

In 1938, a year after Holder had left for Columbia University, the SGA published in its first *Proceedings* a brief, two-page overview of Holder's 1936–1937 in-progress excavations on St. Simons Island alone. There is no evidence that Holder ever expected to publish this little piece, and indeed Setzler had prohibited him from publishing his results. On June 4, 1937, a year before it appeared in print, Lucy McIntire, the division supervisor of WPA archaeological projects in Savannah, had sent a curt note telling him, "Kindly write a brief, not too technical, account of the work done on St. Simons, which would take about 3 minutes to read. Mail it direct to me. Mr. Mallory has asked me to read this paper at the State Archeological Meeting in Columbus on June 12th" (McIntire 1937). Holder quickly complied with the two-page account now considered his sole publication on all the work he accomplished on the Georgia coast (Holder 1938a). "Please forgive the typing," he joked, "as I am not much on that sort of thing especially on hot days." Apologizing that it might take as long as five minutes to read, he declined her invitation to pay his way to Savannah and then travel with her to Columbus to hear his own paper read. He excused himself because "the work at Cannon's Point is now at the stage which demands all of my attention, and I would not feel right about leaving it at this time" (Holder 1937g).

There is no question that this short note in the *Proceedings* is actually the presentation Holder prepared for McIntire. The secretary's report on the Columbus meeting states, "Richard C. Job read a report by Mr. Preston Holder, transmitted by Mrs. Frank P. McIntyre [*sic*], on the excavations on St. Simons Island and vicinity, a copy of which is attached" (Smith 1938:5). It is well to bear in mind, however, that this first issue of the *Proceedings* was by spring 1938 a retrospect. By then Holder had long completed his work on St. Simons Island, including Cannon's Point, and had already excavated the critical five-mound site at Evelyn in Glynn County (the "vicinity" of the article's title), where he found the first demonstrable ceramic stratigraphy in Georgia. Although his WPA efforts are only ever recognized, if at all, for his work in Glynn County, Holder had also finished a five-month campaign directing excavations in Chatham County at the Irene site in Savannah; had written two thorough reports to Kelly with copies to Setzler; had composed a 27-page guide entitled "Archeological Method at the Irene Site" for his successor (Holder 1938b); and had left Georgia for graduate school at Columbia University at the end of January 1938.

## Holder's Excavations at Evelyn and Irene

After Cannon's Point on St. Simons Island and before Irene in Savannah, Holder turned his attention to Evelyn on the mainland in Glynn County, which coastal archaeologists now recognize as an extremely important prehistoric and historic site. Holder learned about Evelyn, Site VI, early in his work on St. Simons; he even gave a fairly full preliminary account in his December 1936 report to Kelly. The version at NAA is only a draft (Holder 1936e), but the entire report with an appendix fortunately survives at the Coastal Georgia Historical Society (Holder 1936j). He sent a follow-up letter to Setzler on December 15, expressing his excitement at the possibility that the mound-and-village complex was the lost village of Talaxe (Holder 1936k). Thinking it was outside of Glynn County, Lucy McIntire did not want Holder to excavate at Evelyn after Cannon's Point, but Holder fortunately prevailed after confirming the locale (Holder 1937h). By the time he sent Kelly his 14-page report in July 1937 on the last three St. Simons Island sites and a brief update on Evelyn (Holder 1937i), Holder had been seriously digging there, plotting profiles, and analyzing pottery for two weeks. Although Holder continued at Evelyn for six or seven more weeks, Kelly pulled him off in early September to begin supervising the Irene Mound site in Savannah on Monday, September 15, 1937. Holder did not have the leisure to send Kelly a follow-up report then, but a handwritten draft of a report or, perhaps more likely, an article in progress, as it has incipient footnotes, survives in his papers at NAA (Holder 1937j). It is apparent that he prepared this draft without checking his detailed field records, because he left blanks to fill in later for the dimensions of Evelyn's five mounds. He likely wrote it in the first two weeks at Irene, as details in it coincide with some in a letter at that time to the social anthropologist Chuck Wagley, who was then a graduate student at Columbia (Holder 1937k). The draft repeatedly cites a map he had made of Evelyn, which still exists among his papers at NAA. A modern neighborhood now exists at Evelyn, but thanks to the pains Holder took to preserve the site for later archaeologists and the care of several subsequent property owners, one can still locate the mounds and other features by overlaying Holder's map with the 1968 survey plat and a topographical map.

Holder considered Evelyn the most important site he excavated on the Georgia coast. There he found the only complete pot decorated with bold and beautiful Swift Creek designs that archaeologists had yet seen. More importantly, he excavated at Mound C the Holy Grail of Southeastern ceramic studies, an unambiguous stratification of wares, "indicating the relative chronological positions of Swift Creek Complicated Stamped, Deptford Linear Check Stamped, and the Coastal Variant of Mossy Oak [i.e., Deptford] Simple Stamped" (Holder 1937j). In reply to inquiries from Ruby Berrie of the Brunswick Board of Trade a year after he had left Savannah for Columbia, Holder said, "You will be glad to know that the material from Evelyn clearly demonstrates it as one of the major sites on the coast." He added that "for now [pending publication of his final report] you can say with pardonable pride that it is equally as important as Irene (if not more so)" (Holder 1939a). He reminded Berrie that circumstances prevented him from completing his investigation but that he was careful to leave most of the site untouched for later archaeologists to excavate.

Imploring Berrie to use her "considerable influence to protect the site from even such well-meaning persons as amateur archaeologists [and] Boy Scouts," Holder emphasized that a "thorough investigation of Evelyn will be absolutely essential for an adequate understanding of the prehistory of the Coastal Area of Georgia" (Holder 1939a). He reiterated these sentiments when he was chairing the Department of Anthropology at Nebraska, after learning in 1968 that the site was under real estate development (Holder 1969). After individual plots began selling, Kelly in a 1973 interview acknowledged that Evelyn was "one of the top ranking sites in the state of Georgia, and we should do what we can to save it" (Williams 1997:6).

Holder's final campaign on the Georgia coast was the Irene Mound in Savannah. At first Holder resisted the overtures of Setzler and Kelly to supervise the Irene site excavation. Although he told Duncan Strong, the professor he intended to work with at Columbia, that Irene would make possible "a fairly complete picture of Coastal pottery typology," he desperately wanted to begin graduate school at Columbia after finishing his work at Evelyn (Holder 1937l). In the end, however, he had to accede to Strong's insistent advice to "take on the Savannah job," which Strong made palatable by saying he might be able to return to work there the next summer (Strong 1937). Holder confided to a friend, the photographer Willard van Dyke, that he had been under "terrific pressure" to supervise the Irene project or, a sobering alternative, to "spend some time (like months or so) with Kelly in Macon trying to get the Coast straightened out for him." He opted for the former because, as he told van Dyke, "the dig at Savannah [was] damned well essential if I am to use this stuff for graduate research" (Holder 1937m). It appears that Setzler had no intention of letting him use his results, however. After Holder agreed to supervise the excavation at Irene, Setzler wrote to Kelly: "I shall be writing Holder and will emphasize again the fact that he must cooperate very closely with you; and I hope that you have been able to convince him of the importance of cooperation, not for anyone's [least of all Holder's] personal attainments, but for the final result of working out a definite chronology in the Southeast" (Setzler 1937).

## Holder's Contributions to Southeastern Ceramic Studies

Doubtless with the prospect of developing a thesis for his dissertation, Holder set up a ceramic repository at Irene for his own research, as well as for training his assistants for the most efficient field and laboratory work. Holder brought to Irene from his excavations in Glynn County a huge collection of classified sherds, representing the full range of ceramic types he had so far discovered, analyzed, and described from the coast (Davis 1938; Holder 1938c, 1938d). As he told Setzler, he left at the Brunswick Visitors Center "a large and representative sample of all types of artifacts (including a large pottery sample and restorable pots)" and shipped the remaining potsherds to Savannah (Holder 1938c). "The sherd samples" sent to Savannah, he continued, "were opened and placed in shoe boxes and classified according to the typology we were developing and stored in shelf space there—since [his successor, Vladimir J.] Fewkes was new to the area I assumed he would want access to these study materials" (Holder 1938c). This is a formidable collection, filling 33 large bins, now located in the Archaeology Laboratory at the University of Georgia, on loan from the NPS. Drawing on his unparalleled knowledge of coastal ceramics, Holder prepared for his assistants and for his successor a series of guides, including a three-page "Survey Method" (Holder

1938e); a five-page "Survey," whose tentative conclusions corroborate the stratigraphy at Evelyn Mound C (Holder 1938f); and a 27-page "Method," outlining every conceivable aspect of the excavation (Holder 1938b). In addition, he sent Kelly (with copies to Setzler, Job, and McIntire's office) unusually detailed reports, including a seven-page summary report of work in progress on November 30, 1937 (Holder 1938g), and a final 12-page report (with copies to Setzler and Fewkes) on January 24, 1938, a week before he departed for Columbia (Holder 1938h). Researchers who compare these documents with the published results of his successors (Caldwell and McCann 1941; Fewkes 1938a, 1938b) may wish that Duncan Strong had followed through and allowed Holder to return to Georgia to complete the excavation. Instead, Strong sent him the following summer to work on a project with the Arikara Indians in South Dakota, which led to his dissertation and ultimately to his well-regarded book *The Hoe and the Horse on the Plains* (Holder 1970).

There is not sufficient space here to do justice to Holder's exhaustive materials from Irene, but an example relating to his interest and expertise in ceramics and the difficulty of working under the constraints of WPA archaeology might be useful. In his 27-page methodology guide, Holder pointed out that "the use of such a great amount of labor, of course, results in the accumulation of a mass of material in a relatively short time. It was felt that the orthodox practice of subsequent museum identification of all materials should be partially dispensed with at this site. Therefore, a rather strict system of field identification of all decorated sherds is enforced." Because he had provided his assistants and technicians with a comprehensive ceramic research repository from Glynn County, Holder decided to attempt "a fairly definitive analysis of the sherd sequences in the field" (Holder 1938b:5b). As he explained, his theory of pottery analysis was that "sequences of easily discernible design types of pottery are indicative of cultural sequences, and by inference of chronological sequences. This method of attack is stressed both in the field and laboratory" (Holder 1938b:5a). In his final report to Kelly, he gave an example of the gratifying results of this approach. "One especially heartening example of progress," he wrote, "is that exhibited by the Laboratory Technician, John Miles, who seems to have picked up a fairly thorough knowledge of the pottery types likely to be encountered at the site. Periodic check-ups on his work indicate accuracy of a high order" (Holder 1938h).

In fact, Holder was widely acknowledged as the reigning expert on coastal ceramics in the 1930s. As Gordon Willey once remarked to him, "you know that you deserve credit for the 'origination' of most of the coastal types" (Willey 1939). James Ford first met with Holder and Willey in late September

1937 at Irene, where Ford proposed that the three of them and Kelly publish a comprehensive handbook of Southeastern pottery types (Holder 1937k). At this organizational meeting, they planned the first Conference on Pottery Nomenclature for the Southeastern United States to be held in Savannah later that fall (Holder 1937e). "Although the conference is to be a closed meeting," Holder told Waring, "there is every likelihood that you will be invited if you will promise not to throw too many monkey wrenches in the machinery. Matt [Stirling] is all for it and will attend I imagine. The thing has A. R. Kidder's OK to [James] Griffin and others so that Jim [Ford] will probably bring Griffin" (Holder 1937e). The usual procrastination, which Gordon Willey attributed to Kelly (Willey 1937), led to its postponement until May 1938, when it was held at the University of Michigan at the Ceramic Repository of the Southeastern United States, instead of at Savannah, and it came to be considered the first meeting of the Southeastern Archaeological Conference, or SEAC. By then Holder was at Columbia and unable to attend, but the proceedings of the conference honored Holder and Willey in absentia as "members of the Conference because of their interest in its purposes and their valuable assistance in developing the idea presented" (Ford and Griffin 1938:22). When soliciting ceramic descriptions for the group's *Newsletter,* William Haag, its first editor, told Holder, "I know of your interest in the pottery conference so the idea behind all this is not new to you at all, but is really yours" (Haag 1939).

Although he could not attend, Holder prepared for Ford and Willey some outstanding material on coastal ceramics for the conference. On a large index card a draft of a table, marked "Confidential Jim + Gordon" and entitled "Very tentative chronology for Coastal Georgia wares," survives among his papers at NAA and shows that he made them privy to his sensitive research in progress. As far as I know, no archaeologist today disagrees with the postulated sequence of wares he shared with them (Holder 1938i). Holder also sent Ford excellent photographs of decorated ceramics with accompanying identifying keys and critical notes for their use at the conference (Figure 11.2). This example collects specimens of Vining Simple Stamped, Deptford Linear Check Stamped, Residual Check Stamped, and an outlier, Weeden Island Check Stamped, all identified with their proveniences from the Airport site, Evelyn Mound C, and Cannon's Point. His notes to "Jim" on another page explain how these wares, except the Weeden Island ones, were "intimately associated at Mound C, Evelyn; at Deptford Site, Savannah; and at Meldrim Site, Savannah." At Evelyn Mound C these wares were "stratigraphically below Swift Creek Complicated Stamped" (Holder 1938j).

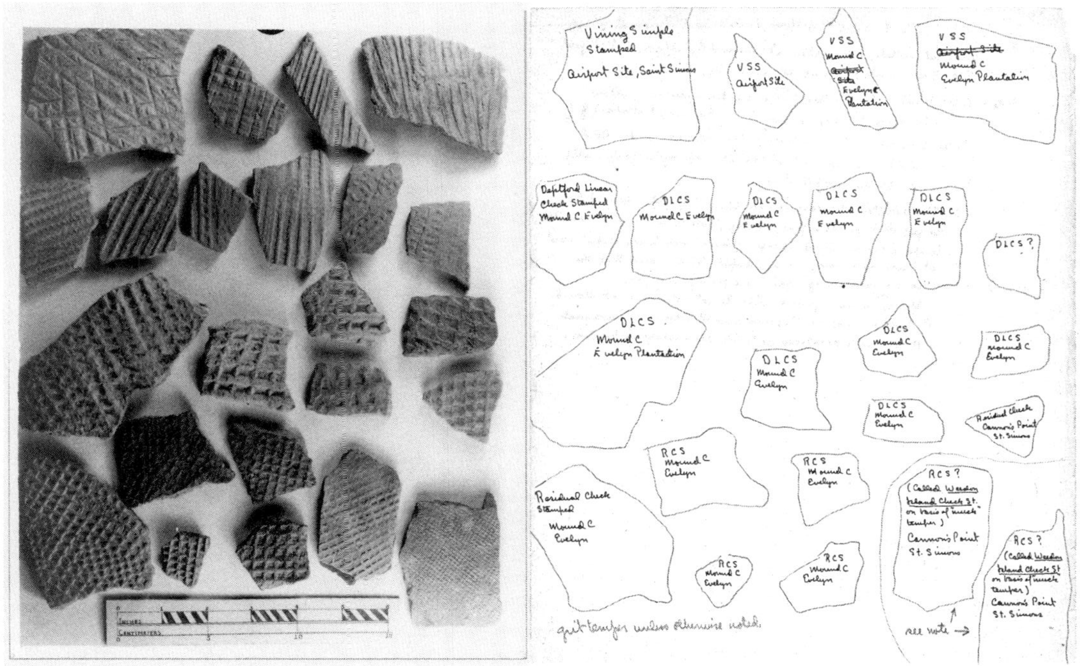


Figure 11.2. Ceramic key for the SEAC conference (Courtesy of the National Anthropological Archives, Smithsonian Institution, MS 3301).

## The Legacy of Holder's WPA Excavations

A study of Holder's amazingly thorough, conscientious, and insightful documentation of his WPA excavations in Glynn and Chatham counties in 1936–1938 can only leave one sadly wondering what prevented him from publishing his work. It is not enough to know that Setzler expected only Kelly to publish all conclusions. Why were Fewkes and Caldwell, for instance, allowed to publish their Irene Mound reports (Caldwell and McCann 1941; Caldwell and Waring 1939a–1939l; Fewkes 1938a, 1938b)? What prevented Setzler, when it became obvious that Kelly would never write his synthesis, from letting Holder at least publish his reports? The Sea Island Company and the Brunswick Board of Trade, the sponsors of the Glynn County excavations, were clamoring for their publication (Berrie 1939; Cate 1940; Gill 1939; Holder 1939a). Vincenzo Petrullo was supposedly intent on publishing Holder's part of the report on the Irene excavation in Chatham County under Holder's name (Petrullo 1938), and Holder duly sent him the requested documents and more (Holder 1939b, 1939c). We know that Setzler had all of Holder's reports at hand. Perhaps, Setzler for some as yet unknown reason suppressed the publication of Holder's findings and concealed his papers under the mysterious designation of MS 3301. Fortunately, Holder's extensive field records, unpublished reports, and correspondence have survived. Today, archaeologists can appreciate the valuable contributions Holder's unsung WPA excavations have made to understanding Southeastern archaeology, especially in the realm of ceramic studies of what are now acknowledged as some of the most important archaeological sites on the Georgia coast.

## Acknowledgments

For their help while I was researching this essay, I wish to thank Alan Bain, Leanda Gahegan, Gina Rappaport, and Daisy Njoku at the National Anthropological Archives of the Smithsonian Institution; and Traci Robison, Katherine Walter, and Mary Ellen Ducey in Archives and Special Collections, Love Library, University of Nebraska at Lincoln. I am also grateful to Bernard K. Means, Keith Stephenson, Fred Cook, R. Morgan Crook, and Aidine Kiernan for their valuable discussions and suggestions.

# 12

# The Resettlement Administration and the Historical Archaeology of the Georgia Piedmont

*James R. Wettstaed*

The Depression-era programs sponsored by the federal government have long been held as significant in the nation's history. Archaeological investigations sponsored by these programs have also had a special place in the history of the field (Lyon 1996). There are, however, programs that indirectly created a significant benefit for archaeological research today. One such program was the Resettlement Administration, which purchased lands from destitute farmers. Detailed records were compiled by the Resettlement Administration regarding the affected regions as a whole, as well as the specific properties purchased. The documents and information compiled by these programs are an invaluable source of data for archaeologists and historians today. They provide a detailed record of the Depression-era landscape, both cultural and natural, that is useful and significant on many levels. The present chapter focuses on the accomplishments and significance of this New Deal program for understanding and interpreting the historical archaeology of the Georgia Piedmont. It will be seen that the New Deal accomplishments are still important today.

## A Land Exhausted: The Oconee National Forest in the 1930s

The Oconee National Forest lies in Greene, Jasper, Jones, Morgan, Oconee, Oglethorpe, and Putnam counties, Georgia, in the Piedmont physiographic province. This is a region of rolling hills located between the flat coastal plain and the rugged mountains of north Georgia. This is also the heart of the so-called Black Belt and historically a significant cotton-producing region. By

1820, most of the settled Piedmont had converted from small subsistence farms to cotton plantations. Prior to the Civil War, the work was conducted by slaves; afterwards, tenant farmers became the principal workforce. By 1900, the majority of the rural population was landless tenants. Fully 60 percent of the farms in Georgia were worked by tenants, compared to 45 percent in 1880. Overproduction of cotton on poor soil destroyed the land; by the early twentieth century, the region was suffering from massive erosion and poor productivity, and farmers cultivated even more land in an effort to stay even (Holmes 1977:257–261; Range 1954:87, 90–102, 152; Wynes 1977:225–231). The boll weevil arrived in the area in 1920 and signaled the end of large-scale cotton farming. Production in Greene County went from 14,024 bales in 1920 to 1,420 bales in 1921. According to Raper (1936:211), there was a small boom in the lumbering industry in the 1920s following the collapse of cotton farming. However, the merchantable timber was quickly cut out. Because cotton farming was essentially over, and the land exhausted, people started abandoning the area. For example, the population of Putnam County dropped 45 percent from 1920 to 1930—from 15,151 to 8,367 residents (Walters 1995:368–371).

In 1935 it was estimated that 87 percent of the land in the lower Piedmont region had been cultivated in the historic period and that over one-half of the uncultivated land was bottomlands. Some fields had been farmed continuously for 60 years or more (Brender 1949:8). Trimble (1974; see also Ferguson 1999:150) estimates that in the Oconee River watershed, 8.35 inches of topsoil was eroded away, while soil loss averaged 7.5 inches across the Georgia Piedmont. In some places 12 inches or more was removed. Garcia and Brook (1996:194) describe the region as "one of the most severely eroded agricultural areas in the United States." Much of the land in the Oconee National Forest does not contain any topsoil, with the sterile clay subsoil exposed on the surface. In the 1930s, most of this land consisted of either abandoned and eroded fields, or abandoned fields that had begun to return to a young second-growth forest (Wettstaed 2009a). Following on the heels of the final collapse of the cotton economy was the Great Depression.

## The Resettlement Administration

In the early 1930s the Roosevelt administration initiated a number of programs to try to get the national economy functioning and to try to help out those who were hurt the most by the conditions. One such federal program was the Resettlement Administration, which was created as a separate agency in 1935. It contained three divisions: the Land Utilization Division, the Resettlement Division, and the Rehabilitation Division. In 1937 the Resettlement Administration was put under the Department of Agriculture's Farm Security Administration, with the Land Utilization Division being separated out and put under the Soil Conservation Service. The purpose of the Resettlement Administration was to combat rural poverty, especially that of tenant farmers in the South. Toward that goal, the agency bought up land and resettled the inhabitants on new property, often communally organized.

Most of the Oconee National Forest (Jasper, Jones, and Putnam counties) was included in the Plantation Piedmont Project of the Land Utilization Division (the Greene, Morgan, Oconee, and Oglethorpe County land was included in a separate project and no information is retained in the forest files). The project was initiated in 1933 and land acquisition was begun in January 1935, with administration being transferred to the Land Utilization Division in May 1935. At that time the plan called for purchasing 125,000 acres and resettling 250 families. A majority of the families were classified as renters (46 percent). Next most frequent were sharecroppers (24 percent), followed by wage hands (19 percent), share-tenants (4 percent), and caretakers (2 percent). Only 5 percent were owner-operators. Of the people living on the tracts considered for purchase, 75 percent were African American and 25 percent were white (Anonymous 1936:13; Hartman 1935:19).

By 1939, 118,657 acres had been purchased or were in the process of being purchased. Of this acreage, 30,000 acres were assigned to the U.S. Biological Survey to manage as an upland game refuge (now the Piedmont National Wildlife Refuge), 4,700 acres were established as the Hitchiti Experimental Forest (administered by the Forest Service), 13,600 acres north of Eatonton were assigned to the Georgia Experimental Station for grazing studies, and the remaining 70,000 acres were administered by the Soil Conservation Service (Anonymous 1939:16–17). This last acreage became the basis of the Oconee National Forest, which was created in 1959 after the land was transferred from the Soil Conservation Service to the Forest Service.

As part of the land acquisition process for the Plantation Piedmont Project, a detailed analysis of the project area was completed (Hartman 1935). This analysis characterized the conditions of the natural environment and collected a great deal of detailed information regarding the social and economic conditions of the area. Within the project area, the population had dropped from 45,000 in 1920 to 26,000 in 1930. Land values dropped from $20–$40 per acre in 1920 to $5–$10 per acre in 1935. While 60 percent of the overall population was African American, the rural population was 75 percent African American and they almost all lived as tenant farmers. Conditions for the residents were very bad. Hartman (1935:8) reported that "these factors have brought about rural standards of living as low as any found in the country." Three-quarters of the families on the land being considered for purchase lived at or below the poverty line, which was considered to be an annual income of $600 (Hartman 1935:29).

The condition of the land was just as bad. At least 50 percent of the land was gullied and less than one-quarter could be classified as crop land in 1935. Severe erosion had "practically destroyed 75% of it [the land] for farming purposes" (Hartman 1935:9). A transect survey of Jasper County revealed that 57 percent of the land was classified as permanently submarginal for farming—85,000 acres of 150,000 in the survey area were severely sheet-eroded and gullied. An additional 46,500 acres were moderately to severely eroded and classified as marginal to submarginal. Only 12 percent of the land was considered suitable for farming. Nearly 50 percent of the land being considered for purchase was abandoned or unoccupied in 1935 (Hartman 1935:16–19).

Because of these conditions, the area was selected to be part of the Plantation Piedmont Project (Hartman 1935:44–47). The program had several purposes: rehabilitate the families living on submarginal land; change the utilization to a more productive use, such as game preserves, recreation, and forestry; eliminate or reduce the expenditures for relief in the area; reduce the overall cotton acreage; and demonstrate the feasibility and desirability of making these changes. In regard to rehabilitating the families, two approaches were followed. Those families that were considered qualified to own and operate farms on their own were offered the opportunity to do so elsewhere. For families that were not so qualified, employment opportunities along with improved housing and school facilities were offered, with the hope that this would lead to their being able to improve their situation. Toward achieving the latter goal, the Resettlement Administration established co-operative resettlement communities. The Briar Patch community was established near Eatonton as one such resettlement community, while the purchased lands were administered by a nonprofit corporation with federal and state control.

Detailed information was compiled for the lands being purchased, including descriptions of the land and improvements that were on it. In some cases the original maps are preserved, while in others only the inventories were retained. At the same time, the federal government employed photographers to document the conditions of the region and the work being done by the Resettlement Administration. The work of these photographers, including Dorothea Lang and Walker Evans, is one of the best-known aspects of the program. The photographs have become classics of American photography,

Figure 12.1. This photograph shows examples of the types of details on people, architecture, and material conditions that are not available through the archaeological record. The original caption in the Forest Service files reads: "Born in slavery still living on same farm" (Courtesy of the Chattahoochee-Oconee National Forest History Files, Gainesville, Georgia).

showing the landscape, houses, and people in a way it is not possible to see through the documents or archaeological record (Figure 12.1). The photographs are also just about the only record available of the architectural history of much of this region. The area of the Oconee National Forest became a particular focus of these photographers. Of the 2,498 Farm Security Administration photographs pertaining to Georgia on file with the Library of Congress, two-thirds of the total (1,655) were taken in the counties containing the Oconee National Forest, and all but 55 of those were taken in Greene County.

All of the records compiled by the Resettlement Administration are an invaluable source of data for cultural resource managers, archaeologists, and historians working in the area. The utility of these records will be demonstrated in two case studies from the Oconee National Forest. In the first, the records are reviewed to provide a broad overview of the area, including farm sizes and details about the structure of farms. The second case study uses the records for a specific tract of land to help analyze archaeological sites recorded on the property.

## Case Study 1: Property Descriptions

The records provided by the Resettlement Administration provide a great deal of information on the properties that were purchased by the federal government. They provide information on farm sizes, house sizes, ages of houses, and data on outbuildings. All of these data can provide an excellent context for evaluating historic period sites recorded in the area. They are also useful for revealing those things we have not been able to learn from the archaeological record.

To highlight the kinds of data available, I examined a sample of 31 land purchase tracts from Jasper County that contained information on structures. Properties purchased from banks were excluded from this comparison because those tracts usually involved thousands of acres that had originally been numerous separate farms. For the 31 tracts examined, there were 5,310 acres purchased from 24 separate owners, for an average of 221 acres per purchase. The actual acreage owned ranged from 28 acres to 688 acres. Regarding residency, 60 percent of the properties sold were owned by residents of Jasper County, while 12 percent lived in adjacent counties and 20 percent lived elsewhere in Georgia. The remaining 8 percent lived in another state entirely. With respect to residents on the properties, 52 percent of the properties were unoccupied, 7 percent were occupied by an owner, and 41 percent were occupied by tenants.

The appraisers recorded the following information concerning structures on each property: type of structure, number of structures, condition (poor, fair, good), construction material, age, size, and assessed value. A total of 28 houses had information provided regarding age. These ranged in age from 10 years old to 110 years old, with an average age of 29 years. Although the average house size was 1,379 square feet, there was quite a range. On the high end, a single house was 2,304 square feet, while there were eight (29 percent) that measured less than 500 square feet. An interesting correlation is that the larger houses tended to be older. Those houses older than 50 years averaged 1,415 square feet, while those 30 years old or less averaged 794 square feet. The older houses may well represent the homes of current or former owners that were later converted into tenant houses. The largest house in the sample was occupied by the owner. It appears that when landowners had to build houses for tenants, they increasingly constructed smaller houses.

All 45 dwellings on these 31 properties were appraised as to value. The average was $145 per house, with a range of $0 to $1,400. As might be expected, the house with the highest value was occupied by the owner. The high-value house throws off the average, because no other house was val-

Table 12.1. Data on structures documented on Tract U-285

| Building | Age (yrs) | Size (feet) | Material | Cost | Condition | Value |
|---|---|---|---|---|---|---|
| Dwelling 1 | 29 | 20 × 44 | Wood | $400 | Fair | $250 |
| Barn D1 | 10 | 10 × 12 | Wood | $20 | Fair | $5 |
| Barn D1 | 20 | 12 × 14 | Log | $15 | Fair | $8 |
| Barn D1 | 10 | 28 × 40 | Wood, tin | $300 | Good | $200 |
| Barn D1 | 20 | 15 × 24 | Wood | $100 | Fair | $40 |
| Barn D1 | 10 | 12 × 16 | Log | $15 | Fair | $7 |
| Dwelling 2 | 20 | 24 × 16 | Wood | $200 | Fair | $125 |
| Barn D2 | 20 | 8 × 12 | Wood | $10 | Poor | $2 |
| Barn D2 | 10 | 16 × 14 | Wood, log | $25 | Poor | $15 |

ued over $500. If that one house is removed from the total, the remaining average is $117 per house. Fourteen houses were valued between $100 and $500, while six had a value of $0 or were listed for salvage.

Regarding water supplies, 14 wells were reported from these properties, along with one spring and one cistern. Among the total of 45 houses recorded, 29, or 64 percent, did not have any water source listed. Many residents were therefore obtaining water from a creek or from a neighbor's house.

There was an overall average of 1.28 outbuildings per dwelling, although there was great variability. Older dwellings (greater than 30 years) tended to have more outbuildings, with an average of 3.25 per dwelling, while younger ones (less than 30 years) had fewer, averaging 1.3. Those properties occupied by an owner also tended to have more, averaging 1.5. The larger number of outbuildings with older dwellings may reflect an accumulation over time.

## Case Study 2: Tract U-285

Land Tract U-285 was purchased in 1936 from Richard A. Tillman of Hillsboro, Georgia. This property was purchased for $1,156.50 and consisted of 140 acres of cropland and 115 acres of forest land, along with two dwellings and seven barns (Table 12.1). The owner did not live on the property, which was occupied by two tenant families. One dwelling (site 9JA413) was 29 years old and associated with five barns, while the second dwelling (site 9JA454) was 20 years old and contained two barns. Locations of houses are shown on a map in the land records, but these structures are not keyed to the ones reported in the files. A single well was reported to be present on the property. The 1930 census (U.S. Department of Commerce 1933) lists Richard A. Tillman as 62 years old, living with his wife Martha (age 53) and sons Lawson (age 18, a laborer) and Marshal (age 10). He is not shown as having an occupation. Both sites were originally recorded in 2004 (Jordan and Quirk 2004) and revisited in 2009 (Wettstaed 2009b).

### *Site 9JA413, the George Griffin House*

Features present at site 9JA413 include a house platform and pier remains, along with a well and two to three outbuildings. Evidence for these outbuildings consists of clusters of rocks that could have served as piers and associated artifact clusters indicated by a metal detector survey of the property. Also present is a single grave with a marble headstone and footstone. The headstone is inscribed "INFANT OF MR. & MRS. G. Y. GRIFFIN." During the 2009 investigations, a total of 36 shovel tests were excavated, with 16 being positive. A distinct midden area was located southeast of the house. The house platform has been disturbed, so it is not possible to estimate the size of the house, although it possibly measured 20 × 44 feet (880 square feet).

A total of 182 historic artifacts were collected from the site. These artifacts include stoneware, refined earthenware, glass tableware, container glass, kitchenware, personal artifacts, architectural artifacts, furnishings, labor and agricultural items, and miscellaneous items. The artifact collection from this site is consistent with the age estimate in the land records (ca. 29 years in 1936).

A 1909 Jasper County map (Jordan and Quirk 2004:Figure 3.1) shows a house along this section of road with the name G. Y. Griffin, which matches the name on the grave. A review of the federal census from 1880 through 1930 reveals that George Y. Griffin appears in this census every year except for the last. In the 1880 census (U.S. Department of the Interior 1883), the name and age of his wife are not clear, but from then on Mary L. Griffin is listed as his wife. In 1900 they had eight children, all of whom were living (U.S. Department of the Interior 1901), while the 1910 census indicates that they had 10 children, with eight living (U.S. Department of Commerce and Labor 1913). Thus the grave dates between 1900 and 1910. According to the census, George Griffin owned his own farm and did not owe a mortgage from 1880 through 1910. In 1920 he is shown living with his son Richard, who is reported to have been renting the farm on which they lived (U.S. Department of Commerce 1922). Mary Griffin had passed away by that time. Neither Griffin appears in the 1930 census (U.S. Department of Commerce 1933).

George Griffin had a large family and employed laborers to help him.

One was listed as living with the family in 1900 and two in 1910. In 1910 his daughter Polly and her five children are shown as living with the Griffin family, and no husband is listed. The family appears to have lost the farm sometime after 1910, as the 1920 census lists Richard Griffin as a renter. The new owner then rented the house out to tenants at some point after 1920.

## *Site 9JA454*

Site 9JA454 is located approximately 160 m south of 9JA413. Shovel testing and metal detecting revealed that there was a distinct sheet midden across the site and a rich depositional midden south of the house. During the 2009 investigations, seven of 23 shovel tests were positive. A single 1.0-×-.5-m test unit was excavated in the vicinity of the richest shovel tests using arbitrary 10-cm-thick levels. Sterile clay was encountered at 24 cm. Above the clay was a loam rich with artifacts.

A total of 432 artifacts were recovered at the site. These artifacts include stoneware, refined earthenware, glass tableware, container glass, kitchenware items, personal artifacts, architectural artifacts, furnishings, firearms, three labor/agricultural items, and miscellaneous unidentified items. Of interest were two sherds from the same blue transfer-printed plate. This design could probably be classified as Classical style, which was popular between 1827 and 1847 (Samford 1997). Jordan and Quirk (2004:85–87) reported finding a piece of blue transfer-printed pottery, but did not provide an illustration or describe the design. It is possible that the sherd found in 2004 comes from the same plate. Because all of the other artifacts indicate a later occupation, this blue transfer-printed plate is believed to represent an heirloom piece.

Problematically, the size of the structure at this site indicated by the house platform and remaining native rock piers (roughly 30 × 33 feet, 990 square feet) does not agree with that reported for the house believed to have been present at this site (24 × 16 feet, 384 square feet). It is possible that some of the structural supports have been disturbed and that is why the apparent house size does not match the reported size. Site 9JA413 was presumed to contain the larger house because that house was associated with more outbuildings (five compared to two) and two to three were identified at that site compared to none at 9JA454. However, the estimated house size (20 × 44 feet, 880 square feet) for that site is much closer to that estimated for site 9JA454. Thus it may be that all outbuildings were found at site 9JA413, while none of the five outbuildings present at site 9JA454 were located.

Another potential problem is that the artifacts from the site indicate that it may have been occupied from the very late nineteenth century through the early twentieth century. No house was shown in this location by the 1909

Jasper County map (Jordan and Quirk 2004:Figure 3.1). The entire area has been surveyed and there are no other sites that could be the one reported in the land records. Thus the age of the site estimated by artifacts appears to be off somewhat, as the land records report that the house was built in approximately 1915. This house was occupied by tenants in 1935.

## Discussion

The land records produced by the Resettlement Administration proved very useful in the analysis of these two sites. Without the records, it would not have been possible to estimate the size of the house at site 9JA413, and an accurate count of outbuildings could not have been obtained. If the larger house was present at site 9JA454, none of the outbuildings were located. Identifying outbuilding locations appears to be rather problematical in the area, most likely due to minimal foundations having been used. Without the Resettlement Administration records, it would not have been possible to get an accurate determination of the site structures.

The artifact collections from these two sites are very similar in appearance (Table 12.2). Comparing these sites with the artifact patterns defined for the area (Joseph et al. 2004:200–201; Joseph and Reed 1991:175; South 1977), both would be classified as falling within the Piedmont Farm Pattern. Joseph and Reed (1991:175) suggest that this pattern reflected a stable occupation in one location for an extended period of time. This contrasts with a pattern of short-term, impermanent occupations that were then converted to agricultural fields, which characterizes the Tenant Farm Pattern. Both sites in this study were occupied by tenants in 1935, although site 9JA413 is believed to have originally been occupied by the owner. At least one-half of the time this site was occupied, however, it was used by tenants. Joseph and Reed (1991:175) do not define what constituted an extended period of time, but based on the data from these sites, tenant sites will be classified with the Piedmont Farm Pattern if they are occupied for 15–20 years.

The one distinct difference between the two sites is that the age of occupation was estimated to have been earlier for site 9JA454. An analysis of the artifacts suggested that the site was occupied from the very late nineteenth century through the early twentieth century, while the Resettlement Administration data indicated that this structure was constructed around 1915. It is possible that this may be due to a reuse (through salvage) of older architectural artifacts (nails, window glass) and a greater curation of other items (such as ceramics and glass) by tenants or by those who constructed ten-

Table 12.2. Comparison of collections from sites 9JA413 and 9JA454 with artifact patterns defined for the region

| | 9JA454 | 9JA413 | Tenant Farm Pattern | Piedmont Farm Pattern |
|---|---|---|---|---|
| Kitchen | 60 | 57 | 70–90 | 45–60 |
| Architecture | 35 | 33 | 2–20 | 35–45 |
| Furniture | 1 | 3 | 1–5 | 1–4 |
| Arms | <1 | 0 | 1–5 | 1–4 |
| Clothing | 2 | 1 | 1–5 | 1–4 |
| Personal | 1 | 2 | 1–5 | 1–4 |
| Tobacco | 0 | 0 | 1–5 | 1–4 |
| Activities | 1 | 4 | 3–10 | 5–10 |

*Note:* Numbers represent percentages.

ant houses (Adams 2003). The age estimate for site 9JA413 was comparable to that provided in the Resettlement Administration data and this house is believed to have originally been constructed by the owner and only later converted to tenant housing. It should be possible to test this theory by examining several other tenant sites for which there are good Resettlement Administration data and comparing their estimated occupation ages based on artifacts with those provided in the records.

## Conclusion

Depression-era programs such as the Resettlement Administration are important on many levels (see Pasquill 2008 for a study of a similar program in Alabama). The modern landscape of many areas exists in its present form because of these programs. Without the Resettlement Administration, the Oconee National Forest would not exist, and many of the sites of the past inhabitants would not have been nearly as well preserved. The preserved records are an important data source for the archaeology and history of the late nineteenth and early twentieth centuries in the Georgia Piedmont. Not only do these records provide site-specific information, but they also provide an excellent regional context. The combination of archaeology and history allows us to better tell the story of those who came before us. We would not be able to do so without the contributions of this New Deal program.

## Acknowledgments

The research discussed herein was supported by the Chattahoochee-Oconee National Forests and the chapter benefited from comments by Bernard Means and Judith Harpole Wettstaed. Any mistakes are those of the author and none of the conclusions or opinions reflect those of the reviewers or the author's employer.

# Conclusion

## Shovels at the Ready: Work Relief and American Archaeology—Today and Tomorrow

*Bernard K. Means*

New Deal excavations by "Forgotten Men and Women" in the 1930s and 1940s are demonstrably of continuing and critical importance to our evolving understanding of America's past. Ordinary Americans during the Great Depression were given an otherwise unimaginable opportunity to make extraordinary finds that both raised contemporary awareness of the nation's rich archaeological heritage and bequeathed a legacy that shapes our understanding of the nation's past today. New Deal archaeology clearly extended well beyond the southeastern Unites States—contrary to what some have inferred from published accounts. However, despite our efforts here, the geographic parameters of New Deal archaeological investigations across America as a whole remain poorly understood. Much research into New Deal archaeology remains somewhat provincial and known largely by archaeologists operating on a fairly local level. We still need to emphasize to American archaeologists practicing in the field today that archaeology across the entire United States benefited from federal work relief programs during the Great Depression. The modern study of New Deal communities by archaeologists is another increasingly prevalent theme that was not fully explored in this volume, although it was addressed directly in the History of Archaeology Interest Group (HAIG) sponsored symposium at the 2010 Society for American Archaeology (SAA) meetings. We also did not explore in this volume whether needs during the unemployment crisis that still characterizes the Great Recession can or are being met by work relief programs akin to those that operated during the Great Depression. I briefly consider each of these issues in this closing chapter.

## Digital Mapping of New Deal Archaeology Projects

I recently undertook an effort to create a GIS of New Deal–funded archaeology across the United States (Means 2011). Digital mapping tools seem ideally suited for achieving a more holistic understanding of the debt modern American archaeologists owe to Depression-era work relief projects. Online access to even obscure journals has made this effort feasible—although much New Deal archaeological work still remains unpublished or minimally published. Original field records are not always readily available and might prove incomplete or even nonexistent. A significant repository of well-organized Works Progress Administration (WPA) accounts can be found at the National Anthropological Archives (NAA) in Suitland, Maryland. These reports reflect a portion of the WPA archaeology actually completed and do not cover work conducted under the auspices of other "alphabet soup" agencies, such as the Civilian Conservation Corps (CCC) or National Youth Administration (NYA). Because WPA funds were dispersed to localities for officials to fund work as they saw fit—as was true for other relief agencies—the records of these excavations are likely somewhat decentralized as well. The NAA curates extensive unpublished records even for published sites. For example, only a few of the hundreds of petroglyphs documented by a WPA crew near Dinwoody, Wyoming, were published in the final report on the project (Sowers 1939a, 1939b, 1941).

The GIS for New Deal archaeology is currently focused on archaeological surveys and excavations. While considerable efforts were expended on stabilizing and reconstructing archaeological parks across the United States during the Great Depression, including these kinds of projects into the GIS is not feasible at the present time. The map as it exists now highlights states where New Deal archaeology took place—and counties within those states when there are sufficient details available to do so—regardless of project size or duration (figure C.1). Searches of online digital journals were most helpful in uncovering forgotten and obscure projects. One rather tangential reference to a NYA archaeology project in Sacramento, California, was found in a journal whose audience was secondary school principals (*NASSP Bulletin* 1940:87–88). My correspondence with California archaeologists has revealed that this work was directed by Jeremiah Lillard, then president of Sacramento Junior College, who played a crucial role in the development of California archaeology in the 1930s by recruiting Robert F. Heizer and Franklin Fenenga to help with his projects in the Sacramento Valley (Wallace 1999). Lillard obtained Federal Emergency Relief Administration (FERA) funds as well as NYA support to aid his archaeological efforts (Lillard et al. 1939; Lillard and

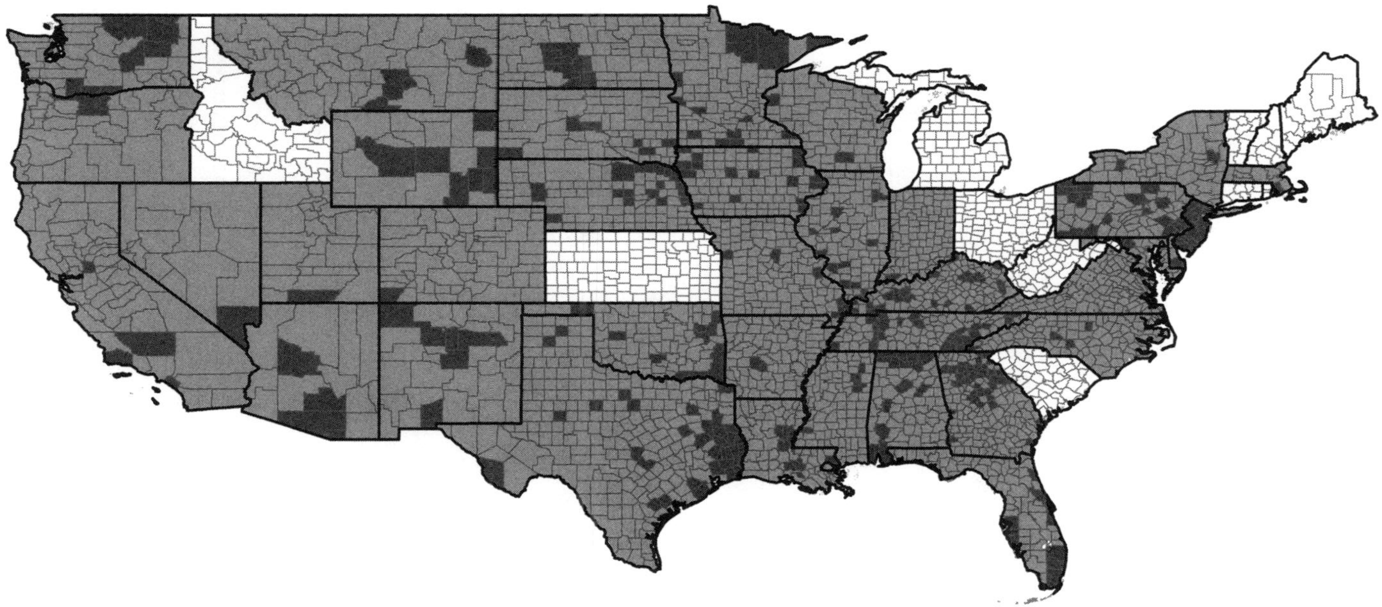

Figure C.1. Map of U.S. states as they existed in the 1930s. States shown in white had no known New Deal archaeological surveys or excavations. Counties within states are shaded when there is sufficient information to indicate work relief archaeology took place in these locations.

Purves 1936). Interestingly enough, Lillard also obtained Public Works Administration support to build his college's library—complete with Mayan-inspired glyphs on either side of the front door—with space to hold artifacts collected by the FERA- and NYA-supported projects (Mary Maniery, personal communication 2011; photographs of the library are available at http://www.loc.gov/pictures/collection/hh/item/CA2248/).

A much more extensive WPA survey and excavation program was also conducted in Orange County, California, largely under the sponsorship of the Board of Education of the Santa Ana City Schools. John Winterbourne directed the excavation and mapping of numerous cave, camp, and more substantial residential sites from 1937 to 1939. Some of these results have been published—decades after the original excavations (Ashby and Winterbourne 1966; Winterbourne 1966a, 1966b, 1967, 1968a, 1968b, 1968c)—but considerable unpublished artifact illustrations, site maps, and photographs are extant at the NAA.

In the adjacent state of Nevada, major work relief excavations were conducted at Anasazi sites to be flooded by Lake Mead following the construction of the Hoover Dam. These CCC investigations were overseen by M. R. Harrington from 1933 to 1935; Harrington had worked earlier in the region for the Heye Foundation (Fowler 1986b:17–18). Harrington apparently faced challenges directing the CCC crews, who were not always careful about what they saved, which limits more recent interpretations of their data (Lyneis 1986:55, 58). CCC crews were also less than helpful to the lead archaeologists on the other side of the United States in Sussex County, Delaware. One of the CCC workers at the Slaughter Creek village site excavated a pit with unbridled enthusiasm and "instead of defining the limit of the pit as requested, dug into it and brought up the entire skull pan on his shovel" from what turned out to be a grave (Davidson 1935:94).

These vignettes provide only a glimpse of the unpublished, underpublished, or forgotten legacy of New Deal archaeology. New Deal archaeology was certainly not an organized and integrated national effort, but it did change how professional archaeologists and lay people alike viewed America's past. The GIS of New Deal archaeology should enhance the modern archaeologist's appreciation for work relief archaeology—especially when the GIS becomes linked to the voluminous collections of New Deal findings emerging in cyberspace, as well as to the locations of significant repositories of artifacts and field records already available for study (e.g., Sullivan and Braly 2011). The GIS is presently in a preliminary state and has already benefited from a dialogue with archaeologists familiar with the New Deal archaeology conducted in their particular regions but who have not considered how these local findings might be integrated into a broader, more synthetic understanding of Depression-era work relief archaeology.

## Archaeologies of the Great Depression

There is increasing archaeological emphasis on the material legacy of the New Deal itself, including modern excavations into archaeological sites created through New Deal programs. Many scholars have turned their attention of late to documenting and excavating CCC camps in particular; regrettably, none of the three papers presented in the HAIG symposium at the 2010 SAA annual meeting were available for this volume. However, I can briefly summarize their major points here. Mason Miller and John Campbell (2010) looked at CCC camps in Texas that were instrumental in developing a state park. Mark Howe, Tim Kelly, and Karen Miller (2010) combined archaeological investigations with oral history to show how CCC camps created the infrastructure for many National Parks and National Forests in California, while incidentally preparing the men to fight in World War II. Carole Nash (2010) drew on modern archaeological testing and remote sensing as an exercise in archaeological methodology devoted to the investigation of ephemeral sites, such as CCC camps in Virginia. A published example of this type of research includes Smith's (2001) study of a CCC camp in Bandelier National Monument, New Mexico.

One of the more intriguing studies into a CCC camp was recently conducted by Jonathan Libbon for his master's thesis at Indiana University of Pennsylvania (Libbon 2010, 2011a, 2011b). He mapped and conducted limited excavations at a CCC camp in the Allegheny National Forest, in Pennsylvania. Libbon's research design focused on consumer behavior under times of cultural and economic stress, including how discretionary spending by CCC enrollees compared with that at contemporary domestic sites. His efforts are more sophisticated in scope and design than studies limited to basic mapping and delineation of CCC camp structural remains and layouts, and they should serve as a model for future studies of CCC camps or other New Deal–era sites.

## Work Relief Archaeology during the Great Recession

Archaeology as it exists today owes a considerable debt to the ordinary men and women who labored at archaeological sites across the United States during the Great Depression under the CCC, WPA, NYA, or other federally funded work relief programs. As I noted in the opening chapter, archaeologists became more professionalized because of their experiences during the New Deal. But, archaeology as it exists today differs in many significant ways from those New Deal–funded efforts. Most importantly, archaeologists today often operate within a regulatory framework, are typically employed by private businesses, and much of their efforts are directed toward compliance with federal, state, or local environmental and other laws on sites to be impacted by construction. The New Deal model for work relief would not benefit most archaeologists today—as that model specifically instructed government agencies not to fund projects that competed with private businesses.

However, the American Recovery and Reinvestment Act (ARRA), signed into law by President Barack Obama on February 17, 2009 (Recovery.gov), certainly generated considerable hope for new work among archaeologists working in the Middle Atlantic states, and presumably other regions as well. At meetings of professional archaeologists that I attended in 2009 and early 2010, some speculated that private archaeological firms would be reinvigorated by ARRA funds spent on construction and the necessary environmental compliance that would precede these federally funded efforts. A few archaeologists even likened this to a new New Deal—except, of course, that professional archaeologists and not ordinary citizens would be provided with employment. Overall, this anticipated renaissance in federally funded archaeology did not take place. However, there are two ARRA-funded projects that are especially evocative of the New Deal, both conducted under the auspices of the U.S. Army Corps of Engineers, St. Louis District (USACE-SLD).

Using ARRA funds, the USACE-SLD contracted with three private cultural resources management firms to work with every USACE district in the continental United States, dividing the country into three districts: John Milner and Associates (Northeast Region); Brockington and Associates (Southeast Region); and Statistical Research, Inc. (Western Region). These companies conducted geoarchaeological and condition assessments of existing sites, among other tasks. They also surveyed USACE properties to locate previously unknown sites—a federally mandated effort that had not been funded in many years—increasing an understanding of prehistory and history throughout the United States. More than 30 states had some ARRA archaeological investigations under the direction of USACE-SLD, which is similar to the number of states investigated during the New Deal. And, of course, the projects provided employment and even led to the hiring of workers, which otherwise would not have been done in the current economy (Majewski et al. 2011). This project to some extent mirrored New Deal work relief programs, with the notable exceptions that those who were employed were professionals and that the effort was coordinated on a national level according to explicit guidelines, even if the latter varied from state to state.

The other program conducted under the direction of USACE-SLD is the Veterans Curation Project (VCP). The goal of the VCP is "to provide veterans with tangible work skills through the rehabilitation and preservation of archaeological collections and to advance the public stewardship of federally owned archaeological collections" (Adams et al. 2011).

The VCP maintains laboratories in Augusta, Georgia; St. Louis, Missouri; and Washington, D.C. (Rubenstein and Riordan 2011:2). As they are rehousing old collections, veterans who have returned recently from combat learn job skills useful in the civilian world, including photography, software proficiency, and records management (Adams et al. 2011), while helping preserve the heritage of the nation they had volunteered to defend. The VCP program is probably closer to the spirit of New Deal archaeology programs than the compliance-funded ARRA project, largely because of the employment of "unskilled" labor to conduct archaeology. Both programs show that there is still a crucial role that federal funds can play in alleviating unemployment and supporting archaeological investigations. Further, while World War II turned some individuals away from archaeology, perhaps a new New Deal can help reinvigorate the close relationship between archaeology and the American people that developed during the Great Depression.

## "If It Is 'Alphabet Soup' Let's Have More of It"

There are certainly varying perspectives on the quality of the archaeological research produced during the New Deal. A decade after the founding of the SAA, and a mere two years after the end of the WPA, the WPA's impact on American archaeology was assessed by the SAA's planning committee, which noted: "In spite of . . . criticisms, the value of work done under WPA is evident. The work which the Committee has done to date supports several statements to the effect that WPA produced more sound archaeological work than has ever been done in a similar period." This statement can be extended to all New Deal archaeological investigations. I close this volume by echoing Pennsylvania's state archaeologist during the Great Depression, who said in 1934: "The past three months have brought Archaeological and Historical research onto a plane never before reached in the history of the country. If it is 'Alphabet Soup' let's have more of it" (Cadzow 1934). As the Great Recession lingers, it may be time to think of new "alphabet soup" programs beyond ARRA that could benefit the American people—and further enrich our understanding of America's past.

## Acknowledgments

I would like to thank the staff at the National Anthropological Archives for opening the WPA collections to me for my research. Without them, the GIS of New Deal archaeology would not have been possible. This GIS would not have been possible without the assistance of Virginia Commonwealth University student Clinton King. John W. Foster of the Archaeology, History, and Museums Division, California State Parks; Mark R. Barnes of Georgia State University; and Mary L. Maniery of PAR Environmental Services should be commended for freely sharing information that helped me understand the role played by Jeremiah Lillard of Sacramento Junior College in New Deal investigations in central California. Bobby Braly of the Frank H. McClung Museum, University of Tennessee, helped me fill in some missing Tennessee counties for the New Deal archaeology GIS. Jonathan Libbon of Coastal Carolina Research was kind enough to provide me with copies of his research on his recent excavations of a CCC camp in Pennsylvania.

# References


Adams, Andrea, Catherine McMahon, Cody Gregory, Lester Stone, and Michael K. Trimble

2011 Veterans and Archaeological Collections: The History and Application of the Veterans Curation Project. Poster presented at the 76th Annual Meeting of the Society for American Archaeology, Sacramento.

Adams, William Hampton

2003 Dating Historical Sites: The Importance of Understanding Time Lag in the Acquisition, Curation, Use, and Disposal of Artifacts. *Historical Archaeology* 37(2):38–64.

Adolph, Henry

1935 Annual Meeting, Society for Pennsylvania Archaeology, Harrisburg, PA., January 17, 1935. *Pennsylvania Archaeologist* 5(1):7–14.

Alex, Lynn M.

2000 *Iowa's Archaeological Past.* University of Iowa Press, Iowa City.

2008 Orr, Ellison James. In *The Biographical Dictionary of Iowa,* edited by David Hudson, Marvin Bergman, and Loren Horton, pp. 390–392. University of Iowa Press, Iowa City.

Allen, Rebecca

1991 Historical Archaeology in Pennsylvania during the Depression. *Pennsylvania Archaeologist* 61(2):18–30.

Almazan, Tristan, and Sarah Coleman

2003 George Amos Dorsey: A Curator and His Comrades. In *Curators, Collections, and Contexts: Anthropology at the Field Museum 1893–2002,* edited by Stephen E. Nash and Gary M. Feinman. *Fieldiana: Anthropology* (Chicago), n.s., 36:87–98.

Anderson, Duane C.

1975 The Development of Archaeology in Iowa: An Overview. *Proceedings of the Iowa Academy of Science* 82:71–86.

1985 Excavations at the Wittrock Site (13OB4): A Compilation of Information Pertaining to Projects Conducted in 1959 and 1965. Research Papers Vol. 10, pp. 1–83. Office of the State Archaeologist, University of Iowa, Iowa City.

Anonymous

1936 *Land Acquisition Project Analysis Report.* Prepared by Analysis and Selection Unit, Project Planning Section, Land Utilization Division. On file, Oconee Ranger District, Eatonton, Georgia.

1939 *Tentative Management Plan, 1939–1940, Plantation Piedmont Project LA-GA-3.* Prepared by the USDA Soil Conservation Service. On file, Oconee Ranger District, Eatonton, Georgia.

Ashby, G. E., and J. W. Winterbourne

1966 A Study of Primitive Man in Orange County and Some of the Coastal Areas. *Pacific Coast Archaeological Society Quarterly* 2(1):3–52.

Augustine, Edgar E.

1935a Untitled report submitted to R. H. Krissinger, WPA District Supervisor, Somerset, Pennsylvania, dated November 22. On file, Pennsylvania State Archives, Harrisburg.

1935b Letter to State Archaeologist Donald Cadzow dated December 4. On file, Pennsylvania State Archives, Harrisburg.

1935c Untitled report submitted to R. H. Krissinger, WPA District Supervisor, Somerset, Pennsylvania, dated December 4. On file, Pennsylvania State Archives, Harrisburg.

1935d Untitled report submitted to R. H. Krissinger, WPA District Supervisor, Somerset, Pennsylvania, dated December 2. On file, Pennsylvania State Archives, Harrisburg.

1935e Untitled report submitted to Sam Kennedy, WPA Labor Management Office, Somerset, Pennsylvania, dated November 18. On file, Pennsylvania State Archives, Harrisburg.

1936a Letter to State Archaeologist Donald Cadzow dated September 18. On file, Pennsylvania State Archives, Harrisburg.

1936b Letter to Banker B. F. Hanna dated September 19. On file, Pennsylvania State Archives, Harrisburg.

1936c Letter to Banker John I. Scull dated September 19. On file, Pennsylvania State Archives, Harrisburg.

1936d Letter to State Archaeologist Donald Cadzow dated October 2. On file, Pennsylvania State Archives, Harrisburg.

1936e Untitled report submitted to R. H. Krissinger, WPA District Supervisor, Somerset, Pennsylvania, dated December 31. On file, Pennsylvania State Archives, Harrisburg.

1936f Untitled report submitted to R. H. Krissinger, WPA District Supervisor, Somerset, Pennsylvania, dated March 11. On file, Pennsylvania State Archives, Harrisburg.

1936g Letter to State Archaeologist Donald Cadzow dated March 12. On file, Pennsylvania State Archives, Harrisburg.

1936h Letter to State Archaeologist Donald Cadzow dated February 26. On file, Pennsylvania State Archives, Harrisburg.

1936i Untitled report submitted to R. H. Krissinger, WPA District Supervisor, Somerset, Pennsylvania, dated November 18. On file, Pennsylvania State Archives, Harrisburg.

1936j Letter to State Archaeologist Donald Cadzow dated August 24. On file, Pennsylvania State Archives, Harrisburg.

1936k Letter to State Archaeologist Donald Cadzow dated March 14. On file, Pennsylvania State Archives, Harrisburg.

1936l Untitled report submitted to R. H. Krissinger, WPA District Supervisor, Somerset, Pennsylvania, dated March 19. On file, Pennsylvania State Archives, Harrisburg.

1936m Untitled report submitted to R. H. Krissinger, WPA District Supervisor, Somerset, Pennsylvania, dated January 3. On file, Pennsylvania State Archives, Harrisburg.

1936n Letter to State Archaeologist Donald Cadzow dated March 23. On file, Pennsylvania State Archives, Harrisburg.

1936o Letter to State Archaeologist Donald Cadzow dated March 24. On file, Pennsylvania State Archives, Harrisburg.

1937a Letter to State Archaeologist Donald Cadzow dated July 20. On file, Pennsylvania State Archives, Harrisburg.

1937b Untitled report submitted to J. Warren Shaver, Assistant Supervisor, WPA, dated June 29. On file, Pennsylvania State Archives, Harrisburg.

1937c Untitled report submitted to J. Warren Shaver, Assistant Supervisor, WPA, dated July 1. On file, Pennsylvania State Archives, Harrisburg.

1937d Untitled report submitted to J. Warren Shaver, Assistant Supervisor, WPA, dated May 4. On file, Pennsylvania State Archives, Harrisburg.

1938a Letter to State Archaeologist Donald Cadzow dated October 24. On file, Pennsylvania State Archives, Harrisburg.

1938b Letter to State Archaeologist Donald Cadzow dated March 14. On file, Pennsylvania State Archives, Harrisburg.

1938c Recent Discoveries in Somerset County. *Pennsylvania Archaeologist* 8(1): 6–12.

1938d Indian Fortifications in Somerset County. *Pennsylvania Archaeologist* 8(2): 41–45.

1938e Somerset County Excavations: The Powell Sites. *Pennsylvania Archaeologist* 8(3):60–63, 71.

1938f Important Research on Peck and Martz Rock Shelter Site in Somerset County. *Pennsylvania Archaeologist* 8(4):83–88.

1939 Fort Hill Site, Quarterly Report: 6/26/39–9/30/39. Somerset County Archaeological Survey, Work Projects Administration. On file, The State Museum of Pennsylvania, Harrisburg.

1940 Fort Hill. *Pennsylvania Archaeologist* 10(3):51–58.

Axel-Lute, Paul

2005 *General Statutes of New Jersey 1895,* Vol. 3. Rutgers, State University of New Jersey, New Brunswick.

Baird, W. David

1974 *The Chickasaw People.* Indian Tribal Series, Phoenix.

Baerreis, David A.

1941a Quarterly Report for McCurtain County, Period Ending September 30, 1941. On file, Sam Noble Oklahoma Museum of Natural History, Norman.

1941b Quarterly Report for McCurtain County, Period Ending December 31, 1941. On file, Sam Noble Oklahoma Museum of Natural History, Norman.

1942 Quarterly Report of McCurtain County, Period Ending March 31, 1942. On file, Oklahoma Archeological Survey, Norman.

Barry, John M.

1997 *Rising Tide: The Great Mississippi Flood of 1927 and How It Changed America.* Touchstone, New York.

Bartram, William

1791 *Travels through North and South Carolina, Georgia, East and West Florida, The Cherokee Country, The Extensive Territories of the Muscogulges or Creek Confederacy, and the Country of the Chactaws.* James and Johnson, Philadelphia.

Bell, Robert E., and David A. Baerreis

1951 A Survey of Oklahoma Archaeology. *Bulletin of the Texas Archeological and Paleontological Society* 22:1–100.

Benn, David W.

2001 Commentary on the Archeological History of Southeastern Iowa. *Journal of the Iowa Archeological Society* 48(1):31–44.

Benn, David W., and Scott Stadler

2004 *Effigy Mounds National Monument Archaeological Overview and Assessment.* BCA 1087. Bear Creek Archeology, Cresco, Iowa. Submitted to Midwest Archeological Center, National Park Service. On file, Office of the State Archaeologist, University of Iowa, Iowa City.

Benson, Fayrene, Jimm Jacobs, and Bob Burke

2004 *Traveling Timber Towns.* Commonwealth Press, Oklahoma City, Oklahoma.

Berrie, Ruby Wilson

1939 Letter to J. D. Compton dated April 21. On file, Bryan-Lang Historical Library, Woodbine, Georgia.

Biles, Roger

1991 *A New Deal for the American People.* Northern Illinois University Press, DeKalb.

Black, Flora

1934 Somerset County Historical Survey, Civil Works Administration, Archaeology Survey: A Progress Report, Jan. 2, to Feb. 15, 1934. On file, Pennsylvania State Archives, Harrisburg.

Bouquet, Henry, Sylvester Kirby Stevens, and Donald H. Kent

1940 *The Papers of Col. Henry Bouquet.* Pennsylvania Historical Commission, Harrisburg.

Bourne, Edward G. (translator)

1904 *Narratives of the Career of De Soto,* Vols. I and II. A. S. Barnes, New York.

Bremer, William W.

1975 Along the "American Way": The New Deal's Work Relief Programs for the Unemployed. *The Journal of American History* 62:636–652.

Brender, E. V.

1949 *Past Land Use History, Hitchiti Experimental Forest, Jones County, Georgia.* U.S. Forest Service, Southeastern Forest Experimental Station, Asheville, North Carolina.

Bronson, Bennet

2003 Berthold Laufer. In *Curators, Collections, and Contexts: Anthropology at the Field Museum 1893–2002,* edited by Stephen E. Nash and Gary M. Feinman. *Fieldiana: Anthropology* (Chicago), n.s., 36:117–126.

Brown, James A.

1976 *Spiro Studies: 4. The Artifacts.* Stovall Museum, University of Oklahoma, Norman.

Brown, Ralph D.

1939–1940 15Bt20 field notes. On file, William S. Webb Museum of Anthropology, University of Kentucky, Lexington.

1947 Letter to the Annis family dated September 14. In the possession of Doris Tichenor, Butler County, Kentucky.

Browman, David L.

2002 Frederic Ward Putnam: Contributions to the Development of Archaeological Institutions and Encouragement of Women Practitioners. In *New Perspectives on the Origins of Americanist Archaeology,* edited by David L. Browman and Stephen Williams, pp. 209–241. University of Alabama Press, Tuscaloosa.

Bryson, Richard A., and David A. Baerreis

1968 Introduction and Project Summary. In *Climatic Change and the Mill Creek Culture of Iowa: Part 1,* edited by Dale R. Henning. *Journal of the Iowa Archeological Society* 15:1–34.

Butler, Brian M.

1991 Kincaid Revisited: The Mississippian Sequence in the Lower Ohio Valley. In *Cahokia and the Hinterlands: Middle Mississippian Cultures of the Midwest,* edited by Thomas E. Emerson and R. Barry Lewis, pp. 264–273. University of Illinois Press, Urbana-Champaign.

Butler, Mary

1936 Recent Archaeological Work in Southwestern Pennsylvania. *Pennsylvania Archaeologist* 6(1):55–58.

1939 *Three Archaeological Sites in Somerset County, Pennsylvania.* Pennsylvania Historical Commission Bulletin 753. Pennsylvania Historical Commission, Harrisburg.

Cadzow, Donald

1934 Editorial. *Pennsylvania Archaeologist* 3(6):23.

1935a The Pennsylvania Historical Commission's Work in Somerset County. *Pennsylvania Archaeologist* 4(4):10–12.

1935b *Report on Archaeological Explorations in Western Pennsylvania 1934.* Pennsylvania Historical Commission Bulletin IV. Pennsylvania Historical Commission, Harrisburg.

1936 Archaeology and the Works Progress Administration in Pennsylvania. *Pennsylvania Archaeologist* 5(4):99.

1938a Letter to Ellen S. Woodward, Assistant Administrator, WPA, Washington, D.C., dated November 2. On file, Pennsylvania State Archives, Harrisburg.

1938b Letter to Ellen S. Woodward, Assistant Administrator, WPA, Washington, D.C., dated July 12. On file, The State Museum of Pennsylvania, Harrisburg.

1938c Letter to Frank Setzler, Smithsonian Institution, dated October 27. On file, The State Museum of Pennsylvania, Harrisburg.

1939 Letter to Mr. Francis J. Nitch, WPA, Johnstown, Pennsylvania, dated May 10. On file, Pennsylvania State Archives, Harrisburg.

1940 Letter to Edgar Augustine dated October 15. On file, Pennsylvania State Archives, Harrisburg.

Caldwell, Joseph, and Catherine McCann

1941 *Irene Mound Site, Chatham County, Georgia*. University of Georgia Press, Athens.

Caldwell, Joseph, and Antonio J. Waring Jr.

1939a Deptford Simple Stamped. In *News Letter of the Southeastern Archaeological Conference* 1(5):4 and plate.

1939b Brewton Hill Complicated Stamped. In *News Letter of the Southeastern Archaeological Conference* 1(5):5 and plate.

1939c Wilmington Heavy Cord Marked. In *News Letter of the Southeastern Archaeological Conference* 1(5):6–7 and plate.

1939d Deptford Linear Check Stamped. In *News Letter of the Southeastern Archaeological Conference* 1(5):8–9 and plate.

1939e Savannah Check Stamped. In *News Letter of the Southeastern Archaeological Conference* 1(5):10 and plate.

1939f Savannah Complicated Stamped. In *News Letter of the Southeastern Archaeological Conference* 1(5):11–12 and plate.

1939g Deptford Bold Check Stamped. In *News Letter of the Southeastern Archaeological Conference* 1(6):1.

1939h Irene Plain. In *News Letter of the Southeastern Archaeological Conference* 1(6):2 and plate.

1939i Irene Incised. In *News Letter of the Southeastern Archaeological Conference* 1(6):3–4 and plate.

1939j Irene Filfot Stamped. In *News Letter of the Southeastern Archaeological Conference* 1(6):5–6 and plate.

1939k Savannah Burnished Plain. In *News Letter of the Southeastern Archaeological Conference* 1(6):7 and plate.

1939l Savannah Fine Cordmarked. In *News Letter of the Southeastern Archaeological Conference* 1(6):8–9 and plate.

Calver, William Louis, and Reginald Pelham Bolton

1950 *History Written with Pick and Shovel: Military Buttons, Belt-Plates, Badges, and Other Relics Excavated from Colonial, Revolutionary, and War of 1812 Camp Sites by the Field Exploration Committee of the New-York Historical Society*. New York Historical Society, New York.

Cate, Margaret Davis

1940 Letter to Preston Holder dated January 30. On file, National Anthropological Archives, Smithsonian Institution, Suitland, Maryland.

Chance, Marsha A.

1974 The WPA Glynn County Project: A Ceramic Analysis. Unpublished Master's thesis, Department of Anthropology, Florida State University, Tallahassee.

Chassé, Kristen

2007 Monongahela Mortuary Practices at the Reckner Site. *Journal of Middle Atlantic Archaeology* 23:117–122.

Clements, Forrest E.

1938 Preliminary Report on Archaeological Work in Oklahoma Done as Projects of the Works Progress Administration. On file, University of Oklahoma Libraries, Norman.

Codrington, Raymond

2003 Wilfrid D. Hambly and Sub-Saharan Africa Research at the Field Museum 1928–1953. In *Curators, Collections, and Contexts: Anthropology at the Field Museum 1893–2002,* edited by Stephen E. Nash and Gary M. Feinman. *Fieldiana: Anthropology* (Chicago), n.s., 36:153–164.

Coe, Joffre L.

1995 *Town Creek Indian Mound: A Native American Legacy.* University of North Carolina Press, Chapel Hill.

Cohen, Allen, and Ronald Filippelli

2003 *Times of Sorrow and Hope: Documenting Everyday Life in Pennsylvania during the Depression and World War II.* Pennsylvania State University Press, University Park.

Cole, Fay-Cooper

1939 Letter to W. C. McKern, Milwaukee Public Museum, dated July 14. On file, Regenstein Library, University of Chicago, Chicago.

1951 Preface. In *Kincaid: A Prehistoric Illinois Metropolis,* by Fay-Cooper Cole, Robert Bell, John Bennet, Joseph Caldwell, Norman Emerson, Richard MacNeish, Kenneth Orr, and Roger Willis, pp. v–vii. University of Chicago Press, Chicago.

Cole, Fay-Cooper, Robert Bell, John Bennet, Joseph Caldwell, Norman Emerson, Richard MacNeish, Kenneth Orr, and Roger Willis

1951 *Kincaid: A Prehistoric Illinois Metropolis.* University of Chicago Press, Chicago.

Collier, Donald

2003 My Life with Exhibits at the Field Museum 1941–1976. In *Curators, Collections, and Contexts: Anthropology at the Field Museum 1893–2002,* edited by Stephen E. Nash and Gary M. Feinman. *Fieldiana: Anthropology* (Chicago), n.s., 36:199–220.

Collins, Henry B., Jr.

1927 Potsherds from Choctaw Village Sites in Mississippi. *Journal of the Washington Academy of Sciences* 17(10):259–263.

Colwell-Chanthaphonh, Chip

2009 *Inheriting the Past: The Making of Arthur C. Parker and Indigenous Archaeology.* University of Arizona Press, Tucson.

Compton, J. D.

1936a Letter to Frank Setzler dated March 7. On file, National Anthropological Archives, Smithsonian Institution, Suitland, Maryland.

1936b Letter to Dr. C. C. Harrold, President of the Society for Georgia Archaeology, dated March 2. On file, Bryan-Lang Historical Library, Woodbine, Georgia.

Coode, Thomas, and John Bauman

1981 *People, Poverty, and Politics: Pennsylvanians during the Great Depression.* Bucknell University Press, Lewisburg, Pennsylvania.

Cotter, John L.

1993 Kentucky Memoir: Digging during the Depression. *Archaeology* 46(1): 30–35.

Claassen, Cheryl

1999 Black and White Women at Irene Mound. In *Grit-Tempered: Early Women Archaeologists in the Southeastern United States,* edited by Nancy M. White, Lynne P. Sullivan, and Rochelle A. Marrinan, pp. 92–114. University Press of Florida, Gainesville.

Clay, Berle

1963 Ceramic Complexes of the Tennessee-Cumberland Region in Western Kentucky. Unpublished Master's thesis, Department of Anthropology, University of Kentucky, Lexington.

Cross, Dorothy

1941 *Archaeology of New Jersey,* Vol. 1. MacCrellish and Quigley Company, Trenton, New Jersey.

1956 *Archaeology of New Jersey: 2. The Abbott Farm.* MacCrellish and Quigley Company, Trenton, New Jersey.

Cushing, Frank H.

1886 A Study of Pueblo Pottery as Illustrative of Zuñi Cultural Growth. *Fourth Annual Report of the Bureau of Ethnology to the Secretary of the Smithsonian Institution, 1882–1883,* pp. 467–521. Washington, D.C.

1896 Pepper-Hearst Expedition: Preliminary Report on the Exploration of Ancient Key-Dweller Remains on the Gulf Coast of Florida. *Proceedings of the American Philosophical Society* 35(153):329–448.

Custer, Jay F.

1996 *Prehistoric Cultures of Eastern Pennsylvania.* Pennsylvania Historical and Museum Commission, Harrisburg.

Davidson, D. S.

1935 Burial Customs in the Delmarva Peninsula and the Question of Their Chronology. *American Antiquity* 1:84–97.

Davis, Alma

1938 Letter to Preston Holder dated November 15. On file, University of Nebraska at Lincoln Libraries, Lincoln.

Davis, Hester A.

1997 New Deal a Good Deal for US Archaeology. *Antiquity* 71:230–233.

Davis, Watson

1937 Letter to W. S. Webb dated July 2. William S. Webb Papers, University Archives, University of Kentucky Libraries' Special Collections, Lexington.

DeJarnette, David L.

1941 Letter to Walter B. Jones, Alabama Museum of Natural History, dated June 5. On file, Alabama Museum of Natural History, University of Alabama, Tuscaloosa.

Dixon, Roland B.

1913 Some Aspects of North American Archeology. *American Anthropologist,* n.s., 15:549–577.

Dorrance, Frances

1931 Report of Committee on Archaeology. In *Fifth Report of the Pennsylvania Historical Commission,* pp. 73–88. Pennsylvania Historical Commission, Harrisburg.

Dorsey, George A.

1894 The Study of Anthropology in American Colleges. *The Archaeologist* 2(12):368–373.

Dowd, Elsbeth L.

2008 Identifying Variation: A Stylistic Analysis of Four Caddo Pottery Assemblages from Southeast Oklahoma. Unpublished Master's thesis, Department of Anthropology, University of Oklahoma, Norman.

2009 New Approaches to Old Collections: Identifying Stylistic Variation among Caddo Pottery from Southeastern Oklahoma. *The Arkansas Archeologist* 49:17–32.

2011 Mountain Fork Archaeology: A Preliminary Report on the Ramos Creek Site (34Mc1030). *Caddoan Archaeology* 21:29–41.

Dugan, Kathleen H. (editor)

1942 *Statistical Abstract of the United States, 1941.* U.S. Government Printing Office, Washington, D.C.

Dunnell, Robert

1986 Five Decades of American Archaeology. In *American Archaeology: Past and Future,* edited by David J. Meltzer, Don D. Fowler, and Jeremy A. Sabloff, pp. 23–49. Smithsonian Institution Press, Washington, D.C.

Dye, David H.

1991 New Deal Archaeology in the Middle Tennessee Valley: 1934–1942. *Louisiana Archaeology* 18:23–59.

2002 The 1936 University of Tennessee WPA-TVA Excavations at the Link Farm Site (40HS6), Humphreys County, Tennessee. Paper presented at the 59th Annual Meeting of the Southeastern Archaeological Conference, Biloxi.

2003 The Link Farm Site (40HS6) in Regional Perspective. Paper presented at the 15th Annual Meeting of Current Research in Tennessee Archaeology, Nashville.

Elizabeth Journal

1931 Form Society for Research, State Museum Committee Members in Westfield. *Elizabeth Journal,* April 25, 1931.

Elliott, Daniel T. (compiler)

2010 *The WPA Glynn County Excavation Project: Phase I—Preston Holder's Paper Trail.* LAMAR Institute Publication Series, Report Number 161. The LAMAR Institute, Savannah, Georgia.

Everson, Gloria

2011 Edward Kennard, the Federal Writers' Project, and Public Archaeology. *The SAA Archaeological Record* 11(3):34–37.

Fagette, Paul

1996 *Digging for Dollars: American Archaeology and the New Deal.* University of New Mexico Press, Albuquerque.

Fairbanks, Charles H.

1946 The Macon Earth Lodge. *American Antiquity* 12:94–108.

1981 *Archeology of the Funeral Mound, Ocmulgee National Monument, Georgia.* Reprinted. Ocmulgee National Monument Association, Macon, Georgia. Originally published 1956, National Park Service, Washington, D.C.

Federal Works Agency

1940 *Under Three Flags.* Incomplete manuscript produced for the Frontier Forts and Trails Survey. Pennsylvania State Archives, Harrisburg.

Ferguson, Bruce K.

1999 The Alluvial History and Environmental Legacy of the Abandoned Scull Shoals Mill. *Landscape Journal* 18(2):147–156.

Fewkes, J. Walter

1924 Archaeological Fieldwork in Florida. In *Explorations and Fieldwork of the Smithsonian Institution in 1923,* pp. 88–98. Smithsonian Miscellaneous Collections 76(10). Smithsonian Institution, Washington, D.C.

1925 Prehistoric Aboriginal Culture of the Gulf States. In *Explorations and Fieldwork of the Smithsonian Institution in 1924,* pp. 92–118. Smithsonian

Miscellaneous Collections 77(2). Smithsonian Institution, Washington, D.C.

1928 The Archaeology of the Piedmont Region of South Carolina. *Explorations and Fieldwork of the Smithsonian Institution in 1927,* pp. 157–164. Smithsonian Institution, Washington, D.C.

Fewkes, Vladimir J.

1938a Irene Mound Excavations, Savannah, Georgia. *Proceedings of the Society for Georgia Archaeology* 1(2):24–31.

1938b News and Notes: Southeastern Area. *American Antiquity* 4:72–73.

Findley, Jim

2010 The Works Progress Administration (WPA) and Its Sub-Agency, the Museum Extension Project. Electronic document, http://digilab.browardlibrary.org/wpa/aboutwpa.html, accessed November 2010.

Ford, James A.

1936 *Analysis of Indian Village Site Collections from Louisiana and Mississippi.* Anthropological Study 2, Department of Conservation, Louisiana State Geological Survey, Baton Rouge.

Ford, James A., and James B. Griffin

1938 Report of the Conference on Southeastern Pottery Typology, May 16–17, 1938. Mimeograph reprinted in the *Newsletter of the Southeastern Archaeological Conference* 7(1):10–22.

Ford, James A., and Gordon R. Willey

1941 An Interpretation of the Prehistory of the Eastern United States. *American Anthropologist* 43:325–363.

Foster, James

1938 Letter to W. S. Webb dated December 6. William S. Webb Papers, University Archives, University of Kentucky Libraries' Special Collections, Lexington.

Fountain, Daniel L.

1995 Historians and Historical Archaeology: Slave Sites. *Journal of Interdisciplinary History* 26:67–77.

Fowler, Don D.

1986a Conserving American Archaeological Resources. In *American Archaeology: Past and Future,* edited by David J. Meltzer, Don D. Fowler, and Jeremy A. Sabloff, pp. 135–162. Smithsonian Institution Press, Washington, D.C.

1986b History of Research. In *Great Basin,* edited by Warren L. D'Azevedo, pp. 15–30. Handbook of North American Indians, Vol. 11, William C. Sturtevant, general editor. Smithsonian Institution, Washington, D.C.

Fowler, Melvin L., and Robert L. Hall

1972 *Archaeological Phases at Cahokia.* Research Series, Papers in Anthropology 1. Illinois State Museum, Springfield.

Fryman, Frank B., Jr.

1967 On the Selection of a Statistically Valid Ceramic Sample. Manuscript on file, William S. Webb Museum of Anthropology, University of Kentucky, Lexington.

Funkhouser, William D., and William S. Webb

1928 *Ancient Life in Kentucky.* Kentucky Geological Survey, Frankfort.

Gage, Abigail

2008 Six Inches Under: Mortuary Behavior at the Phillips Site, a Monongahela Village. *Journal of Middle Atlantic Archaeology* 24:21–26.

Galloway, Patricia

1997 Where Have All the Menstrual Huts Gone? The Invisibility of Menstrual Seclusion in the Late Prehistoric Southeast. In *Women in Prehistory: North America and Mesoamerica,* edited by Cheryl Claassen and Rosemary A. Joyce, pp. 47–62. University of Pennsylvania Press, Philadelphia.

Gamio, Manuel

1913 Arquelogia de Atzcapotzalco, D. F. Mexico. *Proceedings of the Eighteenth International Congress of Americanists,* pp. 180–187. Harrison and Sons, London.

Garcia, Joseph E., and George A. Brook

1996 Reconstruction of the Ocmulgee River, Georgia: 1807–1971. *Southeastern Geographer* 34(2):192–206.

Garland, Elizabeth B.

1992 *The Obion Site: An Early Mississippian Center in Western Tennessee.* Report of Investigations 7. Cobb Institute of Archaeology, Mississippi State University, Starkville.

George, Richard

1983 The Gnagey Site and the Monongahela Occupation of the Somerset Plateau. *Pennsylvania Archaeologist* 53(4):1–79.

Gill, Corrington

1935 Unemployment Relief. *The American Economic Review* 25(1):176–185.

1939 Letter from Assistant Administrator, WPA, Washington, D.C., to Mrs. K. G. (Ruby Wilson) Berrie dated April 4. On file, Bryan-Lang Historical Library, Woodbine, Georgia.

Gladwin, Winifred, and Harold S. Gladwin

1930 *A Method for the Designation of Southwestern Pottery Types.* Medallion Papers, No. 7. Globe, Pasadena, California.

1931 *Some Southwestern Pottery Types. Series II.* Medallion Papers, No. 10. Globe, Pasadena, California.

1934 *A Method for the Designation of Cultures and Their Variations.* Medallion Papers, No. 15. Globe, Pasadena, California.

Gougeon, Ramie A.

2006 Different but the Same: Social Integration of Households in Mississippian Chiefdoms. In *Leadership and Polity in Mississippian Society,* edited by Brian M. Butler and Paul D. Welch, pp. 178–194. Occasional Paper No. 33. Center for Archaeological Investigations, Southern Illinois University, Carbondale.

Green, William

1992 Charles Reuben Keyes and the History of Iowa Archaeology. *Journal of the Iowa Academy of Science* 99:80–85.

Green, William, Larry J. Zimmerman, Robin M. Lillie, Dawn Makes Strong Move, and Dawn Sly-Terpstra

2001 *Effigy Mounds National Monument Cultural Affiliation Report, Volume I.* Research Papers Vol. 26, No. 3. Office of the State Archaeologist, University of Iowa, Iowa City.

Greywacz, Kathryn

1934 Eastern States Archeological Federation: Minutes of the Executive Committee Meeting, February 17, 1934. *Pennsylvania Archaeologist* 4(1): 12–15.

Griffin, James B.

1946 Culture Change and Continuity in Eastern United States. In *Man in Northeastern North America,* edited by Frederick Johnson, pp. 37–95. Papers of the Robert S. Peabody Foundation, Vol. 3. Phillips Academy, Andover, Massachusetts.

1967 Eastern North American Archaeology: A Summary. *Science* 156(3772): 175–191.

1985 The Formation of the Society for American Archaeology. *American Antiquity* 50:261–271.

Griffin, James B. (editor)

1952 *Archeology of Eastern United States.* University of Chicago Press, Chicago.

Grinnell, George Bird

1919 A Buffalo Sweatlodge. *American Anthropologist* 21:361–375.

Gruber, Jacob W.

1986 Archaeology, History, and Culture. In *American Archaeology: Past and Future,* edited by David J. Meltzer, Don D. Fowler, and Jeremy A. Sabloff, pp. 163–186. Smithsonian Institution Press, Washington, D.C.

Guthe, Carl E.

1928 Archaeological Field Work in North America during 1927. *American Anthropologist,* n.s., 30:501–524.

1935 The Society for American Archaeology Organization Meeting. *American Antiquity* 1:141–146.

1936 Report, Society for American Archaeology. *American Antiquity* 1: 310–316.

1937 Letter to Thomas M. N. Lewis, University of Tennessee, dated December 30. On file, Milwaukee Public Museum, Milwaukee.

1952 Twenty-five Years of Archeology in the Eastern United States. In *Archaeology of Eastern United States,* edited by James B. Griffin, pp. 1–12. University of Chicago Press, Chicago.

Haag, William

1939 Letter to Preston Holder dated April 26. On file, University of Nebraska at Lincoln Libraries, Lincoln.

1942 A Description and Analysis of the Pickwick Pottery. In *An Archaeological Survey of Pickwick Basin,* edited by William S. Webb and David L. DeJarnette, pp. 513–526. Bureau of American Ethnology Bulletin 129. Smithsonian Institution, Washington, D.C.

1965 William Snyder Webb, 1882–1964. *American Antiquity* 30:470–473.

1985 Federal Aid to Archaeology in the Southeast, 1933–1942. *American Antiquity* 50:272–280.

1986 Field Methods in Archaeology. In *American Archaeology: Past and Future,* edited by David J. Meltzer, Don D. Fowler, and Jeremy A. Sabloff, pp. 63–76. Smithsonian Institution Press, Washington, D.C.

Hall, James

1976 [1801] *A Brief History of the Mississippi Territory.* Originally printed by Francis Coupée, Salisbury, North Carolina. 1976 publication by The Reprint Company, Spartanburg, South Carolina.

Hally, David J. (editor)

1994 *Ocmulgee Archaeology 1936–1986.* University of Georgia Press, Athens.

Hambly, Wilfrid D.

1930 *Ethnology of Africa, Hall D (Ground Floor).* Exhibit guide. Field Museum of Natural History, Chicago.

Hammerstedt, Scott W.

2005a Mississippian Construction, Labor, and Social Organization in Western Kentucky. Unpublished Ph.D. dissertation, Department of Anthropology, Pennsylvania State University, University Park.

2005b Mississippian Status in Western Kentucky: Evidence from the Annis Mound. *Southeastern Archaeology* 24:11–27.

2007 Mississippian Community and Construction at Annis Village. In *Current Archaeological Research in Kentucky: Volume Nine,* edited by E. Nicole Mills, Richard V. Williamson, and Richard D. Davis, pp. 103–129. Kentucky Heritage Council, Frankfort.

Hammerstedt, Scott W., Amanda L. Regnier, and Patrick C. Livingood

2010 Geophysical Investigations at the Clement Site, McCurtain County, Oklahoma. *Southeastern Archaeology* 29:279–291.

Hanson, Lee, and Dick Ping Hsu

1975 *Casemates and Cannonballs, Archaeological Investigations at Fort Stanwix, Rome, New York.* Publications in Archaeology 14. U.S. Department of the Interior, National Park Service, Washington, D.C.

Harlan, Edgar R.

1910 System in Mound Exploration. *Annals of Iowa* 9(4):311–313.

1914 Proposed Archaeological Survey of Iowa. *Annals of Iowa* 11(5):382.

Harrington, F. P.

1940 Summary of Report on Excavations by the Frontier Forts and Trails Survey on the Site of Fort Le Boeuf. Pennsylvania Historical Commission, Harrisburg.

Harrold, C. C.

1936 Letter to Frank Setzler dated February 19. On file, National Anthropological Archives, Smithsonian Institution, Suitland, Maryland.

Hart, John P.

1993 Monongahela Subsistence-Settlement Change: The Late Prehistoric Period in the Lower Upper Ohio Valley. *Journal of World Prehistory* 7: 71–120.

Hartman, William A.

1935 The Final Plan for the Plantation Piedmont Project for Planned Land Use. On file, Oconee Ranger District, Eatonton, Georgia.

Haskin, Warren E., Stephen E. Nash, and Sarah Coleman

2003 A Chronicle of Field Museum Anthropology. In *Curators, Collections, and Contexts: Anthropology at the Field Museum 1893–2002,* edited by Stephen E. Nash and Gary M. Feinman. *Fieldiana: Anthropology* (Chicago), n.s., 36:65–84.

Hawley, Marlin F.

2006 Introduction. In *Plains Archaeology's Past,* edited by Marlin F. Hawley and Virginia A. Wulfkuhle. *Plains Anthropologist* 51:487–520.

Hefner, Loretta L.

1980 The WPA Historical Records Survey, A Guide to the Unpublished Inventories, Indexes and Transcripts. Society of American Archivists, Chicago.

Heilbroner, Robert, and Aaron Singer

1994 *The Economic Transformation of America: 1600 to the Present.* 3rd ed. Harcourt Brace College, Fort Worth, Texas.

Heimlich, Marion D.

1952 *Guntersville Basin Pottery.* Geological Survey of Alabama Museum Paper 32. University of Alabama, Tuscaloosa.

Heizer, Robert

1949 *A Manual of Archaeological Field Methods; Prepared for Use by the California Archaeological Survey of the University of California and the Department of Anthropology at Berkeley.* University of California, Berkeley.

Henning, Dale R., Amy E. Henning, and David A. Baerreis

1968 1963 Excavations in the Mill Creek Sites. In *Climatic Change and the Mill Creek Culture of Iowa: Part 1,* edited by Dale R. Henning. *Journal of the Iowa Archeological Society* 15:35–106.

Herskovits, Melville J. (editor)

1950 *International Directory of Anthropologists.* 3rd ed. National Research Council, Washington, D.C.

Hinsley, Curtis M.

1976 Amateurs and Professionals in Washington Anthropology, 1879 to 1903. In *American Anthropology: The Early Years,* edited by John V. Murra, pp. 36–68. West Publishing, St. Paul.

1992 The Museum Origins of Harvard Anthropology 1866–1915. In *Science at Harvard University: Historical Perspectives,* edited by Clark A. Elliott and Margaret W. Rossiter, pp. 121–145. Lehigh University Press, Bethlehem, Pennsylvania.

1999 Frederic Ward Putnam. In *Encyclopedia of Archaeology. Part I: The Great Archaeologists,* edited by Tim Murray, pp. 141–174. ABC-Clio, Santa Barbara, California.

Hodge, Frederick W.

1931 Henry Wetherbee Henshaw. *American Anthropologist* 33:98–103.

Holder, Preston

1936a Letter to Frank Setzler dated June 18. On file, University of Nebraska at Lincoln Libraries, Lincoln.

1936b Letter to Frank Setzler dated June 25. On file, University of Nebraska at Lincoln Libraries, Lincoln.

1936c Letter to Frank Setzler dated July 10. On file, University of Nebraska at Lincoln Libraries, Lincoln.

1936d Letter to Frank Setzler dated May 10. On file, University of Nebraska at Lincoln Libraries, Lincoln.

1936e Glynn County Reports to Arthur Kelly for June 2, August 31, October 5, and December 12. On file, National Anthropological Archives, Smithsonian Institution, Suitland, Maryland.

1936f Letter to Arthur Kelly dated May 18. On file, University of Nebraska at Lincoln Libraries, Lincoln.

1936g Letter to Frank Setzler dated June 3. On file, University of Nebraska at Lincoln Libraries, Lincoln.

1936h Letter to Arthur Kelly dated July 13. On file, University of Nebraska at Lincoln Libraries, Lincoln.

1936i Pottery Lab Book—Site I—Airport, St. Simon's [*sic*] Island. On file, National Anthropological Archives, Smithsonian Institution, Suitland, Maryland.

1936j Report to Arthur Kelly dated December 12. On file, Coastal Georgia Historical Society on St. Simons Island, Georgia.

1936k Letter to Frank Setzler dated December 15. On file, University of Nebraska at Lincoln Libraries, Lincoln.

1936–1937 Records of Archeological Excavations in Glynn County, Georgia, for Work Projects Administration 1936–37. NAA Manuscript 3301. National Anthropological Archives, Smithsonian Institution, Suitland, Maryland.

1937a Letter to Julian Stewart dated February 16. On file, University of Nebraska at Lincoln Libraries, Lincoln.

1937b Glynn County Reports to Arthur Kelly for March 11. On file, National Anthropological Archives, Smithsonian Institution, Suitland, Maryland.

1937c Contract with Charles King for Permission to Excavate, dated January 31. On file, University of Nebraska at Lincoln Libraries, Lincoln.

1937d Letter to Antonio Waring dated November 3. On file, University of Nebraska at Lincoln Libraries, Lincoln.

1937e Letter to Frank Setzler dated April 9. On file, University of Nebraska at Lincoln Libraries, Lincoln.

1937f Evelyn Daybook VI. On file, National Anthropological Archives, Smithsonian Institution, Suitland, Maryland.

1937g Letter to Lucy B. McIntire dated June 7. On file, University of Nebraska at Lincoln Libraries, Lincoln.

1937h Letter to Lucy B. McIntire dated January 29. On file, University of Nebraska at Lincoln Libraries, Lincoln.

1937i Glynn County Reports to Arthur Kelly for July 26. On file, National Anthropological Archives, Smithsonian Institution, Suitland, Maryland.

1937j Evelyn Draft. On file, National Anthropological Archives, Smithsonian Institution, Suitland, Maryland.

1937k Letter to Chuck Wagley dated September 27. On file, University of Nebraska at Lincoln Libraries, Lincoln.

1937l Letter to Duncan Strong dated July 25. On file, University of Nebraska at Lincoln Libraries, Lincoln.

1937m Letter to Willard van Dyke dated September 6. On file, University of Nebraska at Lincoln Libraries, Lincoln.

1938a Excavations on St. Simons Island and Vicinity, 1936–1937. *Proceedings of the Society for Georgia Archaeology* 1(1):8–9.

1938b Archeological Method at the Irene Site. On file, Georgia Historical Society, Savannah, Georgia.

1938c Letter to Frank Setzler dated October 23. On file, University of Nebraska at Lincoln Libraries, Lincoln.

1938d Letter to Frank Setzler dated November 20. On file, University of Nebraska at Lincoln Libraries, Lincoln.

1938e Survey Method at Irene. On file, Georgia Historical Society, Savannah, Georgia.

1938f Survey at Irene. On file, Georgia Historical Society, Savannah, Georgia.

1938g Letter to Arthur Kelly dated November 30. On file, Georgia Historical Society, Savannah, Georgia.

1938h Letter to Arthur Kelly dated January 24. On file, Georgia Historical Society, Savannah, Georgia.

1938i Index card addressed to Jim [Ford] and Gordon [Willey]. On file, National Anthropological Archives, Smithsonian Institution, Suitland, Maryland.

1938j Note 1 on Ceramic Key to Deptford Sherds. On file, National Anthropological Archives, Smithsonian Institution, Suitland, Maryland.

1939a Letter to Mrs. K. G. (Ruby Wilson) Berrie dated April 18. On file, Bryan-Lang Historical Library, Woodbine, Georgia.

1939b Letter to Vincenzo Petrullo dated May 20. On file, National Anthropological Archives, Smithsonian Institution, Suitland, Maryland.

1939c Letter to Vincenzo Petrullo dated May 20. On file, University of Nebraska at Lincoln Libraries, Lincoln.

1969 Letter to Mrs. R. H. Newham dated January 10. On file, Bryan-Lang Historical Library, Woodbine, Georgia.

1970 *The Hoe and the Horse on the Plains: A Study of Cultural Development among North American Indians.* University of Nebraska Press, Lincoln.

Holmes, William F.

1977 1890–1940. In *A History of Georgia,* edited by Kenneth Coleman, pp. 255–336. University of Georgia Press, Athens.

Holmes, William H.

1903 Aboriginal Pottery of the Eastern United States. *Twentieth Annual Report of the Bureau of American Ethnology to the Secretary of the Smithsonian Institution, 1898–99,* pp. 1–237. Washington, D.C.

1914 Areas of American Culture Characterization Tentatively Outlined as an Aid in the Study of Antiquities. *American Anthropologist* 16:413–446.

Hotopp, John A.

1973 Phase Three Glenwood Explorations: Preliminary Report. In *Archaeological Explorations along Iowa Highways,* edited by Marshall McKusick, James Boylan, and John A. Hotopp, pp. 27–34. Report submitted to the Iowa State Highway Commission. Office of the State Archaeologist, University of Iowa, Iowa City.

1977 *Archaeological Explorations along Iowa Highways.* Report submitted to the Highway Division, Iowa Department of Transportation. Office of the State Archaeologist, University of Iowa, Iowa City.

1978 Settlement Patterns, Structures, and Temporal Placement of the Central Plains Tradition in Iowa. Unpublished Ph.D. dissertation, Department of Education, University of Iowa, Iowa City.

Hough, Walter

1916 Experimental Work in American Archaeology and Ethnology. In *Holmes Anniversary Volume: Anthropological Essays Presented to William Henry Holmes in Honor of His Seventieth Birthday, December 1, 1916, By His Friends and Collaborators,* pp. 194–197. J. W. Bryan Press, Washington, D.C.

Howe, Mark, Tim Kelly, and Karen Miller

2010 The Civilian Conservation Corps in California: Uncovering Our History. Paper presented at the 75th Annual Meeting of the Society for American Archaeology, St. Louis.

Hume, Ivor Noël

1969 *A Guide to Artifacts of Colonial America.* University of Pennsylvania Press, Philadelphia.

Hunter, William A.

1960 *Forts on the Pennsylvania Frontier, 1753–1758.* Pennsylvania Historical and Museum Commission, Harrisburg.

Inman, Anna R.

2007 Salvaging Prehistory: Archaeological Investigations at the Slayden Site (40HS1), Humphreys County, Tennessee. Unpublished Master's thesis, Department of Earth Sciences, University of Memphis, Memphis.

Iowa State Planning Board

1934 *A Preliminary Report of Progress.* Submitted to the National Resources Board by the Iowa State Planning Board, Des Moines.

1935 *Iowa State Planning Report*. Submitted to the National Resources Board by the Iowa State Planning Board, Des Moines.

Jacobson, Paul B.

1942 How the NYA Helps Youth. *The Phi Delta Kappan* 24:255–257.

Jefferson, Thomas

1782 [1784] Notes on the State of Virginia; Written in the Year 1781, Somewhat Corrected and Enlarged in the Winter of 1782, For the Use of a Foreigner of Distinction, In Answer to Certain Queries Proposed by Him Respecting 1. Its Boundaries ... 23. Histories, Memorials, ... [Paris]. Gale Group, Eighteenth Century Collections Online (accessed via http://galenet.galegroup.com.ezproxy.library.wisc.edu/servlet/ECCO).

Jefferson, Thomas, James Wilkinson, George Turner, Caspar Wistar, Adam Seybert, C. W. Peale, and Jonathan Williams

1799 Circular Letter: The Society Having Appointed a Committee to Collect Information Respecting the Past and Present State of this Country, the Committee During the Last Year Addressed the Following Letter to Such Persons as were Likely, in Their Opinion to Advance the Object of the Society. *Transactions of the American Philosophical Society* 4:xxxvii–xxxix.

Jennings, Jesse D.

1941 Chickasaw and Earlier Indian Cultures of Northeast Mississippi. *The Journal of Mississippi History* 3.

1986 American Archaeology, 1930–1985. In *American Archaeology: Past and Future,* edited by David J. Meltzer, Don D. Fowler, and Jeremy A. Sabloff, pp. 53–62. Smithsonian Institution Press, Washington, D.C.

1994 *Accidental Archaeologist: Memoirs of Jesse D. Jennings.* University of Utah Press, Salt Lake City.

Johnson, William C.

2001 The Protohistoric Monongahela and the Case for an Iroquois Connection. In *Societies in Eclipse: Archaeology of the Eastern Woodlands Indians, A.D. 1400–1700,* edited by David S. Brose, C. Wesley Cowan, and Robert C. Mainfort Jr., pp. 67–82. University of Alabama Press, Tuscaloosa.

Jones, Frank B.

1945 The Archaeological Fields of Southwestern Pennsylvania. In *The Horn Papers,* Vol. 2, pp. 743–754. Herald Press, Scottdale, Pennsylvania.

Jones, George C., Jr.

1873 *Antiquities of the Southern Indians, Particularly of the Georgia Tribes.* D. Appleton, New York.

Jordan, William R., and Phillip W. Quirk

2004 Archaeological Survey of 1,247 Acres in Compartments 113, 114, 118, and 119, Chattahoochee-Oconee National Forests, Oconee District, Jasper County, Georgia. Prepared for Chattahoochee-Oconee National Forests by R. S. Webb and Associates, Holly Springs, Georgia.

Joseph, J. W., Theresa M. Hamby, and Catherine S. Long

2004 *Historical Archaeology in Georgia.* University of Georgia, Laboratory of Archaeology Series, Report No. 39, Georgia Archaeological Research Design Paper No. 14. Athens.

Joseph, J. W., and Mary Beth Reed

1991 Archaeological, Historical, and Architectural Data Recovery at Finch Farm (Indian Road Farm), 38SP101. *In Agrarian Life, Romantic Death: Archaeological and Historical Testing and Data Recovery for the I-85 Northern Alternative, Spartanburg, South Carolina.* New South Associates Technical Report 39. New South Associates, Stone Mountain, Georgia.

Kay, Marvin, and George Sabo III

2006 Mortuary Ritual and Winter Solstice Imagery of the Harlan-Style Charnel House. *Southeastern Archaeology* 25:29–47.

Kelly, Arthur R.

1936a Letter to Preston Holder dated May 22. On file, University of Nebraska at Lincoln Libraries, Lincoln.

1936b Letter to Preston Holder dated July 18. On file, University of Nebraska at Lincoln Libraries, Lincoln.

Kent, Donald H.

1938 Frontier Forts and Trails Survey of Northwestern Pennsylvania. *Pennsylvania Archaeologist* 8(1):3–5.

Keyes, Charles R.

1934 Antiquities of the Upper Iowa. *The Palimpsest* 15(10):321–354.

1935 Field Work in North America during 1934: Iowa. *American Antiquity* 1:65–66.

1937a Notes and News: Iowa. *American Antiquity* 2:223–224.

1937b Iowa. In *The Indianapolis Archaeological Conference: A Symposium upon the Archaeological Problems of the North Central United States Area,* pp. 3–7. National Research Council, Washington, D.C.

1940 Notes and News: Iowa. *American Antiquity* 5:241.

Kidder, Alfred V.

1924 *An Introduction to the Study of Southwestern Archaeology, With a Preliminary Account of the Excavations at Pecos.* Papers of the Southwestern Expedition, Phillips Academy, No. 1. Yale University Press, New Haven, Connecticut.

1931 *The Pottery of Pecos,* Vol. 1. Papers of the Southwestern Expedition, Phillips Academy, No. 5. Yale University Press, New Haven, Connecticut.

Kiernan, Kevin

2008 Edition Production and Presentation Technology (EPPT) Applied to Preston Holder's WPA Archaeology on the Georgia Coast. Paper presented at the Center for Digital Research in the Humanities, University of Nebraska at Lincoln, Lincoln.

2009 The Charlie King Mound: A Little-Known Prehistoric Indian Mound on Saint Simons Island. Paper presented at the Spring Meeting of the Society for Georgia Archaeology, Macon.

2010 A Newly Discovered and Restored WPA Map of the Sea Island Mound. Paper presented at the Symposium on Southeastern Coastal Plain Archaeology, Douglas, Georgia.

Klein, Michael J.

1997 The Transition from Soapstone Bowls to Marcey Creek Ceramics in the Middle Atlantic Region: Vessel Technology, Ethnographic Data, and Regional Exchange. *Archaeology of Eastern North America* 25:143–158.

Kneberg, Madeline D.

1939 Letter to Carl E. Guthe, University of Michigan, dated August 11. On file, Milwaukee Public Museum, Milwaukee.

Knight, Vernon J., Jr.

1996 Introduction: The Expeditions of Clarence B. Moore to Moundville in 1905 and 1906. In *The Moundville Expeditions of Clarence Bloomfield Moore,* edited by Vernon J. Knight Jr., pp. 1–20. University of Alabama Press, Tuscaloosa.

Kooser, Ernest

1935 Letter to J. S. Picking Jr., Personnel Director, WPA, Somerset, Pennsylvania. On file, Pennsylvania State Archives, Harrisburg.

Kroeber, Alfred L.

1916 *Zuñi Potsherds.* Anthropological Papers of the American Museum of Natural History 18, part 1. New York.

1939 *Cultural and Natural Areas of Native North America.* University of California Press, Berkeley.

Krugman, Paul

2009 *The Return of Depression Economics and the Crisis of 2008.* W. W. Norton, New York.

Lambert, Allen C.

1935 Letter to Edgar E. Augustine dated November 30. On file, Pennsylvania State Archives, Harrisburg.

Lattanzi, Gregory Denis

2008 Elucidating the Origin of Middle Atlantic Pre-Contact Copper Artifacts Using Laser Ablation ICP-MS. *North American Archaeologist* 29: 297–326.

2010 The Indian Site Survey 1936–1941: New Jersey's First Stimulus Package. Paper presented at the 75th Annual Meeting of the Society for American Archaeology, St. Louis.

Lebergott, Stanley

1964 *Manpower in Economic Growth: The American Record since 1800.* McGraw-Hill, New York.

Le Page du Pratz, Antoine S.

1976 [1774] *The History of Louisiana or of the Western Parts of Virginia and Carolina.* Edited by Joseph G. Tregle, Jr. A facsimile reproduction of the 1774 edition; published for the Louisiana American Bicentennial Commission by the Louisiana State University Press, Baton Rouge.

Lepley, Sandra

2008 New Deal Archaeology in Somerset County Laid Foundation for Modern-Day Archeologists. *Somerset Magazine* 1(1):38–40.

Leuchtenburg, William E.

1963 *Franklin Roosevelt and the New Deal, 1932–1940.* Harper and Row, New York.

Lewis, R. Barry

1996 Introduction. In *Kentucky Archaeology,* edited by R. Barry Lewis, pp. 1–20. University of Kentucky Press, Lexington.

Lewis, T. H.

1899 Effigy Mounds in Iowa. *Science* 6:453–454.

Lewis, Thomas M. N.

1933 Letter to W. C. McKern, Milwaukee Public Museum, dated December 5. On file, Milwaukee Public Museum, Milwaukee.

1934 Letter to Walter B. Jones, Alabama Museum of Natural History, dated January 3. On file, Alabama Museum of Natural History, University of Alabama, Tuscaloosa.

1937a Letter to W. C. McKern, Milwaukee Public Museum, dated April 21. On file, Milwaukee Public Museum, Milwaukee.

1937b Letter to W. C. McKern, Milwaukee Public Museum, dated May 27. On file, Milwaukee Public Museum, Milwaukee.

1937c Annotations Pertaining to Prehistoric Research in Tennessee. *The University of Tennessee Record* 40(6):1–28.

1938 Letter to William S. Webb, University of Kentucky, dated January 8. On file, Milwaukee Public Museum, Milwaukee.

1939a Letter to W. C. McKern, Milwaukee Public Museum, dated June 23. On file, Milwaukee Public Museum, Milwaukee.

1939b Letter to W. C. McKern, Milwaukee Public Museum, dated June 28. On file, Milwaukee Public Museum, Milwaukee.

1939c Letter to W. C. McKern, Milwaukee Public Museum, dated July 7. On file, Milwaukee Public Museum, Milwaukee.

1939d Letter to James D. Hoskins, President, University of Tennessee, dated August 5. On file, Milwaukee Public Museum, Milwaukee.

1939e Letter to W. C. McKern, Milwaukee Public Museum, dated August 7. On file, Milwaukee Public Museum, Milwaukee.

1939f Letter to Carl E. Guthe, Laboratory of Anthropology, Santa Fe, dated August 17. On file, Milwaukee Public Museum, Milwaukee.

1939g Letter to Carl E. Guthe, Laboratory of Anthropology, Santa Fe, dated August 23. On file, Milwaukee Public Museum, Milwaukee.

Lewis, Thomas M. N., and Madeline D. Kneberg

1941 *Prehistory of the Chickamauga Basin in Tennessee.* Anthropological Papers No. 1. Division of Anthropology, University of Tennessee, Knoxville.

1946 *Hiwassee Island: An Archaeological Account of Four Tennessee Indian Peoples.* University of Tennessee Press, Knoxville.

1947 *The Archaic Horizon in Western Tennessee.* Tennessee Anthropology Papers No. 2. University of Tennessee Record, Extension Series, Vol. 23, No. 4. University of Tennessee, Knoxville.

1959 The Archaic Culture in the Middle South. *American Antiquity* 25:161–183.

Lewis, Thomas M. N., and Madeline Kneberg Lewis

1961 *Eva: An Archaic Site.* University of Tennessee Press, Knoxville.

1995 Manual of Field and Laboratory Techniques Employed by the Division of Anthropology, University of Tennessee, Knoxville, Tennessee. In *The Prehistory of the Chickamauga Basin in Tennessee,* Vol. II, compiled and edited by Lynne P. Sullivan, pp. 603–658. University of Tennessee Press, Knoxville.

Lewis, Thomas M. N., and Madeline Kneberg Lewis, compiled and edited by Lynne P. Sullivan

1995 *The Prehistory of the Chickamauga Basin in Tennessee.* 2 vols. University of Tennessee Press, Knoxville.

Libbon, Jonathan

2010 Life in the Woods: A Study of a Civilian Conservation Corps Camp in the Allegheny National Forest. Paper presented at the Joint Archeological Society of Virginia and Eastern States Archeological Federation Meeting, Williamsburg, Virginia.

2011a Identity and Work: Archaeological Investigations at a Civilian Conservation Corps Camp in the Allegheny National Forest. Paper presented at the Society for Historical Archaeology Annual Meeting, Austin.

2011b We Had Everything But Money: A Study of Buying Strategies at a Civilian Conservation Corps Camp in the Allegheny National Forest. Unpublished Master's thesis, Department of Anthropology, Indiana University of Pennsylvania, Indiana.

Lillard, Jeremiah, R. F. Heizer, and Franklin Fenenga

1939 An Introduction to the Archeology of Central California. *Sacramento Junior College Department of Anthropology Bulletin* 2.

Lillard, Jeremiah, and William K. Purves

1936 The Archaeology of the Deer Creek-Cosumnes Area, Sacramento Co., California. *Sacramento Junior College Department of Anthropology Bulletin* 1.

Lindley, Betty, and Ernest K. Lindley

1972 *A New Deal for Youth: The Story of the National Youth Administration*. Originally published in 1938. De Cap Press, New York.

Listman, John, Christopher Baker, and Susan Goodfellow

2007 *Historic Context: World War II Prisoner-of-War Camps on Department of Defense Installations.* Department of Defense Legacy Resource Management Program Project Number 05-256. Department of Defense, Washington, D.C.

Little, Barbara

2009 Family Resemblances: A Brief Overview of History, Anthropology, and Historical Archaeology in the United States. In *International Handbook of Historical Archaeology,* edited by Teresita Majewski and David Gaimster, pp. 363–381. Springer, New York.

Logan, Wilfred D.

1951 Past Iowa Archeological Research and Future Trends. *Journal of the Iowa Archeological Society* 1:3–10.

1976 *Woodland Complexes in Northeastern Iowa.* Publications in Archaeology 15. U.S. Department of the Interior, National Park Service, Washington, D.C.

Loughridge, Robert H.

1888 Report on the Geological and Economic Features of the Jackson Purchase Region. Kentucky Geological Survey, Lexington.

Lyneis, Margaret M.

1986 A Spatial Analysis of Anasazi Architecture, A.D. 950–1150, Moapa Valley, Nevada. *Kiva* 52(1):53–74.

Lyon, Edwin A.

1996 *A New Deal for Southeastern Archaeology.* University of Alabama Press, Tuscaloosa.

Madlehner, Leo A.

1939 Quarterly Progress Report of Frontier Forts and Trails Survey of Northwestern Pennsylvania. On file, Pennsylvania State Archives, Harrisburg.

Majewski, Teresita, Robert A. Heckman, Joseph F. Balicki, and Thomas G. Whitley

2011 Managing USACE, SLD ARRA-Funded Projects: Challenge and Response. Poster presented at the 76th Annual Meeting of the Society for American Archaeology, Sacramento.

Mann, B.

1938 Letter to Donald Cadzow dated January 11. On file, Pennsylvania State Archives, Harrisburg.

Malakoff, David

2008 A New Deal for Archaeology. *American Archaeology* 12(3):38–42.

Mallory, James M.

1936a Letter to Frank Setzler dated April 30. On file, National Anthropological Archives, Smithsonian Institution, Suitland, Maryland.

1936b Letter to Frank Setzler dated March 4. On file, National Anthropological Archives, Smithsonian Institution, Suitland, Maryland.

1936c Letter to Frank Setzler dated April 20. On file, National Anthropological Archives, Smithsonian Institution, Suitland, Maryland.

1936d Letter to Frank Setzler dated April 22. On file, National Anthropological Archives, Smithsonian Institution, Suitland, Maryland.

1936e Letter to Frank Setzler dated May 4. On file, National Anthropological Archives, Smithsonian Institution, Suitland, Maryland.

Martin, Paul S.

1931 Rare Idol-Like Figure from Illinois Mound. *Field Museum News* 2(6):3.

1932 Navajo Blankets Make Interesting Exhibit. *Field Museum News* 3(6):4.

1933 *Guide, Part 2: Archaeology of North America, Hall B (Ground Floor).* Exhibit guide. Field Museum of Natural History, Chicago.

1934 Toys in the Eskimo Collection. *Field Museum News* 5(5):1.

1936 Ancient Promissory Note Reveals Severe Usury. *Field Museum News* 7(11):3.

Martin, Paul S., Lawrence Roys, and Gerhardt von Bonin

1936 Lowry Ruin in Southwestern Colorado. *Fieldiana: Anthropology* (Chicago) 23(1).

Martin, Paul S., and Elizabeth Willis

1940 *Anasazi Painted Pottery in the Field Museum of Natural History.* Field Museum of Natural History Anthropology Memoirs 5. Field Museum of Natural History, Chicago.

Mason, J. Alden

1941 Aboriginal Sites in Chester County. *Pennsylvania Archaeologist* 11(2):27–35, 45–46.

Mason, Otis T.

1895 Influence of Environment upon Human Industries or Arts. *Annual Report of the Smithsonian Institution for 1895,* pp. 639–665. Washington, D.C.

1905 Environment. In *Handbook of American Indians,* edited by Frederick W. Hodge, pp. 427–430. Bureau of American Ethnology Bulletin 30. Smithsonian Institution, Washington, D.C.

McConaughy, Mark A.

2005 Middle Woodland Hopewellian Cache Blades: Blanks or Finished Tools? *Midcontinental Journal of Archaeology* 30:217–258.

2011 Burial Ceremonialism at Sugar Run Mound (36Wa359), a *Hopewellian* Squawkie Hill Phase Site, Warren County, Pennsylvania. *Midcontinental Journal of Archaeology* 36:73–104.

McConaughy, Mark A., and Janet R. Johnson

2003 Sugar Run Mound (36Wa359) and Village (36Wa2): Hopewell/Middle Woodland in Warren County, Pennsylvania. In *Foragers and Farmers of the Early and Middle Woodland Periods in Pennsylvania,* edited by P. A. Raber and Verna L. Cowin, pp. 101–116. Pennsylvania Historical and Museum Commission, Harrisburg.

McCoy, George D.

1946 *Summaries of Archeological Reports 1934–42.* On file, National Anthropological Archives, Smithsonian Institution, Suitland, Maryland.

McElvaine, Robert

1993 *The Great Depression: America, 1929–1941.* Times Books, New York.

McElvaine, Robert (editor)

1983 *Down and Out in the Great Depression: Letters from the "Forgotten Man."* University of North Carolina Press, Chapel Hill.

McIntire, Mrs. Frank (Lucy B.)

1937 Letter to Preston Holder dated June 4. On file, University of Nebraska at Lincoln Libraries, Lincoln.

McKenzie, Douglas Hugh

1964 The Moundville Phase and Its Position in Southeastern Prehistory. Unpublished Ph.D. dissertation, Department of Anthropology, Harvard University, Cambridge, Massachusetts.

McKern, W. C.

1933 Letter to Thomas M. N. Lewis, University of Tennessee, dated December 29. On file, Milwaukee Public Museum, Milwaukee.

McKinnon, Malcolm B.

1937 Letter co-signed by Preston Holder on November 22. On file, National Anthropological Archives, Smithsonian Institution, Suitland, Maryland.

McKusick, Marshall B.

1971 Foreword: The Man Behind the Reminiscences. In *Reminiscences of a Pioneer Boy,* by Ellison J. Orr. *Annals of Iowa* 40:530–535.

1973 *The Grant Oneota Village.* Report 4. Office of the State Archaeologist, University of Iowa, Iowa City.

1979 Documenting Iowa Prehistory: 1928–1964. *The Wisconsin Archeologist* 60:3–25.

McVicker, Donald

2003 A Tale of Two Thompsons: The Contributions of Edward H. Thompson and J. Eric S. Thompson to Anthropology at the Field Museum. In *Curators, Collections, and Contexts: Anthropology at the Field Museum 1893–2002,* edited by Stephen E. Nash and Gary M. Feinman. *Fieldiana: Anthropology* (Chicago), n.s., 36:139–152.

Means, Bernard K.

1998 Archaeological Past and Present: Field Methodology from 1930s Relief Excavations in Somerset County, Pennsylvania and Its Relevance to Modern Archaeological Interpretations. *Journal of Middle Atlantic Archaeology* 14:39–63.

1999 Monongahela Mortuary Practices in Somerset County, Pennsylvania: Observations and Implications. *Pennsylvania Archaeologist* 69(2):15–44.

2000a Mapping a New Future for the Past: Further Insights into Depression-era Archaeological Excavations in Southwestern Pennsylvania. *Journal of Middle Atlantic Archaeology* 16:155–166.

2000b Archaeology in Black and White: Digging Somerset County's Past during the Great Depression. *Pennsylvania Heritage* 26(3):6–11.

2000c An Archaeology of Archaeology: Recent Investigations into the 1938 Martz Rock Shelters Excavations. *Pennsylvania Archaeologist* 70(1):45–80.

2000d Toward a Model of Monongahela Village Community Organization: Analyzing Pit Feature Data Recovered from the 1934 to 1940 Somerset County Relief Excavations. *North American Archaeologist* 21:35–61.

2001 Circular Reasoning: Ring-shaped Village Settlements in Late Prehistoric Southwestern Pennsylvania and Beyond. *Journal of Middle Atlantic Archaeology* 17:109–131.

2002 Revisiting Mary Butler's "Three Archaeological Sites in Somerset County, Pennsylvania" for Continuing Insights into Depression-era Archaeology in Southwestern Pennsylvania and Late Prehistoric Monongahela Social Organization. *Pennsylvania Archaeologist* 72(2):8–46.

2003 Deliver Me from Mononga-Hell: Thinking beyond the Culture History Paradigm to Examine the Temporal and Spatial Parameters of Somerset Monongahela Village Settlements. *Journal of Middle Atlantic Archaeology* 19:37–58.

2005 New Dates for New Deal Excavated Monongahela Villages in Somerset County. *Pennsylvania Archaeologist* 75(1):49–61.

2006 Circular Reasoning: Drawing on Models of Ring-shaped Village Spatial Layouts to Examine Villages in Late Prehistoric Pennsylvania. Unpublished Ph.D. dissertation, Department of Anthropology, Arizona State University, Tempe.

2007 *Circular Villages of the Monongahela Tradition*. University of Alabama Press, Tuscaloosa.

2008 Resurrecting a Forgotten Monongahela Tradition Village, the Phillips (36Fa22) Site. *Journal of Middle Atlantic Archaeology* 24:1–12.

2010 Two Archaeological Sites in Fayette County, Pennsylvania. *Pennsylvania Archaeologist* 80(1):1–16.

2011 The Future Meets the Past: Digital Mapping of New Deal Archaeology Projects across the Lower 48 States. *The SAA Archaeological Record* 11(3):29–33.

Means, Bernard K., and Laura J. Galke

2004 Making a Future for the Past: New Dating Meets New Deal Archaeology. *Pennsylvania Heritage* 30(1):6–11.

Mehta, Jayur M.

2007 A Study of Sweat Lodges in the Southeastern United States. Unpublished Master's thesis, Department of Anthropology, University of Alabama, Tuscaloosa.

Meltzer, David J.

1985 North American Archaeology and Archaeologists, 1879–1934. *American Antiquity* 50:249–260.

Meltzer, David J., Don D. Fowler, and Jeremy A. Sabloff

1986 Editors' Introduction. In *American Archaeology: Past and Future,* edited by David J. Meltzer, Don D. Fowler, and Jeremy A. Sabloff, pp. 7–19. Smithsonian Institution Press, Washington, D.C.

Merry, Carl A.

2009 OSA Submits Nominations to the National Register. *Newsletter of the Iowa Archeological Society* 59(3&4):11.

Messner, T. C.

2008 Woodland Period People and Plant Interactions: New Insights from Starch Grain Analysis. Unpublished Ph.D. dissertation, Department of Anthropology, Temple University, Philadelphia.

Milanich, Jerald T.

2007 Gordon R. Willey and the Archaeology of the Florida Gulf Coast. In

*Gordon R. Willey and American Archaeology: Contemporary Perspectives,* edited by Jeremy A. Sabloff and William L. Fash, pp. 15–25. University of Oklahoma Press, Norman.

Miller, Mason, and John Campbell

2010 The CCC and Garner: Archeological Inventory of the Materials and Aesthetics from the Creation of One of Texas' Most Prized State Parks. Paper presented at the 75th Annual Meeting of the Society for American Archaeology, St. Louis.

Miller, Randall M., and William Pencak

2002 *Pennsylvania: A History of the Commonwealth.* Pennsylvania State University Press, University Park, and the Pennsylvania Historical and Museum Commission, Harrisburg.

Milner, George R.

2004 *The Moundbuilders: Ancient Peoples of Eastern North America.* Thames and Hudson, London.

Milner, George R., Thomas E. Emerson, Mark W. Mehrer, Joyce A. Williams, and Duane Esarey

1984 Mississippian and Oneota Period. In *American Bottom Archaeology,* edited by Charles J. Bareis and James W. Porter, pp. 158–186. University of Illinois Press, Urbana.

Milner, George R., and Virginia G. Smith

1986 *New Deal Archaeology in Kentucky: Excavations, Collections, and Research.* Occasional Papers in Anthropology No. 5. Program for Cultural Resource Assessment, University of Kentucky, Lexington.

Mitchell, Broadus

1947 *Depression Decade: From New Era through New Deal, 1929–1941.* Rinehart, New York.

Moeller, Roger

2008 Tired of Being Typed? Or the Potsherd Says What? Paper presented at the Middle Atlantic Archaeological Conference, Ocean City, Maryland.

Moore, Clarence B.

1915 Aboriginal Sites on Tennessee River. *Journal of the Academy of Natural Sciences of Philadelphia,* 2nd series, 16:170–304.

1916 Some Aboriginal Sites on Green River, Kentucky; Certain Aboriginal Sites on Lower Ohio River, Additional Investigation on Mississippi River. *Journal of the Academy of Natural Sciences of Philadelphia* 16.

Mott, Mildred

1938 The Relation of Historic Indian Tribes to Archaeological Manifestations in Iowa. *Iowa Journal of History and Politics* 36:227–304.

Myer, William E.

1921 Archaeological Explorations in Tennessee. *Explorations and Fieldwork of the Smithsonian Institution in 1920,* pp. 113–120. Smithsonian Institution, Washington, D.C.

1924 Archaeological Field-Work in Tennessee. *Explorations and Fieldwork of the Smithsonian Institution in 1923,* pp. 109–118. Smithsonian Institution, Washington, D.C.

1928 Two Prehistoric Villages in Middle Tennessee. *Forty-First Annual Report of the Bureau of American Ethnology to the Secretary of the Smithsonian Institution 1919–24,* pp. 485–614. Washington, D.C.

Nash, Carole

2010 The Civilian Conservation Corps and the Archaeology of the Recent Past in Virginia. Paper presented at the 75th Annual Meeting of the Society for American Archaeology, St. Louis.

Nash, Charles H.

1935 Original unpublished field notes on projects in Humphreys County, Tennessee. On file, Frank H. McClung Museum, Knoxville.

1968 *Residence Mounds: An Intermediate Middle-Mississippian Settlement Pattern.* Occasional Papers No. 2. Memphis State University Anthropological Research Center, Memphis, Tennessee.

Nash, Stephen E.

2003 Paul Sidney Martin. In *Curators, Collections, and Contexts: Anthropology at the Field Museum 1893–2002,* edited by Stephen E. Nash and Gary M. Feinman. *Fieldiana: Anthropology* (Chicago), n.s., 36:165–178.

2010 A Conflicted Legacy: Paul Sidney Martin as Museum Archaeologist 1925–1938. *American Anthropologist* 112:104–121.

Nash, Stephen E., and Gary M. Feinman (editors)

2003 Curators, Collections, and Contexts: Anthropology at the Field Museum 1893–2002. *Fieldiana: Anthropology* (Chicago), n.s., 36.

NASSP Bulletin

1940 The Student-Aid Program: Distribution of Youth by Type of Work, Academic Year 1939–40. *NASSP Bulletin* (National Association of Secondary School Principals) 24:43–104.

National Archives and Records Administration

1918 Military Records for Thomas McDowell Nelson Lewis. National Personnel Records Center, St. Louis.

Nelson, Nels C.

1914 *Pueblo Ruins of the Galisteo Basin.* Anthropological Papers of the American Museum of Natural History 15, part 1. New York.

1916 Chronology of the Tano Ruins, New Mexico. *American Anthropologist* 18:159–180.

Neumann, Georg K.

1936 Unpublished field notes and progress reports on projects in Humphreys County, Tennessee. On file, Frank H. McClung Museum, Knoxville.

New Jersey State Museum

1939 Quarterly Report of the Indian Site Survey—December 1939. On file, New Jersey State Museum, Trenton.

Newham, Mrs. R. H. (Marjorie)

1968 Letter to Preston Holder dated November 18. On file, University of Nebraska at Lincoln Libraries, Lincoln.

Nichols, D. G.

1936a Letter to Preston Holder dated July 8 [signed by Lucy B. McIntire]. On file, University of Nebraska at Lincoln Libraries, Lincoln.

1936b Letter to Preston Holder dated November 17 [signed by Lucy B. McIntire]. On file, University of Nebraska at Lincoln Libraries, Lincoln.

Nichols, Roy F.

1967 *The Pennsylvania Historical and Museum Commission, A History.* Pennsylvania Historical and Museum Commission, Harrisburg.

Nitch, Francis

1939 Letter to Edgar Augustine dated May 8. On file, Pennsylvania State Archives, Harrisburg.

O'Brien, Michael J., and R. Lee Lyman (editors)

2001 *Setting the Agenda for American Archaeology: The National Research Council Archaeological Conferences of 1929, 1932, and 1935.* University of Alabama Press, Tuscaloosa.

Olinger, Danny E., and A. Eric Howard

2009 In the Beginning . . . . In *TVA Archaeology: Seventy-five Years of Prehistoric Site Research,* edited by Erin E. Pritchard with Todd M. Ahlman, pp. 17–34. University of Tennessee Press, Knoxville.

Olsen, Stanley J.

1963 Dating Early Plain Buttons by Their Form. *American Antiquity* 28:551–554.

Orr, Ellison

1936a Report of Reconnoissance [sic] Survey and Excavation of Indian Mound Groups and Cemeteries in Valley of Upper Iowa and Mississippi River under Project 1047 of the Iowa Planning Board, by Party under Dr. Charles R. Keyes, June 11 to Sept. 16, 1934. Iowa Archaeological Reports Vol. 1. On file, Office of the State Archaeologist, University of Iowa, Iowa City.

1936b Report of a Statewide Reconnoissance [sic] Survey of Indian Mound Groups and Excavations of Camp Sites, under Project 1047 of the Iowa Planning Board, by Party under Dr. Charles R. Keyes, Sept. 17, 1934 to Mar. 7, 1935. Iowa Archaeological Reports Vol. 2. On file, Office of the State Archaeologist, University of Iowa, Iowa City.

1936c Report of Surveys and Excavations of Mound Groups along the Mississippi River Bluffs and Terraces from McGregor to Clinton, Iowa, under Project 1047 of the Iowa Planning Board, by Party under Dr. Charles R. Keyes, Apr. 8 to Aug. 10, 1935. Iowa Archaeological Reports Vol. 3. On file, Office of the State Archaeologist, University of Iowa, Iowa City.

1942a Survey and Excavation of Indian Mounds, Village Sites and Cemeteries in the Valleys of the Upper Iowa and Mississippi Rivers, 1936. Iowa Archaeological Reports Vol. 5. On file, Office of the State Archaeologist, University of Iowa, Iowa City.

1942b Report of an Archaeological Survey of Mills County, Iowa, Sponsored by the Iowa State Planning Board, WPA Project 3600, April 12 to Dec. 5, 1938. Iowa Archaeological Reports Vol. 10. On file, Office of the State Archaeologist, University of Iowa, Iowa City.

1942c Report of an Archaeological Survey of the Broken Kettle and Kimball Pre-Historic Indian Refuse-Mound Village Sites, 1939. Iowa Archaeological Reports Vol. 11. On file, Office of the State Archaeologist, University of Iowa, Iowa City.

1963 *Iowa Archaeological Reports 1934–1939 with an Evaluation and Index by Marshall McKusick.* In *Archives of Archaeology,* edited by David Baerreis. Microcard Series 20, Society for American Archaeology. University of Wisconsin Press, Madison.

Paige, John C.

1985 *The Civilian Conservation Corps and the National Park Service, 1933–1942: An Administrative History.* U.S. Department of the Interior, National Park Service, Washington, D.C.

Parker, Arthur C.

1916 The Origin of the Iroquois as Suggested by Their Archeology. *American Anthropologist* 18:479–507.

1920 *Archaeological History of New York.* 2 vols. New York State Museum Bulletins 235–238. New York State Museum, Albany.

Pasquill, Robert G., Jr.

2008 *Planting Hope on Worn-out Land: History of the Tuskegee Land Utilization Project, Macon County, Alabama, 1935–1959.* New South Books, Montgomery, Alabama.

Patterson, Thomas C.

1991 Who Did Archaeology in the United States before There Were Archaeologists and Why? Preprofessional Archaeologies of the Nineteenth Century. In *Processual and Postprocessual Archaeologies: Multiple Ways of Knowing the Past,* edited by Robert W. Preucel, pp. 242–250. Occasional Paper No. 10. Center for Archaeological Investigations, Southern Illinois University, Carbondale.

Peebles, Christopher S.

1979 *Excavations at Moundville. 1905–1951.* University of Michigan Press, Ann Arbor.

1981 A Precious Bequest: Contemporary Research with the WPA-CCC Collections from Moundville, Alabama. In *The Research Potential of Anthropological Museum Collections,* edited by Anne-Marie E. Cantwell, James B. Griffin, and Nan A. Rothschild. *Annals of the New York Academy of Sciences* 376:433–447.

Pennsylvania Archaeologist

1932a Archaeological Research on a Broad Scale to be Done by the State. *Pennsylvania Archaeologist* 3(1):11.

1932b Editorial. *Pennsylvania Archaeologist* 3(2):20.

1935 Editorial. *Pennsylvania Archaeologist* 5(3):58.

Pennsylvania Historical Commission

1915 *First Report of the Historical Commission of Pennsylvania.* Press of The New Era Printing Company, Lancaster, Pennsylvania.

Pennsylvania State Archives

2010 RG-13—Series Descriptions—PA Historical and Museum Commission. Electronic document, http://www.phmc.state.pa.us/bah/dam/rg/sd/r13sd4.htm, accessed December 12, 2010.

Perry, Michael J.

2007 Ancient Waterman Creek. *Iowa Heritage Illustrated* 88(3):99–109.

2008 Keyes, Charles Reuben. In *The Biographical Dictionary of Iowa,* edited by David Hudson, Marvin Bergman, and Loren Horton, pp. 282–284. University of Iowa Press, Iowa City.

Pestle, William J., Karen Wilson, Stephen E. Nash, and Sarah Coleman

2006 Reconciling the Past: A Catalogue of Scattered Collections. In *Archäologie und Computer, Kulturelles Erbe und Neue Technologien.* Stadtarchäologie Wien, Vienna.

Petrie, W. M. Flinders

1899 Sequences in Prehistoric Remains. *Journal of the Royal Anthropological Institute of Great Britain and Ireland* 29:295–301.

Petrullo, Vincenzo

1938 Letter from National Consultant, WPA, Washington, D.C., dated November 29. On file, University of Nebraska at Lincoln Libraries, Lincoln.

Pevarnik, George, Matthew T. Boulanger, and Michael D. Glascock

2008 Instrumental Neutron Activation Analysis of Middle Woodland Pottery from the Delaware Valley. Paper presented at the 74th Annual Meeting of the Eastern States Archeological Federation, Burlington, Vermont.

Philadelphia Record

1936 WPA Crews Digging for a "Jersey Adam." *Philadelphia Record,* March 19, 1936.

Phillips, Philip

1970 *Archaeological Survey in the Lower Yazoo Basin, Mississippi, 1949–1955,* Part 1. Papers of the Peabody Museum of Archaeology and Ethnography, Vol. 60. Harvard University, Cambridge, Massachusetts.

Phillips, Philip, James A. Ford, and James B. Griffin

1951 *Archaeological Survey in the Lower Mississippi Alluvial Valley, 1940–1947.* Papers of the Peabody Museum of American Archaeology and Ethnology No. 25. Harvard University, Cambridge, Massachusetts.

Polhemus, Richard R.

2002 Introduction: Clarence B. Moore's Research on the Tennessee, Green, and Lower Ohio Rivers, 1913–1916. In *The Tennessee, Green, and Lower Ohio Rivers Expeditions of Clarence Bloomfield Moore,* edited by Richard R. Polhemus, pp. 1–45. University of Alabama Press, Tuscaloosa.

Pykles, Benjamin C.

2008 A Brief History of Historical Archaeology in the United States. *The SAA Archaeological Record* 8(3):32–34.

2011 A New Archaeology in the New Deal: The Rise of Historical Archaeology in the 1930s. *The SAA Archaeological Record* 11(3):38–41.

Rafinesque, Constantine S.

1824 *Ancient History, or Annals of Kentucky: Introduction to the History and Antiquities of the State of Kentucky.* Privately published, Frankfort, Kentucky.

Range, William

1954 *A Century of Georgia Agriculture, 1850–1950.* University of Georgia Press, Athens.

Raper, Arthur F.

1936 *Preface to Peasantry: A Tale of Two Black Belt Counties.* University of North Carolina Press, Chapel Hill.

Redman, Samuel

2011 The Hearst Museum of Anthropology, the New Deal, and a Reassessment of the "Dark Age" of the Museum in the United States. *Museum Anthropology* 34(1):43–55.

Reed, Alfred, Jr.
1938 A Review of the Past—A Plan for the Future. *Oklahoma Prehistorian* 1(1):2–5.

Regnier, Amanda L., and Elsbeth L. Dowd
2010 The McDonald Site: A Caddo Farmstead(?) in McCurtain County, Oklahoma. Paper presented at the Annual Meeting of the Caddo Conference, Tyler, Texas.

Roberts, Frank H. H., Jr.
1935 Indian Mounds on Shiloh Battlefield. *Explorations and Fieldwork of the Smithsonian Institution in 1934,* pp. 65–68. Smithsonian Institution, Washington, D.C.

Rogers, J. Daniel
1978 Federally-Sponsored Archaeological Work in Oklahoma before World War II. On file, Oklahoma Archeological Survey, Norman.

Rubenstein, Paul, and Jennifer Riordan
2011 The US Army Corps of Engineers' Mandatory Center of Expertise for the Curation and Management of Archaeological Collections. *Department of Defense Cultural Resources Program Cultural Resources Update* 8(1):1–2.

Ruppé, Reynold J.
1953 The Present Status of Iowa Archaeology. *Journal of the Iowa Archeological Society* 3(2):16–24.
1955 Progress Report on the Excavation of the Phipps Site. *Newsletter of the Iowa Archeological Society* 5:1–3.

Samford, Patricia M.
1997 Response to a Market: Dating English Underglaze Transfer Printed Wares. *Historical Archaeology* 31(2):1–30.

Schermer, Shirley J., Linda Forman, Robin M. Lillie, Jill Robinson, and Larry J. Zimmerman
1998 *NAGPRA Inventory and Consultation: Human Remains and Funerary Objects in the Charles R. Keyes Collection.* Research Papers Vol. 23, No. 1. Office of the State Archaeologist, University of Iowa, Iowa City.

Schoff, Harry L.
1936 Activities of the Archaeological Division of the Frontier Forts and Trails Survey, 1937 and 1938. *Pennsylvania Archaeologist* 8(3):69–70.

Schoolcraft, Henry Rowe
1854 *Information Respecting the History, Condition, and Prospects of the Indian Tribes of the United States, Part IV.* Lippincott, Grambo, Philadelphia.

Schroder, Alan M.

1981 History, Analysis and Recommendations Concerning the Public Programs of the Iowa State Historical Department, Division of the State Historical Society. On file, Office of the State Archaeologist, University of Iowa, Iowa City.

Schroeder, Sissel

2005 Reclaiming New Deal Era Civic Archaeology: Exploring the Legacy of William S. Webb and the Jonathan Creek Site. *CRM: The Journal of Heritage Stewardship* 2:53–71.

2006 Walls as Symbols of Political, Economic, and Military Might. In *Leadership and Polity in Mississippian Society,* edited by Brian M. Butler and Paul D. Welch, pp. 115–141. Occasional Paper No. 33. Center for Archaeological Investigations, Southern Illinois University, Carbondale.

2007 Angelly Phase Mound Construction at Jonathan Creek. In *Current Archaeological Research in Kentucky: Volume Nine,* edited by E. Nicole Mills, Richard V. Williamson, and Richard D. Davis, pp. 131–150. Kentucky Heritage Council, Frankfort.

2009 Viewing Jonathan Creek through Ceramics and Radiocarbon Dates: Regional Prominence in the Thirteenth Century. In *TVA Archaeology: Seventy-five Years of Prehistoric Site Research,* edited by Erin E. Pritchard with Todd M. Ahlman, pp. 145–180. University of Tennessee Press, Knoxville.

2011 An Investigation of the Origins of Variation in Perishable Architecture at Jonathan Creek. *Southeastern Archaeology* 30:311–336.

Schwartz, Douglas W.

1967 *Conceptions of Kentucky Prehistory: A Case Study in the History of Archaeology.* University of Kentucky Press, Lexington.

Scull, John I.

1936a Letter to State Archaeologist Donald Cadzow, Pennsylvania Historical Commission, dated October 1. On file, Pennsylvania State Archives, Harrisburg.

1936b Letter to Whom It May Concern dated September 22. On file, Mary S. Biesecker Public Library, Somerset, Pennsylvania.

1938 Letter to Edgar Augustine dated March 1. On file, Pennsylvania State Archives, Harrisburg.

Setzler, Frank M.

1934 A Phase of Hopewell Moundbuilders in Louisiana. *Explorations and Fieldwork of the Smithsonian Institution in 1933,* pp. 38–47. Smithsonian Institution, Washington, D.C.

1936a Letter to J. D. Compton dated March 11. On file, National Anthropological Archives, Smithsonian Institution, Suitland, Maryland.

1936b Letter to Richard C. Job, Managing Secretary, Brunswick Board of Trade, dated May 6. On file, National Anthropological Archives, Smithsonian Institution, Suitland, Maryland.

1936c Letter to Arthur Kelly dated May 16. On file, National Anthropological Archives, Smithsonian Institution, Suitland, Maryland.

1936d Letter to Arthur Kelly dated June 12. On file, National Anthropological Archives, Smithsonian Institution, Suitland, Maryland.

1936e Letter to Preston Holder dated June 10. On file, University of Nebraska at Lincoln Libraries, Lincoln.

1937 Letter to Arthur Kelly dated August 17. On file, National Anthropological Archives, Smithsonian Institution, Suitland, Maryland.

1943 Archaeological Explorations in the United States, 1930–1942. *Acta Americana* 1:206–220.

Setzler, Frank M., and Jesse D. Jennings

1941 *Peachtree Mound and Village Site, Cherokee County, North Carolina.* Bureau of American Ethnology Bulletin 131. Smithsonian Institution, Washington, D.C.

Setzler, Frank M., and William Strong

1936 Archaeology and Relief. *American Antiquity* 4:301–309.

Skinner, Alanson, and Max Schrabisch

1913 *An Archaeological Survey of Trenton, NJ.* Geological Survey of New Jersey, Trenton.

Smith, Harlan I.

1910 *The Prehistoric Ethnology of a Kentucky Site.* Anthropological Papers of the American Museum of Natural History 6, part 2. New York.

Smith, Kevin E.

1992 The Middle Cumberland Region: Mississippian Archaeology in North Central Tennessee. Unpublished Ph.D. dissertation, Department of Anthropology, Vanderbilt University, Nashville, Tennessee.

Smith, Monica

2001 The Archaeology of a "Destroyed" Site: Surface Survey and Historical Documents at the Civilian Conservation Corps Camp, Bandelier National Monument, New Mexico. *Historical Archaeology* 35:31–40.

Smith, Richard W.

1938 Secretary's Report, Columbus Meeting, June 11–12, 1937. *Proceedings of the Society for Georgia Archaeology* 1(1):5–7.

South, Stanley

1977 *Method and Theory in Historical Archaeology.* Academic Press, New York.

Sowers, Ted C.

1939a Wyoming Archaeological Project Quarterly Report for July, August, and September. Work Project No. 885. Official Project No. 665-83-3-17.

Sponsored by the University of Wyoming. On file, National Anthropological Archives, Smithsonian Institution, Suitland, Maryland.

1939b *Petroglyphs and Pictographs of Dinwoody.* On file, National Anthropological Archives, Smithsonian Institution, Suitland, Maryland.

1941 *The Wyoming Archaeological Survey.* University of Wyoming, Laramie.

Spaulding, Albert C.

1985 Fifty Years of Theory. *American Antiquity* 50:301–308.

Spears, Joseph F.

1941 Letter to W. S. Webb dated July 26. William S. Webb Papers, University Archives, University of Kentucky Libraries' Special Collections, Lexington.

Spier, Leslie

1917 *An Outline for a Chronology of Zuñi Ruins.* Anthropological Papers of the American Museum of Natural History 18, part 3. New York.

Squier, Ephraim G., and Edwin H. Davis

1998 [1848] *Ancient Monuments of the Mississippi Valley.* Bartlett and Welford, New York. 1998 edition edited and with an introduction by David J. Meltzer. Smithsonian Institution, Washington, D.C.

Staller, John E.

2003 Donald Collier: A Curator's Life. In *Curators, Collections, and Contexts: Anthropology at the Field Museum 1893–2002,* edited by Stephen E. Nash and Gary M. Feinman. *Fieldiana: Anthropology* (Chicago), n.s., 36:189–198.

Starr, Frederick

1897 Bibliography of Iowa Antiquities and Summary of the Archaeology of Iowa. *Proceedings of the Davenport Academy of Science* 6:1–24, 53–124.

Stelle, J. Parish

1871a An Account of Aboriginal Ruins at Savannah, Tennessee. In *Annual Report of the Board of Regents of the Smithsonian Institution, Showing Operations, Expenditures, and Conditions of the Institution for the Year 1870,* pp. 408–415. Government Printing Office, Washington, D.C.

1871b Account of Aboriginal Ruins on the Williams Farm, in Hardin County, Tennessee, Two Miles below Savannah, Tennessee. *Annual Report of the Smithsonian Institution for 1870,* pp. 416–419. Washington, D.C.

Stevens, Sylvester Kirby, and Donald H. Kent

1940 *The Venango Trail.* Pennsylvania Historical Commission, Harrisburg.

Stewart, R. M., and G. Pevarnik

2008 Artisan Choices and Technology in Native American Pottery Production. *North American Archaeologist* 29:391–409.

Stirling, Matthew W.

1932 The Pre-Historic Southern Indians. In *Conference on Southern Pre-history,* pp. 20–31. National Research Council, Washington, D.C.

1935 Smithsonian Archaeological Projects Conducted under the Federal Emergency Relief Administration, 1933-34. *Annual Report of the Smithsonian Institution for 1934,* pp. 371–400. Smithsonian Institution, Washington, D.C.

1936a Letter to Preston Holder dated March 10. On file, University of Nebraska at Lincoln Libraries, Lincoln.

1936b Letter to Preston Holder dated April 22. On file, National Anthropological Archives, Smithsonian Institution, Suitland, Maryland.

1936c Letter to Preston Holder dated March 9. On file, National Anthropological Archives, Smithsonian Institution, Suitland, Maryland.

1940 The Historic Method as Applied to Southeastern Archaeology. In *Essays in Historical Anthropology of North America,* pp. 117–124. Smithsonian Miscellaneous Collections 100. Smithsonian Institution, Washington, D.C.

Stokes, B. Jo

1995 Annis Village (15Bt20) Chronological, Ceramic Analysis: Comparisons of Angel Phase and Caborn-Welborn Phase Ceramics to Date a WPA Excavation. Manuscript on file, William S. Webb Museum of Anthropology, University of Kentucky, Lexington.

Strong, W. Duncan

1933 The Plains Culture Area in the Light of Archaeology. *American Anthropologist* 35:271–287.

1935 *An Introduction to Nebraska Archaeology.* Smithsonian Miscellaneous Collections 93(10). Smithsonian Institution, Washington, D.C.

1937 Letter to Preston Holder dated July 28. On file, University of Nebraska at Lincoln Libraries, Lincoln.

Stuiver, M., P. J. Reimer, E. Bard, J. W. Beck, G. S. Burr, K. A. Hughen, B. Kromer, G. McCormac, J. van der Plicht, and M. Spurk

1998 INTCAL98 Radiocarbon Age Calibration, 24,000–0 cal BP. *Radiocarbon* 40:1041–1083.

Sullivan, Lynne P.

1987 The Mouse Creek Phase Household. *Southeastern Archaeology* 6:16–29.

1995 Mississippian Household and Community Organization in Eastern Tennessee. In *Mississippian Communities and Households,* edited by J. Daniel Rogers and Bruce D. Smith, pp. 99–123. University of Alabama Press, Tuscaloosa.

1999 Madeline D. Kneberg Lewis: Leading Lady of Tennessee Archaeology. In *Grit-Tempered: Early Women Archaeologists in the Southeastern United States,* edited by Nancy M. White, Lynne P. Sullivan, and Rochelle A. Marrinan, pp. 57–91. University Press of Florida, Gainesville.

2007 A WPA Deja Vu on Mississippian Architecture. In *Architectural Variability in the Southeast,* edited by Cameron H. Lacquement, pp. 117–135. University of Alabama Press, Tuscaloosa.

2009 Archaeological Time Constructs and the Construction of Hiwassee Island Mound. In *TVA Archaeology: Seventy-five Years of Prehistoric Site Research,* edited by Erin E. Pritchard with Todd M. Ahlman, pp. 181–209. University of Tennessee Press, Knoxville.

Sullivan, Lynne P., and Bobby R. Braly

2011 Correspondence among Colleagues: WPA Archaeology in Letters. *The SAA Archaeological Record* 11(3):42–46.

Swanton, John R.

1911 *Indian Tribes of the Lower Mississippi Valley.* Bureau of American Ethnology Bulletin 43. Smithsonian Institution, Washington, D.C.

1946 *The Indians of the Southeastern United States.* Bureau of American Ethnology Bulletin 137. Smithsonian Institution, Washington, D.C.

Tandarich, John P., and Loren N. Horton

1976 A Memorial Bibliography of Charles R. Keyes and Ellison J. Orr. *Journal of the Iowa Archeological Society* 23:45–142.

Taylor, Nick

2008 *American-Made: The Enduring Legacy of the WPA: When FDR Put the Nation to Work.* Bantam Books, New York.

Taylor, Walter W.

1948 *A Study of Archaeology.* Memoir No. 69. American Anthropological Association, Menasha, Wisconsin.

Tennessee Valley Authority (TVA)

1951 *The Kentucky Project: A Comprehensive Report on the Planning, Design, Construction, and Initial Operations of the Kentucky Project.* Technical Report No. 13. U.S. Government Printing Office, Washington, D.C.

1964 *Tennessee River Navigation System: History, Development, and Operation.* Technical Report No. 25. Tennessee Valley Authority, Knoxville.

1983 *A History of the Tennessee Valley Authority.* 50th anniversary edition. Tennessee Valley Authority, Knoxville.

2010 Kentucky Reservoir. Electronic document, http://www.tva.gov/sites/kentucky.htm, accessed December 13, 2010.

Thierman, Sue

1955 Bones Are His Meat. *Courier-Journal* (Louisville), November 13.

Thiessen, Thomas D.

1999 *Emergency Archeology in the Missouri River Basin: The Role of the Missouri River Basin Project and the Midwest Archeological Center in the Interagency Archeological Salvation Program, 1946–1975.* Special Report No. 2. Midwest Archeological Center, National Park Service, Lincoln, Nebraska.

Thiessen, Thomas D., and Karin M. Roberts

2009 The River Basin Surveys: A Legacy for American Archaeology. *Plains Anthropologist* 54:121–136.

Thomas, Cyrus

1894 Report on the Mound Explorations of the Bureau of Ethnology. *Twelfth Annual Report of the Bureau of Ethnology to the Secretary of the Smithsonian Institution, 1890–91,* pp. 3–742. Washington, D.C.

Tiffany, Joseph A.

1981 The Keyes Archaeological Collection: A Finder's Guide. Iowa State Historical Department, Iowa City.

1986 Curating the Charles R. Keyes Archaeological Collection. *Council for Museum Anthropology Newsletter* 10(2):15–22.

Tiffany, Joseph A., Shirley J. Schermer, and Debby Zieglowsky-Baker

1990 Documenting Archaeological Sites in the Charles R. Keyes Collection. *Journal of the Iowa Archeological Society* 37:88–92.

Townsend, A. O.

1936a Letter from Clerk, Commissioners Roads and Revenue, Glynn County, Brunswick, Georgia, dated April 28. On file, National Anthropological Archives, Smithsonian Institution, Suitland, Maryland.

1936b Letter from Clerk, Commissioners Roads and Revenue, Glynn County, Brunswick, Georgia, dated April 28. On file, University of Nebraska at Lincoln Libraries, Lincoln.

*Trenton Sunday Times*

1936 Survey of Mercer Trails Is Planned. *Trenton (New Jersey) Sunday Times,* March 21.

Trigger, Bruce

1986 Prehistoric Archaeology and American Society. In *American Archaeology: Past and Future,* edited by David J. Meltzer, Don D. Fowler, and Jeremy A. Sabloff, pp. 187–215. Smithsonian Institution Press, Washington, D.C.

2006 *A History of Archaeological Thought.* 2nd ed. Cambridge University Press, Cambridge.

Trimble, Stanley Wayne

1974 *Man-Induced Soil Erosion on the Southern Piedmont 1700–1900.* Soil Conservation Society of America, Ankeny, Iowa.

U. S. Department of Commerce

1922 Fourteenth Census of the United States, Taken in the Year 1920: Population. Government Printing Office, Washington, D.C.

1933 Fifteenth Census of the United States, Taken in the Year 1930: Population. Government Printing Office, Washington, D.C.

U. S. Department of Commerce and Labor

1913 Thirteenth Census of the United States, Taken in the Year 1910: Population. Government Printing Office, Washington, D.C.

U. S. Department of the Interior

1883 Population Schedules of the Tenth Census of the United States, 1880. Government Printing Office, Washington, D.C.

1901 Twelfth Census of the United States, Taken in the Year 1900: Population. Government Printing Office, Washington, D.C.

Vega, Garcilaso de la

1951 *The Florida of the Inca,* translated by John G. Varner, and Jeanette J. Varner. University of Texas Press, Austin.

Walker, S. T.

1879 Report on the Shell Heaps of Tampa Bay, Florida. *Annual Report of the Smithsonian Institution for 1880,* pp. 413–422. Washington, D.C.

1883 Mounds, Shell Heaps, Ancient Canal, etc., Florida. *Annual Report of the Smithsonian Institution for 1881,* p. 685. Washington, D.C.

1885 Mounds and Shell Heaps on the West Coast of Florida. *Annual Report of the Smithsonian Institution for 1883,* pp. 854–868. Washington, D.C.

Wallace, William J.

1999 Franklin Fenenga and California Archaeology. *Journal of California and Great Basin Anthropology* 21(1):2–5.

Walters, Katherine Bowman

1995 *Oconee River: Tales to Tell.* The Reprint Company, Spartanburg, South Carolina.

Ward, Duren

1903 Historico-anthropological Possibilities in Iowa. *Iowa Journal of History and Politics* 1:47–76.

1905 The Problem of the Mounds. *Iowa Journal of History and Politics* 3:20–40.

Watkins, T. H.

1993 *The Great Depression: America in the 1930s.* Little, Brown, Boston.

1999 *The Hungry Years: A Narrative History of the Great Depression.* Henry Holt, New York.

Webb, William S.

1937 Letter to Thomas M. N. Lewis dated April 10. On file, University of Kentucky Library, Lexington.

1938a *An Archaeological Survey of the Norris Basin in Eastern Tennessee.* Bureau of American Ethnology Bulletin 118. Smithsonian Institution, Washington, D.C.

1938b Letter to James Foster dated December 8. William S. Webb Papers, University Archives, University of Kentucky Libraries' Special Collections, Lexington.

1939 *An Archaeological Survey of Wheeler Basin on the Tennessee River in Northern Alabama.* Bureau of American Ethnology Bulletin 122. Smithsonian Institution, Washington, D.C.

1952 *The Jonathan Creek Village.* Reports in Anthropology 7(1). University of Kentucky, Lexington.

Webb, William S., and David L. DeJarnette (editors)

1942 *An Archaeological Survey of Pickwick Basin in the Adjacent Portions of the States of Alabama, Mississippi, and Tennessee.* Bureau of American Ethnology Bulletin 129. Smithsonian Institution, Washington, D.C.

Webb, William S., and William D. Funkhouser

1932 *Archaeological Survey of Kentucky.* Reports in Archaeology and Anthropology 2. University of Kentucky, Lexington.

Webb, William S., and C. G. Wilder

1951 *An Archaeological Survey of Guntersville Basin on the Tennessee River in Northern Alabama.* University of Kentucky Press, Lexington.

Wedel, Mildred Mott

1959 Oneota Sites on the Upper Iowa River. *Missouri Archaeologist* 21(2–4).

Wedel, Waldo R.

1938 *The Direct-Historical Approach in Pawnee Archaeology.* Smithsonian Miscellaneous Collections 97(7). Smithsonian Institution, Washington, D.C.

1952 The Keyes Collection of Archeological Materials in the State Historical Society of Iowa: An Appraisal of Its Present Conditions and Its Scientific Possibilities. On file, Office of the State Archaeologist, University of Iowa, Iowa City.

Weener, Carol G.

1986 Pennsbury Manor: A Study in Colonial Revival Preservation. Unpublished Master's thesis in Historic Preservation, University of Pennsylvania, Philadelphia. Available online at http://openlibrary.org/books/OL23325000M/Pennsbury_Manor.

Welch, Paul D.

1998 Middle Woodland and Mississippian Occupations of the Savannah Site in Tennessee. *Southeastern Archaeology* 17:79–92.

2006 *Archaeology at Shiloh Indian Mounds, 1899–1999.* University of Alabama Press, Tuscaloosa.

Welsch, Robert L.

2003 Albert Buell Lewis: Realizing George Amos Dorsey's Vision. In *Curators, Collections, and Contexts: Anthropology at the Field Museum 1893–2002,* edited by Stephen E. Nash and Gary M. Feinman. *Fieldiana: Anthropology* (Chicago), n.s., 36:99–116.

Wetmore, A.

1936 Letter to H. T. McIntosh, District Chairman, National Resources Board,

Albany, Georgia, dated March 10. On file, Coastal Georgia Historical Society on St. Simons Island, Georgia.

Wettstaed, James R.

2009a *Land Use History of Oconee Ranger District: A.D. 1000–1935.* Forest Service Report R2010-08-03-08-003. On file, Chattahoochee-Oconee National Forests Supervisor's Office, Gainesville, Georgia.

2009b Heritage Resource Investigations for the Compartment 113 Second Stewardship Project, Oconee Ranger District, Chattahoochee-Oconee National Forests, Jasper County, Georgia. Forest Service Report R2009-08-03-08-001. On file, Chattahoochee-Oconee National Forests Supervisor's Office, Gainesville, Georgia.

White, Carolyn L.

2005 *American Artifacts of Personal Adornment 1680–1820: A Guide to Identification and Interpretation.* AltaMira, Lanham, Maryland.

Willey, Gordon R.

1937 Letter to Preston Holder dated November 20. On file, University of Nebraska at Lincoln Libraries, Lincoln.

1939 Letter to Preston Holder dated May 5. On file, University of Nebraska at Lincoln Libraries, Lincoln.

1984 Archaeological Retrospect 6. *Antiquity* 58:5–14.

Willey, Gordon R., and Jeremy Sabloff

1995 *A History of American Archaeology.* 3rd ed. W. H. Freeman, San Francisco.

Williams, Aubrey

1939 The Work of the National Youth Administration. *Living* 1:65–66.

Williams, Lorraine E., David C. Parris, and Shirley S. Albright

1981 Interdisciplinary Approaches to WPA Archaeological Collections in the Northeast. *Annals of the New York Academy of Sciences* 376:141–59.

Williams, Mark (editor)

1997 *In His Own Words: An Interview with Dr. Arthur Kelly (1900–1979).* Interviewed by Marilyn Pennington, Summer 1973. LAMAR Institute Publication 44. University of Georgia, Athens.

Williams, Stephen

1960 A Brief History of the Southeastern Archaeological Conference. *Newsletter of the Southeastern Archaeological Conference* 7(1):2–4.

Wilson, Greg D.

2005 Between Plaza and Palisade: Household and Community Organization at Early Moundville. Unpublished Ph.D. dissertation, Department of Anthropology, University of North Carolina at Chapel Hill, Chapel Hill, North Carolina.

2008 *The Archaeology of Everyday Life at Early Moundville.* University of Alabama Press, Tuscaloosa.

Winterbourne, J. W.

1966a The 1935 Adams-Fairview Excavation, Orange County Historical Research Project. *Pacific Coast Archaeological Society Quarterly* 2(3):24–29.

1966b The WPA Excavation of the Sunny Hills Site #1 (1939). *Pacific Coast Archaeological Society Quarterly* 2(4):8–49.

1967 Report of the Goff's Island Site Excavation, May 1, 1939 to January 22, 1940 (WPA). *Pacific Coast Archaeological Society Quarterly* 3(2/3):1–156.

1968a Orange County Historical Research Project, Newland Hillside Excavation (1935). *Pacific Coast Archaeological Society Quarterly* 4(2):1–9.

1968b Orange County Historical Research Project, Report of Banning Estate Excavation (Norris Property), 1935. *Pacific Coast Archaeological Society Quarterly* 4(2):10–17.

1968c Orange County Anthropological Project, Report of the Excavations of the Griset Site at Costa Mesa, Orange County (1938). *Pacific Coast Archaeological Society Quarterly* 4(2):18–68.

Witthoft, John

1950 The History and Present Status of Pennsylvania Archeology. *Proceedings of the American Philosophical Society* 94(3):301–307.

Wissler, Clark

1914 Material Cultures of the North American Indians. *American Anthropologist* 16:447–505.

Woodward, Ellen S.

1938 Letter to J. Banks Hudson, State Works Progress Administrator, Harrisburg, Pennsylvania, dated June 22. On file, Pennsylvania State Archives, Harrisburg.

Wyman, Jeffries

1868 On the Fresh-Water Shell-Heaps of the St. John's River, East Florida. *American Naturalist* 2:393–403.

1973 [1875] *Freshwater Shell Mounds of the St. John's River, Florida.* Originally published by the Peabody Academy of Science, Salem, Massachusetts. AMS Press for Peabody Museum of Archaeology and Ethnology, Harvard University, New York.

Wynes, Charles E.

1977 1865–1890. In *A History of Georgia,* edited by Kenneth Coleman, pp. 205–254. University of Georgia Press, Athens.

Yastrow, Ed, and Stephen E. Nash

2003 Henry Field, Collections, and Exhibit Development, 1926–1941. In *Curators, Collections, and Contexts: Anthropology at the Field Museum 1893–2002,* edited by Stephen E. Nash and Gary M. Feinman. *Fieldiana: Anthropology* (Chicago), n.s., 36:127–138.

Young, Bennett H.

1910 *The Prehistoric Men of Kentucky.* Filson Club Publications 25. Louisville.

Young, Jon N.

1962 Annis Mound: A Late Prehistoric Site on the Green River. Unpublished Master's thesis, Department of Anthropology, University of Kentucky, Lexington.

# Contributors

**John L. Cordell** is employed at the University of Iowa Office of the State Archaeologist (OSA) in Iowa City, Iowa. He has worked at the OSA since 1983 and has been repository manager since 1990. He has day-to-day responsibility for managing the approximately 4,000,000 items housed within the State Archaeological Repository at the OSA. These items include the Keyes Collection, much of which was derived from WPA-funded excavations.

**John F. Doershuk** is employed at the University of Iowa Office of the State Archaeologist (OSA) in Iowa City, Iowa. He has been state archaeologist since 2007 and was previously with the Contract Services Division of the OSA. As state archaeologist, he has found the history of archaeological investigations in Iowa an increasingly interesting and relevant topic. He has also found researching the efforts of his predecessors personally satisfying and the knowledge gained about the context and aims of their work informative regarding how and where to steer the future of Iowa archaeology.

**David H. Dye** is a professor of archaeology in the Department of Earth Sciences at the University of Memphis. He is the author of *War Paths, Peace Paths: An Archaeology of Cooperation and Conflict in Native Eastern North America* and the editor of *Cave Archaeology of the Eastern Woodlands: Essays in Honor of Patty Jo Watson*. His research interests include cooperation and conflict in the past, eastern North American prehistory, and archaeological photography.

**Scott W. Hammerstedt** is a member of the research faculty at the Oklahoma Archeological Survey at the University of Oklahoma. He received his Ph.D. from the Pennsylvania State University in 2005. His current research focuses on the archaeology of late prehistoric Mississippian and Caddo societies in what is now the southeastern and midwestern United States.

**Janet R. Johnson** is a curator in the Section of Archaeology at the State Museum of Pennsylvania, Pennsylvania Historical & Museum Commission. She is responsible for the curation management of nearly five million artifacts from throughout Pennsylvania representing 16,000 years of occupation. Her specific research interests have focused on the Contact period and the influence of European trade on native lifeways.

**Kevin Kiernan** is an emeritus professor of English at the University of Kentucky, where he taught as a medievalist for 35 years. He now lives on St. Simons Island, where his interests have centered on the history and the history of archaeology of the Georgia Coast.

**Gregory D. Lattanzi** is an assistant curator for the Bureau of Archaeology & Ethnography at the New Jersey State Museum in Trenton, New Jersey. He obtained a B.A. in Anthropology from the State University of New York at Binghamton and an M.A. in Anthropology from the City University of New York, Hunter College. His current research focuses on the chemical characterization of prehistoric copper artifacts and their implications on trade and exchange and social complexity in the Middle Atlantic region.

**Patrick C. Livingood** has a Ph.D. from the University of Michigan and is an associate professor of anthropology at the University of Oklahoma. His research interests include the Mississippian Period in the southeastern United States, including the archaeology of the ancestral Caddo in eastern Oklahoma and adjacent states. He is the author of *Mississippian Polity and Politics on the Gulf Coastal Plain: A View from the Pearl River, Mississippi* and co-editor (with Mark A. Rees) of *Plaquemine Archaeology,* both from The University of Alabama Press.

**Anna R. Lunn** attended the University of Memphis, receiving a B.A. in anthropology in 1998 and an M.S. in earth sciences in 2007. Since graduation, she has worked for a cultural resources management firm as an archaeologist, a lab director, and a GIS specialist, and has served on projects in Tennessee, Mississippi, Missouri, Arkansas, and Louisiana. She is currently co-editing a volume on New Deal archaeology in the Tennessee River Valley.

**Bernard K. Means** currently teaches anthropology at Virginia Commonwealth University and is director of the Virtual Curation Laboratory, which is creating three-dimensional digital models of archaeological objects. He has a B.A. in Anthropology from Occidental College and a Ph.D. in Anthropology from Arizona State University. Dr. Means's scholarly interests include cross-cultural studies of village spatial and social organizations, the research potential of archaeological collections, and the history of archaeology across the Americas, especially during the Great Depression. He is author of *Circular Villages of the Monongahela Tradition* from The University of Alabama Press.

**Stephen E. Nash** is chair of the Department of Anthropology and Curator of Archaeology at the Denver Museum of Nature & Science. He is the author or editor of five books on the history of archaeology and the history of museums, and recently served as co-editor of the journal *Museum Anthropology*. He earned his Ph.D. from the University of Arizona in 1997 and worked at the Field Museum from 1997 until 2006.

**Amanda L. Regnier** is a member of the research faculty at the Oklahoma Archeological Survey, University of Oklahoma. She has a Ph.D. from The University of Alabama. Her research interests include Caddoan archaeology, social and ethnic composition of southeastern Mississippian and Protohistoric societies, ceramic analysis, archaeological theory, and multivariate statistical analysis.

**Sissel Schroeder** is a professor in the Department of Anthropology at the University of Wisconsin, and a faculty affiliate of the American Indian Studies Program, the Center for Culture, History, and the Environment, and the Nelson Institute of Environmental Studies at the University of Wisconsin. Her archaeological research explores the spatial distribution of ancient people in relation to inconstant and heterogeneous social, natural, and anthropogenic landscapes in eastern North America. Much of her research is focused on the Jonathan Creek site in western Kentucky and on Mississippian-era settlements in the vicinity of the Cahokia site in the Mississippi River valley, near modern-day St. Louis.

**James R. Wettstaed** is forest archaeologist/tribal liaison for the Chattahoochee-Oconee National Forests in Georgia. After obtaining his M.A. in anthropology from Wichita State University in 1989, he has worked in National Forests in Montana, Missouri, and Georgia. His research interests span the prehistoric and historic archaeology of the southeastern United States, but most of his publications have focused on the historic period of the Ozarks and Georgia.

# Index